THE KEY TO NUMEROLOGY

1 AGGRESSION
2 BALANCE
3 EXPRESSION
4 STEADINESS
5 ADVENTURE
6 DEPENDABILITY
7 MYSTERY
8 SUCCESS
9 POWER

THE COMPLETE
ILLUSTRATED BOOK OF
The Psychic Sciences

THE COMPLETE
ILLUSTRATED BOOK OF
The Psychic Sciences

WALTER B. GIBSON

and

LITZKA R. GIBSON

DRAWINGS BY MURRAY KESHNER

BELL PUBLISHING COMPANY
New York

This 1988 edition is published by Bell Publishing Company, distributed by Crown Publishers, Inc., 225 Park Avenue South, New York, New York 10003, by arrangement with Doubleday & Company, Inc.

Printed and Bound in the United States of America

Library of Congress Cataloging-in-Publication Data

Gibson, Walter Brown, 1897-
    The complete illustrated book of the psychic sciences / by Walter B. and Litzka R. Gibson.
    p.   cm.
    Reprint. originally published: Garden City, N.Y. : Double-day, 1966.
    Includes index.
    ISBN 0-517-67152-2
    1. Occultism.   2. Psychical research.   I. Gibson, Litzka R.   II. Title.
BF1411.G5   1968
133—dc19   88-14615
                                                                        CIP

ISBN: 0-517-67152-2
h g f e d c b a

Contents

Introduction

The lure of the unknown and the lore of hidden things have long intrigued the human mind. Along with such skills as throwing rocks and fashioning flintstone spearheads, primitive man developed more subtle crafts, as foretelling the weather by the ways the birds flew or the winds blew. From those beginnings came modern sciences like ballistics and meteorology; and the same applies in many other instances.

Two factors were present in most primitive sciences; the psychic and the occult. The practitioner of a craft usually claimed and often believed that he possessed a special faculty not given to ordinary mortals, enabling him to gain unique results and issue reliable forecasts. He backed this by professing knowledge of secret subjects which he was pledged not to reveal.

This combination of psychic power and occult learning has persisted into modern times. Skilled artists often regard their work as "inspired" or rely on "trade secrets" for results. So the pattern is similar, even though many things that once created awe and wonderment are explainable by modern science. Now the cycle may be bringing us to new wonders, perhaps including some revivals from the past.

The science of alchemy, which flourished in the Middle Ages, has been styled the "father of chemistry," and it is interesting to note that the efforts of the alchemists to transmute one metal into another have been realized in our modern laboratories, though not as the alchemists anticipated. But that should not reflect too greatly on alchemy, for according to some authorities, it was not the alchemists, but their imitators, who stumbled upon the more important discoveries that founded modern chemistry.

Similarly, astrology, as the forerunner of astronomy, may have had its faults. But any absurdities of astrologers were outmatched by the erroneous theories held by astronomers, until the invention of the telescope proved that they were wrong.

This is not a defense of outmoded beliefs founded on ignorance and superstition. It is all the more reason why such notions should be discarded, as they often have been. But theories that have an intelligent basis, those that have stood the test of time and gained popular acceptance, were and are worthy of continued consideration. Had they not been, chemistry, astronomy, and other modern sciences would have died in infancy, whenever some new finding disproved the old.

There is such a thing as being both right and wrong. Columbus proved that when he sailed westward and thought he had discovered the East Indies, but blundered into America instead. Today, the Caribbean islands are called the West Indies, which is a classic misnomer. But nobody doubts their existence.

As to psychic and occult sciences, those that have won continued interest are worthy of consideration, as astrology or numerology. So are those that have sprung to public acceptance, as graphology and physiognomy, which are newer than some of our standard sciences. All these have been included in this volume because of their own merits.

But always, we have followed this purpose:

Each psychic or occult science is treated as it stands today, in the light of modern knowledge and interest. All have been simplified and updated for the reader's convenience. These constitute the great portion of this volume, but as preliminary, we have cataloged an array of ancient psychic and occult sciences as well as modern:

Aeromancy, or divination from the air and sky, goes beyond the range of weather prognostications and concentrates more upon cloud shapes, comets, spectral formations, or other phenomena not normally visible in the heavens. Even in modern times, such visions have caused speculation and consternation among viewers.

Alchemy is the science of transmuting base metals into gold or silver with the aid of a mysterious substance termed the "philosopher's stone." Alchemists also claimed to prolong human life indefinitely by means of a secret elixir.

Alectryomancy is a form of divination whereby a bird, usually a black hen or a white gamecock, is allowed to pick grains of corn from a circle of letters, thus forming words or names with prophetic significance. Another method is to recite the letters of the alphabet, noting those at which a cock crows.

Aleuromancy requires slips with answers to questions. These are rolled in balls of dough, which are baked, then mixed. One is chosen at random and presumably will be fulfilled. Modern "fortune cookies" are a survival of this ancient ritual.

Alomancy, or divination by salt, accounts for some of our modern superstitions; so does *Alphitomancy,* which utilizes special cakes that are digestible by persons with a clear conscience, but are distasteful to others; while *Anthropomancy* is an ancient and long-outlawed form of human sacrifice.

Apantomancy covers forecasts from chance meetings with animals, birds, and other creatures, which can be updated to include modern omens of the "black cat" variety. A classic case was the founding of Mexico City on the spot where Aztec soothsayers saw an eagle flying from a cactus, carrying a live snake; this represents the Mexican coat-of-arms today.

Arithmancy or *Arithmomancy* is the ancient form of Numerology and applies chiefly to divination through numbers and letter values, as discussed in the section on Numerology. *Astraglomancy* or *Astragyromancy* was worked with crude dice bearing letters and later numbers; this, too, has developed into a modern diversion, detailed under Fortune Telling by Dice.

Astrology, as the ancient science of the stars, was basically a form of divination, as persons who could foretell changes in the heavens naturally felt capable of predicting the smaller affairs of mankind. Modern astrology makes no such extravagant claims, but has retained enough of the old tradition to become a fascinating subject in its own right, and it is so treated in this volume.

Augury is the general art of divination, covering many forms included in this list, and applying chiefly to interpretations of the future based on signs and omens.

Austromancy refers to divination by a study of the winds. *Axiomancy* requires an ax or hatchet, which answers questions by its quivers when driven into a post, or points out the direction taken by robbers or other miscreants, according to the way the handle falls.

Belomancy, one of the most ancient types of divination, required the tossing or balancing of arrows. *Bibliomancy* involves divination by books; while *Botanomancy* requires the burning of tree branches and leaves to gain desired answers. *Bumpology* is a strictly modern term, a popular nickname for Phrenology.

Capnomancy is the study of smoke rising from a fire and is performed in varied ways. *Cartomancy* is fortune telling with cards, covered specially under that heading, with a discussion of modern methods. *Catop-*

tromancy was an early form of crystal gazing, utilizing a mirror that was turned to the moon to catch the lunar rays.

Causimomancy involves divination from objects placed in a fire. If they fail to ignite, or burn more slowly than anticipated, it becomes a good omen.

Cephalomancy refers to divinatory procedures with the skull or head of a donkey or goat. *Ceraunoscopy* draws omens from the study of thunder and lightning. *Ceroscopy* is a fascinating form of divination in which melted wax is poured into cold water, forming bubbles which are duly interpreted.

Chiromancy, or divination from the lines of a person's hand, is the companion of *Chirognomy*, the study of traits through general hand formation; together, these compose modern Palmistry, which has its own chapter.

Clairaudience or "clear hearing" and *Clairvoyance* or "clear seeing" are also "twin" subjects with divinatory features. These have come under intensive study in modern parapsychology, which regards them as forms of extrasensory perception.

Cleromancy is a form of lot casting, akin to divination with dice but simply using pebbles or other odd objects, often of different colors, instead of marked cubes.

Clidomancy, or *Cleidomancy* is worked with a dangling key that answers questions. *Coscinomancy* is similar, utilizing a hanging sieve. These are primitive forms of radiesthesia, discussed in a separate chapter.

Critomancy is the study of barley cakes, in hope of drawing omens from them; while *Cromniomancy* finds significance from onion sprouts. *Crystallomancy* is a term for crystal gazing, which is discussed in another chapter. *Cyclomancy* pertains to divination from a turning wheel.

Dactylomancy is the early form of radiesthesia, with a dangling ring indicating words and numbers by its swings. *Daphnomancy* requires listening to laurel branches crackling in an open fire; the louder the crackle, the better the omen.

Demonomancy refers to divinations through the aid of demons; while *Dendromancy* is associated with both the oak and mistletoe. *Divining rods* and *Dowsing* are discussed in the chapter on Radiesthesia.

Gastromancy was an ancient form of ventriloquism, with the voice lowered to a sepulchral tone as though issuing from the ground. Prophetic utterances were thus delivered in a trance state. *Geloscopy* was the art of divination from the tone of someone's laughter. *Genethlialogy* was the calculation of the future from the influence of the stars at birth.

Geomancy began with tracing figures in the ground and later was extended to include random dots made with a pencil, which were interpreted according to accepted designs, practically a predecessor of our modern "doodles."

Graphology, the analysis of character through handwriting, was studied in ancient times and given a psychic significance. Its modern version is detailed in a special chapter.

Gyromancy was performed by persons walking in a circle marked with letters, until they became dizzy and stumbled at different points, thus "spelling out" a prophecy.

Halomancy is another term for Alomancy, or divination by salt. *Haruspicy, Hieromancy, Hieroscopy*, all had to do with observing objects of ancient sacrifice and drawing prophetic conclusions from them. *Hippomancy* was a form of divination from the stamping and neighing of horses. *Horoscopy* pertains to the casting of an astrological horoscope.

Hydromancy, or divination by water, covers a wide range of lesser auguries, such as the color of water, its ebb and flow; or the ripples produced by pebbles dropped into a pool, an odd number being good, an even number, bad. Our modern "tea leaf" and "coffee ground" readings date from this, as Hydromancy also included close study of water and figures formed therein.

Ichthyomancy involved fish as factors in divination. *Lampadomancy* signifies portents from lights or torches. *Lecanomancy* involved a basin of water in the divinatory process; while *Libanomancy* requires incense as a means of interpreting omens.

Lithomancy utilizes precious stones of various colors. In its more modern form of divination, these are scattered on a flat surface, and whichever reflects the light most vividly fulfills the omen. Blue, good luck soon. Green, realization of a hope. Red, happiness in love or marriage. Yellow, disaster or betrayal. Purple, a period of sadness. Black or gray, misfortune. Colored beads may be used instead of jewels.

Margaritomancy was a procedure utilizing pearls which were supposed to bounce upward beneath an inverted pot if a guilty person approached. *Metagnomy* is a comparatively modern form of intuitive divination covering past, distant scenes of present, and future events while viewed during a hypnotic trance.

Meteoromancy lists omens dependent on meteors and similar phenomena. *Metoposcopy* is the reading of character from the lines of the forehead. Based on Astrology, it has factors akin to Palmistry, but belongs under the head of Physiognomy. *Molybdomancy* draws mystic inferences from the varied hissings of molten lead; and *Myomancy* concerns rats and mice, the cries they give, the destruction they cause, all as prophetic tokens.

Numerology, though of ancient origin, is a modern form of interpreting names and dates in terms of vital numbers, all indicative of individual traits. This popular subject is discussed in its own chapter.

Oculomancy is a form of divination from the eyes; while *Oinomancy* utilizes wine in determining omens. *Oneiromancy* is the interpretation of dreams, and the modern phase of that significant science is discussed in a separate chapter. *Onomancy* answers the question of "what's in a name" by giving meanings for names of persons and things, but has comparatively little importance as a divinatory art.

Onomantics is a development of Onomancy, applied to personal names. Some of these are obvious in meaning, as Hope, or Victor. Others are easily translatable, as Sophia for wisdom, or Leo for lion-hearted. Others have been extended or elaborated, but their basic meanings can be found in many dictionaries or standard reference works, and they lack the deeper significance of psychic or occult interpretation, hence there is no need to list them here.

Onychomancy is a study of the fingernails in the sunlight, looking for any significant symbols that can be traced. *Onyomancy* is similar and somewhat more practical, being an interpretation of personal characteristics from the nails, as a minor phase of Palmistry.

Oomantia and *Ooscopy* are terms applied to ancient methods of divination by eggs. *Ophiomancy* covers divination from serpents; while *Orniscopy* and *Ornithomancy* are concerned with omens gained by watching the flight of different birds. *Ovomancy* is another form of egg divination.

Palmistry is one of the most interesting of psychic sciences and has reached a high state of modern development. It is covered in detail in a separate chapter of this volume. Long known as the "language of the hand," it interprets the lines and general formations according to well-accepted rules.

Pegomancy requires spring water or bubbling fountains for its divinations; while *Pessomancy* involves pebbles. *Phrenology,* which deals in head formations, is a modern form of psychic science treated in a separate chapter. *Phrenopathy* is a similar subject incorporating hypnotism.

Phyllorhodomancy is an intriguing type of divination dating from ancient Greece. It consists of slapping rose petals against the hand and judging the success of a venture according to the loudness of the sound.

Physiognomy, covered as a complete subject here, is highly modern in its treatment and deals with character analysis through physical appearance of the features. It has older roots, but all of a practical nature.

Precognition is an inner knowledge of things to come, which may lead to *Prediction,* which is the announcement of such events, or *Premonition,* a foreboding of the future. These are combined in *Prognostication,* which goes into specific details, or the greater art of *Prophecy,* which connotes inspired knowledge of important events, with their fulfillment almost certain.

Psychography is a form of mysterious writing, usually of a divinatory type. *Psychometry* is the faculty of gaining impressions from a physical object, either regarding its owner, or the history of the object itself. *Pyromancy* and *Pyroscopy* are forms of divination by fire, wherein powdered substances are thrown on the flames; if these kindle quickly, it is a good omen.

Rhabdomancy is divination by means of a wand or stick. Of ancient origin, much of its history is obscure, but it was the forerunner of the divining rod, discussed in the chapter on Radiesthesia. *Rhapsodomancy* is performed by opening a book of poetry and reading a passage at chance, hoping it will prove to be an omen.

Sciomancy is a term for divination gained through spirit aid. *Sideromancy* is the burning of straws on a hot iron and studying the figures thus formed, along with the flames and smoke. *Sortilege* is the casting of lots in hope of a good omen; this has many phases and variations dating from antiquity and is still practiced today.

Spodomancy provides omens from cinders or soot. *Stichomancy* is another form of opening a book, hoping that a random passage will give inspiration, something that many people follow today. *Stolisomancy* draws omens from oddities in the way people dress.

Sycomancy is performed by writing messages on tree leaves; the slower they dry, the better the omen. A more modern way is to write questions on slips of paper, roll them up, and hold them in a strainer above a steaming pot. Whichever unrolls first will be answered; but a blank slip should always be included in the group.

Tephramancy is the seeking of messages in ashes; tree bark is often burned for that purpose and the diviner looks for symbols as with tea leaves. *Tiromancy* is an odd form of divination utilizing cheese.

Xylomancy is divination from pieces of wood. Some diviners pick them up at random, interpreting them according to their shape or formation. Others put pieces of wood upon a fire and note the order in which they burn, forming conclusions as to omens, good or bad.

THE COMPLETE
ILLUSTRATED BOOK OF
The Psychic Sciences

1

Astrology

Introduction

From the dawn of antiquity, Astrology has played its part in the affairs of mankind, and its popularity persists today. The term means "knowledge of the stars" and as such, astrology not only served in forecasting coming events, it included as a by-product the subject now called astronomy. Small wonder that people believed themselves to be controlled by the signs of the heavens when the courses of the stars and planets could be calculated to exactitude!

New civilizations inherited astrology from the old; and with it, the scope of the ancient science was extended. Birthstones were associated with the constellations forming the signs of the zodiac. Metals were identified with planets; gold with the sun; silver with the moon; mercury, because of its elusive quality, with its namesake, Mercury. Everything mundane was interpreted astrologically.

All sciences therefore owe much to astrology. When they branched out on their own, astrology was not discredited; it merely returned to its original purpose, that of determining the shape of things to come. It is an interesting fact that when Tycho Brahe, the great astronomer of his time, sighted the comet of 1577 and classed it for what it was, he did not even guess at the year when it would next appear.

Instead, he used the comet as the basis of an astrological calculation from which he predicted that a prince to be born in Finland would become a great Swedish king and would invade Germany, meeting his death in the year 1632. That astrological forecast was fulfilled by the career of King Gustavus Adolphus of Sweden. But astronomers haven't yet found out if Tycho's comet ever did come back.

However, skeptics insist that predictions of latter-day astrology depend mostly on coincidence or guesswork, as did some of the early findings of astronomy. At least, the abstruse calculations of astrology are of little interest to the public. People want to know what their birth signs and planetary influences may mean to them, if anything. Often, they would like to check those findings for themselves. That can be done, through a study of the pages that follow.

The Signs of the Zodiac and Their Significance

Among the many constellations that stud the night sky, there are twelve which form a great belt around the earth. Each of these represents a month in the astrological year that runs from March 21 on through the succeeding March 20. These are called the signs of the zodiac.

The signs of the zodiac

Each month, the Sun enters a new sign, and all persons born during that period have it as their birth sign. According to astrology, there are twelve types of persons thus represented, as all individuals born under a given sign become imbued with its inherent traits.

The signs and the dates when they exert their individual influences are as follows:

Aries or the Ram—March 21 through April 19
Taurus or the Bull—April 20 through May 19
Gemini or the Twins—May 20 through June 20
Cancer or the Crab—June 21 through July 22
Leo or the Lion—July 23 through August 21
Virgo or the Virgin—August 22 through September 22
Libra or the Scales—September 23 through October 22
Scorpio or the Scorpion—October 23 through November 21
Sagittarius or the Bowman—November 22 through December 21
Capricorn or the Goat—December 22 through January 20
Aquarius or the Water Carrier—January 21 through February 19
Pisces or the Fish—February 20 through March 20

The twelve charts that follow describe the basic traits attributed to each of these signs, and in many cases they fit the individual with surprising exactitude. All persons differ to some degree, however, and their variable traits will be discussed in later chapters, which cover in-between periods as well as planetary influences and their significance. These apply not only to the astrological month, but to the day and year of birth.

ARIES—THE RAM
March 21–April 19

Headwork is the chief factor of this sign. Persons born under Aries are keen, creative, and highly adaptive; but they are also impetuous and headstrong. This is accentuated by the governing planet, Mars, which adds an aggressive touch to an already active and ambitious nature. Their incessant drive gets them off to a good start on any project, but they are apt to become diverted and scatter their further effort.

Though quick to anger, Aries people often calm easily. They are naturally humorous and quick of wit; they enjoy music and entertainment. They say the right thing at the right time; and as students, they are often keen and have the ability of applying whatever they learn to

Aries

good advantage. They like new things and have a way of rousing and swaying other persons to work along with them. In all fields, however, there is a frequent disinclination to "stay with it" once the novelty wears off.

Coincident with this is an Aries tendency of giving ideas to other people and also leaving detail work to others. This is seldom a mark of generosity or confidence on the Aries person's part, but more the desire to see things carried through without effort on their own part. There is a strong ego in the Aries nature, which causes them to become visionary and idealistic, thereby rising to positions of importance and esteem.

Conversely, they can let their impatience ruin them, turning them into fickle, self-centered individuals, foolish or false in their generosity. Unable to attain their high aspirations, they may value money only as a means to such a goal, spending it foolishly and extravagantly.

Thus misguided by their own impetuosity, Aries persons become angry when plans fail. They may find fault or interfere with their subordinates, blaming them instead. They often regard their own ideas as perfect and sometimes set up their own standards of right or wrong, even to the extent of sheer fanaticism. This can prove disastrous to their careers.

When well controlled, Aries people foster friendship and promote both harmony and beauty, which they relish to the degree of luxury. They show loyalty and are willing to fight for what they consider right; all the more reason why they should set high and worthy standards. Being natural leaders, Aries people do not like to take orders from others; but they should at least accept advice if they hope to attain their ambitions.

In business, Aries determination spells success, if good choice is shown toward opportunities and issues are squarely faced. Aries people are specially suited to the Atomic Age, as they shine in new and undeveloped fields, due to their eagerness to lead the way. In more prosaic pursuits, they are good salesmen and their drive is valuable in real estate, insurance, banking, and other financial fields. Professionally, they are fine actors, capable lawyers, and statesmen. They are also qualified for literary and artistic work.

Due to their strong executive ability, Aries people usually do better on their own, rather than entering into any partnership. However, they need business associates to a degree and their surest choice is someone born under Taurus. While Aries teams well with Sagittarius, Aquarius, and Pisces, any of those are apt to profit more from the association unless the Aries person is strongly dominant. Any association between Aries and Capricorn or Aries and Scorpio may prove highly productive of problems.

In marriage, Aries persons frequently find harmony and understanding with those born in Leo, Sagittarius, or under their own sign. Marriages with Gemini or Libra are regarded as specially suited to the Aries temperament.

TAURUS—THE BULL
April 20–May 19

Strength is the predominating feature of this sign. With it, however, there is a stubborn, firm-set nature that is difficult to change. The governing planet, Venus, emotional and fraught with primitive urge, furthers these Taurian trends rather than repressing them. At the same

Taurus

time, it accounts for the sympathetic side of this strong-willed nature. Taurus people are won over through emotion, rather than by reason.

Taurus persons are opportunists, but they take what comes along, rather than go after it. They absorb ideas and retain them, due to the remarkable memory so often found with persons of this sign. Being practical-minded, they plan ahead and usually carry their purposes through to a finish. By then, they regard any ideas that they have borrowed as being something all their own.

The instinct of the Taurian nature is counterbalanced by its ability to acquire knowledge. Sometimes these faculties are combined; in other instances, they operate independently. Whatever the case, the Taurian's sense of understanding is not only deep, but long-lasting. Taurus persons are well-liked and become the best of friends. Their generosity is genuine and when they make money, they are liberal with it, particularly among friends.

This is because their natures appreciate creature comforts and they seek the best in life, not only for themselves, but to share with others. Their tastes, however, may be simple. Games, outdoor sports and activities, music, anything dramatic or artistic, are apt to satisfy them far more than luxury or ostentatious display.

With Taurus persons, their own interests usually come first; they become big-hearted afterward, though they may go all out for someone any time they are emotionally aroused. Though slow to action, the Taurus nature, once stirred, can overcome all obstacles. Opposition can arouse them to unreasonable fury in which friendships and promises may be thrown to the wind.

Taurians therefore should seek to be slow to anger rather than action. They must curb their stubborn and self-willed natures, which are often stirred by jealousy or prejudice. They should never make decisions when excited or oversympathetic to someone else's viewpoint. Their own honest opinions are best when properly weighed, because Taurians are normally faithful and trustworthy, their own strength sometimes becoming their chief weakness.

In business, the practical mind of Taurus is suited to constructive fields. They can succeed in all mechanical lines, as engineers, builders, and contractors. Their sustained effort makes them good in chemistry and research, while some have become famous as explorers. Often mathematical-minded, they are capable cashiers and accountants; here, their trustworthy nature, once recognized, may raise them to high position in financial circles. They are good teachers, due to their natural sympathy. Their artistic ability is often on the practical side, producing photographers, designers, sculptors, and landscape architects.

In partnerships, Taurus persons do well with those born under Aries or Gemini. An Aries partner can supply the initial drive, which Taurus carries on. From a Gemini individual, a Taurian will gain a variety of ideas, some of which are sure to be suited to the practical mind of Taurus. Good business associations for Taurus are frequently found with Scorpio, Capricorn, or Pisces.

In marriage, Taurus and Scorpio often prove ideal, each being strong or forceful, while supplying qualities that the other needs. Taurus and Virgo are well suited, because of the latter's analytical ability. Taurus may do well with Libra, who adds good judgment to the union, but there is often an element of uncertainty here. Taurus and Capricorn are a very fine marital combination.

GEMINI–THE TWINS
May 20–June 20

Adaptability is the keynote of this sign. Gemini people are not only versatile, they are quick to grasp situations and will act on the spur of the moment, often very effectively. The governing planet, Mercury, is a strong factor in the "Act now, explain later" policy so prevalent with this sign; but Gemini persons are so naturally adaptable to any turn of affairs, that they frequently come up with answers during the course of action.

Gemini

Duality of nature is a concomitant of the Twin sign, and while cases of split personality are comparatively rare, the Gemini mind runs to contradictions. When they go to such extremes, they manage to make their policy sound plausible, at least to their own satisfaction. As well as being imaginative, they are generous and affectionate; but their frequent desire for a change makes them dissatisfied with existing conditions.

Once the urge for anything has lessened, or the project itself seems outworn, a Gemini person will drop it for something newer or more intriguing. These people are popular, quick to acquire new skills; but as a result, they are content with superficial knowledge and halfway results. They are clever, witty, and have an easy way of covering or excusing their faults, without ever intending to correct them.

Gemini people can drive good bargains, and while they look out for themselves, they are very helpful to other persons, often giving them ideas and offering them opportunities. In short, the Gemini individual is free with what he doesn't need or doesn't want and may frequently neglect or reject much that is useful and valuable through his insatiable urge to invade new fields.

Experience means little to the Gemini people; they feel sure of themselves without it. With them, achievement of ambition may be a prelude to disappointment. Hence they should use will power to curb their scattering of activity or it will tell upon them and deny them the contentment that should reward their effort. If they can find the right niche and concentrate their varied abilities upon that goal, happiness will be theirs.

Gemini people have a way of going from hot to cold, like the swing of a pendulum. Their friendly attitude may shift to mistrust when they encounter problems. They are often unconventional as well as skeptical; and their keen foresight may suffer through overenthusiasm, causing them to let real opportunities languish while they go after something else. Above all, they should never waste what they have gained, for though they picture each success as building to something bigger, they overlook the obstacles that can ruin such hopes.

Being born under not just one lucky star, but two, Gemini people should make the most of it while they can, remembering that even double luck can run out and result in nothing.

In business, Gemini people fit almost anywhere. They are good salesmen, promoters, and often successful speculators. They do well in advertising, publishing, television, transportation, and other fields where they must keep up with modern trends. Indeed, this is a lush era for Gemini folks, who find industries changing so rapidly that they are worthy of the quick answers which these people can supply.

As teachers, writers, artists, and also as politicians, Gemini people have both the right attitude and aptitude. In business associations, they do well with Taurus, for persons of that sign are receptive to Gemini notions and will see them through. The balanced nature of Libra and the straight-aiming qualities of Sagittarius, make both of those signs good partners for those born under Gemini. One of the strongest combinations in the zodiac is that of versatile Gemini and conservative Cancer, provided the latter serves strictly as a counter-balance rather than a drag.

In marriage, Gemini and Libra are well suited, as are Gemini and Aquarius; but some restraining force is needed, due to the wavering natures in both cases. Gemini gains drive from an Aries marriage; and exuberance from a mate born under Leo. Gemini and Sagittarius form an unusually good marital combination.

CANCER—THE CRAB
June 21–July 22

Here we find people who are tried and true, who cling to tradition as though they were a part of it. Yet their moods and even their purposes may become as changeable as the sign's ruling planet, the Moon. This self-contradiction is understandable, when recognized as part of the individual's innate nature.

Cancer

These people are home-loving, fond of family life and domestic tranquillity, but they also enjoy travel and adventure. They love the past and sometimes practically live in it, which accounts for the way they seek the new, yet always come back to the old. Persons born under this sign are very sensitive, though they frequently do not show it. Argument wears them down, criticism hurts them and crablike, they crawl into their shells.

Though strongly conservative, they are fond of amusements and social life. Their moods may differ by day or night and even changes of weather affect their restless natures. But beneath that variable surface, they are steadfast, disapproving sudden or radical changes. Their loyalty to friends and family is constant, unless broken by some actual hurt or imagined slight; then they may never feel the same toward a person.

Both imaginative and affectionate, Cancer folk are not apt to show these emotions outwardly, hence they are too often misunderstood or go unappreciated. They should avoid any spite of jealousy, because these can become their greatest faults. Also, they should be expressive of their sympathy and loyalty, otherwise their friends may regard them as fickle.

These people are frequently vivacious and are humanitarians as well, devoting themselves to worthy causes. But they have letdowns and can become too opinionated to understand another person's viewpoint. Then they begin to wonder why they have been neglected or ignored, never willing to admit that the blame may be theirs. Sometimes their firmest decisions will be abandoned without reason, another indication that they are swayed by moods.

Despite these contradictory characteristics, this can be developed into one of the best of signs by persons who subordinate the morbid side and refuse to dwell in the past. They have strong determination and great perseverance, otherwise they would not go to the extremes that they do. If they put these faculties to constant effort instead of futile conflict, they can attain great goals and free themselves of worry and despondency.

In business, people of this sign succeed along established lines. They do well as manufacturers and merchants, for with them, quality is important and they are proud of their name and whatever they produce. They must learn to be progressive, however, for they can vacillate in business as well as other fields and find themselves left far behind.

Professionally, they are good teachers, librarians, historians, and scientists. They are capable lawyers and politicians. Many rise to high rank in art, literature, and music. They may miss opportunities, though, because of their inherent changeability, and this applies particularly to those in subordinate positions who are too content to think of what they might have been instead of becoming what they should be.

Proper business associations can do much to rectify this. Cancer and Capricorn are opposite enough to form a strong combination. There is an affinity between Cancer and Aquarius that also marks them as good business partners. An association with Gemini is excellent, if the Cancer individual can keep his versatile partner under due restraint. In contrast, a teaming with exuberant Leo is very effective, provided Leo is allowed to dominate in the matter of decisions.

In marriage, the home-loving nature of Cancer is a highly important factor, but it must be remembered that Cancer mates can suffer through neglect. As in business, Cancer and Capricorn are usually admirably suited to matrimony. Cancer and Pisces are a good combination; while Scorpio and Libra also mate well with Cancer.

LEO—THE LION
July 23–August 21

This is the sign of exuberance, denoting powerful personality and born leadership. Both ambition and idealism are present under Leo, for the brilliance of this sign reflects the grandeur of its governing planet, the Sun. But Leo, as well as being high-minded, can be high-handed. When persons of this type fall victims to their own shortcomings, the result can prove disastrous. Worse, it is usually not noticeable until after the crash.

Leo

There is little of the negative in Leo. That is what makes this sign deceptive and sometimes deceitful. Leo people are impulsive, generous, and brave, quick to follow their own intuition. Their success is furthered by their marked influence upon all persons that they meet, often winning over those who oppose them by their sheer magnetic qualities. But if their efforts are wrongly directed, this can result in false idealism. The Leo benefactor is sometimes only a hairsbreadth from a tyrant.

Leo people insist upon charting their own course and do so with an inherent vigor. They like everything that is active, including outdoor life, for they crave the warmth of the sun that is so predominant in their sign. They ride over their own faults so naturally, that apparently they are not aware of them. Their very exuberance makes them show-offs, but they feel they are above such criticism.

By an odd quirk, indolence is the greatest of drawbacks to the Leo temperament. They will revel in ease and luxury until they are forced to action either through necessity or their own self-imposed demands. They love the spotlight, perhaps because to them it is the sun in miniature. They seek appreciation and affection as quickly as they give it, but they form their own conclusions without considering whether they are right or wrong.

As a result, when they honestly think that they are right, they assume that all critics must be wrong. There are no halfway measures in such exuberant natures. They stand up for their friends and family in the same impulsive way and are ready to denounce all who disagree. Hence, the higher they rise, the more convinced they become of their own importance and the less they care about the opposition. Leo's power can override anything.

Leo personalities do not show jealousy. Instead, they invite it, which throws the burden on their critics. But they are easily flattered and make the mistake of trusting false friends. They are above petty things and gain results through their own personality and charm. But if they find themselves slipping, they will justify whatever measures they need to take in order to retain what they honestly feel is rightfully theirs.

In business, Leo offers unlimited prospects. The men of this sign are fine physicians, the women excellent nurses, because of the influence they hold upon their patients. They succeed in many other professions, because they have a flair for showmanship, which can sway clients quite as effectively as audiences. Many noted actors were born under this sign; and in the literary field, they have had a strong trend toward the dramatic, all part of the Leo makeup.

In the strictly commercial lines, Leo people star in special fields. Anything requiring promotion or enthusiastic development comes in their domain. They are capable hotel men, restaurateurs, real estate developers, sales managers, and executives, for their enthusiasm is contagious. As partners, they team well with persons of all signs, but do particularly well with those born under Cancer, Virgo, and Aquarius.

In marriage, the Leo exuberance is also generally helpful, though not always harmonious. Perhaps they are best suited to Aries, Sagittarius, or Aquarius; but Leo also has excellent marital prospects with Cancer and Virgo, as well as those of their own sign, Leo.

VIRGO—THE VIRGIN
August 22–September 22

This is the sign of analysis. Under it are found some of the most capable and yet most difficult personalities in the entire zodiac. The governing planet, Mercury, may be the cause of this, for it supplies quickness to a nature which could well afford to be more deliberate and given to deeper purposes. Added to the keen Virgo mind, it produces good reasoners and convincing talkers, though they are apt to spend too much time over trifling details and also to talk a subject dry.

Virgo people have inquiring minds that will not rest until they have learned all they want to know about something. They are skilled at drawing information from people, then filling in from other sources or rationalizing facts into a complete and remarkably accurate picture. Often they pick up essential data without anyone realizing what they are about.

Virgo

Along with keen analysis, they have remarkable memories, otherwise they could not form the exact comparisons that they do. They have prolific memories, seem to retain all that they read, and have the ability to express it in new and elaborated form. Their analytical ability causes them to find fault with people and projects, and while their purpose is generally constructive, they are often regarded both as overcurious and too critical. This is unfortunate as it causes misunderstandings and lost opportunities.

Order and harmony are essential to the Virgo mind. Therefore, Virgo people should simplify their lives and purposes, or they will bog down under a mass of detail that their exacting minds cannot ignore. The less little things to bother them, the greater their capacity for higher aims. Virgo people are usually tolerant, but once blind to their own faults, they may become even more opinionated than those whom they criticize.

Imagination rules the Virgo mind, making them fearful of accidents, illness, and financial problems. They are sensitive to pain and any kind of suffering, which makes them superficially sympathetic to persons who experience misfortune. Actually, they are anxious to dismiss misery from their minds. Their mental quickness, their ability to concentrate on some other subject, can aid them to shake off any morbid spells. But unless they do so, they will fall victims to their own imagination.

Usually, Virgo people are alert, hard-working, and given to intellectual pursuits. They depend upon their ego as a driving force, but should show the same understanding of others that they expect for themselves. In short, they should never become self-centered, or they may resort to deceit, double-dealing, and other crafty devices to attain what they regard as a justifiable goal. Usually, they can rise above such faults, once they are aware of them, for they have great self-control if they will only exercise it. Defeat only stirs them to new purposes and their minds are quick to envision coming success.

In business, Virgo people are suited to special lines, where their quick minds see new opportunities or productive deals. They are good at analyzing business conditions and market trends. They become good writers, editors, lawyers, professors, because they size up things quickly and apply them ingeniously. Many become architects or designers. As actors, lecturers, and showmen they must overcome their self-consciousness to succeed. The same often applies in salesmanship.

Virgo's analytical ability teams well with Leo's exuberance, where a business partnership is concerned. Virgo also gains much from Libra's judgment and intuition; but here, Virgo may chafe under restraint. Virgo also does well with Pisces; and sometimes Scorpio. In fact, Virgo gets along in business with nearly every other sign; but many of them are apt to gain far more from the Virgo person than they give in return. Therefore, Virgo people must be very careful in choice of business associates.

Marriage presents problems for Virgo, because of the exacting, fault-finding, and sometimes demanding nature evidenced by this sign. One of the best marital combinations for Virgo is with another of the same sign, as each may understand the other's critical moods. Virgo should find great happiness with Pisces; while Aries, Taurus, and Capricorn should prove compatible. Virgo and Libra should be helpful to each other, but their strong minds too often come in conflict, making this a dubious combination.

LIBRA—THE SCALES
September 23–October 22

This is the sign of justice, indicative of persons who balance every-thing to a nicety, always trying to promote good will and friendship, even if they must go to extremes to do so. This is actuated by their inherent love of harmony and beauty, as reflected by the beneficent gleam of the sign's ruling planet, Venus.

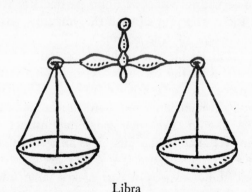

Libra

Sympathy and understanding are paramount with Venus. They are never deaf to an appeal from family or friends and they will often side with total strangers if they seem to represent a deserving cause. The Libra person tends to champion the underdog, even against their sounder judgment. Again, this seems due to their urge to equalize matters and produce harmony.

Intuition is a guiding force with Libra and often enables them to ferret out deceit and insincerity, no matter how much it is glossed over. But if Libra folks prejudge a matter, or listen to persons in whom they trust or sympathize, they can be carried far astray. They are so susceptible to influence of those who impress them, that they will imitate the manners of such persons and actually pick up their traits.

Everything in Libra has to do with balance; hence the susceptibility of the Libra individual is counterbalanced by a strong-mindedness that can become firm and unflinching in purpose. Librans become dissatisfied with anything wherein they are disregarded, even if it is to their own best interest. If they are not consulted on a matter, they consider it unfair play and their high sense of impartiality is offended.

Though imitative in conduct, they are original in ideas and often quite farsighted because of their intuitive qualities. Their motives are always of the highest, but they will act upon impulse when they deem it right. They are generous and expect that quality in others; hence they are inclined to regard a mere slight as a rank injustice, causing rifts between them and the persons thus involved.

Libra people like amusements and excitement. Their love of harmony makes them fond of music. They should learn to accept criticism, otherwise their sense of justice can become warped and they will argue themselves into accepting wrong as right, particularly when they yield to the wiles of those who prey upon their sympathy, rather than listening to the blunt words of true friends.

In business, Libra people rise to high positions, as their judgment, properly exercised, is of the executive type. Similarly, their sympathy toward subordinates can prove a powerful asset. Their intuitive ability makes them excellent merchants and their hunches aid them in speculative fields. They should curb their gambling instinct or it may run away with them, yet at the same time, it is an asset in certain fields.

Libra people are often inventors, and they are good researchers and historians. Their ability to play a part makes them fine actors. They are excellent musicians and singers. They are also mathematical-minded and are suited to many arts and crafts. Since they rely on their own judgment, they should be wary of business partnerships. They team well with Gemini, Virgo, or Scorpio, provided any of those agree to rely on the Libra judgment. Many other signs are too cautious to team up with Libra, especially Pisces.

In marriage, Libra does well with Aries, because of the latter's drive. Libra gains exuberance from marriage with Leo. Perhaps the susceptible Libra and the jovial Sagittarius are the best mating of all; but Libra also harmonizes with Aquarius and gains something from Gemini or Scorpio.

There is a natural attraction between Libra and Virgo, but conflicts of interests may result. Libra and Pisces are seldom a suitable combination.

SCORPIO—THE SCORPION
October 23–November 21

Here is the sign of bold enterprise, a fearless nature guided by self-control and confidence, but geared for action when the time demands. The governing planet, Mars, provides the power with which this sign is packed, denoting the will to surmount all obstacles.

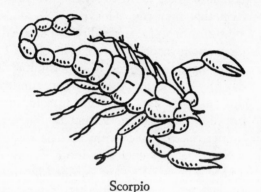

Scorpio

Theodore Roosevelt, who was born under Scorpio, once quoted the adage, "Speak softly and carry a big stick; you will go far." That aptly sums the characteristics of this sign. Scorpio people are quiet, even secretive in manner, yet highly observant. Once roused to action, they are determined, aggressive, and dominant, always ready to champion a cause.

When they work for the good of others, they rise to great heights and are much respected, but Scorpio people, always well-satisfied with themselves, can become domineering and arrogant. When seeking reform, they show little mercy toward those who oppose them, and it is not uncommon for Scorpio folks to stretch a point and justify their actions regardless of honest opposition.

If Scorpio folks apply their forceful determination solely to making money, particularly in fields which have no regard for human welfare, their fine traits will give way to selfishness, petty jealousy, and even ruthless action. Once they think only of material gain, they lose their natural sympathies along with their dignity and self-control.

Scorpio people are blunt, argumentative, and natural fighters, but their coolness under fire deceives the opposition and adds to the Scorpio strength. Always, in the showdown, Scorpio is apt to have the upper hand. That is why they should control their tempers as well as their actions.

Added up, this means that Scorpio people should develop their talents and take an interest in the better things of life. They should never let their remarkable capability for calm deliberation degenerate into procrastination. They should direct their interests toward the benefit of humanity, remembering that their ability to overcome obstacles will enable them to attain any goal; therefore, the finer their purpose, the greater the ambition that they can achieve.

In business, a powerful Scorpio personality can succeed in practically any line. They range from managers of branch offices to the head of a great industry. They have the greatest of opportunities in the expanding world of today, for as heads of bureaus, committees, and other investigative groups, no other sign can begin to equal them. Scorpio is the sign of the future, a fact that should not be forgotten. Professionally, those born under Scorpio frequently become great physicians.

In partnership, Scorpio's best choice is Libra, for the bold projects of the Scorpio mind will be weighed and certified by Libra's judgment. Scorpio sometimes does well with Sagittarius, if they can agree upon their policy. Each has the quality needed by the other, if they can solve the question of togetherness. Virgo, Taurus, and Cancer do well with Scorpio, if needed. Always remember that Scorpio can do quite well alone.

In marriage, Scorpio finds three strong choices: Taurus, Cancer, and Pisces. Scorpio's crusading spirit is admirably seconded by Taurus. The Scorpio boldness carries along the wavering Cancer disposition, and brings the strong points of Pisces to the fore. Scorpio may also find a harmonious marriage with Virgo; while Scorpio's power and Leo's exuberance may prove a satisfactory marital combination. The success of such unions, however, depends greatly upon the individuals involved.

SAGITTARIUS—THE BOWMAN
November 22–December 21

Activity is the keynote of this sign, and while the persons born under it are often capable in many ways, they have the faculty of concentrating upon the project of immediate importance. Like the bowmen, they aim for their target and are apt to score a hit. Add to that a cheerful, happy disposition, stemming from the governing planet, Jupiter, and Sagittarius has the makings of an excellent sign.

Sagittarius

However, there are pitfalls. The natural energy which gains such good results can be wasted through overzeal or the feverish excitement that too often accompanies their work. Sagittarians wear themselves out in their anxiety to get things done; therefore they should seek projects worthy of their efforts, offering full-time prospects. The saying, "Not failure, but low aim, is crime," applies strongly to Sagittarians.

Being workers, not seekers, these people can accomplish twice as much as others and will apply themselves to charitable or helpful causes with the same energy that they devote to their own aims. When their time is thus divided, they are often happiest, because by doubling their effort—as they like to do!—they can still handle their own affairs along with someone else's.

When confronted by adversity or failure, these people can usually stage a remarkable "comeback" by stepping up their activity or their output. But it is that very nervous impatience to be always doing more that causes them to stumble or flounder in the first place. They are naturally intuitive with keen foresight, so when they feel sure that something "can't go wrong" they yield to impulse and in their excitement or enthusiasm overlook new problems that arise. Also, because their natures are versatile, they pick up new things too quickly, thinking they have learned all there is to know about them.

Sagittarius people mind their own business, but sometimes go so far afield that they conflict with others. They are very outspoken and often offend more sensitive persons without realizing why. Being so frank and forthright, they assume that any one who is at all secretive must be hiding something that is wrong. As a result, Sagittarians can become scathing in their accusations, making mountains out of molehills.

Impulsive acts cause Sagittarians great trouble, clear on through middle age, when they become irritable and develop unruly tempers, which can only be soothed or restrained by persons whom they trust. Sometimes they literally wear themselves down until their impulsiveness is merely spasmodic. With stamina gone, they fuss from one minor project to another, getting nowhere.

But at their best and strongest, Sagittarius people insist on seeing things through and their impulsive actions are contagious, bringing them great popularity and a host of followers. Those who achieve success under this sign are usually neat, methodical, and orderly.

In business, Sagittarians succeed in anything that provides a multitude of outlets for their active, versatile minds. They like to travel and do well as prospectors, mining engineers, air pilots, and sea captains. Imports and exports are good lines for their progressive, systematic minds. They do well as bankers and financiers, but in all well-established endeavors they should avoid too many side interests, remembering that time is money.

Inventors, writers, stock raisers, and large farm operators are all found under Sagittarius. They are very strong in scientific and mechanical fields, and in partnership with Aries or Gemini they can gain great results. The impulsiveness of Sagittarius and the exuberance of Leo is also an effective combination, though it may prove less sustained.

Partnerships between Sagittarius and slower-moving signs are generally unproductive. There is one exception: Sagittarius supplies the impulsive fervor that Capricorn needs, making that a good combination. The impulsiveness of Sagittarius also combines with the deliberation of Scorpio, but chiefly in big enterprises. In lesser projects they may disagree.

In marriage, Sagittarius is aptly called "the bachelor sign" because these freedom-seeking folk can get along quite well on their own. But being cheerful, considerate, and willing to share burdens, they often prove to be fine spouses. Sagittarians do well to marry someone born under their own sign, or a person born in Gemini, due to the mutual urge toward varied interests. Sagittarius also may marry well with Aries or Leo, which are themselves impulsive to a degree. Sagittarius and Libra are often a good marital team, due to their mutual recognition of intuitive qualities.

CAPRICORN—THE GOAT
December 22–January 21

This is the scholarly, intellectual sign, producing deep thinkers and philosophers, yet with it, Capricorn people apply themselves to practical things. This helps them to shake off the gloomy moods caused by their governing planet, Saturn. As a result, Capricornians are generally regarded as extremists, though often they are simply striving to strike a proper balance.

Capricorn

These people are calm and deliberate in method and action. They approach new subjects in a scholarly fashion and instinctively try to increase their range of knowledge. They are good organizers as well as philosophers and they like to think things out alone. Here, they show the Saturnian love of solitude, which is good when practically applied, but should be avoided if it produces morbid trends.

Capricornians have something resembling a psychic sense and are often quite aware of it. Fear of ridicule often curtails their expression of their views, making them secretive, but in a defensive way. They take a dark view of many projects, feeling that they are too difficult; this, in turn, causes Capricornians to shun the world and seek solitude.

To the practical philosophy of Capricorn, nothing succeeds like success. Thus they are inspired by appreciation and advancement. Once fully self-reliant, they will fight for further success along a chosen or recognized line. Opposition and criticism worry them; and they must learn to meet such challenges through patience and perseverance.

Capricornians need encouragement early in life, so as to gain confidence and develop their genial and witty qualities. The more gregarious they become, the more diversified and practical their interests, the better they can elude the ever-haunting factors of gloom and despair.

Intellectual Capricornians who fail to broaden their views or accept the more practical side of life, are apt to become morose and give themselves over to reckless dissipation. Those who fail to develop their studious qualities at all and who have no benefit of early cultural training, may become utterly despondent and totally unable to combat adverse conditions.

Self-interest is strong in Capricorn, for these people are used to finding their own way; but those who are well developed are by no means selfish. Fear of the future often makes them economical, but they share their possessions with others, sometimes too generously. Once a gloomy mood has passed, a Capricorn person often manages to forget it. Their desire for success is usually so determined that it rouses petty jealousy on the part of others. If Capricornians do not fall victims to despair, they can outlast their problems and overcome all limitations, becoming true optimists.

In business, people of this sign are good managers, superintendents, bookkeepers, and accountants. Their practical foresight makes them good financiers. They succeed in many professions, as lecturers, teachers, and lawyers, to name a few. They usually evidence strong literary qualifications.

Capricorn and Sagittarius may make exceptional business partners, combining foresight with impulse. Capricorn finds good business associates in Taurus or Virgo. Capricorn and Aquarius do well, provided Aquarius does not hold Capricorn back. The same applies with Capricorn and Cancer, a combination that is pleasant, but apt to fail through Cancer's timidity.

In marriage, Capricorn probably does best with Virgo, though Capricorn and Taurus may prove an equally fine combination. Capricorn and Aries also promise good marital prospects. All three of those signs have qualities which are helpful to Capricorn's changing moods.

AQUARIUS—THE WATER CARRIER
January 21–February 19

This has been styled the humanitarian sign because many persons born under Aquarius dedicate themselves to causes, take on great missions, and advance the affairs of humanity in general. Their governing planet, Saturn, supplies them with a reticence or natural reserve which enables them to accomplish things in a quiet, surprising way. It also has a studious influence and helps to endow them with fine and useful memories.

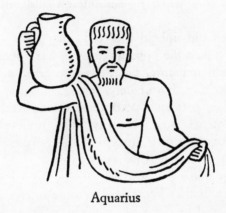

Aquarius

Primarily, Aquarians are simple, unassuming persons. They absorb knowledge readily and show a frank and friendly attitude that makes them popular. They often like to be alone, but not for morbid reasons. They use solitude to concentrate on new ideas and to make important decisions. Also, much of their real work is done when they are by themselves.

Aquarians who develop the honesty and kindly sentiments of this sign will attain great heights. They have mild dispositions and can curb their tempers. They are both active and volatile and once their ambitions are aroused, they can scale to unprecedented heights. Their greatest fault is indolence, for if they delay or treat life lazily, they will never get anywhere. They must also maintain their natural, quiet dignity; for without it, they may become boastful and surly, losing the popularity which may carry them far.

More famous persons have come from this sign than any other and in the great majority of cases they have risen from obscurity or have made up for early failure, sometimes succeeding despite insurmountable odds. Invariably they have done this on their own, through the full application of all that they have learned and usually more. Self-reliance, confidence, and the belief that they are right are the qualities that spell their success.

The humanitarian urge is very apparent in the careers of scientists, musicians, reformers, poets, pioneers, and explorers born under this sign. These are the real "water carriers" who supply the human race. Others have risen to high and commanding positions, so that rather than water carriers they have become standard bearers around whom many people rally. Still, their devotion to humanity is strong, even though they may be spurred by self-interest and criticized as being self-important.

All Aquarians should uphold the credo that right makes might, as the few who have taken the opposite attitude have done great damage. In short, the Aquarian nature, once given to arrogance and bombast, will brook no opposition. Fortunately, few such Aquarians attain great heights. Instead, they pass up opportunities, ask advice but never follow it, and seldom emerge from obscurity. The undeveloped Aquarian promises much but does little, except in a confused and sometimes fanatical way that defeats its own ends.

In business, Aquarians are good bargainers, keen buyers, and make capable auctioneers, as they know how to rouse interest. They are great promoters and do well in law and especially politics. They have great mechanical skill and noted scientists as well as famous inventors have been born under this sign.

Business partnerships are valuable to Aquarians, who seldom press their opportunities themselves, but require the cooperation of others. They guide Aries people to opportunities and rouse the latent force of Pisces. Aquarians have a steadying effect on Gemini or Libra, which can prove of mutual advantage.

In marriage, Aquarius does well with most signs, for the Aquarian has an understanding nature. Gemini, Leo, and Libra are especially good as they respond strongly to the sympathies of Aquarius.

PISCES—THE FISH
February 20–March 20

Here is the most modest and unassuming sign of the zodiac. Pisces people acquire knowledge, then fail to show it, often regarding it of little consequence and believing that other people who brag about their ability must actually know more than they do. Their governing planet, Jupiter, has much to do with this, for it endows these Pisces people with a nature so generous that it becomes overtrustful.

Pisces

Because of their unselfish dispositions, persons of this sign fail to realize their own possibilities. The greater their honesty, the more doubtful they become as to their own ability. This produces fear of the future, which in turn causes them immediate worry. Hence, Pisces people are perhaps the most cautious of all, where their own affairs are concerned.

In contrast, however, they rely upon the promises of other people and are frequently and easily duped. Though they themselves are sincere and trustworthy, they are often blamed for the mistakes of others, who shunt the burden onto the kindly Pisces person. Often, a Pisces individual becomes the victim of a subtle, cunning plot, which he never even begins to suspect.

There are two saving factors to this sign. One is the optimistic trend inspired by Jupiter. Most other planets would be deadly if they held chief sway over Pisces. But thanks to their jovial dispositions, people of this sign ride over deep troubles almost as trifles. The other factor in their behalf is that their true worth is appreciated by real friends and good people, who help them to bring out their strong points and even serve as a buffer against unscrupulous persons.

Calmness is a great trait of Pisces and should be used to fight off worry and imaginary problems. These people should weigh vital questions beforehand; then be sure that they act on sound judgment. They should never listen to persuasive appeals to their generosity, but should study solid facts, come to a conclusion, and if need be, take the advice of proven and impartial friends.

There is determination in the Pisces nature, and it becomes stronger the more it is aroused. Pisces people should cultivate this for their own good. If they are accused of being stubborn, that is all right, too, as long as it makes them more determined. If they yield on minor points, they should never let that become a wedge for a greater play upon their sympathies.

Pisces people are deep in their devotion to friends and causes, even under the most hopeless circumstances. There is no downing their optimism, and they imbue others with the same confidence. A Pisces person is fortunate indeed, when he or she finds a right niche in life; and those who depend upon them are still more fortunate in having such a stalwart friend.

In business, Pisces people belong with large organizations where their honesty and executive capacity can be appreciated. They do well in government jobs and scientific pursuits. Many of them succeed as engineers. They are interested in historical subjects and all forms of nature.

Pisces and Aries form a good team in business. Association with Taurus, Virgo, and Aquarius also furnish attractive prospects. Pisces, with its reliability, and Capricorn, with business judgment, make a good partnership in enterprises where each can handle the part to which he is best suited.

While a marriage between two persons born under Pisces is harmonious, it is difficult for one to bring out the other's stronger qualities. Pisces does well with Cancer, Virgo, and Scorpio; and other signs often prove helpful, with the exception of Libra, which is too prone to weigh the Pisces shortcomings.

The Cusps

Persons born "on the line" between two signs of the zodiac partake of qualities found in both those signs, or more strictly speaking, have a blend of traits that may compose an individual nature. Due to variations in astrological calendars, this may become apparent during the last few days of a departing sign, but the "cusp," as it is termed, pertains chiefly to the first week of the incoming sign.

While the new sign is gaining its ascendancy, the influence of the old persists, but gradually loses its hold day by day, until by the seventh day, the new sign is in full control. So in the descriptions of the cusps and their significance, the approximate dates of the first week are given. The names of both signs are included and persons born on or near the line should refer to the chart of each sign for a summary of personal traits, at the same time remembering that the strength of the latter sign is more evident with each successive birth date.

The cusps follow:

PISCES—ARIES
March 20 to 27

Inherent caution and foresight restrain the natural drive and ambition of the Aries sign. It is an excellent combination, since Jupiter, as governing planet of Pisces, supplies an ambition of its own, in the form of deep determination, which Mars, ruler of Aries, will further in an assertive way.

Such people are quick to accept new ideas, but generally reconsider them before venturing too far, since the Pisces nature abhors failure. They also regret hasty action, and when roused to anger, under the Martian urge, they cool down rapidly and worry over their brief display.

The same applies when they become boastful, or even too talkative. They feel that they have let their enthusiasm carry them beyond their capability and they try to retrench. This applies to new business ventures. Their Aries nature takes them into active, challenging, and even speculative fields, though always with honest purpose. But unless they gain immediate results, they will fall back on something tried and true.

This is because the Jupiterian carry-over from Pisces causes them to value the opinion of other persons ahead of the self-esteem which Mars furthers through Aries. Persons born at this period are fighters, but must be sure of their ground. They are good promoters and developers of new ideas, but only when those are founded upon established facts or principles. Then, the native of this cusp has the firm conviction needed to proceed.

ARIES—TAURUS
April 19 to 26

The Martian carry-over from Aries gives this cusp an impetuous touch that can become both powerful and dangerous through the self-willed and often stubborn nature of Taurus, with Venus as its emotional, pleasure-loving governing planet. However, they can become doubly strong and purposeful.

When these people act impulsively and their plans suffer, they seldom give up. Having started as go-getters, they become bullheaded and see it through. Often, they take up enterprises just to prove that they can put them across, and usually they do. Because of this, they should exert their powers along honest, worthwhile lines. Their self-esteem is exceeded only by their urge for self-gratification, which will make them unreasonable and overbearing unless they develop self-control.

Briefly summed, this is an excellent blend of natures provided a person chooses undertakings that are not only worth the effort involved, but are also worthy of it. Here is a chance to turn initial drive into sustained power, particularly because those born on this cusp are suited to all the occupations given under Taurus, but should have greater prospects in those fields than the average person of that sign.

They should remember, though, that their strength does not lie in the creation of ideas, but in their development, which is all the more reason for choosing well in the first place.

TAURUS–GEMINI
May 19 to 26

The firm-set Taurian nature with Venus in control acts as a counterbalance to the activity of Mercury, with its quick, Mercurian ways. The desire to try new things is in the ascendant, because of Gemini, but there is an inherent reluctance to give up the old, a carry-over from Taurus. This is a factor toward stability.

However, too much of this can hamper the Gemini nature. It may mean trying to do two things at once, to the detriment of both. It also can make a person stubborn about lesser things, even when he knows very little about them. Self-control is strongly needed, and once acquired, it will enable the individual to correct another lack, that of concentration, which is essential to this highly adaptable but somewhat contradictory type.

Active employment is a "must" with those born in this cusp. It is the only way to keep their quick but forceful minds at work and to develop their unusual talents. They are free with money and can become wasteful unless they are purposeful. But they can succeed at almost anything if they try.

GEMINI–CANCER
June 20 to 27

Because of Gemini and its ruler, Mercury, there is a desire here to take up new projects and switch occupations, which can greatly influence the restless nature of Cancer, with its own conflicts and contrasts. With the Moon in the ascendant, this period needs stability. Oddly, however, the flashback to Gemini provides it in a way.

People born in this cusp become extremely active during the daytime and all other working hours, thus overcoming their restlessness at night. Their strong sense of conservatism also restrains them from taking on unwise or questionable enterprises, a usual Mercurian fault. These people just won't gamble or take undue risks beyond a well-defined point.

They have quick wits, however, and are so intrigued with things about them and find so much happiness in their own activity, that they manage to shake off the retrospective moods that are such a handicap to others born under the sign of Cancer. Once they have attained an aim, they move on to something else, feeling that the more they do in the future, the more satisfied they will be when it becomes the past.

In brief, these people create their own traditions, thus conforming to their innate love of the old while accepting and enjoying the new. They are suited to any of the occupations given under Cancer, with greater chance of success in most of those lines—as well as others—due to the high activity provided by their Gemini background. They must, however, curb any tendency toward excitability and overindulgence in diversions, particularly at times when the Moon is on the wane.

CANCER–LEO
July 22 to 29

Here, exuberant Leo, with its powerful governing influence, the Sun, takes almost full control over uncertain Cancer with its flickery, fickle governor, the Moon. But the lesser force is present and can evidence itself, just as the Moon occasionally eclipses the Sun.

People born at this time should regard themselves as Leo subjects, striving to shake off any lunar weaknesses that may prove to be their undoing. If they become retrospective, they should consider the past and its traditions purely as a guide toward a greater future. If they are moody, they should snap from it and think in terms of ambition. When they become sympathetic to suffering, they should take immediate steps to better the condition of such persons.

Otherwise, the brilliant, intellectual qualities of Leo can become warped or dissipated. Fascinated by their own brilliance and eloquence, persons of this period can become self-hypnotized to the point where they consider themselves masters of right or wrong. From high-minded reformers, they can become unscrupulous spellbinders. Their self-confidence will cause them to ridicule their own conservatism.

Once the Leo mind drops its idealism and falls prey to indolence or deceit, the lunar forces will take over in the worst way, stirring the restless mind with jealousy. This can all be avoided, however, by fostering the natural exuberance of Leo and turning it to progressive channels. Leo people born during this early period can rise high in professions such as medicine and law, as well as becoming fine educators, because their human sympathies are strongly furthered by the lunar undercurrent.

LEO–VIRGO
August 21 to 28

Exuberance, indicated by Leo's ruler, the Sun, combines with the quickness that Mercury applies to Virgo's analytical ability. The result is an intuitive nature, wherein the Sun brings out the favorable side of Mercury while Virgo's harmony counteracts Leo's chief weakness, indolence.

Virgo's curiosity is tempered by Leo's sympathy, keeping these people open and above-board in their dealings; but they can suffer through their own self-importance. The more their good points, the quicker they recognize them through their ability at self-analysis, and their egotism is apt to swell proportionately. The fact that it is justified only makes it worse for them, if it rouses the animosity and jealousy of others.

People born in this period are good actors, writers, and lawyers, but are less likely to become physicians, due to the oversympathy of their highly imaginative minds. They are good businessmen with great executive prospects, as they are forceful enough to command interest and respect.

The closer to the line, the more basic the Leo traits, with Virgo turning them to practical application not found in the usual Leo nature. The Virgo nature takes over rapidly during its ascendancy, but good na-

ture persists and produces willing workers. They must curb their desir
for display and smug self-satisfaction.

VIRGO–LIBRA
September 21 to 29

The shrewd, quick ruling force of Mercury and the analytical sign
of Virgo have a marked influence that carries through this period, giving
a sharp perception to the Libra nature, which with its governing planet,
Venus, is impressionistic and relies on judgment rather than analysis.
Generally considered, it is a fine combination, giving Libra the elements
that it needs most. It is largely a case of studying the faults of Virgo and
guarding against them, as the sharper Mercury may prove injurious to
the softer, more understanding qualities of Venus.

Otherwise all is for the best. This cusp shows the Libra sense of
judgment coupled with a quick ability to size a situation and back a
decision with sound logic. Trivialities should be avoided, as minor issues
will bring worry, particularly over what other people will think or do.
But there is logic in the minds of those born at this time, enough to enable them to modify their judgment in the light of later facts.

Fortunately, their tendency is one of self-criticism in minor matters,
which keeps them quite steadfast where more important things are at
stake, and if they systematize their efforts in big directions, they will automatically overcome lesser complications. They are suited for many of
the occupations of the Virgo type as well as those recommended for
Libra.

LIBRA–SCORPIO
October 21 to 29

The fair judgment of Libra, with its sympathetic ruler, Venus, adds
intuition to the cool, precise skill of Scorpio with its aggressive governor,
Mars. The result is a very remarkable combination if care is taken in
its development. Along with the Libra craving for excitement, there is
the bold, pleasure-seeking Scorpio mind, strong in self-control and determination, ready to carry into action whatever seems worthwhile.

The ability to turn ideas into accomplishment often produces a
marked egotism among people of this period, which is all the more reason why they should seek higher things in culture, education, and social
life. Whatever they achieve, they cling to with tenacity, so the un-

developed Scorpio with a Libra background may become narrow-minded and unscrupulous. They are easily flattered, especially by popular acclaim, and flare into anger toward those who oppose their schemes.

With their intuition and judgment developed to the full, they are not only dynamic but are endowed with the rare presence of mind found in physicians and military men. They are generous in disposition, but should develop their natural ability to think and act promptly, as their tendency to delay or mull things over can prove costly.

SCORPIO–SAGITTARIUS

November 20 to 28

The boldness of Scorpio with its aggressive ruler, Mars, is helpful indeed to the active, versatile nature of Sagittarius, with the highly magnetic qualities gained from its governing planet, Jupiter. Here are people who can accomplish the most difficult things and meet almost any emergency.

The Sagittarian zeal offsets any procrastination from Scorpio, producing a strength of purpose and accomplishment that seems far beyond them. They are frank and open-minded, perhaps too much so, but they usually manage to curb their ego to the simple point of self-satisfaction over true accomplishment.

This is the type that can succeed at whatever they undertake, as executives, engineers, physicians, explorers, and the like. No obstacles seem to stop them, except that overconfidence in their own ability. If they lapse into the Scorpio tendency to delay, they will make it up with Sagittarian fervor, often expending too much effort in their project.

In short, the fiery Sagittarius nature can burn itself out, when it has watery Scorpio as its damper. Fire and water, properly separated, produce steam, with steady as well as powerful results. Those born in the early part of Sagittarius should aim for such consistency.

SAGITTARIUS–CAPRICORN

December 20 to 28

Jupiter as ruler of Sagittarius provides a jovial influence, plus the sign's own activity, that is of great value to the practical, yet self-effacing Capricorn nature, with its moody governing planet, Saturn. From that blend, persons born in this period can develop a versatile type of intellectuality which few others can match.

Persons born in this cusp learn things easily and at the same time constantly crave for knowledge, taking up all subjects that appeal to them. Here, they show intelligent choice, in keeping with the Capricorn sign, so that they shine in specific fields, ranging from professional to home life.

They do well, however, to keep such fields interrelated, applying what they learn from one in another, rather than becoming jacks-of-all-trades. Usually, they follow this efficient Capricorn pattern, avoiding the wasteful expense of energy, which is a Sagittarian carry-over.

They should live up to the motto, not merely to try, but to accomplish. Thus they may attain much in a comparatively short time. They have great patience and are very fond of children. They also know the importance of wealth, hence aim for the high positions which they can and do attain.

Overwork is something they should avoid, particularly when it induces the dissatisfaction or despondency that is the Capricornian pitfall. Along with maintaining that underlying joviality gained from the preceding sign, they should avoid speculative projects, as failure disturbs them.

CAPRICORN–AQUARIUS
January 19 to 26

This is a curious cusp, because the same planet, Saturn, rules each of the two signs. Far from being baleful, this can prove very helpful, for it rounds out the planetary influence, producing a powerful intellectuality which can cope with almost anything except its own forebodings; and even those can be pitted against one another.

The Aquarian interest in people should be furthered to the utmost, with avoidance of the solitude found both in Aquarius and Capricorn, for such a double dose means almost sure gloom. The self-consciousness of Capricorn, understandable to itself, can prove a serious drag on the Aquarian disposition. However, the self-reliance of Capricorn can strengthen Aquarius.

People born during this period are inclined to the fantastic and often support illogical ideas. Being extremists, they will labor long on things that interest them, then will give up and become idle, due to frustration or lack of results. Therefore, their great purpose should be consistency, with stress on every optimistic trend. They should never lapse into careless ways or try to overcome despondency by extravagance.

They are brilliant as scientists and writers, as well as successful in businesses that appeal to their intellectual natures. They do well in art, music, and drama. With them, success stimulates success.

AQUARIUS–PISCES
February 18 to 26

The humane sign of Aquarius, with its scholarly planet, Saturn, lends a helpful influence to the modest nature of Pisces, giving it special attributes that befit the dignity of its governing planet, Jupiter. Though people born in this sign are changeable, that helps to curb their over-caution, stirring them to firm decisions.

They make allowances for people as well as circumstances, returning good for evil until they feel that the time has come for a proper accounting. Then they come out well, unless they have let themselves become embittered during the waiting process. Often they win esteem through their patience and become very popular without realizing it.

Concentrated effort is needed here. By blending caution with business ability, success, though sometimes slow, is generally assured, for people born in this period live up to their promises and make it evident. They are good office-holders and fulfill all positions of trust, but are apt to be satisfied in subordinate capacities, even when capable and deserving of some higher place.

The Decans and Their Planets

To give fuller interpretation to the signs of the zodiac, they have been divided into periods of approximately ten days, called the "decans" or "decantes" which cover modifications of individual traits. These are attributed to minor planetary influences, which temper or blend with the ruling influence of the period. A study of these is therefore helpful in forming the individual horoscope, but they are always to be regarded as subordinate to the ruling planet.

The ten-day periods are somewhat arbitrary in order to allow for the five—and sometimes six—extra days in the year beyond the 360 required for the thirty-six decans. These have been added according to accepted procedure, to form various six-day periods instead of five.

The decans and their planetary influences follow:

ARIES: *Ruling Planet:* Mars

First Decan: March 21–30. *Planets:* Mars and Jupiter
Aries, as the fiery head of the zodiac, begins with its own planet,
Mars, as the prime influence of the first decan. This means simply that
persons born in this period will have the firm, assertive disposition that
marks the Martian drive. The influence of Jupiter, a carry-over from the
previous sign, adds brilliance to the Arian nature; but any trend toward
triviality will weaken this. Here is a fearless nature that should guard
against becoming too headstrong.

Second Decan: March 31–April 9. *Planet:* the Sun
Here is an excellent combination, with the Sun supplying generosity,
nobility, and leadership to the aggressiveness of the Martian temperament. Negative factors are the only problem. The dignity and magnetic
qualities of the Sun may give way to vainglory, if the aggressive Martian
nature is allowed to rule.

Third Decan: April 10–19. *Planets:* Venus and Jupiter
Venus tempers the Aries nature, but allows it to become rash and
headlong, ready to take up any cause because of sentimental reasons.
This is a pleasure-seeking period, which must be controlled. Cultivation
of the Jupiterian sincerity and generosity is all-important.

TAURUS: *Ruling Planet:* Venus

First Decan: April 20–29. *Planets:* Mercury and Mars
The natural sympathy of this period is roused to quickness and over-
activity which can lead to worry and dissatisfaction. Trivial matters and
immediate aims can disturb the romantic side of the individual nature.
The Martian trend is responsible for angry moods that are disturbing to
the normal trend. Be tactful, rather than aggressive.

Second Decan: April 30–May 9. *Planets:* the Moon and Mercury
Here, the Venusian nature must be stanch and steady, pushing the
strength of Taurus to the full. The lunar influence, with its changeability, can induce the indolence that is the great weakness of the
Venusian nature. The Mercurian impulse is helpful in this decan, as it
can snap you from the doldrums. But don't take up things you don't
like, or your Venusian nature will rebel and fail to make the most of

them. People born in this period need a goal and must avoid petty jealousy while seeking to attain it.

Third Decan: May 10-19. Planet: Saturn

All the combined sympathy and self-will which characterize the Taurian nature can falter through doubt and worry if they are allowed to take over. You can avoid them, for this is a strong, impulsive sign that overrides obstacles. Just be yourself and shake off morbid moods. You will never know that Saturn was around, except for your studious desires. Take advantage of them, but don't let them keep you from whatever you like better.

GEMINI: Ruling Planet: Mercury

First Decan: May 20-29. Planets: Venus and Jupiter

The influence of Venus carries over into the cusp of this sign and is strongest during the first five days. Persons born at that time will find that their versatile Gemini natures are apt to become purposeless and indolent. They find sympathetic listeners for all their ideas and spend their time in planning things that may never work out. This leads to deceit and discouragement. Here, everything should be done to concentrate on a single purpose and take advantage of the self-discipline that comes from Jupiter, the planetary influence that forestalls failure.

Second Decan: May 30-June 8. Planets: Mars and Venus

This is an aggressive period, wherein the versatile Gemini nature shows a powerful and unexpected drive, once the Martian influence is allowed to take over. It is strictly Gemini, but "stepped up" to a high degree, which may reach the ruthless point. The quick, scheming ways of Mercury are hitched to the bulldozing tactics of Mars, with no more questions asked. Such effort, however, can be directed toward good instead of wasteful purposes. Here, the sympathetic understanding of Venus should be cultivated. The bigger and better the purpose, the more you should stick to it, avoiding distractions and unnecessary details.

Third Decan: June 9-20. Planets: the Sun and Saturn

Gemini here has opportunity to combine its many talents toward one goal, with the Sun's influence helping to make that purpose high. Saturn supplies knowledge and scholarly effort seldom found in the more fickle Gemini nature. But Saturn brings worry that can curb the Sun's exuberance. If these two influences conflict, the individual will fall into the Gemini habit of switching to whatever comes along, good or bad. Ambition will be frustrated and study will be wasted. These people should strive for the greatest things they can attain and they should avoid worry in the process.

CANCER: *Ruling Planet:* the Moon

First Decan: June 21–July 2. *Planets:* the Moon and Venus

The influence of Mercury is already apparent in this period, which represents the cusp of Gemini and Cancer. But the Moon, itself, is doubly strong and is only partially swayed by the minor influence of Venus. It is a period of swift changes, and the stronger the element of Venus, the more radical they become. Sociability will swing to the extreme of suspicion. There is an urge for romance and adventure; but this may switch suddenly to self-sufficiency. People born at this time are very capable, but do so many things that they fail to recognize their own faults. They are very diplomatic, keeping much to themselves.

Second Decan: July 3–12. *Planets:* Mars and Mercury

Mars gives a bold but willful manner to the indecision of this period. When action is taken, it is determined; but such persons can become stubborn on other points. They are also forceful when opposed. Hasty action may lead to gloomy spells, hence people born in this decan should curb the quick impulses of the Mercurian influence. The strength of Mars and the skill of Mercury should be combined to balance the wavering moods of Luna.

Third Decan: July 13–22. *Planets:* Jupiter and the Moon

The influence of Jupiter is very strengthening in this period; and it needs to be, because the Moon is greatly increased in intensity. Jupiter supplies good judgment and steadiness to this otherwise fluctuating period and stirs the individual to action, when it is needed. Commercial success may come to many people of this decan, provided they are not too swayed by the vacillating lunar influence. Otherwise, they will become egotistical and talkative, too concerned with trifles to accomplish great things.

LEO: *Ruling Planet:* the Sun

First Decan: July 23–August 1. *Planet:* Saturn

The Sun's influence is dominant in this decan, but any waverings will allow the gloom of Saturn to set in. Hence people of this period may become boastful and arrogant, sometimes resorting to violence if their ideas are opposed. Through control of such moods, Saturn's knowledge can be added to the Sun's power, culminating in a generous, steadfast nature, free from worry and able to override misfortune.

Second Decan: August 2–11. *Planet:* Jupiter

One of the strongest of all periods. Common sense is often accompanied by a generous disposition that is both openminded and openhearted. Here is the Solarian "will to win" coupled with the Jupiterian ability to see it through. People of this period are understanding and tactful in dealing with others. Their great fault is overconfidence, which often induces conceit and may cause them to put self-interest above the honesty that this period normally represents.

Third Decan: August 12–21. *Planet:* Mars

Here, the dominance of the Sun is most forceful. It betokens a brave and virile disposition, a thirst for real adventure, along with honesty and strength of purpose. The danger lies in becoming too impulsive and too dominating in disposition. This can result in serious rivalries in both business and social fields. Friendship is important to persons of this period and they should further it by showing appreciation of others, rather than boasting of their own achievements.

VIRGO: *Ruling Planet:* Mercury

First Decan: August 22–31. *Planet:* the Sun

This period marks the cusp of Leo and Virgo, where the Sun's exuberance carries over from the previous sign, often to Virgo's benefit. The added influence of the Sun marks this as a period of fame and perhaps fortune, for it betokens inventive genius and scientific achievement. These are often devoted to humanitarian causes, rather than profit. The greater the influence of the Sun, the more it controls and guides the cleverness of Mercury into favorable channels.

Second Decan: September 1–10. *Planets:* Venus and Saturn

Here is a neat, orderly nature; both friendly and patient. Mercurian aptitudes are directed toward helping others, through the Venusian influence, while knowledge and refinement are supplied by Saturn. Volatile Mercury and harmonious Venus draw the best from Saturn. The one weakness is overcaution, particularly in money matters. Success usually comes to these persons but is often long delayed.

Third Decan: September 11–22. *Planets:* Saturn and Venus
Somewhat the reverse of the previous period. Here, Mercury utilizes the Saturnian thirst for knowledge in inventive and ingenious ways. People born at this time are bright, talkative, and usually sincere, due to the influence of Venus. But though they make friends, they may become meddlesome and their artistic skill may suffer through gambling instincts. Their Mercurian liveliness pulls them from Saturn's moods, but they will have their ups and downs, which often deter them from the success they deserve.

LIBRA: *Ruling Planet:* Venus

First Decan: September 23–October 2. *Planet:* the Moon
The kindliest of natures, but highly oversensitive. A strong sense of justice causes persons of this period to go "all out" for a losing cause. The Venusian sympathy goes to extremes because of the Lunarian influence. Artistry, soulful meditation, and fondness for the deeper things in life are very evident in this decan.

Second Decan: October 3–12. *Planet:* Saturn
Persons born in this period are fair-minded and have a flare for scientific knowledge, but they are unsettled in disposition. Their ability to understand other people makes them natural leaders, but they are often shrewd enough to turn them to their own advantage. When swayed by Saturn's moods, they show it chiefly in impatience, and will often use considerable daring in an effort to attain immediate goals.

Third Decan: October 13–22. *Planets:* Mercury and Jupiter
Here is a nature fond of luxury and social life, with good nature and generosity as continuous expressions of friendship. Wide interests and the ability to make friends quickly often leave doubt as to the sincerity of persons born in this period. They have a marked fondness for persons of the opposite sex, and if they lose old friends they have no trouble finding new ones. The Jupiterian influence supplies an idealism, which is helpful to this overchangeable temperament.

SCORPIO: *Ruling Planet:* Mars

First Decan: October 23–31. *Planets:* Mars and Venus
This is the most forceful, self-willed period in the entire year and nothing can stop its drive, whether for good or bad. Usually, it is for good, even though the planetary influence of Mars is at double strength, for this nature is too virile to be selfish. Its strong will is also accompanied by will power and a desire to explore the unknown. The influence of Venus is very helpful, tempering the Martian aggressiveness with a love and appreciation of family and friends.

Second Decan: November 1–10. *Planets:* the Sun and Jupiter
Here, the forceful Scorpio nature becomes strong-minded and set in purpose, capable of meeting enemies and opposition. The influence of the Sun, even when strong, does not ease this situation, but intensifies it, making the individual feel that he is all the more right, which he often is. The Jupiterian influence is therefore better, as it eases tensions and lessens the need of outright combat, and also shows a scientific turn of mind. Usually one or the other predominates—the Sun or Jupiter—but seldom both.

Third Decan: November 11–21. *Planets:* the Moon and Venus
Here we find a haughty, though fair-minded nature, gifted with remarkable energy, yet unyielding to the extreme. Such people make sure that they are right; then decide that whatever they do must be right. Since they are subject to the caprices of the ever-changing Moon, this can present problems. However, they are usually well liked, due to the friendly presence of Venus, which adds a fondness for pleasure and amusement.

SAGITTARIUS: *Ruling Planet:* Jupiter

First Decan: November 22–December 1. *Planet:* Mercury
This is generally an excellent period as the optimistic, purposeful Jupiterian nature brings out the best in Mercury. Quickness and aptitude are applied to learning, but often of a practical, scientific type rather than the academic sort. Keen, quiet thinking and careful preparation of plans characterize this period. Being on the cusp, with the influence of Mars still present, such planning will result in action.

Second Decan: December 2–11.   *Planets:* the Moon and Mars

The Jupiterian influence is weakened by the changeability of the Moon, but this seldom produces conflict in the individual nature. Jupiter adds some purpose to each mood, so that people with this combination thrive on new scenes and varied interests. Luck seems to favor them, but they take too many things for granted and are too apt to avoid important issues. The influence of Mars, though comparatively slight or generally neglected, gives them a fighting spirit when needed. They should learn to use it.

Third Decan: December 12–21.   *Planets:* the Sun and Saturn

This is a self-sufficient period, though by no means self-centered. All the high qualities of Jupiter are intensified by the Sun's strong influence, often to the point of inspiration. Science, research, and experimental work are furthered by the scholarly presence of Saturn, which here can be utilized to its best. Dangers are overwork, neglect of outside interests, and failure to establish friendships.

CAPRICORN: *Ruling Planet:* Saturn

First Decan: December 22–January 1.   *Planet:* Jupiter

Most of the characteristics of this period conform closely to the description of the cusp of Sagittarius and Capricorn, since the planetary influences are identical. However, those born in the first five days (December 22–26) are more strongly Jupiterian. They are very dependable, fair-minded, and of the highest integrity, making the most of their scholarly attainments. Those born later put greater stress on study and are more limited in outlook, with a greater tendency to worry over the future.

Second Decan: January 1–10.   *Planets:* Mars and Venus

Vigor and independence enter into the retiring nature of this sign, but such activity is apt to be impractical and wasteful. Eagerness for action should be subordinated to scholarly pursuits and social life. Venus brings out the best in Saturn, but care must be taken to avoid false friends, as this nature is easily duped.

Third Decan: January 11–20.   *Planets:* Mercury and the Sun

Here, the retiring Saturnian nature is stirred by the Mercurian craving for action, which may take place in small but futile ways. Self-confidence is needed by people of this type in order to gain the leadership they seek. The Sun in their nature gives them dreams of dominance, but they shy from responsibility and either revert to the role of a frustrated Saturnian, or indulge in exaggerated talk. People of this period should seek advancement and make the most of it. Once they have plunged themselves into an opportunity, their path will be plain. Suspicion and skepticism often handicap people of this decan.

AQUARIUS: *Ruling Planet:* Saturn

First Decan: January 21–30. *Planet:* Venus
Venus brings out the friendly, agreeable side of this steady-going, plodding nature, but not always for the best. The tendency here is to be easily led, yet easily discouraged. Once such people go against their own interests or wishes, they become stubborn and get nowhere. Being kindly, they often back other persons but forget themselves. They are both artistic and scientific, so their best plan is to develop their own abilities and go on from there.

Second Decan: January 31–February 9. *Planet:* Mercury
Here, quick thought and lively manner add impulse to the Aquarian nature. People born in this period make many friends, because they show interest in other persons and apply good common sense. Deep-set ambition is brought to the fore through self-expression. But contacts are important to success. Persons born in this period should never become self-centered, or they will lose their greatest asset.

Third Decan: February 10–19. *Planets:* Venus and the Moon
This is a highly changeable period, in which wild imagination can result in utter disappointment. Venus adds a pleasure-loving side to the otherwise practical Aquarian nature, which is too apt to result in extravagance or waste. The changeable qualities of the Moon cause the stanch Aquarian to vary his activities, which can be equally disastrous. The only road to triumph is through common sense, with which Aquarius is fortunately endowed. Apply it and make sure each new step is in some way progressive. Then, the lesser planetary influences may prove helpful.

PISCES: *Ruling Planet:* Jupiter

First Decan: February 20–29. *Planet:* Saturn
People of this decan conform closely to the cusp of Aquarius and

Pisces. Should the Saturnian influence be overstrong, as it too often is, it can produce a worried type of individual who will forget all ambition and drift into obscurity. Such persons should set their sights on a goal and never stop until they attain it, thus pushing their Jupiterian to the fore, letting studious Saturn lend a helping hand.

Second Decan: March 1-10. Planet: the Moon

Here, the good fortune of Jupiter can be lost through indecision or by delving into too many minor interests, particularly those pertaining to other people. Indulgence is a Jupiterian weakness, so don't let the Lunarian influence carry it to extremes. People of this decan should trust their own judgment and uphold their own ideas. Fortunately, the Jupiterian influence is often doubly strong at this period, and if all the virtues of Pisces are brought to the fore, the presence of the Moon can be readily counteracted.

Third Decan: March 11-20. Planet: Mars

The Jupiterian ambition is handicapped in this period, for Mars provides a bold but too aggressive disposition. These people often overvalue their personal opinions and attempt impossible achievements. Once they are on the wrong track, it is difficult to set them straight, for they are argumentative enough to try to prove their point, and the more they talk, the more they convince themselves. Though somewhat fickle, people of this decan are generally friendly, and they should learn to accept and follow advice of those they trust. Then, the strong points of Pisces can be built to the full, with the Martian influence being used as an added impulse.

Summary of Decans

The planetary influences described under the decans are valuable in shading the traits of many persons, but they are generally subordinate to the stronger characteristics detailed under the Signs of the Zodiac. In some persons, the traits of the decans are only slightly traced; with others, they are very marked.

As a rule, a person's sign details his characteristics with surprising exactitude. That is one reason why astrology has persisted through the centuries and has retained its popularity with each new generation. But where individual traits may seem at variance with the accepted pattern of the sign, the answer may be found in that person's Decan. Also, a study of the decans may reveal hidden factors to which a person may be susceptible, even though his major traits are fully delineated under his sign.

The Planets and Their Influences

From the earliest days of astrology, special note was given to the planets, or "wanderers," which followed their own special paths among the fixed stars or constellations that form the signs of the zodiac.

These planets, seven in number, were simply the members of the Solar System that were continually visible from Earth: namely, the Sun, the Moon, Mercury, Venus, Mars, Jupiter, and Saturn.

Each sign of the zodiac was regarded as under the control of one special planet. The Sun became the governing influence of Leo; the Moon held sway over Cancer. The other planets were each given two signs, Mercury controlling Gemini and Virgo; Venus influencing Taurus and Libra; Mars dominating Aries and Scorpio; Jupiter ruling Sagittarius and Pisces; Saturn governing Capricorn and Aquarius.

There are persons who could be typed as Solarians, Jupiterians, and the like, according to the planet ruling their sign. In fact, the study of "planetary types" was probably quite common several centuries ago, because the nomenclature used in palmistry was derived from the astrological teachings of that period.

Seldom, however, are the planetary qualities fully apparent in an individual. Rather, they imprint themselves in varying degree upon the attributes of the separate signs, which are of a fixed and firmer nature. In a sense, the planetary influences simply activate the signs, rather than exert a direct force of their own.

Also, the planetary influences are subject to modifications, which the signs are not. Even with persons born on the cusp—or the "line" between two signs—it is the carry-over of the preceding planetary influence that makes the real difference.

Consider the marked contrast between two individuals born in Gemini and Virgo. Both are Mercurians; often, they brim over with that quality. But almost invariably, Gemini veers to the versatile and Virgo toward the analytical, showing the inherent traits of their respective signs. Many examples could be given to stress this point.

So diverse can these planetary influences become that some modern astrologers have substituted newly discovered planets for the older ones. Thus, Saturn is kept as the governing planet of Capricorn; but Uranus has been assigned to Aquarius. Similarly, Jupiter has been retained as the ruler of Sagittarius, but Neptune has been put in charge of Pisces.

This last is in keeping with mythology, as Neptune, god of the sea, was the reputed overlord of all the fishes therein and Pisces is the sign of the fish. But it is rather confusing in astrology, which has done quite well with the original seven "planets" for some five or six thousand years. Nor has anyone yet found a proper place for the planet Pluto, which would only confuse the situation all the more.

Adhering to the seven traditional planets, we find not only the major influences, which directly activate the zodiacal signs; but we have minor influences as well, which apply to portions of those signs known as the "decans" or "decantes"—each representing an approximate ten-day period. These have been treated under a separate heading of their own.

Highly important and worthy of their own classification are the planetary influences of the day of birth as well as that of the birth year, which in turn are modified by a cyclic influence. These will be treated individually and discussed in the formation of the horoscope. In every case, such influences conform in varying degree to the general planetary influences now to be described.

That is just one more reason why it is preferable to classify all influences under the seven original heads that follow:

THE SUN
Ruler of the sign Leo

This is the strongest of all planetary influences, so forceful that it can seldom be repressed, though its fine qualities may be neglected or dissipated.

Acquisition of knowledge and artistic achievement are keynotes of this influence. The Solarian nature is one that puts ideas into practice, often riding over all obstacles. Often, they are regarded as lucky, but that is because their inherent optimism will not allow them to accept temporary setbacks as failure.

Along with such attributes toward success, the Sun denotes a dignity of manner, integrity of nature, and loyalty to a cause. It carries the gift of good speaking and a magnetic personality, if effort is made toward their development. These are the positive aspects.

The weakness of this nature is found in the neglect of small things, or pressing for personal glory rather than high achievement. Solarians should avoid becoming high-handed as well as high-minded. Pride, desire for domination, and general arrogance are the negative aspects.

Physically, the Solarian influence indicates a strong, virile appearance, with well-formed and sometimes handsome features; keen of eye and smiling in manner. The height of the well-developed Solarian should run average, with proportionately good physique.

The Sun directly activates the sign of Leo, providing the exuberance found in many persons born in that period; but the Solarian qualities can become dynamic wherever else they appear. The influence of the Sun is therefore favorable and should always be encouraged.

THE MOON
Ruler of the sign Cancer

Like the lunar orb itself, this planetary influence is changeable, yet understandable and therefore controllable. Imagination is its chief trait and one that can be carried to almost fanciful extremes.

On the one hand, the Lunarian exhibits that insight known as intuition; on the other, overimagination can lead to worry and hysteria. In between, there is a restless, ever-changing trend, which may run the gamut from idle dreaming to compelling urge for purposeless travel.

Being pliable, the Lunarian nature is receptive and adaptable to almost any circumstance. It betokens sympathy, sound economy, and intelligent planning, except when indecision takes hold. Such fluctuation is the great danger of the Lunarian influence.

Hence, this nature needs strengthening, which can be gained by making the most out of other planetary influences, provided they do not produce conflict or add to the moodiness that is so typically Lunarian.

Lunarians vary in height, but there is one type which is more than average, often stout in build and dreamy in gaze. Lunarians, in later years, draw into themselves, as though living in another world.

The Moon activates the sign of Cancer and is responsible for the uncertainty of that period. Hence the influence of the Moon is regarded as unfavorable. It should be subordinated or adapted to more helpful planetary influences.

MARS
Ruler of the signs Aries and Scorpio

Physical drive and energy are basic in the planetary influence of Mars. There is no stopping the Martian nature, which can be brave to the point of becoming foolhardy, unless tempered by other influences. It gives aggressiveness to the signs where it predominates: Aries and Scorpio.

Fortunately, the Martian influence can be diverted. With it, attainment of an immediate goal is so important that other purposes can be shelved. Here is a fighting instinct that knocks down all obstacles, small and large. Keep them small when they do not matter; large, when they are important, and you have the ultimate in Martian development.

Sports, adventure, love of outdoor life all are found in the Martian personality. Travel, military affairs, any form of new and virile experience appeals to those who come under this influence. Skill and mechanical ability are part of the Martian setup; and as natural concomitants, honesty and reliability go into such a nature. Such are the positive aspects.

In contrast, the Martian influence can breed impatience, savagery, boastfulness, and a tendency toward useless, wasteful combat. Action is just another word for Mars, in the full sense of the term. In order to obtain it, persons swayed by this influence may become destructive. When they are prone to envy, nothing can stop their rash, impetuous nature, except their own power of reason, which fortunately is strong and therefore helpful.

Physically, the typical Martian is well above average size and strength. Some are tall, but others are stocky, oversized in bulk. Their faces are usually broad and strong-jawed, their physique heavy. They are both bold and gallant in manner, when intelligent and cultured; otherwise, they may be coarse and cruel.

Mars controls the signs of Aries and Scorpio. To both of these it supplies impulse, but they must seek elsewhere for foresight, which is the one faculty lacking in the Martian nature. Chiefly on that account, the influence of Mars is unfavorable and must be greatly tempered to turn its iron will into fine steel.

JUPITER
Ruler of the signs Sagittarius and Pisces

This is perhaps the finest and most beneficial of all planetary influences. Though it lacks the inspiration of the Sun, it more than makes up for it in a practical way. People swayed by this influence are friendly and generous, appreciative of others and therefore cooperative.

Sincerity and sympathy go into the Jupiterian nature. Hence they are honest, charitable, impelled by high ideals. They have open minds and are always ready to take up a worthwhile cause. This automatically makes them popular, and their very frankness often makes them wonder why they are so well liked. Such are the positive aspects of Jupiter.

It would seem that a nature so influenced would be free from all faults, but such is not the case. With a Jupiterian, natural generosity leads to extravagance. Since Jupiterians like people, they in turn like to be liked. Hence they are easily influenced and will waste their ability as well as their resources in futile, worthless effort. They become careless both of themselves and of their future.

Wastefulness is therefore the negative aspect of the Jupiterian nature. Recognition of this can lead to simple yet vital ways of correcting the fault; but often, other planetary influences are needed to insure such a result. By all means, Jupiterians must avoid the pitfalls of less fortunate influences, for in itself Jupiter is highly favorable.

In physical appearance, the highly developed Jupiterian is strong, personable, and often handsome. Jupiterians are often tall or rugged of physique. In every case, the Jupiterian influence produces a cheerful, winning personality, capable of great development.

Jupiter controls the signs of Sagittarius and Pisces, giving wisdom and integrity to each, provided of course that wasteful ways are avoided. In all cases, the Jupiterian influence is regarded as highly favorable.

SATURN
Ruler of the signs Capricorn and Aquarius

Gloom and Saturn are synonymous, but do not let that deceive or discourage you! Far from being baleful, the Saturnian influence is scholarly and scientific, made to order for the Atomic Age into which the modern world has been precipitated.

With its urge for knowledge, the Saturnian nature cultivates other desirable qualities. Such people are patient, serious, and reserved in manner. They often remain calm under stress, depending upon their training and intelligence to carry them through. They are sticklers for punctuality and accuracy; and they are usually quite thrifty. These are the positive aspects, but they are innate, rather than active.

Therein lies a weakness. When the Saturn influence impels someone to "get up and go," they too often turn the wrong way. Or, in another sense, they simply accentuate their normally passive inclinations to the point where they become unbearable, not only to others but to themselves.

Constant study can cause Saturnians to draw themselves apart from the world. Patience can lead to procrastination. Seriousness can make them skeptical; their reserve may become a form of mistrust. Their thrifty ways may turn stingy; and they may resort to deceit to protect their interests. All this can add up to the moodiest of natures.

These aspects, though negative in result, are in a real sense positive Saturnian expressions. Hence this is one influence that must be curbed, not merely tempered, in order to meet life's challenge. It is either that, or the choice of an ascetic or sheltered existence, where the Saturnian urge for knowledge, research, and service can be developed without emotional conflict.

Since every Saturnian has other planetary influences, those should be developed along constructive lines, thus utilizing the intellect and serious side of Saturn to full advantage. All speculations and risks should be avoided where Saturn is involved, for the result may be an outright waste of both talent and resources.

Physically, Saturnians are often tall, but they are inclined to be thin, with high foreheads and long jaws. Some are imposing in appearance, but outwardly they may show the result of inner conflict. A hollow countenance, stooped shoulders, and lack of response are typically Saturnian.

MERCURY
Ruler of the signs Gemini and Virgo

Here is a planetary influence so marked in contrasts that it is often unpredictable, though its attributes and faults can always be noted. It shows skill, quick observation, and ability to talk convincingly. Often, the Mercurian influence produces a clever nature and commercial ability. It stands for swift action and indicates a convincing speaker. Mercurians think fast, act fast, and talk fast. Given a dash of superficial knowledge, they can make it look like intellectual attainment. They are adaptable to almost any circumstances or conditions.

Such are the positive aspects of this planetary influence; positive aspects from the standpoint of the Mercurian himself, since he stands to profit thereby. It is how these natural abilities are applied that marks the good or bad in the Mercurian. When engaged in cooperative, worthwhile efforts, these traits are strongly positive. But if the "go ahead" is put into "reverse," the negative aspects appear.

Skill becomes cunning; cleverness is turned into deceit. Convincing speech takes the form of glib talk. Their adaptability enables them to "get by" with little or no effort and to further their own purposes at the expense of others. Schemers and gamblers are prevalent among Mercurians, for when they once begin to take advantage of their friends and acquaintances, it can become a regular habit.

Even the best of Mercurians are apt to make deals or resort to subterfuge; and conversely, the worst are not always too bad. They all have the tendency to "give and take" and it is the preponderance of "give" or "take" that marks the demarcation between the positive and negative aspects of this planetary influence.

Physically, Mercurians are apt to be under average height, but their stature, as well as their general appearance, may vary according to other planetary influences, as Mercurians are very susceptible to outside conditions. They are usually youthful in appearance, generally personable, and frequently handsome. They are sound and sometimes strong of physique; and they are both brisk and witty in manner.

Mercury activates the signs of Gemini and Virgo, being responsible for their basic traits; but as already specified, these vary according to the purposes of the individual and are very responsive to other planetary influences. Mercury, therefore, is one planet whose influence can be regarded as both favorable and unfavorable.

VENUS
Ruler of the signs Taurus and Libra

In its highest form, Venus provides the finest of all planetary influences. It denotes a kindly, harmonious nature, with a desire for happiness and comradeship. Beauty, charm, love of music and gaiety, all belong to the Venusian makeup. Persons under this influence will spare no effort in the creation of comfortable surroundings. They enjoy home life and form firm and lasting friendships. Such are the positive aspects.

In contrast, lack of harmony is disturbing to Venusians. They become emotional over disputes. Being kindly, they are easily offended and will resent even slight neglect. Unless they are careful in their choice of friends or those upon whom they shower their affections, misunderstanding may result.

Venusians sometimes become careless and indolent. They give way to useless pleasure and love of show. Theirs are affairs of the heart, not the head. Unless their affections are reciprocated, they may turn to new friends and new fields. These negative aspects cause Venusians to appear paradoxical to those who do not understand them.

Many Venusians have what has been termed the ideal physical appearance, with finely molded features and well-proportioned physique. They take pride in their appearance and have an ease of manner and a natural charm by which they show themselves at their best.

Venus activates the signs of Taurus and Libra; hence the likable qualities of this influence are commonly found among persons born at those periods. In fact, the predominance of Venus is responsible for a mutual attraction between persons with those birth signs. However, the "touch" of Venus is found wherever this planetary influence occurs, and is a strong factor in the blending of a personality; hence it is a valuable adjunct in every horoscope. This marks Venus as a highly favorable planet.

The Ruling Planet of the Day

In recognizing seven planets, ancient astrologers linked them to different days of the week, in the following order: the Sun, the Moon, Mars, Mercury, Jupiter, Venus, Saturn.

These became the Sun's Day for Sunday; the Moon's Day for Monday; but the names of the Roman gods became mixed with their Teutonic equivalents. For example, Woden is used instead of Mercury for Woden's Day, or Wednesday; while Thor is used instead of Jupiter for Thor's Day or Thursday.

The French, however, have adhered more closely to the Latin origins, with such names as *mardi*, for Mars' Day or Tuesday; *mercredi* for Mercury's Day or Wednesday; and so on.

Astrologically speaking, each planet is the ruler of its respective day of the week, so the seven conform to the following order:

The Sun is the ruling planet of Sunday.
The Moon is the ruling planet of Monday.
Mars is the ruling planet of Tuesday.
Mercury is the ruling planet of Wednesday.
Jupiter is the ruling planet of Thursday.
Venus is the ruling planet of Friday.
Saturn is the ruling planet of Saturday.

According to astrology, the planetary influences are strongest on the day of a person's birth. Each individual thereby partakes of the planet governing his birth sign, and any controlling the particular decan or ten-day period in which he was born.

But he also comes under the direct influence of the ruling planet of the exact day on which he was born. This is a factor in its own right; and whether it proves to be a dominating force or simply a modifier of the indications of the birth sign depends to a great degree upon the planets involved and their varied effects upon one another.

It is essential therefore to know the day of the week upon which a person was born in order to determine the ruling planet of his birthday. This can be quickly ascertained by utilizing the following chart:

Year 1900—Value 1
Other years in 1900's and their values:

```
01 02 03 04 05 06 07 08 09 10 11 12 13 14 15 16 17 18 19 20 21 22 23 24 25 26 27 28
29 30 31 32 33 34 35 36 37 38 39 40 41 42 43 44 45 46 47 48 49 50 51 52 53 54 55 56
57 58 59 60 61 62 63 64 65 66 67 68 69 70 71 72 73 74 75 76 77 78 79 80 81 82 83 84
85 86 87 88 89 90 91 92 93 94 95 96 97 98 99

 2  3  4  5  0  1  2  3  5  6  0  1  3  4  5  6  1  2  3  4  6  0  1  2  4  5  6  0
```

Years in italics (04, 08, etc.) are *leap years,* and 1 point must be added to their values for any date from March 1 on through the year. Thus for a date in January or February 1972, the year's value would be 6; for a date in any other month, 7.

Regular Monthly Values

January	0	April	6	July	6	October	0
February	3	May	1	August	2	November	3
March	3	June	4	September	5	December	5

Daily Values
Add from 1 to 31, inclusive, according to exact date.

Ruling Planet as Represented by Total Values

the Sun	the Moon	Mars	Mercury	Jupiter	Venus	Saturn
1	2	3	4	5	6	7
8	9	10	11	12	13	14
15	16	17	18	19	20	21
22	23	24	25	26	27	28
29	30	31	32	33	34	35
36	37	38	39	40	41	42
43	44	45	46	47	48	49

For dates in the 1800's, add 2 toward total value.
For dates in the 1700's, add 4 toward total value.

The following examples will clarify the process:

April 5, 1957. Year ('57) = 2. Month (April) = 6. Day (5th) = 5. Total values: 2 + 6 + 5 = 13. Ruling planet: Venus.

May 13, 1964. Year ('64) = 3 + 1 (leap year). Month (May) = 1. Day (13th) = 13.
Total values: 4 + 1 + 13 = 18. Ruling planet: Mercury.

September 12, 1897. Year ('97) = 3. Month (September) = 5. Day (12th) = 12. Added value for date in 1800's = 2.
Total values: 3 + 5 + 12 + 2 = 22. Ruling planet: the Sun.

To find the ruling planet of George Washington's birthday:
February 22, 1732. Year ('32) = 5 + 0 (leap year but before March 1.) Month (February) = 3. Day (22nd) = 22. Add value for date in 1700's = 4.
Total Values: 5 + 3 + 22 + 4 = 34. Ruling planet: Venus.

Note: Washington's birthday—and others prior to 1752—were originally figured according to the obsolete Julian calendar. The correct date (February 22, 1732) conforms to the Gregorian calendar, which should be used in all astrological calculations.

Influences of Ruling Planets

Having determined the ruling planet of a person's birthday, its influences can be studied according to general planetary indications (as already listed) as these apply in all combinations of planets. However, the planet of the day is a strongly individual factor, so it is possible to list its influence on the various signs. Here are the principal indications:

RULING PLANET: THE SUN

The Sun has a strengthening and often beneficent influence on the planets governing each sign, often promising high achievement in fields to which the individual is most suited, but at the same time producing a great intensity which may lead to overeffort.

In Aries, the Sun, combined with Mars, develops the drive found in this sign, urging the individual to great achievements. It also intensifies his ideas of right and wrong, often resulting in a crusading spirit that goes beyond normal bounds and defeats its own interests.

In Taurus, the Sun, combined with Venus, adds great warmth to an already friendly nature. It increases the natural strength of this sign, tempering it with honesty and self-control.

In Gemini, the Sun develops the favorable side of Mercury, adding power of concentration and generally inducing the native of Gemini to turn his versatility to good use. Great eloquence and striking personality may result from this combination.

In Cancer, the Sun and the Moon produce a highly variable combination of brilliancy and restlessness. The Sun curbs the imaginative disposition of this period and generally strengthens any good traits.

In Leo, the Sun doubles its power, as this is its own sign. A very fortunate period, with good traits predominant, but sometimes subject to overzeal. Early brilliancy may fail to mature, though fame is often attained.

In Virgo, the Sun combined with Mercury puts power of analysis to good use, with great results if applied to important aims. Wasted talent may result through trivial detail and too much self-pride.

In Libra, the Sun steadies the temperamental side of Venus, making these the most likable of people, stressing their fair judgment and providing originality. Overconfidence may produce strongly formed opinions, which often should be avoided.

In Scorpio, the Sun with Mars produces dignity and adds exuberance to the natural energy and determination of this sign. It promises great success but tends toward arrogance.

In Capricorn, the Sun modifies the gloom of Saturn, lessening the self-conscious factors of this sign and strengthening its self-reliance. It also turns the propensity for knowledge toward high attainment.

In Sagittarius, the Sun adds brilliance to the magnetism of Jupiter, making this fiery sign powerful but overforceful.

In Aquarius, the Sun again stimulates Saturn, causing persons of this sign to rise from obscurity and develop high-minded purposes and strong character. Honesty and popularity are furthered by this combination.

In Pisces, the Sun combined with Jupiter promises fame and fortune as well as happiness. The Sun develops all the fine but latent qualities of Pisces. The reliability found in Pisces can lead to great honor through the powerful influence of the Sun. In all, this is one of the finest combinations.

RULING PLANET: THE MOON

The Moon has a weakening effect on other planets and is therefore generally unfavorable when it predominates, unless the individual can rise above it, which is often possible when his horoscope shows minor planetary influences of a strengthening sort.

In Aries, the Moon gives impatience to Mars, resulting in changeable, self-defeating action. The keen minds of this sign are often diverted into foolish channels.

In Taurus, the Moon and Venus further soften an already indulgent nature. Personal gratification and similar faults are apt to retard development.

In Gemini, the Moon hinders the favorable aspects of Mercury. This produces a temperament that is always on the jump, never taking time to develop a given talent. The Moon, however, makes the mind receptive; and its influence fades in the face of stronger indications.

In Cancer, which is the Moon's own sign, the lunar influence is doubly strong, but often works on the principle of "two negatives make a positive," thus bringing out all the better qualities of the sign.

In Leo, the Moon has little effect upon the Sun. It gives an individual a hesitant, uncertain trend, but the Leo nature usually shakes off such moods.

In Virgo, the Moon combines with Mercury. Here, its receptive quality is a great adjunct to the Virgo ability at analysis, enabling a person to apply his talents in new ways. Its danger is overimagination, leading to constant worry.

In Libra, the Moon combines unfavorably with Venus. Natural sympathy is stimulated, producing the kindliest of natures; but there is a craving for excitement, acceptance of new fads, and a generally careless disposition.

In Scorpio, with Mars, the Moon curbs the overdominant trend of this sign, making the individual receptive and therefore more understanding. But it weakens the urge for action, causing hesitation when drive is needed.

In Sagittarius, the Moon joins Jupiter to aid individual adaptability and to improve the sign generally. A fine combination if a person can stay with his ideals and purposes despite occasional restless spells.

In Capricorn, the Moon and Saturn tend to increase moodiness, but the changeability of the Moon can turn the mind to new channels. The only question is how helpful those changes may be, as the dual influence forces some persons to extremes.

In Aquarius, the Moon and Saturn may lead to many disappointments. The restless quality of Aquarius is overstressed and must be curbed. Receptivity aids the trend toward knowledge, and people so influenced can attain great popularity.

In Pisces, the Moon blends naturally with Jupiter. The lunar influence adds adaptability, but may otherwise be weakening, though its effect is often negligible.

RULING PLANET: MARS

In Aries, Mars doubles its influence, this being its own sign. The Aries nature becomes proportionately strong, with impetuosity its predominant trait.

In Taurus, Mars adds strength to Venus, but increases the sensual, pleasure-loving trend of this sign, without counteracting undesirable traits.

In Gemini, Mars adds drive to Mercury, increasing the unfortunate aspects of this sign. The Gemini nature, already active, can become violent and sometimes unpredictable.

In Cancer, Mars dominates the weaker Moon, arousing action which can be used to good advantage, but only if controlled. Otherwise, this combination can prove very dangerous.

In Leo, Mars combines with the Sun to give active purpose to this sign. But it also increases aggressive qualities and the desire to domineer.

In Virgo, Mars and Mercury are usually favorable, as Mars adds action to the analytical nature of Virgo. Dubious schemes should be avoided.

In Libra, Mars unites with Venus to add strength and activity to this sign, but it may narrow many purposes at the expense of fair judgment, lessening the Libra sympathy.

In Scorpio, the Martian influence is definitely doubled, producing arrogance and forcefulness at the expense of all else. A dangerous combination.

In Sagittarius, Mars adds activity to Jupiter, which absorbs such influence, generally to excellent advantage. All Sagittarian traits are strengthened.

In Capricorn, Mars gives purpose to the moody Saturn. The combination furthers the development of the Capricorn traits, but this sometimes applies to bad as much as good. So be wary of the Martian influence.

In Aquarius, Mars again combines with Saturn, often quite effectively, as purpose is needed in this sign. The chief danger lies in scattering of effort.

In Pisces, Mars and Jupiter combine almost to perfection, as this sign needs Martian activity and is definitely capable of shaping it. Here, the Martian drive can be given full play in the development of natural traits.

RULING PLANET: MERCURY

In Aries, Mercury makes Mars unfavorable. It adds scheming ways to a keen, ambitious nature, turning it to selfish interests.

In Taurus, Mercury retards Venus, often turning the sympathy of this sign into jealousy and intrigue. Natural abilities are generally quickened, sometimes in a helpful way.

In Gemini, Mercury accentuates all the characteristics of its own sign. This can be very dangerous unless modified by lesser influences.

In Cancer, Mercury and the Moon produce a quickening of the sign's natural traits, often to disadvantage. Overaction defeats receptivity, resulting in an incompetent, unreliable nature. Though people of this sign are seldom schemers, they may be swayed and used by others.

In Leo, Mercury and the Sun add quickness to the exuberance of Leo. An excellent combination, except when given to double-dealing or deceit.

In Virgo, Mercury has double strength, increasing the cleverness and analytical ability of this sign, while lessening its quality of imagination. Scheming tendencies must be curbed, as they are very marked under this double influence.

In Scorpio, Mercury and Mars are a bad combination, developing the negative and unscrupulous aspects of this sign. Self-control is strong, but is often used to further self-interest. Other planetary influences are needed to modify this combination.

In Sagittarius, Mercury enlivens Jupiter, producing an active, energetic sign. All good traits are strengthened, except for a tendency to jump to conclusions too quickly.

In Capricorn, Mercury and Saturn are bad. The intellect of this sign is often diverted to morbid, sordid channels and dangerous, unprofitable adventure.

In Aquarius, Mercury and Saturn somewhat counterbalance. Quickness and ease of accomplishment stress the lack of incentive so common to this sign. Honesty and scholarly urge usually control the deceptive ways of Mercury, giving insight to this sign.

In Pisces, Mercury combines well with Jupiter, overcoming the caution of Pisces and finding outlets for the abilities that are usually too latent in this sign. Jupiterian integrity controls the more wayward Mercury.

RULING PLANET: JUPITER

Jupiter, as a favorable planet, combines well with the others, except in a few instances that will be noted under their respective signs.

In Aries, Jupiter gives purpose to Mars, so that this sign shows true daring and sincere ambition. Conformity to accepted standards is advisable in order to control a rebellious trend which should be confined to worthy causes.

In Taurus, Jupiter and Venus are very favorable. Strength is added to all good traits of this sign, and stubborn, pleasure-loving trends are overcome.

In Gemini, Jupiter provides Mercury with a frank, direct approach, which is helpful to this often unpredictable sign.

In Cancer, Jupiter steadies the Moon, adding to the dignity of this sign and turning the conservative, uncertain nature into constructive purposes.

In Leo, Jupiter and the Sun are a very fine combination. Jupiter supplies dignity and idealism to the enthusiastic qualities of this sign, with tremendous prospects of success and esteem.

In Virgo, Jupiter helps Mercury, causing the keen Virgo mind to seek high callings and honorable professions in which the skill of this sign functions to the full. Integrity must be maintained, however, or persons with this combination may become shallow and superficial.

In Libra, Jupiter adds strength to Venus, confining the judgment of this sign to important affairs and turning the affections and sympathies of Libra to worthy persons and commendable causes.

In Scorpio, Jupiter adds integrity and sympathy to Mars, but does not restrain the boldness of this sign.

In Sagittarius, the double influence of Jupiter gives great strength to the natural qualities of the sign, generally for the best, though any bad traits must be doubly watched.

In Capricorn, Jupiter strongly influences Saturn, bringing out the best found in this sign. People with this combination seem typical Capricornians but seem luckier and more intelligent than most, due to Jupiter's presence.

In Aquarius, Jupiter visibly influences Saturn, giving persons of this sign a popularity that they seldom have. It also adds to their ambition.

In Pisces, Jupiter has double strength, but needs other planetary influences to attain high purpose; for without them, the indolence of the sign may prevail.

RULING PLANET: VENUS

Invariably, Venus supplies sympathy to any nature and often in a helpful way. But this planetary influence must be controlled or it can disintegrate into maudlin sentiment and its attendant faults.

In Aries, Venus combines with Mars. This supplies a kindly quality to the natural drive of Aries, but does not add the self-control and patience needed in this sign. This combination may run wild without other planetary influences.

In Taurus, the influence of Venus is doubled, producing a sympathetic rather than a stubborn type; but love of pleasure will be over-evident and detrimental.

In Gemini, Venus and Mercury add to the superficial trend of this sign. Things of the moment will prevail, and persons of this type will use sentiment to further their own desires.

In Cancer, Venus and the Moon increase emotional uncertainty of this sign, but turn its loyalty and home-loving qualities into a steadying factor.

In Leo, Venus combines with the Sun to add charm to exuberance, understanding to loyalty, greatly strengthening this sign, though self-restraint is often lacking. There is also a tendency to take life too easily.

In Virgo, Venus and Mercury give creative artistry to the skill of this sign. The combination adds friendliness and understanding to the Virgo temperament, but often results in wasted effort. The combination is generally good.

In Libra, Venus exerts a double influence, increasing the traits of Virgo to an exaggerated extent. Good or bad, sink or swim, is the indication here, depending much on the individual and which traits he develops.

In Scorpio, Venus and Mars give amorous ardor to this sign. Sympathy tempers the harsh Scorpio nature but intensifies the desire for pleasure.

In Sagittarius, Venus with Jupiter softens the somewhat irritable nature of this sign, but lessens its energy. Most Sagittarian faults are controllable through Venus.

In Capricorn, Venus combines with Saturn to rouse the Capricorn nature from moodiness to sociability, but this often results in jealousy and misunderstanding.

In Aquarius, the combination of Venus and Saturn is usually bad, tending to dissipation, extravagance, and reckless ways.

In Pisces, Venus and Jupiter produce an optimistic outlook, resulting in a happy, cheerful disposition. People with this combination are simple and truthful.

RULING PLANET: SATURN

Though Saturn is generally regarded as unfavorable, its intellectual qualities can prove a valuable influence in most planetary combinations. Faults are usually intensified by Saturn; hence other planetary influences must be stressed to counteract them.

In Aries, Saturn with Mars gives Arians a petulant, impulsive disposition that hampers their best efforts. Efforts to think things out hampers the natural foresight of this sign and may lead to unwise speculations.

In Taurus, Saturn with Venus adds intellectuality to a pleasure-loving nature, but may increase the stubborn disposition of this sign. This can result in extremes of self-gratification.

In Gemini, Saturn and Mercury can develop the mentality of Gemini to the point of real genius. This is harmful when such inventive talent is diverted to unscrupulous purposes as is too often the case. This can be a very dangerous combination.

In Cancer, Saturn combines with the Moon, which is seldom helpful to this sign. Restlessness, uncertainty, and moodiness are accentuated and need other planetary influences to temper them.

In Leo, Saturn combines with the Sun to give wisdom to idealism, but often retards the exuberance of this sign, producing periods of gloom and dissatisfaction.

In Virgo, Saturn combines with Mercury to turn the analytical ability of Virgo into skeptical channels. People under such influence become argumentative, applying their knowledge to useless and sometimes base purposes. Here, again, other influences are needed.

In Libra, Saturn with Venus can hamper the good judgment of this sign, often turning sympathy to jealousy. Much effort is needed to counteract this.

In Scorpio, Saturn and Mars are sometimes helpful to this sign, giving wisdom to courage, adding intellectuality to drive. Any gloom or cynicism may bring out the faults of Scorpio, in the form of greed and self-will.

In Sagittarius, Saturn curbs the zeal of Jupiter, adding a scholarly touch to the varied energy of this sign.

In Capricorn, the influence of Saturn is doubled, adding to the practical foresight of this sign. Defeatism, in its turn, is more evident. Other planetary influences can be used to activate the high qualities of this sign.

In Aquarius, the double influence of Saturn accentuates the intellectual and humanitarian qualities of this sign, but they can build a double-thick shell as well. High aim, good associations, are a "must" with this type.

In Pisces, Saturn provides Jupiter with the needed intellectuality to produce a strong philosophy in persons of this sign. They can usually ride over disappointments, and if they can shake off morbid moods, this combination should bring them fame as well as popularity.

Ruling Planets of the Years

In astrology, the years have been grouped in cycles of thirty-six years each, with a ruling planet for each cycle, following the order of the days in reverse. The first year of each cycle is governed by its own planet; and every seventh year thereafter. The in-between years are ruled by other planets in this order: the Sun, Venus, Mercury, the Moon, Saturn, Jupiter, Mars, continuing in rotation.

Once the cyclic planet is listed, these are easily calculated, but for convenience they are given here from the year 1729 through 2016. It must be remembered that the astrological year begins on March 21. Thus the year 1729, first year in the cycle of the Sun, ran from March 21, 1729 through March 20, 1730. The same applies to all succeeding years.

Cycle of the Sun

Yearly Rulers	(1729–1764)
the Sun	1729, 1736, 1743, 1750, 1757, 1764
Venus	1730, 1737, 1744, 1751, 1758
Mercury	1731, 1738, 1745, 1752, 1759
the Moon	1732, 1739, 1746, 1753, 1760
Saturn	1733, 1740, 1747, 1754, 1761
Jupiter	1734, 1741, 1748, 1755, 1762
Mars	1735, 1742, 1749, 1756, 1763

Cycle of Saturn

Yearly Rulers	(1765–1800)
Saturn	1765, 1772, 1779, 1786, 1793, 1800
Jupiter	1766, 1773, 1780, 1787, 1794
Mars	1767, 1774, 1781, 1788, 1795
the Sun	1768, 1775, 1782, 1789, 1796
Venus	1769, 1776, 1783, 1790, 1797
Mercury	1770, 1777, 1784, 1791, 1798
the Moon	1771, 1778, 1785, 1792, 1799

Cycle of Venus

Yearly Rulers	(1801–1836)
Venus	1801, 1808, 1815, 1822, 1829, 1836
Mercury	1802, 1809, 1816, 1823, 1830
the Moon	1803, 1810, 1817, 1824, 1831
Saturn	1804, 1811, 1818, 1825, 1832
Jupiter	1805, 1812, 1819, 1826, 1833
Mars	1806, 1813, 1820, 1827, 1834
the Sun	1807, 1814, 1821, 1828, 1835

Cycle of Jupiter

Yearly
Rulers   (1837–1872)

Jupiter   1837, 1844, 1851, 1858, 1865, 1872
Mars   1838, 1845, 1852, 1859, 1866
the Sun   1839, 1846, 1853, 1860, 1867
Venus   1840, 1847, 1854, 1861, 1868
Mercury   1841, 1848, 1855, 1862, 1869
the Moon   1842, 1849, 1856, 1863, 1870
Saturn   1843, 1850, 1857, 1864, 1871

Cycle of Mercury

Yearly
Rulers   (1873–1908)

Mercury   1873, 1880, 1887, 1894, 1901, 1908
the Moon   1874, 1881, 1888, 1895, 1902
Saturn   1875, 1882, 1889, 1896, 1903
Jupiter   1876, 1883, 1890, 1897, 1904
Mars   1877, 1884, 1891, 1898, 1905
the Sun   1878, 1885, 1892, 1899, 1906
Venus   1879, 1886, 1893, 1900, 1907

Cycle of Mars

Yearly
Rulers   (1909–1944)

Mars   1909, 1916, 1923, 1930, 1937, 1944
the Sun   1910, 1917, 1924, 1931, 1938
Venus   1911, 1918, 1925, 1932, 1939
Mercury   1912, 1919, 1926, 1933, 1940
the Moon   1913, 1920, 1927, 1934, 1941
Saturn   1914, 1921, 1928, 1935, 1942
Jupiter   1915, 1922, 1929, 1936, 1943

Cycle of the Moon

Yearly Rulers	(1945–1980)
the Moon	1945, 1952, 1959, 1966, 1973, 1980
Saturn	1946, 1953, 1960, 1967, 1974
Jupiter	1947, 1954, 1961, 1968, 1975
Mars	1948, 1955, 1962, 1969, 1976
the Sun	1949, 1956, 1963, 1970, 1977
Venus	1950, 1957, 1964, 1971, 1978
Mercury	1951, 1958, 1965, 1972, 1979

Cycle of the Sun

Yearly Rulers	(1981–2016)
the Sun	1981, 1988, 1995, 2002, 2009, 2016
Venus	1982, 1989, 1996, 2003, 2010
Mercury	1983, 1990, 1997, 2004, 2011
the Moon	1984, 1991, 1998, 2005, 2012
Saturn	1985, 1992, 1999, 2006, 2013
Jupiter	1986, 1993, 2000, 2007, 2014
Mars	1987, 1994, 2001, 2008, 2015

The Influence of the Yearly Planet

Each yearly planet can be studied much the same way as the daily planet, where astrological influence is concerned. First note the general indications of the planet of the year; then check it against the person's birth sign, as with the planet of the day, using the same list.

Opinions vary as to comparative values, but many astrologers feel that the planet of the day is more definitive and therefore should be considered first. Where the daily influence appears strong, the yearly indication may be regarded mostly as a modifying influence.

But there are times when the planet of the day has little effect upon the birth sign, or may be a weakening influence. In such cases, the planet of the year, if strong, may automatically be a helpful influence; or the individual may take its indications as both a standard and a guide toward higher achievement.

Sometimes a yearly indication combines with that of the decan, adding needed strength to the over-all pattern. Much could be written on the blending of the different influences, and some of these will be detailed in the sample horoscopes that follow. But mostly, it is a matter of good judgment based upon a knowledge of planetary indications and the characteristics of the twelve birth signs. This is what makes astrology a fascinating study.

The planet of the cycle has little direct effect upon the individual, beyond his being attuned to its conditions. The cycles affect mankind in general, a significant example being the fact that both World War I and II occurred during the cycle of Mars; and that unrest and continuous change immediately followed during the cycle of the Moon.

But it is obvious that a person's birth sign and planetary indications will show whether he is fitted for war, peace, or whatever cyclic conditions may prevail.

The cyclic influence of the planets is clearly defined in American history. The nation's rise to a power in its own right began in the cycle of the Sun (1729–1764) and was followed by the trials and struggles of the cycle of Saturn (1765–1800) when hopes were at a low ebb, but intellect prevailed and won.

The era of eloquence and statesmanship was coincident with the cycle of Venus (1801–1836) but showed a typical weakness as well. The cycle of Jupiter (1837–1872) began the period of expansion, with the establishment of Texas as a republic, and continued on through the Civil War and the subsequent migration to the West.

The cycle of Mercury (1873–1908) ushered in the era of big business, keen competition, panics, and corruption that resulted in trust-busting tactics. All was then set for the cycle of Mars (1909–1944), which resulted in this nation becoming the mightiest military power ever known. The cycle of the Moon (1945–1980) will go down on record as the nation's greatest era of change.

All of which simply highlights the importance of astrology to the individual. The saying that "The stars impel but do not compel" is indeed appropriate, when everyone is trying to find his proper place in the complex scheme of the modern world.

Forming a Simplified Horoscope

The casting of a complete, detailed horoscope is not only difficult; in many cases it is practically impossible due to a lack of data regarding the exact time of a person's birth, which, according to most professional astrologers, should be calculated not only to the day, but to the hour and the minute.

Because of that, many persons are content to go by the indications of their birth signs, classing themselves as a Gemini, a Leo, or a Virgo type, as the case may be. Often, such readings run remarkably true to form, but there is no reason why they should be so limited. It is quite easy to extend the astrological findings pertaining to a person's birth date by means of a simplified horoscope.

The procedure is as follows:

1. Study the general characteristics of the birth sign or cusp under which the individual was born. These include the influence of the planet governing that period.

2. Note the lesser traits listed under the decan or ten-day period which is subordinate to the sign, due chiefly to the planetary influences of that particular decan.

3. Find the planet governing the day of the week on which the person was born. These are usually listed in a special section, together with a chart for finding the correct day of the week for any date in the past three centuries. Study the influence of that planet and apply it as an important factor.

4. Note the planet ruling the year of the person's birth, which is listed in another section. This can be considered as an added influence, usually of a modifying nature, and its indications should be gauged accordingly.

5. Check the ruling planet of the cycle, which is also listed, to learn how well it harmonizes with the previous influences. This is of comparatively small importance, but can account for slight differences in individuals, due to favorable or unfavorable combinations.

From these indications you can blend a personality chart far more comprehensive than a mere monthly reading. In many instances, its practical interpretations will approach those of a very elaborate horoscope. However, the more careful the analysis, the greater the shading of the various influences, the better the result.

This should be remembered when preparing horoscopes for various persons. As with every occult science, a full interpretation of accepted indications requires skill and judgment which can only be gained through effort and experience.

2

Cartomancy or
Fortune Telling with Cards

The Origin of Playing Cards

Though the origin of playing cards is shrouded in the past, it is almost certain that they were originally designed to foretell the future, and they have been used for that purpose ever since they began. Some authorities claim that they evolved from Chinese divining sticks; others, that they were adapted from the pages of a legendary "Book of Thoth" used by ancient Egyptians.

Whichever the case, they were supposedly brought to Europe by wandering tribes of gypsies, some time after the year A.D. 1300. The gypsies presumably came from India by way of Persia, where playing cards of a picture type called *atouts* were already in vogue. The gypsies, to give themselves status, intimated that they were of Egyptian origin and spoke of their homeland as "Little Egypt," so it would not be surprising if the Persian cards had been purposely attributed to Egypt instead. There probably never was and never will be a gypsy camp without a pack of cards of some sort, and a member of the tribe who is capable of interpreting them. As for the cards themselves, the packs that first developed in Europe were called *tarots* and consisted of seventy-eight cards. Of these, fifty-six were suit cards similar to those of modern packs, except that the suits were swords, cups, coins, and rods, and that there were four court cards to each suit, namely, king, queen, knight, and knave (jack). The "spot" cards, which bore the symbols mentioned, ran from ten down to one (ace).

The additional twenty-two cards all bore symbolic pictures and corresponded to the *atouts* of the Persian packs. These cards were of various types, but generally speaking, they depicted similar personages and themes. One typical list ran as follows:

1. the juggler. 2. the high priestess. 3. the empress. 4. the emperor. 5. the hierophant. 6. the lovers. 7. the chariot. 8. Justice. 9. the hermit. 10. Fortune. 11. Strength. 12. the hanged man. 13. Death. 14. Temperance. 15. the devil. 16. Lightning. 17. the stars. 18. the Moon. 19. the Sun. 20. Judgment. 21. the world. 22. the fool.

These cards constituted the "greater arcana" and each had its special divinitory significance. Since the pictures were upright, they were often inverted when dealt, changing their interpretation, frequently for the worse.

The "suit" cards, swords, cups, coins, and rods, formed the "lesser arcana" and these had their own interpretations. Their original designs were also "one-way," allowing them to be reversed when dealt, so that their readings could be variable.

In full form, these were used chiefly for telling fortunes, and when card games were developed, the pack was cut down to four suits, and four cards—the knights—were eliminated, reducing the pack to fifty-two cards.

In France, the suits were changed to spades, hearts, clubs, and diamonds. English and American cards adopted the new pattern, resulting in the playing cards of today. Oddly, one card managed to survive from trumps major, as the greater arcana was also known. That card was the fool, and it forms the joker of our modern packs.

These departures from the original tarots had little effect upon the card readers. They continued to interpret them in terms of past, present, and future, with the usual results. Mademoiselle Lenormand, a famous cartomancer during the Napoleonic era, was credited with some fantastic revelations which particularly impressed the Empress Josephine. At that time the pack popularly used in France was the thirty-two-card piquet pack (aces down to sevens), and presumably she used those in some of her divinations.

With the development of "double-ended" court cards, the type now in vogue, it became impossible to note if they were reversed when dealt. Cards of French and English design always presented that problem with the diamond suit, which has spots that look alike both ways. The other suits, too, lost their reversible quality when printed with spots pointing opposite ways, like the two of spades, in modern packs.

One answer was to mark the "top" end of each card, thus telling when it was reversed. That course was adopted during the vogue of

1 LE BATELEUR א

2 LA PAPESSE ב

3 L'IMPERATRICE ג

4 L'EMPEREUR ד

5 LE PAPE ה

6 L'AMOUREUX ו

7 LE CHARIOT

8 LA JUSTICE

9 HERMITE

10 LA ROUE DE FORTUNE

11 LA FORCE

12 LE PENDU

13. LA MORT

14. LA TEMPÉRANCE

15. LE DIABLE

16. LE FEU DU CIEL

17. LES ETOILES

18. LA LUNE

19 LE SOLEIL

20 LE JUGEMENT

21 LE MONDE

22 LE FOU

the thirty-two-card pack, which was used almost exclusively by many cartomancers who followed Mademoiselle Lenormand. But with the emphasis on games demanding a fifty-two-card pack, fortune-telling systems fell into the same groove, and today there are enough "full pack" methods to supply the demand. These eliminate all the nuisances and uncertainty of "reversed" card interpretations, which in some instances is an arbitrary factor. So in the pages that follow, you will find instructions for full pack readings exclusively, in conformity to the modern trend.

Devotees of the tarot pack still regard it with a sentiment akin to awe, but it is hard to share their view. The art of cartomancy lies more in the skill and insight of the interpreter than in the cards themselves. Mademoiselle Lenormand did right well with the cards of her day and followed it up by putting out her own fortune-telling pack, with her favorite instructions printed on the appropriate cards. Such packs have been printed ever since, some attributed to the Great Lenormand and others with titles of their own.

During the centuries, gypsies and other gifted folk have been reading whatever cards come to hand, whether tarots, circular cards of Hindu origin, or cards of various European countries with their different symbols. Readers can try their own hands with available cards and learn for themselves the spell of the unknown as revealed by the ever-changing pasteboards that could still be the mystic pages from the unbound Book of Thoth!

Fortune Telling Simplified

Fortune telling with cards is a fascinating pastime, which—more often than not—produces surprises that have all the semblance of predictions. How seriously a person cares to take this, depends—like the interpretation of the cards themselves—upon the mood of the individual.

Many systems have been used with card fortunes, and some have become obsolete or confusing. Therefore it is best to adhere to those that are simple and direct, or which have proven their value in the past and have stood the test of time. Such systems are given in the following pages.

The fact of primary importance is this:

Each card in the pack has acquired a traditional meaning, which is subject to various modifications. The seer—or person telling the fortune —should know all these meanings, or have them ready for reference.

Next: Each card must be interpreted in terms of certain other cards with which it appears in the layout or face-up deal. This helps clarify the particular meaning of a card.

For example, a card specifying the immediate receipt of something would be modified by a card pertaining to "love" to mean that the "something" would be an engagement ring. Whereas if the modifying card had to do with "business," we could expect money as the "something" due to be received.

Often, too, the consultant—or person whose fortune is being told—can help in the interpretation. Do not look upon card fortunes as an effort to astound or outwit someone, nor even as a guessing game. It should be considered a sincere attempt to learn what the cards themselves may reveal. So treated, the results will often become phenomenal.

The question invariably arises: How often should the cards be consulted?

The answer is: As often as you want, provided that they are read only a few times at one sitting—for the same consultant—and the repeat deals should be intended purely to clarify or verify something that was indicated in the original interpretation.

If the same card or token appears conspicuously in a repeat deal, it becomes a very important omen. Also, some new interpretation may interlock with one that arose before. This rule applies if the same consultant has his or her fortune told over within a few days.

Ordinarily, an entirely new consultation should not be sought by an individual within a week or more—and even then, it should be interpreted in terms of immediate happenings rather than some distant date.

The significations of the various cards are given in the following list:

Table of Card Significations

HEARTS

Ace: Pertains to one's home and domestic happiness. Can signify visitors, change of residence, or word from members of the family. Often helpful but can indicate home problems.

King: A man of influence and good intentions. Generous and likable, but more hasty than wise. Not reliable as an adviser. Watch out for arguments and hot temper, as these are the indications.

Queen: A faithful, loving woman, often representing a trustful wife, or a man's true love. In a woman's fortune, this card looms as a potential rival, but always one who is kindly and plays fair.

Jack: Someone very close to the consultant; a bosom friend or confidant. Not necessarily a man, but usually a person of long-standing acquaintance, sometimes a childhood sweetheart or a school chum.

  10:   A highly favorable card, promising success and good luck to any project. Sometimes indicates a big surprise, always fortunate. It adds strength to good cards close by and counteracts bad ones.

   9:   A card of fulfillment promising harmony and success to projects indicated by accompanying cards. Often called the "wish card" that makes dreams come true. Bad cards with it mean temporary obstacles, sometimes serious.

   8:   The party card, presaging a happy occasion when all should "eat, drink, and be merry." Generally, it refers to an event already anticipated or planned, so check the surrounding cards to see how they will help or harm it.

   7:   This is a card of false hopes and hasty promises. Never depend on other persons in plans influenced by this card, as they are always apt to change their minds. With bad cards you can expect anything, even outright enmity, so count on nothing.

   6:   This shows weakness in the consultant, a warning that he may be easily imposed upon, particularly in ways indicated by accompanying cards. It signifies an overgenerous nature, or conniving associates.

   5:   A card of indecision. Inability of the consultant to make up his mind regarding specific subjects. Occasionally shows change in surroundings due to a desire to escape issues.

   4:   This is a "bachelor" or "old maid" sign, though often indicating a long-delayed or much-postponed marriage, sometimes as a result of a reconciliation. Due often to the consultant's fussy disposition.

3: A card denoting hotheaded action on the part of the consultant. Impetuous, unwise decisions will threaten or spoil favorable enterprises and can produce disaster when other bad cards are present.

2: This is the success card, promising great fortune, often beyond all expectations. Bad cards will delay it and often force the consultant to consider other projects instead of those where obstacles appear.

CLUBS

Ace: This is the card of wealth, financial success, and with it, fame in a chosen profession. It is also an indication of many friends, all helpful to the consultant throughout life.

King: Represents an individual of constant and valuable friendship. With a man, sometimes a rival but a generous one. With a woman, this man may be a relative or family friend, but always an honest, loyal, and sincere adviser.

Queen: A kindly, lovable woman, sometimes temperamental but always true, whether in love or in friendship. To a man consultant, this card may indicate a wife; to a woman, a lifelong confidante.

Jack: A friend who will prove both generous and sincere. Not necessarily a man, this may represent any friend of either a male or female consultant. The card also indicates flattery but only when well-intended.

10: A very strong good luck card. It brings fortune from an unexpected source and sometimes promises a long, successful journey. A card of happiness, warding off any evil influences.

9: A real trouble card. If it brings gifts or rewards, the person may lose a friend as a result. Otherwise it means frequent disputes among friends that will cause harmful results. Ambition injured by obstinacy.

8: An overwhelming urge for money. A good token of friendship, if persons are independent, or a project offers sufficient gain for all. Otherwise friends will be sacrificed for profits. Denotes a person who will gamble borrowed money with his own.

7: A card of great good luck provided there is no interference, particularly from the opposite sex. This card needs favorable ones accompanying it to insure its proper success.

6: This is the partnership card, a sure sign of successful business based on friendship. On any scheme indicated by accompanying cards, be sure to consult friends or seek their financial aid.

5: A marriage card usually represents marriage with a wealthy mate. In any case, it offers a prosperous future to both parties. Should be considered carefully in relation to other projects.

4: A danger card showing sudden misfortune or failure of a project. Watch out for false or inconstant friends. They may injure any good prospects otherwise indicated.

3: A sign of a second marriage and often of a third, with good prospects. Sometimes indicates a long engagement to one person followed by a marriage to someone else, after a friendly parting.

2: A card of direct opposition. Do not count on support from friends or business associates. They may be the ones who will oppose you. It takes a lone wolf to beat this card.

DIAMONDS

Ace: This card signifies an important message. It could be a letter, as indicated by an accompanying card. Or it may mean money or a gift, the latter sometimes in the form of an engagement ring.

King: A dangerous man. In business, often a ruthless competitor; in love, a bitter rival. With women, this card can mean a deceitful lover, or a bad-tempered husband.

Queen: A flirtatious woman, who will interfere in love and business, where a male consultant is concerned. Given to gossip and scandal where other women are concerned. Dangerous, attractive, and with very persuasive powers over the male sex.

Jack: A selfish person, usually a man. Sometimes a messenger bringing bad news. Occasionally a jealous relative or unreliable friend. Seldom dangerous to a male consultant, but bad toward women—except when good cards also appear.

10: This card means money—though you may not get it. It can indicate a journey, with money as the objective. It might also mean an unexpected marriage, usually with money involved.

9: A card of adventure, the wanderlust. Here, too, money is the objective. It may mean a necessity to move from one place to another, always in hope of advancement. Can be unexpected news regarding money, good or bad, according to the accompanying cards.

8: This card relates both to travel and a marriage late in life. Sometimes the two are closely associated, such as a journey resulting in a courtship. This card indicates country life.

7: A card of bad aspects. It indicates the gambler, usually a heavy loser. It also concerns false rumors and unfair criticism. It can be regarded as bad luck with any enterprise or purpose.

6: This card denotes an early marriage. It also threatens an unhappy ending to such a marriage. It likewise bodes ill for a second marriage. The adjacent cards may reveal the reasons.

5: This is a card of prosperity in business or marriage, perhaps both. With business, long, enduring friendship would be gained through honest transactions. With marriage, pride in family and children.

4: A quarrelsome card applying both to friendship and family. It shows forgotten or neglected friendships. In marriage, frequent quarrels and interference from relatives.

3: This is a card of disputes and quarrels. It means disagreements in business, lawsuits. The same applies in the home, this being a sign of separation and perhaps divorce.

2: Here we have the token of a serious love affair; whether resulting in marriage or interfering in it, the other cards will determine. Certainly it will interfere in other matters indicated.

SPADES

Ace: This is the card of misfortune sometimes termed the "death card." It does not always apply to the consultant but more generally refers to bad news, particularly tidings of death. It causes emotional conflicts in love, family, and friendship.

King: Represents an ambitious man who will prove dangerous, injuring business or marital relationships. For a woman consultant, this is a warning against a man who may prove to be worthless or incompatible, according to the nearby cards.

Queen: The card of a treacherous person, often a woman who is ruthless and cruel. With men, it is a warning against a "merry widow" type. With women, it means betrayal by a "very dear" friend.

Jack: This is the card of the "hanger-on." It shows a pretended friend, or a useless partner who may be sincere but is lazy and will hinder the consultant in any enterprise.

10: A very unlucky card. The best that can be said for it is that it merely nullifies good omens. When found with bad cards it doubles their misfortunes.

9: Regarded as the worst card in the pack. It can mean illness, loss of money, or misery—even amid the best of cards. Just hope for the best but don't depend upon it in any project influenced by this card.

8: A card of opposition. False friends may become your enemies. Fortunately, most of the trouble predicted by this card can be avoided if its warning is observed. Check all your affairs immediately.

7: Sorrow and quarrels revealed by this card, sometimes a combination of both. Avoid misunderstandings with friends and relatives; you may regret them later. Let things ride until bad luck rolls by.

6: This is the card of much planning and little result. It is associated with discouragements. Perseverance may triumph, however, unless accompanying cards are very bad. Frequently this card brings luck despite failure.

5: Business success and a happy marriage are both shown by this card, but they will be gained only after many reverses. The person may be overwhelmed and too easily discouraged, particularly if other odds are present.

4: Minor misfortunes. A short illness, temporary financial reverses, envy, and petty jealousy—one's own or that of others—will retard any projects suggested by the surrounding cards.

3: This is an unhappy card. Often it designates misfortune in love or marriage. Such troubles must be forgotten or they will nullify all other good omens pertaining to the consultant.

2: This is an indication of complete change or separation. It may mean loss of home, a separation from loved ones, a departure to a distant land, or a death. Its effect on the accompanying cards is usually very marked.

General Significances

A study of the individual significances of each card shows that those of certain suits bear a marked affinity—whether for good or bad.

This is something that must be remembered when interpreting cards in groups. If any card is flanked by two of a certain suit—or if any suit predominates the layout—a special significance results.

In brief, this interpretation of an individual card, or the whole mood of the consultation, must be tempered accordingly. These general significances are:

HEARTS: These are a complete symbol. They show a full, wholehearted nature, but with it a strong emotional force. Therefore hearts point to high success. They indicate an integrity that will nullify evil; they soften most adverse signs—except where love and close friendship is concerned. There, hearts are a symbol of grief and suffering under strenuous conditions.

CLUBS: These symbolize friendship. They indicate the importance of influence. With good cards, clubs are reminders that friends must be kept to insure success. With bad cards—as in business—they signify that friends may help to overcome obstacles. Where the cards portend very bad luck, however, clubs may mean that friends will desert the consultant when things go wrong—so be warned!

DIAMONDS: These indicate the practical side of life—including money.

Diamonds represent difficulties. They also stand for halfway achievements that require something more to complete them.

Thus, diamonds flanking a success card may mean that money will be needed to insure that success. Or they can point to friction such as success in business where there is danger of serious competition.

They may mean lawsuits, temporary reverses, many other things that will interfere with success. On the contrary, diamonds sometimes soften the significance of bad cards by indicating that money—or wealth—if obtainable, can conquer that adversity that those cards indicate.

SPADES: Far from being bad cards, spades are often warning tokens signifying hazards or misfortunes which, by that very fact, may give the consultant a chance to counteract them. When spades appear they betoken bad luck, interference, and losses generally, so no matter how good a card may be, don't expect too much.

Where certain cards signify enemies, business problems, or other troubles, count on them as being doubled when spades are around. To be forewarned is to be forearmed, and that is half the battle!

Methods of Fortune Telling

Three methods of telling fortunes by cards are given here. In each instance the interpretations of the cards follow those given in the preceding tables. Sample interpretations are included.

THE SEVEN TRIPLETS

The seven triplets are also called the "seven sisters" or the "seven fates." This system requires twenty-one cards from a shuffled pack of a full fifty-two. After the shuffle, the pack should be cut into three heaps by the consultant, who, for some ceremonial reason, should always do this with his or her left hand.

Three cards are then dealt face up, one from each heap, forming a cluster. This is followed by a deal of three more and so on, until seven heaps have been dealt in all. Each of the heaps is then interpreted according to the cards that compose it. The center card of each group (the one coming from the middle heap) is the focal card about which the prediction is centered. The triplets illustration shows a typical example. Follow it closely and note the interpretations.

Triplets

Interpretation of the cards:

1. *For a male consultant:* An influential friend or partner (K H) will advise you regarding a business venture which will prove successful (5 D) only after considerable argument that may break up your marriage—if an early one (6 D).
For a female consultant: Avoid the unwise advice of a well-meaning man (K H) regarding your marriage. Your future hopes are great, both for yourself and your children (5 D), provided you do not let your marriage—particularly an early one—be disturbed (6 D).

2. *For a male consultant:* Curb your tendency to gamble (7 D), as it will result in utter disaster, including the loss of any legacy you receive (A S), and will force you into a marriage for money (5 C).
For a female consultant: Don't take chances with the man you love (7 D). You may lose him and your money as well (A S), leaving you no choice but poverty or a marriage for money instead of love (5 C).

3. *For a male consultant:* You will lose the one you love to a rival (K C), as you have the worst possible card in the pack (9 S)—with spades doubled (9 S + 3 S)!
For a female consultant: Confide your troubles of love and marriage to an old family friend, who is the only person able to help you reclaim anything from what is sure to be disaster.

4. *For a male consultant:* You have many friends whose eagerness for your success will offset the unfair business practices of a dangerous competitor who will call in an equally ruthless man to aid him.
For a female consultant: Be warned by your many friends against a man who will try to cover up for a deceitful lover or a faithless husband.

5. *For either consultant:* You can depend on your friends—or one friend in particular—to show you the road to opportunity. You may have to travel far to get it, but good news may already be on the way and you can look forward to a great celebration.

6. *For either consultant:* Do not worry about a trifling misfortune or slight illness. A good friend will solve your problems, thus terminating all your indecision.

7. *For either consultant:* You are easily imposed upon and this will lead to unhappiness and quarrels either with business associates or at home.

A fortunate turn of events will resolve the issue and ultimate success and happiness will be yours.

THE LUCKY THIRTEEN

Take a joker or some odd card and place it face up to represent the consultant. Around it add twelve more cards face down, exactly as shown here.

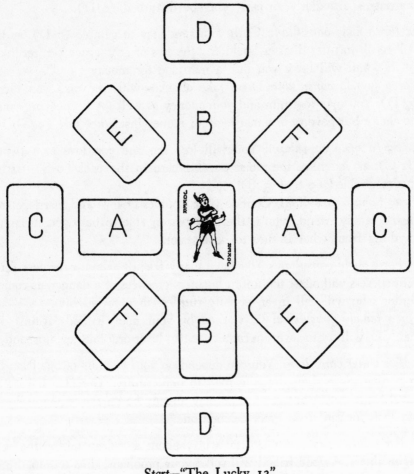

Start—"The Lucky 13"

The letters on the cards show the way they are to be paired. Turn up the two marked "A" and interpret them in terms of the consultant. Do the same with the pair marked "B." These represent the closest influences to the consultant.

Pairs "C" and "D" come next. They are either "futures" or represent strong influences that are blocked by "A" and "B" respectively. Finally, turn up the "E" and "F" pairs. They are secondary influences, helpful or harmful as the case may be.

Here is an example:

Finish—"The Lucky 13"

Interpretation: A loyal friend of long standing (J H) is constantly working to keep your home life (A H) happy and harmonious. This is very helpful to your welfare and can overcome all other influences. (The "A" pair.)

This is very important because you personally are trying to escape issues, due to your own indecision (5 H). You are greatly bothered by temporary financial problems, occasional illness, or petty worries (4 S). (The "B" pair.)

An overambitious man (K S) may try to interfere in your future success, but you will win despite him, thanks to the help of other friends (A C) and your own merit. (The "C" pair.) Also—and this is quite important—your loyal friend (J H) is blocking the troublemaker (K S).

Despite failure of certain projects (4 C) you can count on a future acquaintance—to bring you a new opportunity leading to the success already indicated and thus insuring it (2 H). (The "D" pair.)

Do not expect to get along without opposition (2 C). You are sure to meet with it, particularly in business and also from persons who call themselves friends. You can depend upon a loyal, kindly woman to combat this opposition (Q C). With a male consultant, the woman might represent his wife. With a female consultant, her closest friend. (The "E" pair.)

Both business success and happy marriage (5 S) may be marred or retarded by a serious love affair (2 D), which can also threaten the success that this reading presages. (The "F" pair.)

TRIPLE NINES

This is a very intriguing form of card consultation, requiring three deals, which some cartomancers interpret in terms of past, present, and future, but which can be made into a general reading quite as effectively. This, as with all such auguries, depends much on the mood of the consultant and whatever questions he or she may want answered.

Briefly, the pack is dealt into five rows of face-up cards, nine to each, with an added row of seven. The consultant's appropriate card, which is decided upon beforehand, is then located and a count begun from it, toward the right of the row in which it appears. Reaching the end of that row, you move to the row below and continue the count to the left.

The ninth card thus reached is duly interpreted. The count then is resumed toward the left of that row, continuing to the right in the row below, to reach another ninth card. This continues, stopping on every ninth card, and upon reaching the bottom row you simply go up to the top and continue the zigzag process there.

This means an interpretation of six cards in all—or in some cases, only five. So the pack is gathered, shuffled, and dealt again for further interpretation in the same fashion. That is done a third time, thus completing what is usually a very satisfactory reading. Always, the consultant's card is the starting point and you count with the first card to the right, going left on the row below.

Here are three sample layouts and their readings, with the Q D as the consultant's card:

First Layout

K C	8 C	4 S	8 H	Q S	A S	A H	7 S	3 D
J D	5 C	4 C	4 D	K S	J S	9 H	10 H	Q H
10 D	6 H	7 C	9 D	5 S	5 H	9 C	7 H	2 D
3 H	7 D	6 D	Q C	J C	K H	2 H	Q D	10 C
8 S	4 C	9 S	6 S	10 S	3 S	A C	4 H	5 D
	A D	6 C	J H	2 S	K D	2 C	8 D	

Counting right from the Q D and then left in the row below, the ninth card (4 C) shows misfortune or failure of plans through indifference of false friends. Continuing left, then right along the bottom row, up to the extreme right of the top row, a count of nine ends on the 3 D, showing disputes at home, or in business, probably attributable to that influence.

Another count of nine reveals a likely source of the trouble (J D) as a selfish person—possibly a jealous relative or unreliable friend—who may bring bad news. This is specially applicable with a woman as consultant. Nine to the right along the second row and down to the third produces a romantic angle (2 D) which may prove to be more serious than it appears.

Counting nine to the left and down to the next row, the 3 H shows an impetuous action on the part of the consultant which may have brought this all about, or which promises immediate trouble. The main point is, don't blame other people for conditions which can be improved through personal attention. Once the factors are recognized, the consultant should be able to control them through calm, intelligent procedure. There is no further count of nine as the Q D interrupts it.

88

Second Layout

A C	5 C	9 D	3 S	10 H	6 S	3 C	J H	10 D
K H	Q H	2 S	4 S	8 H	9 H	3 D	9 S	A D
8 C	7 H	3 H	J D	5 S	Q D	10 S	K C	2 D
A S	5 D	4 C	6 H	J S	7 D	8 D	K D	2 H
9 C	7 C	Q C	A H	5 H	6 C	6 D	7 S	4 H
	J C	10 C	4 D	Q S	K S	8 S	2 C	

Starting to the right from the Q H, a count of nine reaches the K C, who may be a tall, dark, and possibly handsome man, but is just as apt to be simply a good adviser. At any rate, the consultant should trust his judgment and sincerity. This is necessary toward prosperity (5 D) whether in social or financial affairs, so the consultant should make sure of the person indicated.

That is because misunderstandings loom (7 S) at home or at work, and all friction should therefore be avoided. It is very helpful to have the right person available in this situation where high hopes are in the balance. Another count of nine shows that money is involved (10 C) and that collecting it may prove a problem; in fact, it may be wiser to forget it.

This is confirmed by continuing the count to the 6 S, which indicates discouragement through frustrated plans. Its promise of eventual success goes with the helpful friend (K C) and the prosperous sign (5 D), which should be played to the full against the baleful indication of the 7 S. No more cards are involved as the count comes to the Q H.

Third Layout

6 H	7 H	5 D	Q C	9 C	5 H	Q D	8 S	J D
Q S	K S	2 C	A S	5 S	7 C	2 S	10 D	8 C
4 C	10 H	7 D	4 D	J C	8 D	A H	10 C	6 S
J S	4 S	6 C	8 H	3 H	9 S	2 D	3 D	9 D
3 C	A C	4 H	7 S	K D	6 D	10 S	9 H	K C
	J H	Q H	2 H	A D	3 S	5 C	K H	

From the consultant's Q H, she is immediately confronted by indecision (5 H), even with an urge to get away from things. Another count of nine (left along the top line and right along the second) reveals the probable source of trouble, the A S, which signifies bad news and often the presentiment of some misfortune.

A change of surroundings (8 D) and a possible journey may change this. Here, the application of the card depends greatly on the consultant's age, circumstance, and any existing problem. It may be helped by the next ninth card (8 H), with its promise of a pleasant event with a happy outcome, but the consultant should be cautious where matrimony is concerned, as the count ends on the 6 D.

The Mystic Cross

This is a brief but sometimes pointed method of prognostication that should be interpreted strictly in terms of the consultant's own interests in order to be most effective. Don't expect the cards to come up with something totally out of character, but count on them to answer something close at hand or already in mind.

That way, this will prove a very useful system that can be repeated at fairly frequent intervals, particularly after one prediction has been at least partially fulfilled.

Thirteen cards are used, but they are laid in cross rows of seven each, so that any bad luck may be offset by good. However, luck will be seen in the cards themselves as soon as they are dealt face up.

Before the deal, you must decide upon the consultant's card, which we will suppose in this case is the king of spades, representing a consultant with dark hair and dark eyes. We will assume that he is either happily married or is planning matrimony and that he is ambitious or engaged in a reasonably profitable business.

Hence the cards will be studied in those terms, and the first to look for is the consultant's own card, which is always a good sign if it appears among the mystic thirteen. Aces also have special significance, but are detrimental, particularly if more than one appears.

The presence of the consultant's K S is helpful, and the absence of aces is equally favorable, as it means that any luck will hold. Next, you note the center card, because it has a bearing on both rows. In this case, it is the 7 C, which is a very lucky card, if properly accompanied.

To learn its full status, you first read the vertical row from top to bottom; then the three cards at the left, which modify the fortune for good or bad; and finally, the three at the right, which may provide the unexpected.

The interpretation follows:

Since the consultant's card appears (K S) conditions favor his plans

The Mystic Cross

and he may be luckier than he would ordinarily suppose (7 C). Reading downward, he will meet opposition (2 C) which he may already anticipate, but the presence of his own card (K S) shows that he is quite capable of handling it, and should ignore any aid offered by a false or incapable friend (J S). He can count on luck (7 C) and can rely on the loyalty or intuition of his wife or sweetheart (Q H) to help him attain his great wish or long-sought ambition (9 H). The 5 C confirms this, as it promises a happy and prosperous marriage.

If above the center, the "wish card" (9 H) would almost automatically gain fulfillment, but toward the bottom it is shaky and therefore doubtful. Working in from the left, quarrels can be expected (4 D) and may delay the great success promised by the next card (2 H), but the balance will be swung in the consultant's favor (10 H), and perhaps through some great surprise.

Working in from the right, the consultant should realize that he is being imposed upon (6 H) and that his domestic happiness may be long delayed (3 C) or even broken up through further quarrels (3 D). By referring back to the full significance of these cards, you will readily see how greatly their interpretation hinges on the consultant's existing status.

If young and so far uncommitted as to his future, he may be at the parting of the ways, with everything pointing toward the best for all concerned. But if older and with much at stake, he may be threatened with personal disappointments that might outweigh achievement of delayed ambition.

3

Colorology

From the dawn of antiquity, color has been a strong yet subtle force in the shaping of human behavior. So prevalent is color in our natural surroundings that primitive man not only was swayed by its variations; he tried to imitate them and to seek their aid in furthering his luck or warding off evil.

The ancients coupled colors with natural forces. To them, red symbolized fire, because of its ruddy glow. Orange or golden yellow represented the sun; green, the foliage of springtime; blue, the sky and sea. Even in modern times, savages have donned war paint to frighten enemies, and they have traded away property and belongings for beads and cloth of gay hues.

More enlightened people have developed many forms of mysticism concerning colors. Astrologers, in an effort to identify the planets with things mundane, chose gold as the metal of the Sun, and silver as that of the Moon, because of the similarity in colors. Various colors were ascribed to the other planets: red for Mars; green or light blue for Venus; dark blue or purple for Jupiter; black or brown for Saturn; variable colors for Mercury.

In linking the planets with gems, colors were sometimes the determining factor, which may account for some of our modern birthstones. The modern choice of the alexandrite as a birthstone for Gemini is indeed appropriate, for Mercury is the ruling planet of that sign, and the alexandrite is a gem that changes color in different kinds of light.

Colors also have been given numerical values. One list covers the nine basic numbers used in numerology, as follows:

1, black; 2, yellow; 3, purple; 4, orange; 5, blue; 6, green; 7, gray; 8, brown; 9, red. In this list, gold is regarded as the equivalent of orange (4) and silver the equivalent of gray (7).

In astrology, various colors have been assigned to each sign of the zodiac, and some even to each ten-day period or decan. This stresses the importance that colors play in everyday life. This is all the more reason that they should be considered as a subject of their own. The modern science of "colorology" is therefore an answer to an ancient question.

According to occult science, both stars and numbers exert a vibratory influence over human affairs. The same applies to colors, but here, the psychic phase is confirmed by physical science, as it is a recognized fact that the apparent color of an object depends upon the wavelength of the light that it reflects. The psychic theory assumes the existence of a human aura, or an ethereal emanation issuing from everyone, like swirls or darts of colored lights, each indicative of an individual mood.

Only persons gifted with an inner sight are able to see those emanations clearly, though many people may gain glimpses of them or sense their influence. But interpretation of such colors is not only limited to the chosen few; the colors themselves are not necessarily an index to the character of the person from whom they emanate. Often, they are the outgrowth of a temporary condition, and as such they are apt to be charged with undue intensity, which further lessens their reliability.

Everyone at times gives way to fits of anger. When this manifests itself in the form of righteous indignation, it is all the stronger. That is when you are most apt to sense it, and perhaps misjudge it. That applies to other moods, which must also be sufficiently intensive to register. You may get a recurrent color vibration from someone who is continually exerting it, but usually such persons reveal that trait in other ways, too. Color radiation may be just a follow-up to normal expression.

To put colorology to practical use, try to decide what color you like best. Accepting that as your vibratory color, you will have a key to your natural trends. You can also analyze your friends by learning their favorite colors. But they should not give snap judgment as an answer. Let them be sure of the color before they name it. In case of doubt, you can take two colors, combining the traits under one with those of the other.

Some students of the occult claim that a deep-set aura never changes. If right, they are speaking of extreme cases. In childhood, there is a tendency to admire bright and sometimes garish colors; but that lessens as taste is developed. So you cannot type a person too soon.

Also, every color has modifying shades, so it is possible to undergo a personality change within one color's realm. Also, the impulses of any given color are quite controllable. So be careful to weigh your favorite color according to your full inclinations.

The Vibratory Colors

Red is the most forcible of colors, with a constantly active urge. It does not necessarily denote a headstrong nature, despite such phrases as "seeing red," for it may be cool and calculating as well as vigorous. People who like red are stalwart and their bravery is often evidenced. But if badly goaded, they may become vengeful. Analysts are therefore apt to regard this as a fiery color, whereas it actually represents virility, so flare-ups by persons with red preference may result from normal experiences. Being challengers, they frequently have encounters with persons who are just as determined as themselves.

Red is the most popular of colors, and when we realize that it is greatly favored by primitive tribes and persons of low mentality, it is easy to see how it has mistakenly been regarded as a symbol of brute force. Actually, red is the most controllable of colors, so no one should hesitate to admit it as a preference.

Instead, persons with red proclivities should make the most of them. Consider first that red includes such traits as passion, drive, endurance, boldness, and other qualities that lead to joy of life and love of adventure. Add to that the fact that the vibratory influence of red, like that of other colors, may run from the extremes of the utter physical to that of the sheer mental. You will then realize how rarely all the red elements are embodied in one personality.

You will find heroes and hero-worshipers both responsive to red vibrations; the same with great athletes and avid sports fans. Men of action may have little time for anger; while persons of tempestuous moods may show it in bluster, nothing more. People who actually choose red as a color to wear are usually optimistic and high-spirited.

The very power of the red wave length causes it to reflect the individual's nature more vividly than with other colors, where preference may be governed by more rational notions. Red, being an instinctive choice, characterizes people who need guidance in their development; and here, a study of shades and their significance is highly important.

Maroon, with its deep hue, shows stamina along with strength. Purpose and restraint are in this color, but perhaps more than any other, it represents the true fighting spirit, especially in the face of odds or adversity. It is a color of warmth and cooperative effort; though given to moody spells, it is strongly recuperative. This color itself has variance in shades; the richer it is, the better; too much brown restricts it to mundane affairs and selfish action.

Crimson shows the optimistic, go-getter traits of red. Here is the challenging, competitive nature, eager for success and always ready to champion a cause. Here we have action and aggressiveness on the intellectual plane, and its very drive carries the individual on to greater things. Often this volatile nature demands the satisfaction of desire regardless of consequences, but the ability to sway opinion and the promise of the future makes up for such shortcomings. Affectionate dispositions characterize this hue.

Scarlet is the most impassioned of red hues and can produce a nature more likable or more spiteful than any other type. Sudden temper can flare with those who hold this color preference, and often their action lacks purpose, being largely the result of a restless mood. Their affection is often superficial, a mere cover-up for their own selfish urge. Yet this is a gay, volatile hue that teems with vivacity and rules out the despair that so often handicaps other red shades.

Pink is the ultimate in light red shades, showing love rather than mere affection and a willingness to serve and help others. It has the activity of red, but it indicates a nature so softened that jealousy and spite cannot become a part of it. True pink is a delicate shade, however, and people who respond to its vibration can be easily hurt, though they recover readily.

The darker the red hue, toward brown or black, the more its violence must be controlled. The lighter the hue, the more loving and humane the nature, with calm moods amid the action. Bright tints show buoyancy; dull tints, glumness.

Orange is a color of high aspiration. People with that vibration are proud and self-sufficient, yet by direct manner and approach they impress other persons strongly. The drive of red is found in the orange aura, but it is high-minded and usually restrained or deficient on the sensual side, its one aim being ambition.

That handicaps the orange nature, for it shows a lack of warmth. The orange temperament is social, because it wants success. So orange folk go out of their way to gain popularity, which may cause people to mistrust them. Orange rides over opposition, however, through sheer exuberance and inventive ability. Orange people get what they want, and if conceited, they are also contented. Whatever their course, they justify it in their own minds, which gives them confidence, but often narrows their outlook.

With orange as your color, you must learn to recognize your own limitations. You must realize that intelligence and logic are not the only things that count in life. To make people like you, first you should like them.

Yellow is a much maligned color that actually deserves the highest rating, but only as a strong, full-bodied hue. Where orange leans to intelligence, yellow shows intellectuality. It is the color of the sun, and Oriental mystics use it to dispel evil, as the sun's rays banish the dark. In more practical terms, yellow denotes the scientific mind that overcomes ignorance. Yellow also denotes artistry.

As your color, yellow gives you wisdom and marks you as creative, but to what degree is the question. Many persons admit that the yellow which appeals to them is not the golden glow, but a paler, duller shade. With such a yellow, wisdom is restrained by caution. This shows a retiring nature, given to wishful thinking, too timid to take the risks that would lead to success. Vivid yellow, in contrast, shows the person who will take a chance with confidence and win.

Dull yellow marks a selfish individual, too introspective to make the most of opportunity. Yellow-brown is worst, literally both muddy and muddly. If such a color appeals to you, it is time to think in better shades of your favorite color, yellow.

Green is the great color of nature, and those who emanate that aura are not only adaptable to circumstances, but are generally both sympathetic and sentimental. Those factors are perhaps their greatest weakness. They are fond of companionship and therefore inclined to take life too easily. If they don't succeed as they should, they naturally blame everybody and everything except themselves.

As the diametric opposite of red, green is slow to anger and restrained of action. People with this vibration are as firm, as immutable as nature itself. Their power grows slowly but formidably, and there is no way of repressing their friendly but determined spirit. They are conformists, but in their own way. Once they feel that they are right, nothing can force them to change their opinions.

If green is your color, you may be a bit "green" at times, but people will like you all the better. Just don't fritter away idly, as this calm color vibration is apt to let you do. Seek action, because you should be capable of it. However, the shade of your aura may have some bearing there.

Emerald, the strong, rich green, is the most volatile expression of this aura. It raises adaptability to the status of adventure, and persons with that powerful vibration have all the vigor found in red and other colors. They find situations and make the most of them, in a forthright, indomitable way that still sways sentiment and sympathy.

Olive, in contrast, is a weak, dull hue, avoiding issues, seeking excuses. This may be a "negative" vibration, too close to nature. It is evasive, unable to express itself or to help the person who adopts it.

Apple green, a few shades higher, has a happier faculty, a hopeful, pleasant vibration, striving for the sympathy that characterizes the full-fledged color. Yet it is still too light, and therefore oversentimental.

Sea green is much darker than the others, including emerald; but with its strength, it carries envy. Instead of caution, which features the greens that are on the yellowish side, this deep green shows cunning and defeats its own purpose.

With greens, shades make the difference, more so perhaps than with any other color. Various other hues could be mentioned, but the general rule will suffice. Toward yellow, green becomes unstable; toward blue, it turns oversmart. Find the balance point and focus your vibration there if green is your favorite color.

Blue is a powerful vibratory influence, living up to the expression of "true blue" and at the same time going far beyond such scope. It is a color that mixes sensitivity with fervor, so eager to do right that it may take the wrong way to that purpose.

The sky is blue, but it varies from the light hue of azure to the near-black of midnight. Thus do the moods of the blue vibration vary. Not only that, it is difficult to find a person whose blue aura maintains a constant shade. It may descend to the depths of the "blues" and then rise to the inspired heights that come "once in a blue moon." So with blue, you should try to find your most suitable hue and hold it.

Generally speaking, all blue shows some measure of devotion. You make friends readily, but often in a formal way. Blue is a cold color, with a certain self-sufficiency, but persons with this aura recognize the value of cooperative effort and therefore exert it.

Where red responds to warm, primitive urge, and green absorbs the vitality of nature, blue turns to the sky and sea for inspiration. In seeking higher, deeper things, blue has become the predominant color in modern life. In business, social, and educational circles, blue far exceeds red as a motivating color, making blue the favorite color of many thinking persons.

Azure, or sky blue, is a truly heavenly hue, chosen by many who forego the world and dedicate themselves to noble causes. This is the token of unselfish personalities, as well as those whose self-interest has been absorbed by the desire for spiritual attainment.

Navy blue is a dark, strong hue, showing faithfulness, trust, and a constancy of purpose. There is a self-sufficiency in this darker shade, but always in a cooperative way. Strength and reliability are characteristic of this and approximate hues.

Indigo or *ultramarine* are borderline colors, with a purplish tinge. They have the basic qualities of blue, but they lean less to devotion and more to affection, finding outlets for their ideals by helping other people. Moodiness is more apt to grip such persons than those who favor lighter hues.

Admixtures of other colors disturb the steadfast trend of blue. A leaning to black or brown shows morbid or selfish inclinations. A strong tinge of gray creates uncertainty and even fear. A leaning to green, found in some shades of turquoise, shows an impetuous trend.

Violet is a color of grandeur and importance, often too strongly so. Its very richness seems to sway persons with this aura, and many people shy away from it as a favorite color, perhaps for that very reason. Like blue, this color has high ideals, but violet is given more to ritual than to devotion. Its self-esteem is so pronounced that people tuned to this vibration try to influence others accordingly. Sometimes that works out, but often the violet vanity proves its own undoing.

Usually, persons who favor violet are unaware of their own faults, as they habitually avoid criticism. They turn their idealism into a form of perfectionism, living in their own world of illusion, often to their own full satisfaction. With violet, the term "out of sight, out of mind" applies to anything they do not like. Violet, as a result, is a soothing, harmonious color, with its meditative side.

People with the violet aura often have literary, artistic, or dramatic ability, and they are highly imaginative and creative. This increases their self-satisfaction, for once aware of their genius, they are apt to flaunt it. But they are by no means self-effacing; the term "shrinking violet" refers strictly to the flower, not the color.

Less persons emanate this aura than any other, but that is all the more reason why violet folk regard themselves as different, if not unique. Often they have a yearning for the mystic, for theirs is the hue of twilight, denoting the transition from day to darkness. Turning fantasy into reality is a common violet practice.

Lavender represents the mild side of the violet nature. People with this aura have sweet dispositions, but a precious, precise manner. They are self-centered, insistent upon ruling their own little domain; hence they are intensive and exacting, willing to let many small things pass only as a way of gaining their main issue, which is often small in its own right. Hence lavender is often the mark of affectation.

Purple is the royal hue, and here we find violet at its strongest, with pomp and ceremony predominant. There is no limit to the height that a person with this aura will seek to attain. Indeed, many persons, swayed by success, purposely take on the purple aura, as it gratifies their sense of superiority. Given enough prestige and power, they will live up to it; but when it is mostly inflationary, such people dwell in a world of empty grandeur.

Magenta or other colors wherein violet or purple have a strong tinge of red often show a practical as well as a pompous nature. Such people have a "down-to-earth" attitude that enables them to couple lofty notions with practical results, despite their tendency to show off their importance.

White, as a color, has long been a symbol of purity. Actually, preference for white does denote an untrammeled mind, though its vibration may be largely neutral. Persons who choose white for their color are fastidious, careful in detail and in manner, but understanding of others. They are sincere and fair, but apt to be overcritical.

Gray is the color of uncertainty, running the gamut from fear, as shown in its lighter shades, through false bravado of the middle hues, to the selfish dark gray, which is dangerous because of its intensity. This is a deceptive color, as those who prefer it appear to be strict conformists with self-effacing ways, though often they are simply biding their time before pressing their own interests at the expense of others. When gray shows a decidedly silvery tinge, it becomes stronger and more constant, gaining a fine quality, which persons with this aura should seek.

Black is by no means a glum aura, as it is highly understanding, in a quiet way. Black is properly a symbol of formality and convention. It supplies dignity without false pride, and is a color that commands respect. It can become dynamic, enabling a person to drive home facts and purposes emphatically. But black is strong chiefly in its own right. If it simply tinges other colors, it becomes too heavy a restraint, curbing their natural trends. That accounts for some of the gloom attached to black.

Brown is a comparatively rare aura, but it is firm and definite. Otherwise, few persons would develop such a nature, as it seldom rises to great heights. It shows a plain, practical disposition; hence persons strongly of that type exhibit an affinity for brown because it is their obvious choice.

Dull, reddish brown is a token of a sensual trend. An average or medium brown shows a grasping personality. A dark brown indicates an irascible, fault-finding temperament. Yet brown often plods along successfully, and persons with this aura certainly do not wear false colors. They are solid folk who may get places through their plain-spoken, honest manner, despite their shortcomings. However, brown, as a tinge, hurts other colors, clouding out some of their finer points.

Color Combinations

A highly interesting and informative phase of colorology is the study of color combinations. To list these in detail would be superfluous, as by comparing the charts just given it is easy to analyze a person's composite traits. Here, however, you are moving from the psychic phase into the physical field, where subtle forces are supplanted by personal preferences.

So far we have been dealing primarily with the aura. This is something that can at times be sensed. It is possible to type a person by color impressions, and sometimes a golden glow may be disturbed by spots of red; or a purple cloud may be streaked with brown, like an approaching storm. Then analysis becomes intuitive, being centered on the more definitive color, but with special interpretations for the intruding hues.

A balanced or composite analysis is applied to the effect of color combinations on persons; that is, outward causes are used to study inward reactions. This goes with school colors, which rouse sentiment and enthusiasm; national emblems, which stimulate loyalty and patriotism; colors of nature, as a golden sunlight against a purple twilight, which awaken inspiration.

From the combinations a person favors strongly, you have a good index to individual temperament. Add up points for each color, allowing for conflicts, and you have it. In such analysis, white is often a contrast. A person favoring "red and white" is obviously responsive to red, but the white may show an appreciation of the finer side of the red vibration, such as fair play combined with virility.

There must be a reason for white, however, say as a trimming, or emphasis for the stronger color. Otherwise, the white influence may be weakening, particularly when a person, in naming it, deliberately rejects some other color. Where three colors are named in combination, white, if one of them, is almost always the balancing element, and a very valuable factor.

Gray is a good modifying color; in fact, it finds its best expression in combination, for there it is definitive, representing wise caution rather than doubt and uncertainty. Brown, too, shows its strong points with another color accompanying it, as brown is solid and unswayed, thereby lending consistency to its companion color.

An interesting commentary on the effect of colors in shaping the popular mind and the spirit of entire nations is found in comparative studies of World Wars I and II, where the national emblems of the contesting forces were concerned.

In World War I, France, Great Britain, and the United States, on the Allied side, all had flags with the colors red, white, and blue. So did others of the Allies, notably Russia, until with defeat she declared a separate peace and switched to plain red. Various smaller nations joined the Allied cause and some of those had flags with colors red, white, and blue.

But not one of the Central Powers and their satellite nations had national colors of red, white, and blue!

With World War II, France, Great Britain, and the United States were again among the Allies. Among the nations drawn into the conflict on the Allied side were the Netherlands and Norway, both with colors of red, white, and blue.

Again, not one of the opposing Axis Powers had red, white, and blue as colors; but that was not all. Of the nations that had been on the Allied side in World War I, but switched over to the opposition in World War II, none had flags of red, white, and blue.

Certainly, those colors must seemingly have a mutual and unchanging effect upon all who come within their constant and consistent influence!

4

Dice Divination or
Fortune Telling by Dice

Rules of Dice Divination

Fortune telling by dice dates back to antiquity, and this modern version of that divinatory art can be used as an intriguing form of entertainment. As to the accuracy of its answers, that is something that experiment best can prove.

The procedure is as follows:

Study the list of questions and choose whatever one you wish. Keep it constantly in mind while you shake a pair of dice, preferably in a cup or glass, though they may be shaken back and forth between the hands, which should be kept close together.

Roll the dice on the table and note the combination of spots that comes up. Refer to the list of answers headed by that combination. Find the answer with the same number as your question.

Example: A consultant chooses question 8, which asks, "Which friend or person shall I believe?" He rolls the dice and spots "2" and "3" appear. In the list of answers headed by combination "2-3" he finds number 8, which states, "The one whom you have known longest."

According to traditional rules governing this type of divination, only three questions should be asked by one person on a single occasion. Also, once a question has been asked, a person should wait a reasonable period of time for the answer to be fulfilled, before asking the same question again.

The Mystic Oracle

This may be used instead of actual dice, when seeking answers to questions. It consists of a chart of twenty-one squares or units, each one containing one of the twenty-one possible combinations of dice. Lay the chart flat, take a pencil, and close your eyes while you place the pencil point on a square at random. The dice combination depicted on that square is used to find the answer, using the proper list, just as when rolling a pair of dice.

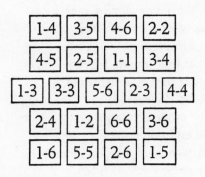

Somewhat significantly, the divinatory qualities of dice have gained some credence through modern parapsychology tests wherein persons have successfully "willed" a certain number to appear most often over an extended series of "throws" made with a group of dice. Therefore:

In theory, at least, it would be possible for a "dice diviner" to take a random question, choose the best answer through clairvoyance, and apply a psychokinetic force to make the dice come up with the number or combination required. The same would apply in varying degree with the "mystic oracle."

It is doubtful, however, that the average consultant would take it that seriously or have the ability to carry it that far. The preferable course is to treat it all in a spirit of good fun. But if results go beyond chance expectations, don't be surprised!

List of Questions

1. In what field does my future success lie?
2. Shall I be happy in love?
3. Does danger threaten me?
4. Where may I find the lost or missing article?
5. Will my proposed enterprise be successful?
6. Will my present wish be fulfilled?

7. What subject should now influence my thoughts?
8. Which friend or person shall I believe?
9. Should I change my occupation?
10. Does the one I love, love me?
11. Shall I become involved in legal affairs?
12. Are my opinions of a certain person well founded?
13. Shall I receive the money owed me?
14. What does next year mean to me?
15. Shall I receive the present I expect?
16. Shall I hear from my absent friend?
17. Shall I meet with many adventures?
18. Will my secret be discovered?
19. Shall I take my proposed journey?
20. Shall I achieve my ambition?
21. What does marriage hold in store for me?
22. How shall I know my future lifemate?
23. How many romances shall I have?
24. What does the immediate future mean to me?
25. What precept now applies particularly to me?
26. When will the traveler return?
27. Where shall I find real happiness?
28. What period of the coming year should be most favorable to me?
29. Shall I ever achieve wealth?
30. Should I travel or remain at home?

Answers (1-1 has been rolled)

1. Steadfast adherence to your present occupation.
2. Yes, if you behave unselfishly.
3. Not if you act cautiously.
4. In a room or a closet.
5. If it does not depend on other people, yes.
6. It depends entirely upon yourself.
7. Elevation, high position, progress, a leader.
8. The one who makes the most objections.

9. Only if you see a real opportunity.
10. If your love is sincere it will be reciprocated.
11. To your disadvantage, if you are not careful.
12. They are exaggerated.
13. Only if you press for it.
14. It will be a period of progress.
15. You may never receive it.
16. Not until you write to that person.
17. Not many, but a few important and exciting ones.
18. Probably not.
19. Yes.
20. You must work to achieve it.
21. Misunderstandings, but eventual happiness.
22. He or she will be the one most interested in your ambitions.
23. Three to five.
24. Unexpected news.
25. Discretion is the better part of valor.
26. When the moon is full.
27. In a foreign country.
28. The month of your birth.
29. Not while you long for riches.
30. Travel is advisable.

Answers (1-2 has been rolled)

1. Where you can act in an advisory capacity.
2. You should be.
3. No.
4. Somewhere in the house, perhaps in a closet.
5. Yes, if you have a capable associate.
6. It is too extravagant.
7. Travel, the future, absent persons, art.
8. One who flatters you the least.
9. It would be inadvisable at present.
10. Yes, if that one is certain of your love.
11. If you do, it will be as a minor witness.

12. No. They have been influenced by chance occurrences.
13. Not for a long time to come.
14. Happiness and enjoyment, but no great achievement.
15. You are expecting too much.
16. Yes, very unexpectedly.
17. Very few, if any.
18. Very probably. Too many know it already.
19. Not as soon as you expect.
20. You have too high an object of attainment.
21. Happiness, unless you deliberately destroy it.
22. One who is your opposite.
23. One too many.
24. Several enjoyable events.
25. Procrastination is the thief of time.
26. When he makes his fortune.
27. In your own home.
28. The month of June.
29. Only through an inheritance.
30. You will travel frequently, but not far.

Answers (2-2 has been rolled)

1. Where courage is needed.
2. Yes, if your love is true.
3. It is always near, but never great.
4. In a hallway, a passage, or among documents.
5. Yes, if you begin at once.
6. Eventually.
7. A personal matter, illness, fear, or anger.
8. The one whose reliability you have tested.
9. Not for at least three months.
10. Not now, possibly later.
11. Only to your own advantage.
12. They are true except for a few minor details.
13. Part of it, but do not expect the whole amount.

14. Increased income, but also increased expenditures.
15. Yes, when there is a full moon.
16. Not until your friend returns.
17. Some, when you least expect or desire them.
18. Not until it can be of little harm.
19. Yes, perhaps sooner than you may have planned.
20. Probably, but overdesire may prevent it.
21. Trying times, but eventual happiness if you persevere.
22. One who is both wise and cheerful.
23. One, that you will long remember.
24. A message you have long awaited.
25. Perseverance is a virtue.
26. When he is no longer welcome.
27. In the "great outdoors."
28. Late autumn and early winter.
29. Not while you spend money as carelessly as you do.
30. Travel indicates much money for you.

Answers (1-3 has been rolled)

1. Steady work and constant attention to detail.
2. More than if you love not.
3. No, and not for a long time to come.
4. You may not have lost it. Look again.
5. You will not lose by it, but do not expect great gain.
6. After you have given up hope for it.
7. Home, family, affairs of the heart, a new project.
8. The one who believes you.
9. No, your present one should be satisfactory.
10. Your love will not be returned for many months.
11. You should avoid all court proceedings.
12. They have been influenced by false information.
13. Yes, during the next month.
14. Disappointment, but of a temporary nature.
15. Yes. The next big holiday.

16. When you are ready to resume your friendship.
17. No, because you instinctively avoid them.
18. Probably not. Few people wish to know it.
19. Exactly as you have planned.
20. After you have modified it, you may succeed.
21. A large family and many responsibilities.
22. One whose birth number corresponds to yours.
23. Very few.
24. An unpleasant surprise.
25. Rome was not built in a day.
26. When he is least expected.
27. In your future work.
28. All periods are about equal.
29. Only through long effort.
30. You will not profit by travel.

Answers (1-4 has been rolled)

1. Travel and new lines of work.
2. Temporarily.
3. Much less than you believe.
4. You may find it unexpectedly.
5. At first, but be prepared for unexpected loss.
6. Yes, but you may regret the fulfillment.
7. Marriage, harmony and understanding, new ventures.
8. The oldest and wisest.
9. You will have no choice in the matter.
10. Yes, at present; but you must strive to keep the love.
11. Too often.
12. They were a month ago; but they are not now.
13. Yes, when you have fulfilled your obligation.
14. Unexpected changes and new scenes.
15. It is due you, but has been forgotten.
16. Yes, through an unexpected meeting.
17. Yes, under strange circumstances.

18. It will be learned while you are absent.
19. Sooner than you have planned.
20. No, but you will gain a new one.
21. Many surprises, disagreements, and reconciliations.
22. One whom you will meet in a distant place.
23. As many as a dozen.
24. A succession of surprises, some good, others bad.
25. A rolling stone gathers no moss.
26. When his mission has been fulfilled.
27. In pleasant company.
28. The late summer.
29. Probably, but you will not retain it.
30. You will find much that you want is in foreign lands.

Answers (2-3 has been rolled)

1. A partnership, or cooperative business enterprise.
2. More and more as time progresses.
3. To a slight extent, but it will not be serious.
4. On a shelf, stand, rack, or in a small room.
5. Not if it is of a hazardous nature.
6. Very soon, if it is practical and tangible.
7. A close relation, travel, similar things, news.
8. The one whom you have known longest.
9. Not unless it offers immediate increase of income.
10. You can find out only by asking.
11. Not for the next two years.
12. They are true except for a few details.
13. Only after long and persistent demand.
14. A period of moderate progress.
15. When you next hear from or meet the giver.
16. As soon as he or she needs your aid.
17. Not unless you seek them.
18. Not if you guard it.
19. Not unless a new reason for the trip presents itself.

20. Not unless you receive unexpected assistance.
21. Wealth, but doubtful happiness.
22. One whom you meet through an old friend.
23. Three or four of brief duration.
24. A slight obligation to an old friend.
25. Fine feathers do not make fine birds.
26. Just before a wedding.
27. In a place of quiet and solitude.
28. The third week after a severe disappointment.
29. Your opportunity is present, if you can grasp it.
30. Travel only to make a permanent change of residence.

Answers (1-5 has been rolled)

1. Inventive or mechanical lines.
2. Partly, but never as much as you hope.
3. Slightly, but much less than you believe.
4. Through a friend or a servant; after a long search.
5. It should be; but you may demand too much.
6. Not if it depends upon someone else.
7. A building, water, a change, buried things, mystery.
8. One who comes to you secretly and unexpectedly.
9. Not if many people advise it.
10. You will probably never know.
11. Only through a quarrel with family or friends.
12. They are due largely to prejudice and imagination.
13. Yes, you will receive it in small payments.
14. Mysterious happenings and unexplainable occurrences.
15. When the person you expect it from has been reminded.
16. In a peculiar way, through a mysterious message.
17. Not many, but surprising ones.
18. Not if you conceal all evidence of it.
19. A peculiar happening will detain you.
20. Only if you make it known.
21. Misunderstandings with your in-laws.

22. He or she will be an only child.
23. Few who really care for you.
24. A disagreement resulting in a necessary change.
25. All is not gold that glitters.
26. When he has spent all his money.
27. In study and research.
28. When most of the holidays come at the turn of the year.
29. Not unless you sacrifice love and ambition.
30. If you travel you may never return.

Answers (2-4 has been rolled)

1. An old and established business.
2. Not if you are content with things as they are.
3. Only if you deliberately ask for it.
4. On a shelf, a floor, or some flat place.
5. Not unless it is well established.
6. Its fulfillment is already under way.
7. Ancient or foreign things; distant scenes; philosophy.
8. One who is in accord with your present plans.
9. Vary your present one, if you wish, but do not change it.
10. Not if your likes and dislikes are opposite.
11. None of your own making.
12. They are true, but too critical.
13. Not unless you have a receipt for it.
14. Steady progress, but an unexpected loss.
15. It will follow a letter.
16. A message is already on the way.
17. No, you should try to avoid them.
18. It will be difficult to prevent it.
19. Exactly as you have planned.
20. Only unexpected misfortune can prevent it.
21. A change in life; new interests, to which you will become adapted.
22. One whom you meet in time of trouble.
23. No more than you have or have had.

24. A period of quiet, with possible achievement.
25. Beauty is only skin deep.
26. When he has received a letter from home.
27. In a new business.
28. The second week after a holiday.
29. Probably not; but if you do, it will be great.
30. Travel only when absolutely necessary.

Answers (3-3 has been rolled)

1. Enterprise and leadership.
2. Only through marriage.
3. It lurks at every corner, but you can avoid it.
4. A child has it or knows about it.
5. It should be highly successful.
6. Beyond your expectations.
7. Loss, misfortune, retaliation, restitution, new plans.
8. The one who is willing to do what you wish.
9. Yes, if a real opportunity presents itself.
10. With a greater love than yours.
11. Those who seek to involve you will be disappointed.
12. You hold the person in too high esteem.
13. Yes, with interest.
14. A new and successful enterprise.
15. When you need it most.
16. Only through the efforts of another friend.
17. Not very many, but very fortunate ones.
18. Yes, but it will not matter.
19. Yes, and it will be longer than you have planned.
20. Yes, if you do not change your mind.
21. A golden wedding anniversary.
22. One who is nearly your own age.
23. No definite number, but two in particular.
24. The realization of a desire.
25. The early bird gets the worm.

26. On a summer afternoon.
27. Wherever you look for it.
28. The month after next.
29. No; but your closest friend will.
30. Travel only in the summer.

Answers (1-6 has been rolled)

1. An active profession.
2. If you give more than you get, yes.
3. It has, but it is probably past.
4. You are almost certain to get it back.
5. Not if you begin it at once.
6. Only through the efforts of a stranger.
7. Trouble, dispute, lack of agreement, mistaken trust.
8. One who now doubts your sincerity.
9. Not unless someone demands your services.
10. That person doubts your love.
11. Yes, small but annoying ones.
12. They are utterly groundless.
13. Only through an unexpected arrangement.
14. Temporary good fortune.
15. Never.
16. Not for a long time, as there is no reason.
17. Ones that seem important to you but are of little consequence.
18. You will foolishly reveal it.
19. Probably not.
20. Possibly, but it is not to your best interests.
21. Several years of happiness.
22. One whom you now dislike.
23. An average of two a year.
24. Delay and slight disappointment.
25. Pride goeth before a fall.
26. Within a fortnight.
27. In your dreams.

28. The rainiest week of the year.
29. Yes, if other persons fulfill their obligations.
30. Travel only if your friends advise it.

Answers (2-5 has been rolled)

1. Peculiar and unusual occupations.
2. Spasmodically.
3. Very much, but from one source only.
4. Near water, or by means of a journey.
5. The chances are greatly against it.
6. Only after disappointment.
7. Property, real estate, source of income, money.
8. No one is particularly reliable.
9. To do so will mean either great success or disaster.
10. No, but another does.
11. If you do, you will regret it.
12. Not in regard to money or financial affairs.
13. In the next month or not at all.
14. A new interest, of doubtful value.
15. After you no longer need it.
16. A misunderstanding must first be mutually forgotten.
17. More than you desire.
18. Not if you caution a close friend not to reveal it.
19. No, because another will take its place.
20. No, not to the degree you now hope.
21. Either great happiness, or divorce.
22. One who will render you a great service.
23. That depends entirely upon yourself.
24. A doubtful acquaintanceship.
25. Time and tide wait for no man.
26. On a cloudy night.
27. In the midst of excitement.
28. The first week of spring.

29. Not while you work for other people.
30. Travel will bring you pleasure but not profit.

Answers (3-4 has been rolled)

1. Something requiring persuasion or salesmanship.
2. It is doubtful.
3. In an unexpected way.
4. It is probably safe, as no one has found or taken it.
5. No, but it will lead to a new and better venture.
6. Only if your own efforts can attain it.
7. Comfort, merriment, a pleasant place, companionship.
8. One who will soon make your acquaintance.
9. Not unless your present one is too problematical.
10. Very slightly.
11. Only through an accident.
12. They are wrong on one important point.
13. Not if it has been owing more than a year.
14. Great but unappreciated effort.
15. You have no right to expect it.
16. As soon as that person can communicate with you.
17. Not unless you travel.
18. Not if you confide in those who wish to know it.
19. Very probably.
20. Only after much work.
21. The fulfillment of your desire.
22. Through lack of interest in others you now admire.
23. Plenty.
24. A useless inspiration.
25. A bird in the hand is worth two in the bush.
26. When he receives a telegram.
27. In the memories of long ago.
28. The coming year is not very favorable.
29. Not unless you continually work overtime.
30. Travel now; it may be your last opportunity.

Answers (2-6 has been rolled)

1. Work requiring executive consultations.
2. Your attitude may be indifferent.
3. Not now.
4. Someone has found it. It will be recovered with difficulty.
5. It needs someone with unusual enterprise.
6. Not while you count on it.
7. Speculation, gain, a child, a school, learning.
8. One who is the most doubtful.
9. Not if it means a change of residence.
10. The person concerned knows nothing about your love.
11. They may play an important part in your future life.
12. Not unless other people share them.
13. Yes, quite soon.
14. Small obligations and trifling annoyances.
15. At an appropriate time.
16. You will meet the friend at a social gathering.
17. Only if you travel with strangers.
18. By a child who may not reveal it.
19. Yes, with someone whom you do not expect.
20. Seven years from now, or not at all.
21. A new circle of friends.
22. One who is tall, athletic, and versatile.
23. One in particular who will cause you trouble.
24. An unexpected demand which must be met.
25. A roving bee gathers the honey.
26. He is now on his way and will arrive without delay.
27. In a garden of roses.
28. The first hundred days.
29. Not until you have saved a few thousand dollars.
30. Travel is advisable except by water.

Answers (3-5 has been rolled)

1. Literary or artistic pursuits.
2. Yes, if you are romantic.
3. Only when the moon is in the last quarter.
4. Recovery is doubtful, but search again where you last saw it.
5. It may mean financial loss.
6. It depends upon you.
7. A journey, distant messages, a friend.
8. One who is absent-minded.
9. Not without a more remunerative one available.
10. No. That person's love belongs to another.
11. Possibly, if you undertake new ventures.
12. Time alone can tell.
13. No, but you will receive its equivalent.
14. A renewal of old friendships.
15. On a day when snow has fallen.
16. Not until the person returns.
17. Yes, during the next leap year.
18. Only through an unguarded message or letter.
19. Exactly as you have arranged.
20. Yes, by means of a journey.
21. A great adventure.
22. One who has the same interests that you have.
23. Two, principally: one tall, the other short.
24. Some new accessories.
25. Think twice before you speak.
26. On a holiday.
27. Through a hobby.
28. When the snow is on the ground.
29. Yes, if you locate the source.
30. Traveling is good for everybody.

Answers (4-4 has been rolled)

1. Where personality and persuasive powers are needed.
2. Not during your first experience.
3. You are your only real enemy.
4. A relative may know about it. Search again.
5. Not unless it is well financed.
6. Not if it involves money.
7. Loss, misfortune, disaster, mourning, unhappiness.
8. Only one who offers you financial aid.
9. Decide after long consideration.
10. Yes, because of ignorance of your faults.
11. Yes, where money is concerned.
12. Yes, but they are not complete.
13. After you have forgotten it.
14. Misfortune which may be overcome later.
15. You will receive something entirely different.
16. Yes, when you have paid what you have owed the person.
17. Yes, in strange surroundings.
18. Yes, but you will not know it for a long, long time.
19. Lack of funds will prevent you.
20. Yes, but in a different locale.
21. More than you expect.
22. One who speaks a foreign language.
23. Three of different nationalities.
24. Something that will perplex and amuse you.
25. A fool and his money are soon parted.
26. Saturday night.
27. Where you think you have lost it.
28. When the leaves are falling.
29. You will not be satisfied with what you get.
30. Travel, if the direction is westward.

Answers (3-6 has been rolled)

1. Something involving space or mystery.
2. Not in your own community.
3. Sometimes, at night.
4. Chances of recovery are good, through a stranger or servant.
5. Yes, if it requires travel.
6. No, but another will.
7. Marriage, good fortune, partnership, agreement.
8. Your own opinions are best.
9. Not if it means a business connection with relations.
10. No, but you can win the love you desire.
11. Not if you avoid undesirable strangers.
12. They have been influenced by false appearances.
13. After you have paid all you owe.
14. Comfort and enjoyment, but wasted opportunities.
15. After you have bought something like it.
16. Yes, but you will receive bad news.
17. Yes, if you make a long trip by air.
18. Yes, by one who cannot use it.
19. Yes, but you will alter your plans slightly.
20. It is doubtful.
21. Happiness and moderate wealth.
22. One who has many relatives.
23. Many at one time.
24. An unexpected trip.
25. A stitch in time saves nine.
26. On the first of the month.
27. In working for others.
28. The hunting season.
29. Not unless you already have it.
30. Neither will satisfy you.

Answers (4-5 has been rolled)

1. Matrimony.
2. If you do not expect too much.
3. Not at all.
4. On a shelf, a cabinet, in a drawer or a box.
5. Yes, but others will profit more than you.
6. Very soon, or not at all.
7. Discomfort, illness, a servant, a friend, a problem.
8. One who is distantly related to you.
9. Not unless you have money saved.
10. Yes, but it may not endure.
11. Only through your own desire.
12. Fairly well, but not exactly.
13. Only through legal action.
14. Difficulty in collecting money.
15. When you have renewed an old friendship.
16. Through the newspapers.
17. During one summer.
18. Yes, by someone who will profit from it.
19. Not until you have set your affairs in order.
20. No, but a friend will.
21. The realization of hidden virtues.
22. One whose age is five years different from your own.
23. None of consequence.
24. An idle rumor.
25. Don't cry over spilled milk.
26. At the time he has planned.
27. In collecting butterflies or coins.
28. The football season.
29. You have one chance in a million.
30. You will have no opportunity to travel.

Answers (4-6 has been rolled)

1. Affairs of state.
2. Not unless you change your ambition.
3. Not unless you interfere in other people's business.
4. It is in an automobile or in someone's house.
5. Not financially.
6. A letter may bring its realization.
7. A journey, gold or jewels, love, a brother, a message.
8. Your closest relation.
9. Only upon the advice of the one you know best.
10. Your love is reciprocated.
11. Only after marriage.
12. You should investigate further.
13. You will know within a few weeks.
14. A change in residence.
15. When you have made a journey.
16. Through another person.
17. Yes, but none may please you.
18. It will become known gradually and will do no harm.
19. No, it will be unnecessary.
20. If you persist for many years.
21. Many worries, but much joy.
22. That person will be a childhood sweetheart.
23. Several.
24. An unexpected meeting.
25. Let well enough alone.
26. When he realizes his mistake.
27. You will always be looking for it.
28. The fifteenth of November until the fifteenth of December.
29. Possibly, through foreign investments.
30. If you travel, buy a return ticket.

Answers (5-5 has been rolled)

1. In enterprises that require planning.
2. Yes, if you are willing to settle down.
3. From those who try to flatter you.
4. Not far away, beneath a tree or by a wall.
5. Yes, if you do not have many associates.
6. No, because it is unfair to others.
7. Confinement, imprisonment, a publication.
8. The one who offers nothing.
9. Not now. You will know when the time has come.
10. That person feigns love but may be insincere.
11. Possibly, through a false friend.
12. Regarding ability, yes; reliability, no.
13. You will be given a worthless check.
14. Realization of mistaken opinions.
15. Soon, but think well before you accept it.
16. Yes, but you had better avoid the meeting.
17. A few, but dangerous ones.
18. Not unless you tell a woman.
19. No, an unexpected visitor may change your plans.
20. It is within your reach; but enemies may prevent you.
21. Jealousy and a loss of friendship.
22. Through a letter.
23. More than your share.
24. Temporary good fortune that will not last.
25. Beware of the stranger bearing gifts.
26. When he remembers an appointment.
27. In a theater.
28. The first week of September.
29. Yes, if your present plans materialize.
30. Travel only under sunny skies.

Answers (5-6 has been rolled)

1. In affairs of public benefit.
2. It will not be your fault if you are not.
3. Very seldom.
4. It is probably gone beyond recovery. It may be near water.
5. It is doubtful, as your plans are hardly practical.
6. Yes, when you work instead of wish.
7. Something worn or carried; a highway, means of communication.
8. One who is very impulsive.
9. You may make a foolish step if you do.
10. Not as much as you love.
11. Only if you procrastinate.
12. They are too impartial.
13. You should have had it long ago. Now you may never get it.
14. New friends and new interests.
15. When you cease worrying about it.
16. Yes, by long distance or special delivery.
17. Less and less every year.
18. It is really of little consequence.
19. Yes, but it may bring disappointment.
20. Probably not. You are apt to give it up soon.
21. Harmony, with quiet existence.
22. One who is practical and not excitable.
23. Very few.
24. Nothing unusual.
25. Variety is the spice of life.
26. A few days behind schedule.
27. When you take a vacation.
28. Early July.
29. Not unless you have extraordinary luck.
30. Stay at home while you have the opportunity.

Answers (6-6 has been rolled)

1. Where conditions are harmonious.
2. Not if it restrains you from other interests.
3. Not at present.
4. It is probably in a box or a case of some sort.
5. It may prove to be too speculative.
6. Partly, but not enough to satisfy you.
7. Silver, something white, gain, possessions.
8. The one who is most influential.
9. It should prove greatly to your advantage.
10. Yes, but the person is too susceptible.
11. Possibly, as a material witness.
12. Yes, but you may foolishly change them.
13. Not soon, but it will be more than you expect.
14. Unexpected acquisitions.
15. Not soon, but it will be more than you expect.
16. Your friend has forgotten how to reach you.
17. Not if you search for them. They will come to you.
18. Yes, but surprising events will render it harmless.
19. A more desirable trip will probably take its place.
20. If you really want it, yes.
21. True happiness, but many sorrows.
22. Your first meeting will be at night.
23. A sufficiency.
24. A stroke of wonderful fortune.
25. It's a long lane that has no turning.
26. After many difficulties have been surmounted.
27. Through lasting friendships.
28. Springtime.
29. Yes, but it will be of little use to you.
30. When you travel, go to familiar places.

5

Domino Divination

With a standard set of dominoes, running from double-blank to double-six, fortunes can be read according to the traditional interpretations that follow.

In procedure, the dominoes are placed with their spots downward and are thoroughly mixed about before one is chosen. Some diviners insist on taking the most distant domino, but others feel that fate provides the guiding hand in any case, so either process may be used.

All agree, however, that no one should seek to learn his fortune by this method more than once a month, as the answers will then be meaningless, or even worse, may result in an adverse fulfillment.

Three dominoes are also the prescribed limit for an individual, within that period, or at a single sitting. Any domino drawn should be interpreted, then replaced and thoroughly mixed with the rest, before another is drawn.

If the same domino should come up twice for a person, it is a strong confirmation of its original finding. In that case, the individual is also allowed to draw another domino beyond the prescribed three.

Some students of domino lore refuse to consult them on Mondays or Fridays, claiming that those are bad days that produce doubtful divinations. That rule may not really matter, but those who follow it will have the satisfaction of being on the safe side.

Double-Blank This domino is considered the worst of all, bringing total disappointment to all persons except those who thrive on dishonesty and deceit. Whoever has gained anything by fraud is likely to retain it by turning up this domino. Other people will find it bad in business and in love. It may mean loss of valuables, even loss of a job.

Double-Ace This is a symbol of happiness both in love and marriage. It not only promises harmony and affection but may lead to financial gain or security as well.

Two-Blank Dishonesty and ill luck are designated by this domino. If a woman turns it up, the meaning is applicable to her fiancé, or husband, if she is already married. A son might be dissipating his talents. If travel is the objective of the consultant, the predictions are excellent, indicating a very pleasant and safe journey.

Two-One For a woman, two-one denotes an early marriage that would bring her wealth. However she might become a widow and remarry, this time lasting for many happy years. For a young man, there are no promises of wedding bells, just a life of a gay and popular bachelorhood. In business, guard against an unbalanced budget.

Double-Two Success in business and a happy home life. For those who marry, children will add to their happiness. Thrift leads them to prosperity.

Three-Blank An indication of quarrels. For a man, his wife is often bad tempered. A young girl should be sure that her fiancé is not given to wrangling. If you are going to a social gathering, be careful to avoid an argument or any subject that is controversial.

Three-One Warning that scandal may cause unhappiness and embarrassment. Danger of resulting lawsuits if impropriety should be proven.

Three-Two A lucky combination for love, marriage, money matters such as investments, or just speculation. A propitious time for traveling. Special care should be given to children at this time lest they feel neglected.

Double-Three Large sums of money and great abundance are the predictions of this domino.

Four-Blank Disappointments in love for both men and women. Neither will want to marry in spite of engagements. Anyone who has a secret should not divulge it. If the consultant is a pregnant woman, this domino presages twins, triplets, or more.

Four-One Promise of married bliss with an ample sufficiency of money. Finances will increase with the advent of each additional child. Excellent sign of prosperity.

Four-Two A period of change is denoted by this domino. It may refer to family, money, occupation, almost anything. The change may be slight or it may be greatly different from the present status. Those in love may have a change of heart. Business that has been slow will begin to improve. Whatever the circumstance may be, the four-two indicates a change.

Four-Three Marry young and live a modest, happy life, augurs this domino. It also, in turn, promises at least one child and a very comfortable living.

Double-Four For artisans this is a lucky, fortunate prognostication. For all other people it is unfortunate as far as work or progress is concerned. Socially, it is excellent for everybody, from the very young to the very old. A time for fun and relaxation. A wedding, too, is predicted.

Five-Blank This is a warning to an unmarried girl that she should avoid attentions from a man who is insincere and unworthy of her love. To a married woman it suggests a careful, watchful eye on the family budget. A man turning this domino must fight off selfishness, imprudence, and the urge to gamble. This applies to businessmen too who are very sharp bargainers.

Five-One A busy and very enjoyable social calendar is on the agenda if you draw this one. It also indicates an addition to the family. Moneywise it portends disappointment.

Five-Two Marriage is not conducive at this time, for lovers. If just married, misunderstandings may occur that will take a long time to mend. Patience and tolerance will bring eventual happiness if the consultant is a woman. For a man, he would do well to marry a woman who is industrious and thrifty. If he intends to change his business connections or venture something new, it is best to take time, not be hasty, investigate every channel thoroughly.

Five-Three This is a good domino that portends a calm, rather well-adjusted way of living. The rich man may not get any richer, but he and his family will remain very comfortable. The poor man will have a chance to gain quite sufficient means to improve his way of living. For a young couple it promises ample resources as the years increase.

Five-Four A domino that says a young lady will marry for love, not riches or position; that she may be oblivious to the faults of the man she wants to marry. She should have proof that he can make good, fulfill his promises of security, even grandeur. This domino also threatens loss of money, a poor time for investments.

Double-Five Very successful, no matter what you choose to do. Indicates great enterprise. This domino predicts plenty of money.

Six-Blank This is an unhappy sign, one that signifies financial strain and news of death. This may be a member of the family or someone else of importance to you.

Six-One To the young who draw this domino, it foretells two marriages. To those already married, good fortune will attend them in their later years. Children of these families do not always stay close to their parents since their interests take them far away. There is a chance that one child may prefer the proximity of parental love.

Six-Two A lucky domino for business people who are scrupulous and fair in their dealings. It threatens trouble for the dishonest and the unfair. To a married couple it foretells prosperity and unity of family.

Six-Three The most fortunate draw for lovers. Their marriage vows are the beginning of a fruitful family life and many many prosperous years. Often the draw is considered the best one for riches.

Six-Four Promise of an early marriage, many children, and sufficient income for a comfortable life.

Six-Five Perseverance is the watchword for this domino. If disappointment is about money matters, you may have to start over; if poor health is the trouble, patiently strive for healing; if disappointed in love, there is someone else much more worthy of your affection and devotion. If you are expanding in business, check and double check every detail for your own benefit.

Double-Six This is the domino for good speculation. It promises riches and honor to a girl about to marry. The only good sign for wealth that accrues from speculative ventures.

Mystic Domino Oracle

A chart will serve as a mystic oracle if you prefer or if you do not have dominoes. Draw a chart with twenty-eight squares, one for each of the possible combinations on a domino. In seeking answers, the consultant shuts his eyes and places a pencil point upon a random square among the twenty-eight in the chart. The domino depicted on that square is used for an interpretation, according to the list already given.

As with the actual dominoes, three may be tapped on a single occasion and the other rules, as to frequency of consultation, dubious days, etc., follow the same pattern.

Persons keeping monthly records of domino divination have reported interesting results, and an appreciation of their full significance can be gained in this fashion. Therefore, it is recommended for both individuals and groups affording fun along with fortune.

6

Dreams
and Their Interpretation

Of all phases of human experience, dreams are unquestionably the earliest. With the dawn of intelligence, man began to dream, and from his experiences in that half-real world, he drew conclusions regarding the problems that surrounded him.

Oneiromancy, or divination by dreams, was used in connection with ancient oracles, where measures were taken to induce such visions. Spontaneous dreams were frequently accepted as revelations among nearly all the races of antiquity, often with inspirational or inventive results.

The combined findings of centuries of dream interpretation were summarized by Artemidorus, a Grecian soothsayer, about the year A.D. 150. His four-volume opus, probably the first "dream dictionary," was criticized for the broadness of its rules, which were so liberal that any dream could signify almost anything.

During the centuries that followed, this defect was gradually corrected, and by modern times dreams had become rather well defined, though the authority behind them was open to question. Some interpretations were traditional; others, the results of guesswork; still more, the comparisons of personal experiences.

Then along came Freud, with new and startling theories of dreams and their causes, backed by innumerable examples. His school established the sex motif as fundamental to dream interpretation. This rose to popularity during the early 1900's, only to produce disagreement among Freudians themselves, as well as opposition from outside sources.

It was generally conceded that Freud's methods of analysis applied to psychoneurotic patients whose waking lives were replete with ideas and symbols that carried into their dream experiences. But such people represented a minority, whose dreams could be regarded as the exceptions rather than the rule.

Professor Joseph Jastrow epitomized the general criticism with the succinct statement: "What Freud does not sufficiently recognize is that dreams do not all follow similar courses because dreamers have different psychologies."

This was backed by extensive studies of thousands of dreams which only by extreme distortion or greatly strained assumptions could be interpreted according to Freudian findings. Many psychologists came to the conclusion that the symbolism in dreams may express some direct purpose, rather than serve as the concealment of some suppressed desire.

All this is getting back to the days of Artemidorus, when any dream could mean almost anything. However, this can be winnowed down by classifying the dreamers as well as the dreams. That is what many modern psychologists have done, and by the time personalities, physical conditions, general surroundings, and varied moods have been ruled out, it is possible to place many dreams in seven categories:

1. *Dreams of Affluence.* Here, the dreamer gains or finds some prize, very often money, though it may be fame. A nice type, but disappointing upon awakening.

2. *Dreams of Frustration.* Here, the dreamer can be trying to catch a plane, or pack a trunk, or find his car, all to no avail. He may need money, but have no way of getting it. Awakening from such dreams is a pleasure indeed.

3. *Dreams of Travel.* The dreamer may be going places, or simply flying through the air, or off into space. This may indicate a desire for freedom or an eagerness to possess something.

4. *Dreams of Falling.* These were once fairly simple. The dreamer fell off a cliff or over Niagara Falls, generally waking before landing. Now, you can fall from skyscrapers, bridges, and airplanes in these worry-denoting dreams.

5. *Dreams of Being Chased.* Here, the pursuing force can be a person, an animal, or a flood, an avalanche, or anything big or deadly. This may be traced to some hidden fear, symbolized by the menace in the dream.

6. *Dreams of Being Trapped.* These dreams often involve a cellar, a cave, a prison, or whatever else the dreamer would like to be out of. Similar are dreams of an impending danger, such as an explosion, the col-

lapse of a building, or something that will involve the dreamer in a most unpleasant way. These can denote a hidden fear.

7. *Dreams of Lacking Clothing.* Such dreams have varied interpretations, including frustration on the part of the dreamer. Akin to these are dreams of failing in examinations, forgetting appointments, or other examples of personal oversight or inadequacy.

Other dreams, such as those of water, fire, rescue, or even food, all are traceable to fears, frustrations, or desires. They may also be the result of physical impulses: The ringing of a bell may infringe upon a person's subconscious, causing him to dream of fire; or actual hunger may induce a food dream. In such dreams, there may be very little to be interpreted.

On the contrary, dreams of a prophetic or telepathic nature have been recorded, wherein dreamers have "witnessed" accidents, "read" headlines pertaining to disasters, or have been "told" the name of a horse that turned out to be a winner. These are often too few and far between to be judged accurately, but they constitute an intriguing phase of dream experience.

All this adds up to the fact that many dreams of a general pattern may be translated into more specific terms. That was the opinion of the old-time dream interpreters, and modern psychologists concur to a notable degree. In some instances, the result has actually been cyclic, with the newer interpretations coming around to a close approximation of the old. With others, the differences are more marked.

Some older dreams have lost their former significance. Today, people do not dream of wagons, sleigh-bells, hermits and such, so those listings have been dropped. In contrast, airplanes, automobiles, and other features of modern progress have become highly important as dream material, and have been so listed.

It should also be noted that there have been marked changes in the social viewpoint since the days of Freud. Many taboos and limitations have been lessened during the years between. Thus the psychological interpretations of dreams have undergone a change as radical as those of the traditional type.

One popular phase that has persisted is the translation of dreams into numbers, usually of one, two, or three figures. Such numbers are often regarded as lucky, and have been listed with the dream interpretations, though they do not belong there, as they belong more in the field of numerology than oneiromancy.

For the use of those who are interested in studying and checking the possible significance of dreams in terms of numbers, we have included (at the end of the Dream Dictionary) a number chart based on the standard letter chart used in modern numerology, with a formula for reducing key-words to key-numbers.

DREAM DICTIONARY

Abundance If you dream that you possess great wealth, an abundance of everything, it denotes your desire for independence. Still, you must not neglect your duties to those you love while you strive for more and better assets.

Accident If injured by some object, such as a knife, be very careful when using one lest your dream be realized. Such a dream may mean that you wish to sever relationship with a business alliance or a friend. It also shows that you need sympathy and understanding. A dream of an accident while traveling warns that you should avoid any kind of travel during the next day or two, or take every precaution for safety if you must travel. Accident dreams may also warn of an impending illness.

Accordion Hearing an accordion, disappointment in some plan that the dreamer had scheduled. Playing it, conjugal happiness. Out of tune, an unhappy state of mind.

Accounting Talking with accountants reveals a desire for advancement or a better position. If accounts are presented to you, business entanglements. If you present accounts to others, disagreements or business problems may arise.

Accusations If you are the accuser, you may find yourself quarreling with your associates. If you are the accused, malicious scandal may cause you minor embarrassment.

Acrobat To see an acrobat performing, a dangerous scheme may be presented to you. If the acrobat falls, the scheme should not be undertaken. If you are the acrobat, there is need for personal appreciation, such as a few encouraging words for work well done.

Actor, actress Dreaming of theatrical celebrities indicates a personal desire for fame and recognition of talents. If you are the celebrity in the dream, there is much work to be completed.

Addition Confusion in adding numbers indicates many worries. The dreamer is warned to be careful in dealings with others.

Admiral or *any high official*　A desire for power, often a symbol of some type of authority that the dreamer hopes to attain.

Adultery　A sign of a guilt complex that involves sexual relationship is the meaning of a dream of adultery. It threatens heavy consequences.

Agony　To be tortured in a dream may be the result of some actual physical discomfort; otherwise, fear or jealousy often cause misery in the dream state.

Airplane　If the plane is taking off, bright hopes for the future. If the dreamer is on the plane while it is on the ground, a wish to attain success quickly by shaking off troublesome surroundings. In actual flight, fulfillment of desires. This is a dream of purpose wherein the dreamer gets an idea into action and succeeds, or must surmount obstacles before the completion.

Alley　Squeezing through a tight place like an alley or a doorway is considered a symbol of sexual desire. It is also a very common dream when a person is very pressed for time such as meeting a financial obligation or memorizing a speech, preparing for scholastic examinations, and the like.

Alligator　To dream of an alligator or a crocodile means danger. The dreamer must be cautious.

Altar　A reminder about something that is unsatisfactory. It is also associated with the seriousness of the marriage vows.

Anchor　To the sailor the anchor is the symbol of home. To all others it shows the need for a permanent home and occupation. If the anchor is tied to a ship or boat, it indicates an urge to escape from present obligations.

Angel　An angel in flight, unexpected blessings. In a painting, news of a betrothal or marriage. Frequently the face of the angel is that of the dreamer's mother, thus representing goodness and protection from harm.

Animals　An uncontrollable animal symbolizes the lust for sex. Docile animals such as pets reveal a state of contentment and pleasant companionship, but the pet itself may be in danger. Wild animals such as the bull, leopard, lion, and so on are considered symbols of desire for sexual fulfillment.

Ants　Ants denote petty annoyances to the dreamer. *See* Insects.

Ape Unpleasantness and deceit may lurk behind the apparent friendliness of a person close to the dreamer.

Apples Ripe apples signify good luck; fallen or bad apples, thwarted efforts. The apple is considered a sexual symbol, akin to Adam and Eve.

Arrow Festivity and pleasure are the traditional explanations of this dream. Psychoanalytical interpretations make the arrow the symbol of the male sexual organ, the means of fertility when combined with the female organisms. The physical seems to permeate the dream world whether or not the dreamer wants it.

Asp *See* Snakes.

Attorney The dreamer who sees an attorney is aware that advice would be helpful. Encroaching difficulties are denoted.

Auction Dreaming of auctions and hearing the cry of the auctioneer promises a fair deal in business. For a woman it promises abundance. If the dreamer awakens in an unhappy state, keep a watchful eye on all business dealings for the next few days.

Automobile To dream that you want an automobile stresses a desire for financial gain. The motion of an automobile is associated with physical potency that is relative to sexual tension, hence dreams of actual driving, speeding, or skidding may be classed as sexual desires. Being in a wrecked car or escaping from one may warn you of a rival interest or an impending complication of events. Generally, the automobile like the airplane is an expression of the dreamer's desire to motivate a plan.

Ax The ax foretells of happiness after some kind of struggle, either domestic or financial. A sharp ax promises advancement. A dull ax, possible slowing up in business. A broken ax, disappointment.

Baby A crying baby, sickness or disappointment. A happy, laughing baby, many friends. A sleeping baby, desire for a mate. A baby nursing, a sign of deception by a friend or business acquaintance. To bear a baby, desire to show or prove fertility; the urge for sexual pleasures.

Ball To dream of a gay, elegant ball signifies ambition. Ball, as in games, indicates a keen interest in all activities. *See* Dancing, Sports.

Ballet Infidelity, jealousy, and possible quarrels.

Balloon Frustration of the dreamer's aspirations. More than one balloon, assignments, either too difficult or distasteful. As a symbol of motion, the balloon is also classified as a sex motif.

Banana Eating bananas in a dream is a very old prediction of a minor illness. If they are overripe, boredom with work or partner.

Bandit *See* Gang, Pirate.

Bank, banker, etc. To see a bank, or be in one, business difficulties. To see a teller or a banker, profits may decrease. A bundle of soiled banknotes, a fortunate increase.

Bar, bartender Possible feeling of insecurity with a mixed desire to fraternize and seek good fortune. To see the bartender, looking for a reason to plan a celebration.

Barber Seeing a barber cutting or dressing your hair denotes the ever-present conflict toward prestige and success.

Baseball *See* Sports.

Basket To dream of a basketful of goodies, groceries, and the like augurs good fortune and position. An empty basket, sadness.

Basketball *See* Sports.

Bath, bathing Being in a bath, or taking many baths, reveals an intense interest in the opposite sex. To bathe with other people, gossip about the dreamer may be disturbing. For a widow or widower, remarriage. Bathing in clear water, business expansion or renovation about the home. Physiologically, dreams of bathing may be due to physical discomfort. Psychologically, they imply a guilt complex.

Bats Flying bats augur bad news and sadness.

Battle Dreams of battles signify dissension. If defeated, guard your interests.

Bayonet To see a bayonet indicates fear of someone close to the dreamer. Possession of the bayonet dispels any danger, but warns that the dreamer must be alert to present circumstances.

Beach A dream at the beach, in or out of the water, indicates the need for relaxation and pleasure. Sexual motives are also connected with such dreams.

Beads To dream of wearing beads, desirous of attention. To string beads, arduous work ahead.

Bear To dream of a bear indicates unbelievable odds against any pursuit in the immediate future. For a woman, it is a threat of a rival who is interested in her occupation or the object of her affections.

Bed To dream that you are sleeping in a bed other than your own, new opportunities are foretold. If you are making the bed, new friends will be added to your social circle; also refers to a renewal of wedded bliss. Seeing sick people in bed indicates complications for them and unhappiness for you.

Bedroom Journeys or some happy change of events lie ahead, especially if the room and furnishings are new. Also implies that sensual impulses are uppermost to the dreamer.

Bees Bees buzzing around signify an increase in business, or profits in small amounts. *See* Insects.

Beggar If you give something to a beggar, you are suffering from disillusionment. If you just see a beggar, you may lose something valuable. If you refuse to help the beggar, your economy needs checking.

Bells Tolling bells in a dream foreshadow the death of a friend or relative. Other bells ringing, a perplexing problem must be solved.

Berries Blackberries denote illness. To eat them, loss of money. Raspberries foretell implications that are embarrassing. Strawberries denote a long-awaited pleasure will be yours. Eating them, love and affection will be reciprocated.

Betting To dream of betting on the races forebodes losses in business deals. If betting at the tables, any new undertaking must be carefully investigated before investing.

Bicycle Riding a bicycle downhill warns of misfortune. Riding it uphill, bright outlook for the future.

Bigamist *See* Marriage.

Billiards To see people playing billiards, troubles for the dreamer. If no one is at the table, unseen enemies are working against you.

Birds To see birds perched on a tree or in a cage, unexpected happiness for you. If the birds are flying, prosperity for the dreamer. If you kill a bird, unprofitable months ahead. A wounded bird indicates sadness caused by some member of the family. Singing birds, sadness. Talking birds, a warning to be careful about gossip.

Bird's nest To dream of an empty bird's nest, a gloomy forecast is ahead. Eggs in the nest, good prospects. Baby birds in the nest, excellent business arrangements await the dreamer.

Blind To see a blind person in your dream signifies that someone needs your help. If you yourself are the blind one, the predictions are that you are overlooking personal faults and are due for some changes, either in your occupation or living conditions.

Blindfold To dream that you are blindfolded means temporary disappointment for yourself and those around you.

Blindman's buff Loss of money and humiliation through your own foolishness is the interpretation when you dream of playing the game of blindman's buff.

Birthday *See* Holiday.

Blossom *See* Flowers.

Boa constrictor *See* Reptiles.

Boat *See* Ship.

Bomb To dream of a bomb and hear its explosive noise foretells unpleasant incidents and disputes that place the dreamer in a highly emotional state of distress.

Books Any dream of books is significant of cultural interest that should be pursued for intellectual advancement. Shelves of books indicate the need for more application to your work. Empty shelves warn of losses due to inadequate knowledge. Books in a bookstore presage pleasure that interferes with your regular work.

Bookkeeper *See* Accounting.

Boots *See* Shoes.

Boss *See* Employer.

Bottles Dreaming of bottles that are filled with a clear liquid are omens of prosperity. Cloudy bottles, unhappy incidents with the one you love. Empty bottles, much unexpected opposition to present plans.

Bouquet See Flowers.

Bow and arrow The bow and arrow in a dream infers that the dreamer should be self-reliant, make decisions without the help of other people. All the more important if the arrow hits a bull's-eye. If the arrow misses, disappointment in business affairs.

Bowling See Sports.

Box To open an empty box in a dream foretells frustration over some minor problem. A box filled with earth, plans for traveling may ensue. If filled with money or jewels, a bountiful future is promised. The box is also considered a sex symbol pertaining to a woman.

Boxing Unpredictable worries.

Bracelet Wearing a bracelet on your arm is a sign of a marriage. If you lose it in your dream, a perplexing situation will confront you. A bracelet worn on the ankle, indiscretions. If you find a bracelet, it augurs good luck.

Breads of all kinds To dream of eating fresh bread is lucky. Stale bread or biscuits, illness and an uncomfortable situation. To share bread with others is a favorable indication of great happiness that everyone will enjoy.

Breakfast See Eating.

Bride To dream of being a bride promises good fortune to a young woman. If the bride kisses others, you have many true friends. Bridal dreams are associated with love and marriage, so the people involved with the dream fall into various relationships which the dreamer can usually differentiate. If you see a loved one being married it usually portrays an element of jealousy.

Bridge Crossing a bridge, overcoming difficulties. A long bridge that seems to vanish in the distance, loss of possessions or disappointment in love. Passing under a bridge, weighty problems that require time to solve. *See* Plank.

Broom New brooms indicate thrift and a desire for improvement. If the dreamer is sweeping, do not speculate.

Brush A hairbrush warns a dreamer about carelessness in work and personal appearance. A clothes brush, a weighty assignment is bothering the dreamer. Many brushes, too many interests.

Bugs Dreams of bugs mean confusion because of many daily complications. *See* Insects.

Bugle To hear a bugle, unusual happy turn of events. If you blow a bugle, your dream predicts a pleasant outcome following many rough vexations.

Buildings A dream sequence of large new buildings indicates a need to expand, to travel, to find a new interest. Small buildings, a small but profitable undertaking. Old buildings, threat of failure.

Bull The bull in pursuit, in a dream for a man, signifies competitive business troubles. To a woman, an offer of marriage. A white bull usually indicates an increase in money. *See* Animals.

Burglar If you dream of being burglarized, you will need courage to surmount many difficulties in daily life. These are dreams of fear. To women it has a sexual meaning, that of forced intrusion, which is symbolized by the armed robber.

Burial To dream that you are attending a burial, if the sun shines brightly, is a sign that you will hear of a marriage. If the weather is dismal, adverse news will come to you. Death dreams indicate that the dreamer is dissatisfied subconsciously with some one very close or very dear even though this fact may not be a realization. To dream of one's own burial, or being buried alive, signifies utter frustration.

Butterflies Dreaming of butterflies flitting from flower to flower, prosperity, good news from friends.

Buttons If you dream of losing a button, there will be anxiety over the loss of money or property. Sewing buttons on clothes, a good chance of making money or an advancement. Finding a brass button, invitation to a social gathering; a wooden button, success after much work; a pearl button, travel; silver button, romance; colored button, unexpected pleasure; cloth-covered button, take care of your health.

Cab To dream of riding in a cab, secretiveness is indicated. If a man dreams of riding in a cab with a woman, sexual emotions complicate the secret.

Cabin A ship's cabin in a dream warns of enemies. A log cabin, good luck after much work.

Cage See Box, Birds.

Cakes To dream of cakes generally means social or business pleasures such as entertaining. To dream of a wedding cake, bad luck, in a small way. Pancakes or batter in a dream augur a bonus.

Calendar Dreaming of a calendar means that you must be more careful in your calculations.

Camera Dreaming of a camera indicates a change of environment. For a woman, a very pleasant experience with a male companion.

Camping To dream of camping is a sign that you need to travel. If it is a military camp, there should be news of a wedding.

Candles Candles that burn steadily, in a dream, denote constancy, true love. In an old established family, the lighted candles mean that the dreamer inherits all the attributes of heredity. For a girl, it foretells a proposal of marriage. If she lights the candle, the love is clandestine.

Candlestick If there is a whole fresh candle in the holder, the dream promises a happy and prosperous future. If empty, the reverse.

Candy To dream that you receive a box of candy indicates a general improvement financially. For women it also brings adoration from the sender. If you are the sender of the candy, you must face disappointments. If you are making the candy, you can expect a new adventure.

Cane If you carry a cane in your dream it predicts increased wealth. If you break it, bad luck. If you drop it be extremely careful in all your undertakings. Pointing a cane at some object or person is considered, by some authorities, a symbol of sexual desires.

Cannibal To see or meet a cannibal in your dream denotes fear and bodily discomfort.

Cannon To see or hear a cannon warns the dreamer of struggles not necessarily war, but obviously included.

Canoe Paddling your own canoe in calm waters indicates ability to run your own business. In rough waters, domestic and occupational discontent. In shallow water, a brief period of great happiness.

Cap   To see a cap means an invitation to a social event. For a girl to dream that her fiancé is wearing a cap warns that she must protect her virtue.

Car   *See* Automobile.

Cardinal   *See* Clergy. If the cardinal is a bird, in flight, it signifies an urge for freedom and release from responsibilities.

Cape   Wearing a cape signifies that the dreamer takes on a semblance of authority. If someone else wears the cape, the dreamer must submit to the will of another. A girl would have the protective influence of an older person.

Captain   To dream of seeing a captain indicates noble aspirations. To be one, a desire to command others.

Cards   Playing a game of cards socially denotes a realization of your plans. If it is gambling, you may face economical strain. If you are a loser, you have made an enemy. If diamonds predominate among the cards, the signification is wealth; spades, bad news; hearts, pleasantries and fidelity of a loved one; clubs, petty quarrels with friends.

Carnival   Dreaming of a carnival foretells the advent of some very unusual entertainment. If you are performing in the carnival, you are due for a period of many changes.

Carpenter   To watch a carpenter at work denotes the need for diligent application to your own occupation if you wish to succeed.

Carpet   Walking on carpets in your dream portends luxurious living. If you are cleaning them, your personal affairs need attention. Buying or selling carpets indicates a commercial trend that involves you or your associates.

Carrots   *See* Vegetables.

Castle   To dream of being in a castle, great ambitions and, by pursuing them, great wealth may be yours. If you see an old castle, dilapidated but still beautiful, disappointment and frustration may disturb you temporarily. If you live in a dream castle, tradition promises vast riches and holdings.

Cat   The cat has long been considered the symbol for a woman. A dream wherein the cat attacks you, indicates enemies of the female sex.

If you drive the cat away, no harm can damage your reputation. Another version for a thin cat augurs bad news about a friend. If you chase the cat away, the friend will be safe from danger or illness. A white cat denotes improprieties for the young, losses for adults.

Cave To see a cave indicates that the dreamer is faced with many dilemmas. If the dreamer is in a cave, indifference may alienate friends or family. The cave is a dream symbol of sexual implications.

Cellar If the cellar you dream of is damp, it forebodes property losses and a lack of self-confidence. If it is a wine cellar, a business offer may be imminent. For a girl, the wine cellar promises a betrothal with a man who likes to gamble.

Cemetery Dreaming of a cemetery predicts news from some one long absent. To a widow or widower, the cemetery dream means a chance for a new way of living; to some, another marriage. If the dreamer is elderly, the same dream indicates pleasant journeys.

Chair An empty chair foreshadows heavy obligations that the dreamer must meet. If someone is sitting in the chair, illness or accident may befall that person.

Champion Dreaming that you are a champion signifies a desire to exert all your energy to achieve distinction and take your rightful place in society.

Checkers *See* Games.

Cheese To dream that you are eating cheese denotes stubbornness that creates embarrassment. The dreamer, however, retains friendships and family devotion.

Cherries Cherries always denote good luck. Just to dream of seeing them in any way is a symbol of unselfishness, loyalty to your friends. If you eat the cherries you will see your wishes materialize. Green cherries are a promise of increasing good fortune.

Chess or *checkers* Dreams of chess or checkers indicate difficulties that may lead the dreamer to new friendships. *See* Games.

Chickens Chicks or young chickens indicate the need for concentrated planning. A large brood of chickens in the dream indicates many worries. If you are eating a chicken, selfishness may hinder your prospects of financial prosperity.

Children Many children, playing and laughing, signify great happiness for the dreamer. If the children are unhappy, vexations may be caused by the double crossing of a friend. If a child is very ill, the dream indicates monetary reverses.

Choking If the dreamer is being choked, there is fear of someone in real life. If choking another, hatred of that person.

Church The church or chapel indicates to the devout, a fulfillment of hopes yet unattained. If the church is far away in the dream locale, disappointment is in store. To be entering the church, thoughts of marriage vows and wedded unanimity are portended. A church is also a symbol of a woman, often meaning the mother or protector.

Clergy Dreaming of the clergy denotes a desire to overcome a wrong, to gain strength. *See* Religion.

Climbing Climbing indicates success by overcoming obstacles. On a ladder, setbacks but eventual success.

Clock A clock or a watch indicates the dreamer's fear of loss of time. If you just see the clock, it implies fear of losing a job or rank. If the clock strikes, the fear of death either to self or someone close.

Clouds Dark clouds portend troublesome times. Clouds with a little sunshine foretell that adverse business dealings will end successfully.

Coat To dream that you wear a new coat signifies unexpected honors. If the coat belongs to someone else, a crisis will cause the dreamer to borrow from that person. If you lose your coat, avoid speculations unless you wish to lose what you already possess.

Cock To dream that you hear a rooster crowing in the morning promises a good day. To the unmarried it foretells love and security. To hear the cock crow at night forebodes sorrow for the dreamer. Cockfights in a dream threaten you with family quarrels due to infidelity.

Cocktails Drinking cocktails warns the dreamer to refrain from exaggeration and deception.

Coffee klatch To attend a coffee klatch in your dreams warns of talkativeness that may be detrimental to you.

Coffin A coffin is bad luck for a dreamer. It is a signification of bad debts. If you are in the coffin, failure in business or loss of occupation may threaten you. If the coffin is moved, sickness and death are the warning. For the very young, death of a loved one.

Coins Dreaming of dull silver coins forebodes an unhappy day ahead. Gold coins augur a prosperous time plus the opportunity to travel. Copper coins mean heavy responsibilities. Bright silver coins predict prosperity. *See* Money.

Collar If you dream that you are wearing a tight collar you mistrust and fear someone more powerful than you.

College To dream of a college indicates that you will achieve an ambition. If you are attending college or are back in college you will be successful or gain fame in some profession.

Comb Combing your hair in a dream forebodes illness of a friend or loved one.

Compass If you see a compass in your dream it foretells that you will have prosperity through the aid of many helpful friends.

Concert To dream that you attend a concert or participate in one denotes an inward passion that needs expression in some kind of artistic endeavor.

Confetti To dream of confetti indicates that the way to happiness is by working before playing.

Conjuror To dream of performing feats of legerdemain such as tricks with cards or billiard balls denotes an urge to express one's self or display talent that is latent.

Convent To dream of a convent means a desire to get away from conflicts and troubles that involve responsibility. For a young girl there is an indication of disillusionment and despair that turn her subconscious to the highest form of love and devotion.

Convention To attend a convention indicates an increase in finances.

Cooking If you dream of cooking a meal for others, you desire to make somebody very happy. If you do not serve enough food, frustration, incompletion of responsibilities. If nobody is happy in the dream, disappointing events are to be expected, often in connection with a loved one. To see food cooking, avoid gossip.

Corpse The symbol of a corpse in a dream means death, finality, or termination of something very important to the dreamer. To the businessman it threatens failure or involvements that can destroy his reputation. To a young person, disappointment in love. To dream of being the corpse, a desire for absolution from wrongdoing inflicted upon others; a desire to escape, even by death.

Cradle An empty cradle in a dream presages sickness, often a mental state of insecurity. To be rocking a baby in a cradle foretells marital happiness but many difficulties. Twins in the cradle predict financial gains.

Criminal Associating with a criminal warns the dreamer of harassment and unscrupulous dealings with people who have little respect for ethics. If you, the dreamer, are the criminal it denotes that you have infringed upon the rights of others.

Crying A dream of crying signifies sorrow and distress. Implications of love affairs, corrupt business dealings fall into this classification of crying dreams.

Curtains The opening and closing or pulling of curtains threaten illness such as fever or deliriousness. Soiled curtains, moral disgrace.

Cutting Dreams of cutting indicate emotional fear. To cut someone means that the dreamer mistrusts that person and wishes to sever the relationship. Cutting one's self, the strain of overwork or unpleasant family problems weigh heavily, so the dreamer wants to end it all.

Dagger The dagger seen in a dream is a threat. It is also considered a symbol of the male sex. Anxiety, fear of bodily injury that may leave the dreamer impotent are associated with dagger dreams that are common to men. For women, the implication is one of genuine fear of gossip or slander. If the dreamer takes the dagger away from the assailant, none of the fears will materialize. Both men and women can trace these dreams to some act that threatens their reputation, or a desire for sexual relationship that might harm them morally.

Daisy Daisies in a field indicate good health and security for the dreamer. White daisies bring love. Black-eyed susans, jealousy.

Dancing Old, traditional interpretations of dreams of dancing portend happiness and conviviality. For young dreamers, many pleasures. For adults and the very old, bright vistas in store. Modern interpretations add sexual desires to any dance dream. It is sometimes masked as exhibitionism.

Death See Corpse.

Dentist To dream of a dentist usually indicates a fear complex, a distrust in someone, man or woman, who may appear to be honorable but is, in reality, the opposite.

Desert When the dreamer is in the desert, thirsty and worn, there is need for assistance to salvage the dreamer's possessions. This may be purely a change of mental attitude or may mean rehabilitation.

Detective See Police.

Devil The devil appearing in dreams has the same meaning of evil as in waking hours. To see the devil indicates susceptibility to flattery and temptation.

Diamond The diamond in a dream is an omen of good luck. For men, prosperity. For women, love and marriage.

Dinner See Eating.

Ditch To fall in a ditch portends loss of virtue, integrity, even position, for the dreamer. To jump over the ditch, the dreamer narrowly escapes public condemnation or disgrace.

Divorce Dreaming of a divorce is a warning that there is dissatisfaction with marital relations which need understanding and adjustment.

Doctor Meeting a doctor professionally indicates that the dreamer has a discouraging situation and is seeking help subconsciously. To meet a doctor socially, good news and health. If you dream that you are a doctor, you have a latent desire for power or authority.

Dogs For dog enthusiasts, a dream of friendly dogs portends many friendships and a need for pleasant surroundings. Dogs that attack or bite indicate anxiety. Dream analysts of the Freudian trend consider attacks of mad dogs as symbols of sex expression, an urge for mating. Traditional interpretations foretell less emotional happenings, but nonetheless interesting, such as: Seeing a white dog means marriage for a young lady. For a man, business acumen, enough at least to provide for his family. To hear a dog baying, separation from loved ones, or death of one. A growling dog, resentment and depression about overwhelming circumstances. A dog with many heads, too many diversified interests. Police dogs, fear, guilt, or desire for protection.

Doll A child's dream of a doll indicates loneliness. For a grown-up it is a retrogression of the subconscious to be protected.

Dominoes If a dreamer wins at a game of dominoes, it augurs a desire for adulation that results in selfish expenditures. If you are the loser, it forebodes moral indiscretions that cause painful embarrassment to those you love.

Donkey A child's dream of a donkey indicates a void, such as the need for companionship and the joys of playing. Hearing the bray of a donkey releases the dreamer from a most unpleasant family connection, with the added prospect of a small inheritance. To be leading a donkey reveals a feeling of oppression and a determination to extricate one's self by force. Riding the donkey divulges the sensual emotion for mating. Falling or being kicked by the donkey represent some form of yielding to sex impulses.

Door To see people entering and leaving through a swinging door reveals a loss of money because of the dreamer's mismanagement; that is, letting too many good projects slip by. A closed door means that the one who dreams of it feels divested of happiness. The open door beckons the dreamer to partake in the pleasures that bring new excitement and inspiration.

Drinking Drinking alcoholic beverages is a dream version of escape from distasteful realities. If drunkenness is the theme, the dreamer is losing control of responsibilities and wishes to be relieved. To see someone else drunk, the dreamer looks upon that person as an irresponsible dependent. Drinking water or milk in a dream is often the result of a bodily need, either thirst or hunger.

Driving If you are driving a car in your dream you express the desire for independence, a wish to make your own decisions. If someone else is driving, you, the dreamer, place confidence in that person and are willing to cooperate. If you are speeding away from something, emotional impulses overwhelm you so that you are seeking release in your dream state.

Drowning Water symbolizes birth and life, so a dream of drowning is a selfish desire to be reborn, to live again. It may be due to a lack of love or to the many burdens of living.

Dwarf To dream that you are a dwarf reflects a form of inadequacy or helplessness. If you see a dwarf, it is a foreboding that you wish to disrupt the social status of someone near you.

Dying If the dreamer is dying, it is an indication that there is a sense of guilt or a problem that cannot be avoided any other way. If the dreamer sees someone else dying it is the dreamer's desire to remove all authority from that person, or to literally drive him or her far away.

Eagle To see an eagle represents a dream of high ambitions, one that demands personal acclaim. If the dreamer kills the eagle, frustration and failure may be the result.

Eating When the dreamer eats alone, loss of physical energy may cause inertia. This, in turn, signifies mental depression. A dream of endless eating indicates many worries and a restless, unsatisfactory way of living. If the food is removed before the dreamer has finished with it, domestic or occupational complications must be solved.

Elephant To dream of an elephant means a desire to have great strength. Some analysts interpret this power as a sexual motive, especially if the dreamer is a woman. Elephant dreams are symbolic of power, force, and memory.

Elevator The elevator signifies movement, hence a dream of ascending in an elevator may indicate a desire for advancement and material gain. Descending elevators reveal discouragement and a shrinking away from monetary matters.

Embrace Embracing a lover is a dream of sexual relations. To embrace friends or relatives is a longing to help others.

Employer A pleasant conference with an employer reveals confidence and trustworthiness of the dreamer and a chance to prove ability in the near future. If the employer appears annoyed and disagreeable, the dreamer unknowingly distrusts the employer.

Engine, engineer The engine symbolizes the dreamer's wish to demonstrate power. If the dreamer is the engineer this shows motivation for aggressiveness in occupational duties. The engineer actually driving the engine (motor) reveals an emotional urge to impress another person, either male or female.

Escalator See Elevator.

Escape If you dream of escaping from an accident or a confining area, it is a favorable indication that the dreamer will improve his or her status. If you fail to escape, gossip or slander may cause you much embarrassment.

Eve Eve and the apple are associated with serious temptation, but in a dream, the name may refer to a friendly protector, nothing more.

Execution When a dreamer has a guilt complex it is not unusual to dream of death in one form or another. It is also natural that in face of grave disaster the dreamer would rather die being executed than to live a lonely life of deprivation. If the dreamer is the executioner in the dream it signifies a desire to eliminate or overthrow the authority of another person.

Falling Falling, in a dream, is a very familiar sensation to everyone. It is a symbol of fear. It may be a violation of the moral code, which, to women, is disastrous. Falling may also mean failure in your work, or in the management of your home. It is not an encouraging dream.

Fan A pretty fan reveals vanity and a desire for frivolity. It also predicts good news for the dreamer. An old fan, rivalry.

Farm To dream of a farm is a desire for security. The idea of independence because of the abundance that a farm is supposed to produce is latent in the dreamer's mind. It can also express a desire for solitude and peace of mind.

Father Dreaming of your father indicates some difficulty is bothering you. To a child, the father is a symbol of wisdom and power, so in later years it is not unusual for the mind to revert to the father in times of stress. It is natural to dream of members of the family. Sometimes the dreams express resentment actually unknown to the dreamer while awake. If you dream of killing your father, it signifies repression and a desire to be noticed.

Fear Dreams of fear are numerous. They actually indicate fear of something that is worrying the dreamer. Sexual violence is not excluded because it represents a major fear to many women. These dreams require careful analysis since there are so many variants. The stimuli for such dreams may come from reading, from watching crime pictures, from a culmination of events and circumstances, or from something very personal to the dreamer.

Fence To be encircled by a fence or a wall means that the dreamer is suffering from emotional restraint or denial. If you climb over the fence or knock it down, you will find a way to surmount the problem. For a young woman, the fence can be a symbolic desire for marriage and motherhood.

Fighting To dream that you are fighting, or boxing, indicates the will to be successful in spite of many handicaps, even with an inferiority complex or lack of talent. The dreamer must find an outlet.

Fire A fire is usually a favorable dream. To see your home burn indicates a very happy home life. To see your business building burn, prosperity. To see a large fire in your dream, general good luck. To look at the ruins and aftermath of a fire forebodes many vexing situations that may cause the dreamer to start a new enterprise. A fire dream is also a symbol of sexual impulses.

Fish To see a fish in the water indicates the dreamer is likely to receive unexpected favors. A dead fish warns of losses. The fish is a symbol of life, so, if the dreamer sees a fish swimming away among rocks and small caverns, it shows a desire to retrogress into an abyss of darkness where cares and responsibilities can be forgotten. Fishing quietly is a sign of good luck.

Flying Flying is a symbol of achievement. The dreamer is ambitious. Flying low presents problems. Flying with black wings, disappointments. Flying with white wings, excellent business prospects and a successful marriage. These dreams are also classified as mating dreams, the meeting of the sexes.

Forest To dream that you are alone and happy in a forest is a wish to find a new home. If you are afraid, losses and a desire to get away from them. If the leaves are falling, bad news.

Flag To see a flag means peace of mind for the dreamer. A racing flag warns the dreamer to relax a little. A torn flag, shame because of a misdemeanor.

Flame *See* Candles, Candlestick, Fire.

Flies *See* Insects.

Floating Floating on water or in the air means that the dreamer will achieve personal acclaim after overwhelming obstacles.

Floods Floods indicate danger, but they also predict financial gains after much hard work.

Flowers Flowers growing in a garden mean pleasure and happy working conditions. A bouquet denotes imminent social events. Withered flowers, disappointments, regrets. To gather flowers, a surprise.

Flute To hear a flute denotes many friends and security. To play a flute predicts artistic honors for the dreamer.

Football *See* Sports.

Fox If you see a fox in your dream, your reputation may be assailed. If you chase a fox, you may suffer from bad speculations and unsavory amours.

Frogs Frogs in dreams are a symbol of good luck, good health.

Fruit If you see or eat ripe fruit in your dream it threatens uncertainty in financial affairs. Green fruit warns against haste.

Funeral *See* Cemetery.

Gambling If you gamble in your dreams you are likely to be trusting to luck in everyday life. If you lose in the dream you will lose a friend.

Games Playing a game means attainment of ambition. If you are losing, expect obstacles. Observing games, expect contentment. *See* Sports for outdoor games.

Gang If you dream that you are being robbed or attacked by a gang or gangster or burglar who is armed, it is a symbol of passion, a desire for a sex episode or union. It is a timely fear when the news is rampant with vandalism and hoodlum wars.

Garden To dream of a garden of flowers denotes comfort and peace of mind. A garden of vegetables indicates a need to be careful, frugality. A garden symbolizes growth and expansion.

Gate Dreaming of a closed gate predicts impending difficulties. A broken gate, failure to gain immediate advancement. Swinging on a gate, love of pleasure before work.

Ghost A rare dream, but if the ghost has the resemblance to a parent, it is a warning of danger. If the ghost talks to you, be alert for deception by a trusted friend.

Gift If you dream that you receive a gift, check your finances for any discrepancy. If you send a gift to someone, you need or seek attention or flattery.

Gloves If you wear new gloves in your dream, it is a warning to be economical. Old gloves indicate deceit by others. If you find gloves, a new love interest. If you lose your gloves, you should look for a new interest.

Goat To dream of a goat indicates an extra bonus may be yours if you are cautious with present work. The goat is a symbol of male potency.

Gold If you find gold, this is a dream of competition, one that makes the dreamer more anxious to realize ambitions. If you lose gold, you have suffered from negligence. If you dream that you touch gold, look for a new hobby.

Gooseberries If you see gooseberries, your dream foretells a desire to evade an issue. If you are picking gooseberries, look for the brighter side of everything.

Grapes Eating grapes indicates many hardships for the dreamer. Poisoned grapes represent so many worries and fears that might interfere with success.

Grass Dreams of grass are very prophetic. A beautiful carpet of grass, like a rolling lawn, promises a quick route toward the realization of one's ambition. If the dreamer crushes the grass by walking or running over it, there will be many hindrances before ambition is achieved. To lovers, the velvety vista of lawn augurs a happy union.

Grave A new grave is an unfortunate omen in a dream. If you dig a grave, you are trying to avoid punishment for a wrong that you have already committed. To see a person buried in the grave with the head exposed indicates that there is a disagreement between you and a person represented by that head. If you find yourself in a grave you are due for a new channel of happiness.

Gun To hear the noise of a gunshot warns the dreamer of mismanagement. To dream of shooting a person foreshadows dishonor. The gun, like the pistol, revolver, dagger, or knife, is, by some analysts, considered the sex symbol of the male organism. Hence, the translations of any such dreams can pertain to a sexual impulse.

Gutter The gutter dream can signify immorality. Whatever the aspects of the dream, it forebodes unhappiness to the dreamer and anyone else who might be included in the dream.

Gypsy Dreaming of a gypsy or a life of a gypsy indicates a wish for a change of fortune. If travel is connected with the dream, a restless, unhappy mood has overtaken the dreamer. If there is dancing, the dreamer needs an emotional outlet. If the gypsy is reading your fortune, you are dissatisfied with your present situation.

Hair To comb your hair foretells of worries induced by generosity. If a man dreams of a woman with beautiful long golden hair, he wishes to be her lover. Red hair indicates a desire for a change, for either sex. To dream that your hair was cut very short, it indicates lavish spending. Tangled hair, confusion over money and domestic troubles. Flowers in the hair, lustfulness. Hair is the symbol of virility. Many dreams of hair can be associated with some form of sexuality.

Hairdresser This is a common dream with women because they are very concerned with their appearance. It is a simple matter to have the face of a hairdresser, male or female, confused with that of a friend or a member of the family. These are natural routine dreams such as everyday chores at home or office.

Hammer To dream of a hammer forebodes many discouraging obstacles before your economic balance will be attained.

Hand Beautiful hands promise great distinction to the dreamer. A hand detached from the body, misunderstandings with your own people. Hairy hands, sordid imaginings. Hands that are soiled or blood-stained, envy, jealousy. Holding hands, emotional strain. Hands that are tied, too much restraint.

Handcuffs Apart from a dream of occupation such as an officer of the law, the handcuffs denote rigid ties that are unbearable to the dreamer. The officers naturally dream of their work a great many times. If the dreamer breaks open the handcuffs or is released from them, the stigma of mental incarceration will be removed.

Harp To hear a harp is a prediction of sadness for the dreamer. A broken harp, illness. If you are playing the harp, be careful in all matters of trust and love.

Hat Dreaming that you are wearing a new hat prognosticates a change of place. If you lose your hat it forecasts a very unsatisfactory outlook. The hat is also used as a symbol of the male sex organ and its function.

Holiday Any holiday is a dream that you are coming into a happy, prosperous time. You may also expect good results from existing projects.

Horse To see a white horse while dreaming is an indication of prosperity. To see a black horse, tendency to deception. To see a runaway horse, be careful of misuse of your money. All dreams of riding a horse turn into dreams of fantasy, such as those of children who love excitement and the joy of action.

To adults, these dreams are expressions of passion, such as riding a wild or bucking horse, which represents the active sexual display. For women, it may add the element of fear because they dread the results or because they are not prepared for marital life. Men are harassed with fear of impotency rather than death when they dream of dangerous horsemanship.

Hospital Dreams of a hospital are logical to employees and the medical staff connected with this marvelous institution. They are also common to sick people, but to those who are apparently not ill, a dream of a hospital indicates a fear of confinement, perhaps death itself. If the dreamer is in a hospital bed with the attendance of nurses, the dream is significant of a type of helplessness with a wish to have people wait upon him (or her).

Hotel If you dream of living in a hotel it signifies a desire for a more lucrative life, one filled with gay companions and a continuous change of surroundings. To see yourself as the manager indicates a will to have power over others, to dictate.

House Building a new house means that the dreamer will make many changes in present plans. To dream that you are in a very elegant house, a castle, even a palace, you are subconsciously longing for more wealth than you possess, a higher plane of living or better social status.

If your dream house is falling apart it is a warning that your finances need bolstering. If the house is disagreeable to you, family life may be unharmonious or frustrating, although you may not be aware of it.

The house is a symbol of the human body; hence any action connected with the house can be interpreted in terms of sexual conduct. This includes other people and their actions toward the dreamer as well as storms, fires, vehicles, furniture, and so on, in relative importance.

Husband If an unmarried woman dreams that she has a husband, she is fulfilling a desire that she thinks of in her waking hours. When a married woman dreams of her husband there may be some incident or something very unusual that should be analyzed. Among the possibilities are quarrels that unsuspectingly could mean that the wife herself may be causing uncomfortable situations for her husband; illness or an accident in the dream may be a fear complex on the part of the wife; seeing him with another woman indicates jealousy in the subconscious mind of the dreamer.

Ice Dreaming of ice can be the result of a physical discomfort such as actually being very cold or being so warm that you are thirsty. Floating ice on a river warns the dreamer of jealous associates. Walking on ice warns of many distressing interferences. Icicles warn of despondency, perhaps temporary illness.

Insects Insects such as bees, bugs, flies, and the like are not very serious as omens for the dreamer. They represent small worries that accompany most any task when it becomes irksome.

Island An island in a dream signifies happiness and comfort in varying degrees. If the dreamer is running away from enemies to seek refuge on an island, it indicates a deep wish to escape from present conditions. If there are many people on the island, the dreamer is lonely and seeks new companions. The island represents a desire for unlimited freedom.

Jail, jailer Seeing people in jail foretells small worries for the dreamer, such as disappointment in associates, or losses due to negligence on the part of others concerned. A jailer in the dream is another form of a wish to elude responsibilities that have become unbearable. If the jailer is with other people then the dreamer would like to eradicate them. Just to see a jail may be a guilt complex for some very minor infringement of the law such as a traffic violation.

Jewelry Dreaming of jewelry with fine jewels denotes high ambitions. If the jewelry is broken, disappointments ahead. Tarnished jewelry indicates business problems. If you lose your jewelry, take especial care of your personal property. If the dreamer receives a gift of jewelry, it augurs a happy wedded life.

Journey *See* Travel.

Judge To dream of a judge deciding a case in your favor denotes a successful venture. If the case is against the dreamer it is a fear of injustice relative to a crushing defeat. If the judge is a familiar face it may be someone whom the dreamer resents.

Key A dream about a key foretells a change. A broken key warns of sorrow. Lost keys indicate some unpleasantry that may complicate the dreamer's plans. To find a key in a dream is a lucky sign.

Kill *See* Murder, re persons. To kill an animal is usually symbolic. The dreamer wishes to be rid of a difficult situation that appears to be like an animal. *See* Animals.

King A king is a symbol of authority, waking or dreaming. To dream of being a king is a desire to rule others. To see or talk to a king indicates that the dreamer needs the direction and guiding influence of someone powerful as a king. This is usually interpreted as the father of the dreamer. With elderly people it would mean a consultant or adviser.

Kiss *See* Embrace.

Kite Making a kite warns the dreamer not to speculate. To fly a kite indicates a desire to be an extrovert.

Knife The knife, in dreams, has several associations. It is a symbol of fear, either physically or morally. Dissatisfaction that leads to intensive hate and fear can bring on dreams of violence. People and places involved with the dream must be the means to help interpret the dream.

The knife, by some analysts, is also a sex symbol of men. Generally, the knife signifies quarrels between the sexes resultant from a fear complexity.

Knitting Knitting indicates a need for thrift, especially if the dreamer is knitting by hand. If the knitting is done by machinery, hasty decisions need careful attention.

Knots Knots indicate minor worries. If the dreamer ties a knot, time is needed to be free from an uncomfortable situation.

Ladder The ladder is a symbol of the step-by-step method of achieving success. To dream that you ascend the ladder denotes some fulfillment of an ambition, depending upon the number of rungs that have been climbed. Falling or slipping from the ladder, reverses. A broken ladder threatens failure. *See* Falling.

Lake Dreams of lakes are associated with romance, a time for pleasure. However, accidents modify the happy aspect of such a dream. A storm indicates conflicts; an overturned boat, confusion. A lake surrounded by abundant verdure, a desire to release an emotional or passionate urge. A lake with barren surroundings, fear of a financial crisis.

Lamb The lamb is a symbol of happiness if it is grazing peacefully or rollicking happily in the dream picture. A dead lamb signifies unfortunate news. A lost lamb, uncertainty and a struggle for a little security.

Lamp Dreams of lamps and lights indicate troublesome problems that are distressing because of their complications. One exception is a clear light which radiates a prediction of satisfaction in economic and domestic tranquillity.

Laughing To hear children laughing promises a happy time ahead. If the dreamer laughs, it forebodes tears.

Laundry To launder clothes in a dream indicates trifling problems that should not be ignored.

Lawn *See* Grass.

Lawyer *See* Attorney, Judge.

Letters A letter foretells a disagreement or difficulty. An anonymous letter means that something is troubling the conscience of the dreamer. A letter telling of bad news infers that the dreamer may have been uncomfortable while dreaming or may be anticipating news of someone's health.

Lightning Lightning is a symbol of love; also a desire of the dreamer to thrust that love upon someone.

Lion *See* Animals.

Lobster To see lobsters is a prediction of wealth. To eat them, a desire for prominence and financial security.

Lock To dream of a lock means perplexity, even confusion. If the lock is on a trunk or a door, the dreamer wishes to look beyond the lock so it is necessary to learn what the trunk or the door represent.

If the trunk holds papers, books, or treasures, then anything relative to such a dream would supply the link needed to make the story prophecy.

If the door represents a person, is it a man or a woman? Then, is it a stranger or someone close and familiar to the dreamer? The lock is also a symbol of the sexual organism pertaining to woman.

Lost To dream of being lost indicates frustration because of finances or disappointment in love.

Lottery Dreaming of a lottery is a simple dream, one of wanting money. The dreamer would like to get it fast, without much work. If the dreamer loses money in the lottery, the desire is very tense. Either way, the money must be earned during the waking hours.

Love Dreams that express various emotions and cycles of love usually mean that the dreamer is repressed or denied such love during waking hours.

Machinery Entanglements in love and/or provocations in business dealings are the implications of a dream pertaining to machinery.

Machine gun During war or in military service it is natural to dream of guns, but apart from these situations the machine gun can be considered a symbol of the male sexual organ. *See* Gun.

Mad dogs *See* Dogs.

Magic *See* Conjuror.

Mansion *See* House.

Map To dream of a map denotes discontent with present surroundings. Also, an urge to fulfill certain desires.

Marriage Marriage dreams for the young are numerous. They are naturally significant of a human desire for mating, but do not necessarily foretell that a marriage will be contracted. Traditional interpretations vary. Some are as follows:

To dream of your own marriage, if you are not actually married, means that you will hear something that displeases you. To see a marriage, happiness for the dreamer. If everybody is mournful at the wedding, sadness awaits the dreamer.

For a married person, a dream of another marriage signifies distrust or deep-seated jealousy toward the present mate. A dream of bigamy indicates uncontrollable emotions or suspicion of some other person related to the dreamer.

Mask The mask is a symbol of concealment involving deception. This applies to the dreamer wearing a mask in order to withhold a past action from somebody very important to the dreamer. It can pertain to love, falsehood, theft, anything incriminating.

If somebody else is wearing the mask, the dreamer becomes the victim of the deception or becomes suspicious of the wearer of the mask. To see many people with masks indicates envious friends or associates.

Meals See Eating.

Mice A dream of mice warns of insincerity and deception of friends. Mice and rats are included among the symbols pertaining to sexual passion, so the mouse could represent an attacker with the subsequent fear that might be expressed by a girl or woman. A very old translation about a young girl who dreams of mice warns her of subterfuge and scandal.

Midget See Dwarf.

Milk To drink milk signifies abundance. It is a fortunate sign for a pregnant mother. To spill milk, foretells unhappiness for the dreamer. Sour milk, domestic problems. Hot milk, the dreamer must exert great effort to accumulate money.

Minister See Clergy.

Mirror Mirror dreams are usually fear projections. Looking at yourself in a mirror warns of illness or loss of personal property. A broken mirror augurs death of a friend or relative. To see your betrothed or marriage partner in a mirror foretells disagreements or estrangement.

Money To dream that you see stacks of money indicates a great desire for security. To be the recipient, gratification of a little wish. To lose your money, fear of losing something or someone whom you need. If you steal money in your dreams be careful that you do not drive sharp bargains. This dream also signifies a fear of losing your authority or persuasive powers.

Moon A dream of the new moon indicates harmony and congeniality for lovers. The full moon warns of oversentimentality. A red moon, troubles beyond one's control.

Mortgage Mortgage dreams are often the result of actual financial conditions. Taking a mortgage denotes a lack of good economy for the dreamer. To hold a mortgage on someone else's property indicates a wish for great wealth and prosperity.

Mortician See Mortuary.

Mortuary To dream of a funeral service in a mortuary, or any other edifice, portends unhappiness followed by rejoicing. If the service is for a stranger, anxiety over a perplexing difficulty. If it is a member of the family, it denotes good health in spite of worries, which may have caused the dream.

If the dreamer is happy at the funeral of the relative, any differences that exist between the person represented by the corpse and the dreamer will be rectified.

If the dreamer is mournful over the funeral of the relative, it is a wish cycle from the waking state expressing a desire to be rid of the relative.

Mother Dreams about mother are very common. Starting with childhood there is the dream of protection, love, and our very sustenance. These are the normal, happy dreams of contentment.

One of the earliest interpretations of mother dreams where she is at home in a joyful mood, signifies pleasure and just rewards for the dreamer. To dream of talking with her indicates anxiety. To hear her calling you, sorrow because of her absence, or your guilty conscience.

To see her in an accident or dead is sometimes a wishful dream whereby the dreamer would rather she did not interfere. This last type of dream must be studied carefully because there would be symbols and surroundings that would round out the interpretation.

Mother-in-law The mother-in-law dreams can have more or less the same meanings as the mother dreams, except when quarrels become too involved in the dream, the reality would be the "wished for" reconciliation that lies beneath the dream. An old interpretation of a wife arguing with her mother-in-law indicates that the wife is annoyed with many other people too.

Mountain Mountain dreams are a desire to achieve something, an aspiration. If you climb the mountain, reaching the very top, your wish will be gratified. If you encounter many hazards or carry a burden, you are suffering from countless frustrations. Meeting people on the way may help or hinder depending upon the circumstances in the dream.

Snow, rain, cold, or heat all play a part in the deterrence of the goal of the dream sequence, which, in turn, are indicative of the active, daily life of the dreamer. All this is a warning to try other channels of occupation and recreation to achieve success and contentment.

Movies *See* Theater.

Murder To dream that you murder someone indicates that you do not want interference from that person, not that you really want to kill. If you see someone murdered in your dream, you may be very confused or upset over misdemeanors of other people. A dream that you are murdered is a desire to be released from an objectionable hardship.

Music To hear music that you like, in your dream, augurs prosperity. Music that disturbs the dreamer indicates domestic or emotional uncertainty.

Nakedness These are dreams of exhibition, a desire to be noticed or to gain the attention of other people, sometimes only one person. For some dreamers, nakedness is a symbol for a release of sexual emotions. For others it is a desire to be seen and heard in order to gain success, achieve fame or popularity.

Old translations are as follows: To find yourself naked in your dream warns that you may be involved in a scandal. If you are embarrassed, you will violate the conservative rules of propriety. To see other people partially undressed, the dreamer will yield to immoral temptations. *See* Swimming.

Navy To dream that you are in the Navy indicates a desire to avoid present encumbrances, to seek recreation, or travel. If you dream that you are very unhappy in the Navy, it is a warning of business or marital difficulties.

Necklace When a woman dreams that she receives a necklace it foretells that she will have a brilliant marriage. If she loses the necklace, much sorrow.

Needle Threading a needle in your dream indicates many responsibilities that require patience. Finding a needle, new friends. To break a needle, a desire for seclusion. To be sewing with a needle, by hand, need of a sympathetic friend.

Nets To dream that you are catching something in a net indicates that you want to make a hard, binding contract or deal of some sort. If you are caught in the net, it is a wish to avoid any such contract or entanglement. If the net is torn, loss of money, employment, or property.

Newspaper Dreaming that you are reading a newspaper warns that your reputation is in danger. If you are printing a paper, you wish to make new friends. If you try to read a paper and cannot see the words, the dream indicates business worries.

Nuns To dream of nuns indicates a need for spiritual thought. For a woman to dream that she is a nun signifies daily discontentment.

Nurse To dream of a nurse occupied with her work is an omen of good health. To dream that you are a nurse indicates a desire to have many friends.

Nursing To see a woman nursing a baby is a dream with a desire for parenthood.

Nuts To dream of eating nuts, a prophecy that your wishes will be granted. If you dream that you are gathering nuts it predicts a happy love life.

Oak To dream of an oak tree laden with acorns signifies increased income and a chance for advancement. A forest of oaks is a sign of much prosperity. *See* Forest.

Oar Rowing a boat means sacrifice and disappointment for the dreamer. To lose an oar warns of useless effort to please others.

Oatmeal If you dream that you are cooking oatmeal, it denotes the wish to rule others. To eat oatmeal indicates many pleasant hours with friends.

Oats To dream of a horse eating oats means that any project that you have started should be finished.

Ocean To dream of a calm ocean augurs good fortune. A stormy ocean, warning of danger or enmity. To be on shipboard on the ocean, a great desire to travel far away. The ocean is also considered a symbol of death, a desire to be reborn, or a chance to start over again.

Office To dream that you are working in an office indicates a need for closer attention to money matters. To hold an office, by election, foretells high aspirations and many problems.

Onions To see onions growing in a field indicates opposition to present plans. To be cutting or peeling onions, a need to work harder to avoid defeat or frustration.

Opera To dream that you attend an opera signifies a time to improve or augment any business holdings or personal properties. *See* Actor.

Oranges If a girl eats oranges in her dream she may forfeit the love of her fiancé. For a man, it means unexpected complications with his career. To see many oranges on a tree, good health.

Orchard To dream of an orchard of blossoming trees presages the fulfillment of love. An orchard of ripe fruit, a happy home and an ample income. An unproductive orchard, rough road to achievement.

Orchestra To hear orchestral music indicates much popularity for the dreamer. To be playing in the orchestra, advancement in your occupation.

Organ If you dream of playing an organ it denotes social honor and unusual awards. To hear organ music augurs many friends. If the organ is in a church, warning of a separation or death of a loved one.

Overcoat *See* Coat.

Owl An owl in your dream presages gossip. To hear the hoot or screech of an owl omens ill health or bad news about a friend or relative.

Oysters A dream that you are eating oysters indicates a tremendous desire to attain money and social status.

Oyster shells Gathering oyster shells or any other shells on the beach means fleeting pleasures for the dreamer.

Packing A very common dream is one of packing luggage. It is a repressed desire to travel or to leave one's present home, occupation, or a person. If the packing is never completed, the dreamer is frustrated over something in everyday living.

Pagoda Dreaming that you are in a pagoda with all the luxurious decor indicates a desire for sexual union in ornate surroundings. If you just see a pagoda it is a longing to travel in Oriental countries. *See* House.

Painting To paint a picture is a wish to express the dreamer's ambition or to personify someone to whom he or she cannot convey his emotions.

Panther To kill a panther indicates much rejoicing after a hard, long struggle for wealth or position. To see a panther and try to run away from it may mean disappointment or disgrace to the dreamer. The panther is also the symbol of sexual desire. The panther represents the attacker, the dreamer, the one who is sexually dissatisfied.

Paralysis Paralysis in a dream is frequent to many. Failure to walk, move, talk, or scream is terrifying. It represents indecision to solve a problem, a conflict of some sort that faces the dreamer in waking hours. This kind of dream can continue for years, as long as the situation exists.

Parents *See* Father, Mother.

Parrot *See* Birds.

Party A gay party means pleasure and amusement for the dreamer. A mad, wild party augurs trouble and unwise selection of friends.

Passenger If you are traveling as a passenger in your dream, you are dissatisfied. To see passengers leaving without you, a lost opportunity. To greet them arriving, your lot will improve.

Peaches To dream of eating peaches indicates unattained wealth or love. If the peaches are on a tree, conscientious work will be rewarded with ample gain, whether it be for money or for a family. Peaches are also a symbol of a woman's breasts. *See* Plums.

Pearls A gift of pearls mean a gala celebration for the dreamer and the recipient. To lose pearls or break a string of pearls, misunderstandings.

Pears A dream of pears always promises surprises and good health followed by periods of disappointment and temporary illness. *See* Plums.

Pebbles To dream of pebbles signifies petty jealousy or selfishness.

Pen or *pencil* Either indicates complications of an adventuresome nature. A pen is a symbol of the male reproductive organ.

Penny Counting pennies augurs economical worries for the dreamer. To lose pennies, admonition to be economical. To find pennies, a wish for a more lucrative business. *See* Money.

Piano To dream of an old-fashioned piano is a dream of nostalgia, a retrogressive urge to capture something that has been lost. A broken piano signifies frustration. *See* Music, Orchestra, Organ.

Pictures If you dream that pictures surround you it is a desire for artistic expression. To buy them augurs extravagance. *See* Paintings.

Pilot Dreaming that you are a pilot of an airplane or a ship is a wish to direct others, or to at least manage your own affairs.

Ping-Pong *See* Sports.

Pipe A dream about a pipe is an omen of peaceful living. If, however, the pipe is broken it warns of poor health and lessening finances. Smoking a pipe in the presence of someone who is averse to it means a temperamental difference with a loved one.

Pirate A dream of pirates indicates the dreamer's suspicion of associates. If you dream that you are a pirate it signifies unethical practices.

Pistol The pistol in a dream indicates bad luck. *See* Gun.

Pit A pit represents ventures that are hazardous to occupation or marriage. *See* Pockets.

Pitcher An empty pitcher or one containing liquid refreshment is indicative of the dreamer's actual physical thirst, or, in dream parlance, a generous desire to make new acquaintances.

Plank A plank or a bridge is a means for the dreamer to reach a goal that may be economically out of reach. It concerns handicaps experienced in daily life that appear to prohibit the realization of such dreams, awake or asleep. A broken bridge or plank indicates a major hindrance that the dreamer must overcome. *See* Bridge.

Plow Plowing a level field means steady plodding for the dreamer. Uneven, up-and-down hill, or rocks represent setbacks that can be handled but take more time.

Plums *See* Peaches, Pears for similar interpretation. The exception is the dried plum which becomes a prune indicating that the dreamer should wait a reasonable time before making a decision.

Pockets Pockets like pits warn the dreamer to be cautious lest a serious mistake be made. The pocket is symbolic of the womb. This may signify a desire to retrogress or retreat from the world.

Pocketbook Finding a pocketbook containing money and valuables indicates the dreamer's desire to have more possessions which require an increase in funds. Losing a pocketbook heightens the intensity of the dream and shows great disappointment.

Poison Poison dreams are escape trends whereby the dreamer either wishes to eliminate an unwanted person socially or in business, or to personally eradicate an intolerable situation.

Poker To use a poker in your dream to stir up a fire shows an industrious period is ahead. If the poker is used for defense, the dreamer is aware of an unfair plot that could be ruinous to reputation. For a dream about playing poker, *see* Gambling.

Police To be arrested by the police, though innocent, the dreamer will extricate himself from an unfortunate tangle. Otherwise, it may be a guilt complex. To see an officer, a desire to be protected.

Police dog *See* Dogs.

Police station *See* Police, Judge.

Pool *See* Lake.

Pool (*the game*) *See* Billiards.

Poppies Traditionally known as the flower of seduction, it represents the dreamer's wish to be free of responsibilities so that exotic excitement may be experienced.

Porter To see a porter signifies a desire to travel. If the porter has your luggage, a change seems inevitable but not always travel.

Portfolio A portfolio indicates perplexities and a need of advice for the dreamer. Also a desire for a change of surroundings.

Postman To dream of the postman signifies worries and subsequent complications.

Post office To see a post office is a reminder that the dreamer has already neglected to perform a specific task, still in mind.

Poultry *See* Chickens.

Puppet *See* Mask.

Purse *See* Pocketbook.

Prayers To dream of praying indicates a fear of failure.

Preacher *See* Clergy.

Pregnancy A dream about pregnancy indicates anxiety and impatience with conditions.

Priest *See* Clergy.

Prince, princess A dream of royalty is frequently a wish to aspire to a better way of living. The prince and princess are symbolic of young people who may or may not be related to the dreamer. *See* King.

Prison *See* Jail.

Pursuit Dreams where you are running away from someone show discontentment and a determination to enjoy life more.

Pyramids Pyramids indicate that the dreamer would like a change of venue, a new interest, something that will improve a thirst for higher knowledge.

Quarrels To hear other people quarreling in your dream portends complexities in your waking life. To participate in a quarrel indicates mismanagement at home or at duty.

Queen To dream that you are a queen indicates a little too much ambition. If a queen frowns upon you, this represents your mother admonishing you for some reason. A queen is a symbol for a mother.

Rabbi *See* Clergy.

Railroad To see a railroad with its winding tracks warns the dreamer of the many turns and intricacies that abound in every phase of life. Walking the railroad ties indicates the many steps ahead in any venture whether it be marriage or business. Walking the rails indicates a need to handle your affairs very carefully. *See* Plank, Train.

Rain A summer shower of rain foretells prosperity, if the dreamer is watching it from indoors. If the dreamer is in the rain, slow up of plans. A very bad storm foretells confusion of ideas.

Rainbow The rainbow portends happiness after many singular, unexpected events.

Rape A dream of rape, one in which a woman is sexually attacked by a man, is considered, by some authorities, to be the expression of the subconscious desiring a fulfillment of sexual love contrary to the conscious wishes in the waking hours of the woman.

Rapids To dream that you are riding over or through rapids warns of negligence. *See* Riding.

Raspberries A dream of a raspberry bush forebodes many temptations. Eating raspberries, by an old tradition, means gossip about the dreamer.

Rat To dream of rats indicates deception that offends the dreamer. To kill a rat indicates that the dreamer wishes to be free from an alliance that involves passion and perhaps hatred.

Razor To dream that you cut yourself with a razor portends unexpected troubles. To fight with a razor, many disappointments. *See* Knife.

Religion Dreams of religion are natural to the devout, though pleas to the clergy take on the meaning of guilt or transgression with a subsequent desire for absolution or punishment. It is the subconscious performing against the willful waking mind of the dreamer, who thinks of breaking a law or has already committed a violation.

Reptiles Reptiles in dreams are as dangerous as in real life. To see one snake denotes arguments. Two snakes warn that two friends or associates may deceive the dreamer. Various kinds and numbers of reptiles, conflicting obstacles. Reptiles, especially the snake, are representative of the male reproductive organ. So it is argued that the snake in a dream is indicative of a man and his power.

Restaurant To be dining in a restaurant means that the dreamer would like to be waited upon, to live in luxury. If you have guests, the desire for socializing is very strong, which, in turn, requires money.

Revolver *See* Gun.

Ribbons To see ribbons floating gaily foretells a time of relaxation and fun. If a girl dreams that she is wearing pretty bows she must not take flattery as a serious step toward marriage.

Rice To see rice promises steadfast friends for the dreamer. To eat it, happiness and contentment. To see rice thrown at a bride and groom, a desire to mate. To cook rice, an omen of future wealth.

Riding A dream of riding is considered unlucky. Sometimes associated with illness such as seasickness, the result of motion. All dreams of riding, flying, and climbing are rated as a desire for mating, the natural instinct of the sexes; however, they can be translated as motivation dreams that lead to companionship or a union of minds toward one purpose.

Ring To receive a ring indicates the dreamer will find a new and devoted friend. A broken ring, separation from a loved one. To give a ring, a newly found interest. The ring betokens love and friendship; to the young, marriage.

River A beautiful calm river foretells empty promises for the dreamer. If you are on a boat, make a careful checkup on your finances. A muddy river threatens jealousy.

Road A road lined with beautiful trees and shrubbery promises a delightful surprise. A rough road, new enterprises. If you are driving and lose your road, indecision that may terminate in loss for the dreamer.

Rocking chair To be rocking in a rocking chair signifies joy and contentment for the dreamer. To see someone else in a rocker predicts unexpected bliss for the dreamer. Empty rocking chairs, sorrow or separation from a loved one or a termination of an agreement.

Roof To be on top of a roof complete with garden and luxurious surroundings denotes a chance to achieve success. To be reaching for the roof while running or climbing, a struggle to reach your ambition. If you are building a roof, your income may be augmented through strenuous work.

Room To be locked in a room indicates fear to the dreamer. The room sometimes can be used as a symbol of a woman, so in turn the analyst must study the dream carefully.

Rooster A rooster in your dreams augurs advancement. To hear one crow, conceit. *See* Cock, Chickens.

Ropes To be hanging on to a rope indicates the dreamer is concerned about a risky or extraordinary venture. To climb a rope, perplexing complications. To descend a rope, frustration. To tie ropes, a wish to rule other people. To jump rope, a physical need for excitement or a change.

Roses Roses indicate love and admiration of a sweetheart for the dreamer. To gather roses, news of a marriage. White rose, illness for the dreamer or someone near.

Running Running usually indicates that the dreamer wishes advancement, an increase in earning power, or a better place in society. If the dreamer is running with others, contests or festivities may be subconsciously latent in the dreamer's mind. If the dreamer is running away from someone there is a fear of loss of money or a hatred for that someone.

Saddle A dream about a saddle predicts pleasant news. It is also the dreamer's wish to make a journey.

Sailing To dream of sailing on clear blue water warns the dreamer to be alert even though everything seems to be under control. *See* Ocean.

Sailors Dreaming of sailors indicates a desire to take a long vacation.

Salt Salt forebodes disagreements with associates, even quarrels with the dreamer's family.

Saw If you dream that you are using a handsaw it denotes an industrious and provident nature that makes a good home and increases security. If a woman uses a saw, friends will come to her for advice. The sound of a buzz saw portends frugality and resourcefulness.

Scaffold A scaffold threatens the dreamer that imprudent actions will cause a separation with a loved one.

Scales To dream that you are balancing scales indicates good judgment that will lead to greater prosperity. If a girl weighs her sweetheart, her dream foretells that she has found a faithful man.

School To dream that you are attending school indicates tension over something that requires an examination or a test. If you dream that you are a youngster at school, it is a wish to avoid present duties. To revisit your childhood school indicates frustration.

Schoolteacher   If you dream of a schoolteacher it indicates an interest in higher education. If you are the teacher in the dream it is a desire to be successful in the literary realm.

Scissors   To dream of scissors denotes jealousy and distrust of the marriage partner. If you lose the scissors you may be trying to avoid a disagreeable undertaking. *See* Knife.

Scrapbook   A dream about a scrapbook indicates that the dreamer is living too much in the past.

Scratch   To dream that you scratch somebody warns that you are too critical.

Sculptor   To dream that you are a sculptor predicts a change of occupation, one of your own decision. It may not be as lucrative but it will give you more pleasure.

Sea   *See* Ocean.

Seal   Dreams of seals reveal discontent. *See* Animals.

Searching   Any dream of searching or looking for something or someone is an indication of personal loss or a fear of a possible loss at some future time. These dreams recur frequently, especially when "searching" for a loved one who is dead. So often the dreamer never quite sees or reaches the dream figure.

Serpent   *See* Reptiles.

Servant   To dream that you employ a servant portends good fortune.

Shampoo   To dream that you see someone getting a shampoo warns you not to repeat gossip. If you are getting the shampoo it reveals a desire to have a secret rendezvous.

Shark   To be attacked by a shark forebodes despondency and possible financial losses. *See* Animals.

Shawl   A shawl is a symbol of flattery and a warning not to accept favors. If you lose a shawl it forebodes sadness. *See* Cape, Coat.

Shears   *See* Scissors.

Sheep   To dream that you are shearing sheep predicts good business and profitable months ahead. To see many sheep indicates a good time to make new plans.

Shells A dream wherein you are gathering shells at the seashore warns that you are wasteful and need to practice thrift.

Shelter If you dream that you are making a shelter it foretells a plan to escape from your enemies. If you are looking for shelter you may be deceitful without realizing it.

Shelves Shelves when filled show a good chance of acquiring material things. If empty, probable loss or disappointment.

Sheriff See Police.

Ship A dream of a ship predicts unexpected honors. The motion of a ship tossing on the ocean is symbolic of the rhythm of sexual mating.

Shirt If you dream that you are putting your shirt on you will be tempted to commit adultery.

Shoes Worn and dirty shoes tell the dreamer to be tolerant and thoughtful of other people. To have your shoes shined in your dream predicts important changes ahead. Untied shoes forebode misfortune and quarrels.

Shooting See Gun.

Shot If you dream that you are shot you may be the victim of losses and subsequent despondency. See Corpse.

Shotgun See Gun.

Shovel If you dream that you are using a shovel it is an indication that perseverance and hard work will be your means of achieving your ambition.

Shower A shower of gifts reveals a desire for a change of surroundings. To take a shower bath indicates anticipation of new pleasures. See Bath, Rain.

Silk To be dressed in elegant silk clothes predicts that an amicable arrangement will be made between the dreamer and an alienated associate.

Silverware A dream about silverware indicates discontent.

Skates To watch ice skaters warns that malicious gossip is about to damage the reputation of the dreamer. To be skating foretells a loss of personal belongings or position.

To watch youngsters on roller skates indicates that the dreamer likes to share pleasures and contribute to the happiness of others.

Skeleton Dreaming of a skeleton warns that you may suffer mentally and financially because of enemies. If you dream that a skeleton haunts you it forebodes carelessness that can result in an accident or death.

Skull If you dream of leering skulls, avoid family arguments lest they end in serious quarrels.

Sky Dreaming of a clear sky indicates an appreciation of culture and a desire to be with distinguished persons. If you dream that you are floating high in the sky among the clouds seeing weird people and creatures, it is a sign that you will be disillusioned with love.

Sled, sliding To dream of sledding or sliding predicts imprudence in a love affair or that you will be fooled by flattery.

Slippers A dream about slippers warns of intrigue and scandal. *See* Shoes.

Smoke A dream about smoke reveals a confused state of mind due to many troublesome problems. *See* Tobacco.

Snakes The snake through the ages has been considered a sexual symbol and so can be interpreted to mean a sexual urge in a dream, but it can also mean an enemy or an obsession. *See* Reptiles.

Snow To see snowflakes falling predicts an emotional crisis that may cost the dreamer a considerable amount of money. To be in a snowstorm indicates many frustrations. To be walking or climbing on snowcapped mountains reveals disappointment in business affairs or ambitions.

Soap A dream about soap indicates a desire to get a fresh start, to begin again.

Sold If you dream that you have sold some or all of your possessions it reveals many business worries.

Soldiers Marching soldiers indicate a desire for advancement. Wounded soldiers warn the dreamer of many complications due to bad judgment.

Son If you dream of a dutiful son it foretells that you have high aspirations and crave exceptional honors. If the son is ill or cannot be found in the dream it warns of losses or anguish.

Soup If you dream that you are enjoying a bowl of soup it predicts good news. *See* Eating.

Spade A dream of a spade or a shovel means that there is a lot of tough work ahead.

Spectacles A dream about spectacles augurs a change of plans due to other people.

Spider The spider represents an obstacle that worries the dreamer. It can recur many times, as long as the obstacle remains in the dreamer's mind. The spider can be something that the dreamer lacks and wants very much, or it can be a person who annoys the dreamer. *See* Insects.

Spools Spools of thread signify various intricate tasks that harass the dreamer in waking hours. Empty spools denote unsatisfactory results from such tasks.

Spoons To see spoons in your dream is a promise of happiness and contentment at home. If you lose a spoon you may become an innocent victim of suspicion.

Sports Dreams about baseball, football, hockey, and the like reveal a subconscious desire for harmony and teamwork. Playing a game means you expect a fair deal from others. *See* Games, Tennis.

Spy If you dream that you are a spy it forebodes a misadventure. Spy dreams generally indicate anxiety.

Squirrels To see squirrels indicates a period of rapid progress. If a dog chases a squirrel, the dreamer must be tactful lest friends be alienated.

Stage *See* Theater.

Stain A dream about stains indicates worries over trifling difficulties.

Stairs Dreams of stairs are classed by some psychoanalysts as dreams of mating, walking up the stairs meaning the urge for sexual intercourse. A traditional meaning of the same dream predicts great good fortune and unexpected pleasure. To walk down the stairs, bad luck in business and in love. To fall down the stairs, enemies will cause many obstacles.

Stars Bright stars augur many prosperous years for the dreamer. Shooting stars forebode changes that bring much distress and despondency.

Stealing Stealing reveals the dreamer's desire to possess something almost unattainable. Misunderstandings can be the cause or the foreboding of the dream.

Steps *See* Stairs.

Stones Stones and rocks are symbols of hindrances. To throw a stone in a dream indicates a fear of some person.

Store To dream that you are in a store foretells that you will have many small pleasures in the near future. *See* Shelves.

Storm *See* Rain.

Stove To dream of a stove, an oven, and the like means that the dreamer wants warmth and protection, a sort of prenatal existence with seclusion yet without responsibilities.

Stranger If you dream of a stranger dressed in a cloak, it is a desire to die.

Strawberries Strawberry dreams mean general good luck.

Street Dreaming that you are walking down a street is a desire to achieve something worthwhile. It may also indicate dissatisfaction. *See* Railroad and Road.

Sugar A dream about sugar indicates an irritable disposition that may cause domestic unhappiness.

Suicide To dream that you commit suicide indicates a desire to escape a burden or frustration. To see someone commit suicide means that you are annoyed by another person.

Sun A dream about a sunrise predicts happy times. A sunset warns that it is time to protect all assets. The sun peeking through the clouds foretells a return of prosperity.

Swamp All dreams of swamps reveal unhappiness and uncertainty. If you find a way out of the swamp your problems will be solved after much scheming.

Swan White swans predict new pleasures and prosperity. A black swan warns the dreamer against any involvement pertaining to vice or immorality.

Sweeping To be sweeping indicates the dreamer's intense desire to please all people. It also warns against wild schemes and chances. If sweeping is neglected when the need is great, contention and remorse may be imminent. *See* Broom.

Sweet taste Any taste of sweetness like sugar or syrup indicates self-control.

Swimming A dream of active swimming where the dreamer has a feeling of abounding health and exhilaration indicates an intense desire to enjoy life. If accompanied by one or more swimmers it is a wish to make new friends. If there is discomfort or a struggle in the water it forebodes overwhelming difficulties. *See* Water.

Sword If you are wearing a sword in your dream it augurs honors. If you break the sword, or lose it, disgrace or loss of position is threatened. The sword, like the knife, if seen or being used against another person, as in an attack, can be interpreted as a symbol representing a desire for sexual union.

Table If you dream that you are setting a table for a meal it indicates a desire to please someone.

Tacks A dream about tacks forebodes many small annoyances.

Tea To dream that you are making tea warns of possible indiscretions. To drink tea with friends is a prediction that you would like some changes in your present surroundings.

Teacher To dream that you are a teacher indicates a desire to rule others. If you see or talk to a teacher you are in need of practical advice.

Tears *See* Crying.

Teeth Dreams of teeth that are white and beautiful foretell a gratification of the dreamer's wishes. All other dreams such as the loss of one or many teeth, decayed, broken, dirty, or false, portend a situation that may cause the dreamer much unhappiness. These are symbolic dreams that reflect problems carried over from the waking hours.

Telegram If you dream that you receive a telegram you will hear disagreeable news. To send a telegram foretells disappointments at home or in business.

Telephone To dream that you are talking on the telephone denotes a wish to increase your resources. If you hear the ring of the telephone, someone, long absent, would like to talk to you.

Telescope If you dream that you buy a telescope it signifies a change of heart or a wish to change a business situation.

Television See Actor, Theater.

Tennis To dream that you are playing tennis denotes a yearning for more popularity. If you win, your desires will be temporarily fulfilled. If you lose you will have to work harder before you gain your ambition. *See* Sports.

Tent A dream about tents means that a change of environment would be helpful.

Terror Terror in dreams indicates fear of a person or an existing condition that worries the dreamer.

Theater To dream that you are attending a theater is a desire to get away from monotony or overwork. It can also be a hidden urge to be more important than you are at present. *See* Acrobat, Actor.

Thief If you dream that you are a thief you may subconsciously fear that you have usurped the rights of another person. To see a thief indicates the reverse. These dreams are often synonymous with financial difficulties.

Thimble Thimble dreams denote insignificant personal anxieties.

Thread A dream about tangled or broken thread denotes losses due partially to the dreamer's overkindness. *See* Spools.

Tiger A tiger is symbolic of fear or torment because of a personal problem that involves a disappointment. *See* Animals.

Tobacco To watch someone smoking denotes a successful conclusion to a series of tribulations. To be smoking indicates a will to live in peace and harmony.

Tomato The tomato in a dream symbolizes an urge for socializing. Ripe tomatoes predict a happy married life.

Torpedo Dreams of torpedoes denote a desire to harm, retaliate, or obliterate something that is an obstacle to success. *See* Sword.

Torture Dreams of torture denote struggles and disappointment in love or money matters.

Toy Dreams of beautiful toys foretell happiness. Broken toys forebode sadness and complications.

Train *See* Airplane.

Tramp A dream about a tramp denotes a fear of failure.

Travel Dreams of travel indicate a desire for pleasure. *See* Airplane, Automobile.

Trees Dreams of beautiful trees foretell happiness and success. Dead trees warn of losses. To cut down a tree, a warning to avoid quarrels.

Trunk Packing, closing, or opening a trunk means the dreamer would like a change. If the trunk never gets packed or never gets locked, the dream signifies frustration usually because of thwarted ambitions.

Tunnel To dream that you see a tunnel is an expression of insecurity. To be trapped in a tunnel is a wish to escape responsibilities or some form of bondage. To be traveling through a tunnel is a symbol for sexual interests.

Turkey A dream about turkeys that are walking around in a field signifies abundance. *See* Birds.

Ulcer To dream about ulcers indicates unsatisfactory conditions during waking hours.

Umbrella Dreams about umbrellas and parasols denote difficulties and misunderstandings. If it is raining the umbrella represents a friend who will help solve the difficulties.

University *See* College.

Valentine To dream about a valentine augurs a proposal of marriage or adventure.

Vase A dream about a vase of flowers denotes unexpected pleasures. A broken vase, sorrow.

Vegetables To be eating vegetables portends small ventures that meet with moderate success. Withered vegetables, sadness over some trifling speculation.

Veil If you dream that you are wearing a veil that hides your face you may suffer because of your own insincerity. To see the veil on another person reverses the interpretation. A bridal veil means a new opportunity. Mourning veils, embarrassing monetary troubles.

Vineyard To dream of a fruitful vineyard indicates a time for love and a time for making money.

Ventriloquist See Actor, Theater.

Violets Dreams of pretty violets predict many joyful occasions. See Flowers.

Violin To dream that you are playing a violin denotes honors. A broken violin, separation from a loved one. See Music.

Volcano To dream that you see a volcano indicates that you must control your emotions. See Mountain.

Vote If you dream that you are casting a ballot in a voting booth it means that you should take more interest in civic affairs.

Waiter If you dream of a waiter in a restaurant, serving a meal, it signifies a wish for entertainment and relaxation.

Wake To dream that you are attending a wake is indicative of happiness by the return of a loved one.

Walking To dream that you are walking on rough or winding paths forebodes distress due to misunderstandings. Walking at night, fear of threatening circumstances. See Street.

Wall If you dream that you are enclosed by walls or cannot climb up, it means frustration or inability to attain an ambition. Breaking through a wall, success in spite of obstacles. Jumping over the wall, tremendous effort that reaches the goal.

Wallet A dream about a wallet foretells of pleasures that will require expenditures. See Money.

Waltzing See Dancing.

War Dreaming of war, apart from wartime, forebodes family disputes.

Wasp See Ants, Bees, Insects.

Watch Good news and prosperity are predicted if you dream about a watch. To check the time shows a desire to get ahead by accomplishing more in less time.

Water To dream that you are drinking water signifies that you are actually thirsty, even though sleeping. To see clear water augurs prosperity. Muddy water warns of illness. To play in water, a desire to be loved. Rough water, difficulties before success. Jumping into water, a hope for another chance or opportunity. *See* Drowning, Lake, Ocean.

Web *See* Spider.

Wedding *See* Marriage.

Window Closed windows forebode defeat or frustration for the dreamer. Broken windows, disappointment in love. To crawl through a window, dishonorable intentions. *See* Door.

Wolf To dream about a wolf warns of unprincipled friends who are really enemies. *See* Animals.

Woods If you dream of green woods you will have a lucky change. If the woods are on fire make plans for your welfare and security.

Workshop A dream about a workshop means that the dreamer will use all available means to further an impending project.

Worms *See* Snakes.

Wreath To dream of a wreath of flowers augurs a wonderful plan for a reunion. A wreath of withered flowers, self-pity.

X-ray A dream about an X-ray indicates two things. One, a fear of physical problems. The other, a mental probe into the opposing forces of the dreamer, like family or partner.

Yacht To dream of a yacht indicates a love of freedom, a wish to be released from encumbrances.

Yardstick The yardstick indicates that the dreamer wants to be realistic, or that there is no way of measuring up to the ideals of family or occupation. The yardstick becomes a symbol for an obstacle.

Zebra A dream about a zebra denotes many interests. *See* Animals.

Zoo When you dream of a zoo it reveals a feeling of helplessness whereby you may be trapped despite yourself. It denotes an acceptance of ideas imposed by others.

How to Find the Numerical
Significance of a Dream

1	2	3	4	5	6	7	8	9
A	B	C	D	E	F	G	H	I
J	K	L	M	N	O	P	Q	R
S	T	U	V	W	X	Y	Z	

Use the number chart shown above to evaluate the word representing the chief theme of the dream. Thus, with a dream of a house, the key would be:

H O U S E
8 6 3 1 5

Add each pair of figures in this five-figure number, thus: $8 + 6 = 14$. $6 + 3 = 9$. $3 + 1 = 4$. $1 + 5 = 6$.

With a double figure (14) use only the last (4).

The result is a four-figure number: 4946.

Reduce that to a three-figure number; then to a two-figure number, and finally to a one-figure number.

If any number begins with "o," change it to "1." Whenever "o" appears as part of a number, keep it; but count it as "1" in making the next reduction. If the final reduction comes to "o" count it as "1". Thus:

H O U S E
8 6 3 1 5
4 9 4 6
3 3 0
6 4
1

Hence, the significant numbers with the word HOUSE are 86315, 4946, 330, 64, and 1.

As another example:

C L O U D
3 3 6 3 4
6 9 9 7
5 8 6
3 4
7

With CLOUD, the significant numbers are 33634, 6997, 586, 34, and 7. In this case, there was no need for figure substitutions because no zeros appeared.

But the "o" to "1" is well illustrated with:

P U R S E
7 3 9 1 5
 1 2 0 6
  3 3 7
   6 0
    7

Here, beginning with 73915, we had 7 + 3 = 10. Being the first figure, the "1" was used instead of "o." But with the 9 + 1 = 10, the "o" was retained.

In the reduction of 1206 to 337, the "o" was treated as "1" to form the 2 + 1 and 1 + 6 resulting in 337.

In the formation of the next number (60) the 3 + 3 = 6 is followed by 3 + 7 = 10. So the zero is used for the 60, but in the next reduction it is treated as "1" so that the lone figure, 7, is the result of 6 + 1.

This is probably the most logical as well as the most practical system for determining so-called "lucky" numbers. It allows for zeros and yet varies the reductions, so that anyone can pick a "lucky" number of one, two, or three figures, which seem to be the types most wanted in terms of dream interpretation.

Most other systems are not only illogical, but sometimes incoherent. With this one, you can form your own numbers as required and test them accordingly. But they should be regarded as "significant" rather than "lucky."

With simple three-letter words, the full interpretation is used to obtain the three-figure number. Others reduce as already described. For example:

B O Y
2 6 7
 8 3
  1

7

Graphology or
Handwriting Analysis

There is a message to be found in your own handwriting through the amazing subject of graphology, which is older than the Pyramids of Egypt.

From the day when the first literate man chiseled a hieroglyph in stone as a means of recorded communication, he carved the expression of his individual nature with it.

No signature is needed to identify the paintings of certain Old Masters. You can recognize a speech written by Lincoln or Churchill by the words which flow from the lips of a person who recites it. A lover of literature can tell when he is reading Kipling or Hemingway without looking at the title page of the book.

So it is with *your own* self-expression, as revealed by something which you may use most, yet think about least—your penmanship. Here all the quirks and varying moods invariably show themselves to the student of graphology, the only question being how far and how deeply the subject should be followed to suit the average need.

Many innovations have been introduced in recent years where handwriting analysis is concerned, adding greatly to its scientific status. Some of these demand great attention to small details and often require long or painstaking comparisons of various styles. Other findings, while sound, involve such rare and unusual types of writing that few students will ever encounter them.

It is better, therefore, to stay with fundamentals and study many specimens of handwriting according to long-accepted standards rather than to delve into more exhaustive treatments fraught with complications. Those are better left to persons who intend to specialize in the subject and have time to track down the lesser known quirks that are sometimes revealed.

For practical purposes as well as rapid results, you need simply to note the rules given in the following pages, along with the written samples. Then check the handwriting of your friends against what you have learned and see how right you are!

Remember: these rules are not hard and fast; one may often modify another. But the more you test them, the more you will find out about people—and the more enjoyment you will have!

Lines of Writing

To analyze handwriting almost at a glance, you should first observe the lines themselves, noting the direction which they take—upward, downward, or certain other details that will be given here.

The direction of the lines may be termed the index to personality, though of course other features must be studied to form a solid conclusion. Yet in some striking instances, a whole character may be read by the direction of the lines and a few other equally conspicuous details that practically shout facts about the person who penned them.

LEVEL LINES

(a) Writing in straight, level lines indicates both will power and determination, a strong, well-balanced nature. The purpose behind the personality reveals itself in this form. At the same time, if the lines are absolutely exact, it shows a dominating, sometimes unreasonable person, who is exacting in writing as in everything else.

Slight variations in this style of writing are therefore a good sign. If it appears relaxed, rather than rigid, it shows a nature that is frank and honest, but not too blunt or domineering.

(b) The opposite extreme is a wavery line that maintains a level, but is always wandering from it. This shows a nature that seeks balance but fails to attain it. It is a mark of a careless, changeable, weak disposition —but these faults are never great unless the writing wavers to the extreme.

If only fairly irregular, such writing can be taken as a sign of genius, or skill in many fields. Its very lack of system shows a mind preoccupied with larger things than close attention to trivial details.

UPWARD LINES

Lines that rise regularly and consistently show an ambitious, optimistic nature, with a personality that is always on the go—perhaps too much so. Watch such persons for exaggerations; they are often too sure of themselves and unable to keep up with their boasts or promises.

A slight upward slant is a good sign, showing real purpose. It is when it becomes exaggerated that it indicates exactly that sort of nature. Some people like to dash off notes on the upward slant, either line by line or word by word, and the higher they go, the higher they are apt to regard themselves.

Upward Slant

DOWNWARD LINES

Downward writing shows a moody nature, easily discouraged. Otherwise a comparatively slight downward trend is not bad; in fact, it may indicate a person who maintains a gloomy outlook rather than give way to undue or foolish enthusiasm. Call it caution rather than pessimism, unless the downward slant is extreme, as follows:

Are you moody or discouraged? If you are, your writing may reveal it, by following downward slanting lines like these!

Today the stock market crashed!

Downward Slant

In such cases, you have indications of a despondent, morbid mind, increasing in discouragement proportionately to the line's fall. Remember, that this is normally an *outward* expression of a person's feelings, that a person may be simply dramatizing his or her pessimistic attitude to win the sympathy of others.

The real danger is present when this type of writing shows physical as well as mental weariness. A frail person, or one subject to illness, may let lines fall through sheer fatigue. With mental despondency, this is a bad combination, demanding a fresh outlook on life. It should be accepted as a warning.

IRREGULAR LINES

These are variations of those already given. When writing rises toward the end of a line and particularly near the bottom of the page, it shows a restrained optimism, a nature ready to show exuberance as well as a strong, reliant character that can meet adversity.

I feel much more optimistic in regard to this subject than when I last wrote, as things have picked up ever since.

Rising

In contrast, a "fall off" at the end of lines and at the finish of a page shows a weary, worried nature, easily exhausted and apt to weaken under stress.

I am feeling rather tired and I suppose my writing is showing it quite plainly

Falling Off

A "humped" writing that climbs over the rise and then descends again shows a person of short-lived enthusiasm, who starts projects, then abandons them.

Enthusiasm is apt to rise and fall whenever a writer climbs the "hump" and then drops down before he finishes the line.

Humped

The opposite nature is represented by "dipped" writing. Here you have a person who approaches projects rather glumly, or with no special purpose, but gathers enthusiasm as soon as things get under way.

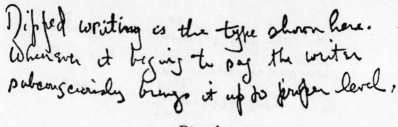

Dipped

Size of Writing

Differences in writing size are quite remarkable, and next to the "over-all" appearance of the lines, size is the most conspicuous thing about a person's penmanship. The examples given run the gamut of sizes, affording easy comparison with any samples you may intend to analyze.

TINY WRITING shows an artistic or literary nature, with great attention to detail. This is the writing of a specialist, a person who becomes more and more centered on a single aim. Such writers never waste time or energy. They are thinkers who embody their thoughts in purpose, but are overly annoyed at trifles.

But you know what the gist is worth!

Tiny

SMALL WRITING marks the scholar, the philosopher, or the statesman— in ordinary life it shows a person of keen observation and executive ability. These writers are the type who go to the top in their chosen fields.

It was good to hear from you, this fine Spring day.

Small

AVERAGE WRITING covers a considerable range of size and in many instances represents just what it is termed: Mr. Average Man. But the analysis should by no means stop at that. This average, in itself, shows balance, plus ability.

I received your letter and I have about finished reading the books that you sent me.

Average

Coupled with other factors, it would indicate a man who would do better in business for himself than as an executive or salesman with a big company. Where learning is concerned, it is the mark of the inventor, the man who acquires knowledge and applies it to new things.

Note if writing of this type tends toward small or large and you will have keys to the individual's personal inclination, a guide to which course he should follow if the choice arose.

LARGE WRITING shows an active, often restless nature, a desire to go places and do bigger things. People who use this style like to attract attention and influence others. They are often big-hearted, self-reliant, and sure of success, but they defeat themselves when they indulge in talk instead of action.

We had the roof on the house reboarded where needed and shingled.

Large

HUGE WRITING is the sure mark of a self-important person, given to grand ideas and unwilling to accept sharp criticism. With this importance, however, there is strict integrity. The very emphasis given to huge writing indicates a person who will back up his convictions.

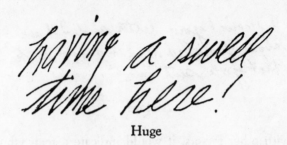

Huge

Angles of Writing

The next and most quickly spotted "at a glance" is the "writing angle" or the slant of a person's penmanship. This feature, however, calls for special study, as many small variations are noticed when writing is studied closely.

A "key chart" or "graphometer" can be used to measure the different angles of writing, and specimens of each type are given here. Their significance is as follows:

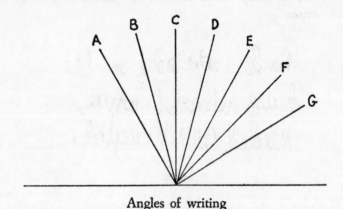

Angles of writing

BACKWARD WRITING

Some experts claim that this style literally represents the past in a person's life—showing someone who thinks in the same backward style. With some, it shows a suppressed nature, a fear of facing the world and its problems. With others, it shows a cold, self-sufficient personality, with very little regard toward people generally.

(A)

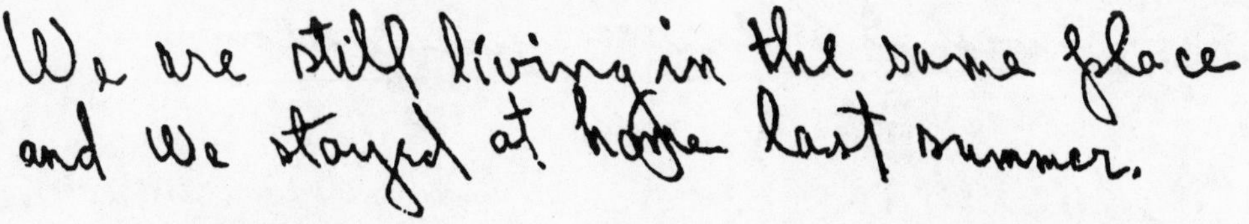

We are still living in the same place and we stayed at home last summer.

(B)

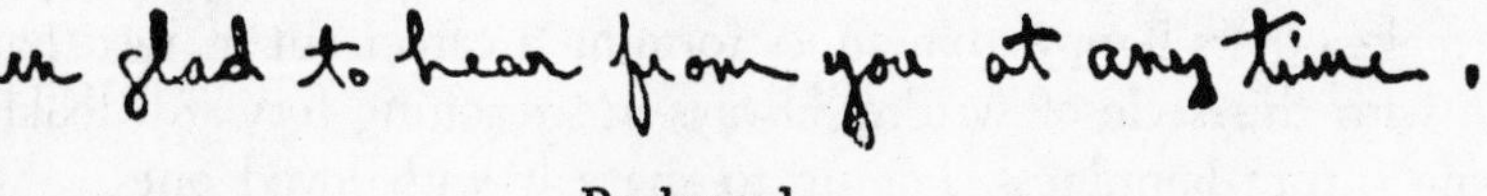

I am glad to hear from you at any time.

Backward

UPRIGHT WRITING

This is a simple, straight up and down style. It, too, shows a selfish nature, with an absolute indifference to surroundings. However, this is also a self-exacting type, showing an analytical mind. Such people, though deliberate, often replace their lack of emotion with sincerity and dependability. They recognize obligations and prove good friends and interesting companions.

(C)

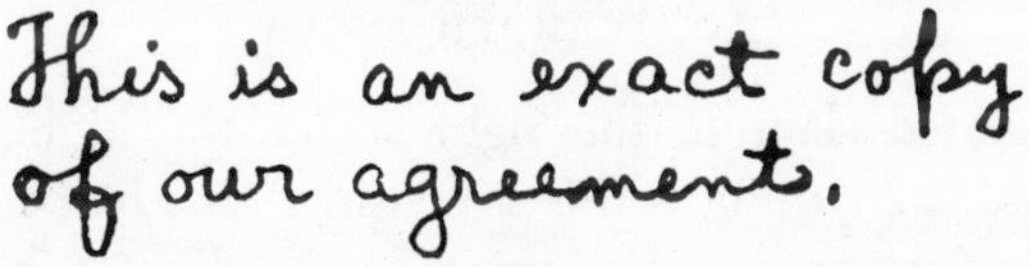

This is an exact copy of our agreement.

Upright

NORMAL ANGLE

Many people adopt this slant through convenience or sheer force of habit, but that tells a story in itself. It consists of a slight tilt to the right. This shows a natural, easygoing disposition, a person inclined to accept things as they are, with a cordial feeling toward other people. There is nothing artificial in the nature of such a writer, and these people are generally quite friendly.

(D)

I wish I could see you to-day —

Normal

FORWARD ANGLE

Here we find a generous, sensitive nature, the person always anxious to make others happy, sometimes forming a career out of just that. People with this style of writing always are reaching forward, looking for some future happiness, hoping to share it with loved ones.

As a result, they are sentimental, easily preyed upon, and occasionally lacking in will power, particularly if it interferes with the expression of some emotion. These are the kindliest of persons and deserve appreciation. Therefore they should be guided by those they trust.

(E)

*Shedding Season's cheer o'er the
Winter snow!"*

Forward

FAR FORWARD ANGLE

This exaggerated slant to the right shows the high-strung person, who never reasons anything and is so sensitive that he becomes a victim of his own imagination, rising to anger on the slightest provocation. Be very careful with people of such intense natures, even when you analyze their handwriting for them. Often, they will not believe how excited they become.

(F and G)

*Owe you a letter that will come
as soon as I get clear*

Far Forward

MIXED ANGLES

Depending upon how variable they are, mixed angles in a person's writing can be the worst sign of all. At least there is some consistency in all the regular types, but a helter-skelter writing indicates a nature in perpetual conflict with itself.

Fortunately, this mixed type seldom goes to complete extremes in its angles, or it would represent a totally unpredictable, utterly scatter-brained personality. Usually it varies between one slope and the vertical, showing indecision in the traits they represent.

When it slopes both backward and forward, this writing shows a wishful yet almost hopeless temperament, a person unable to recognize his own shortcomings. Such people must train themselves to make decisions.

Line Spacing

Spacing between lines of writing is another feature that can often be gathered by a quick glance, and it shows how important it is for the analyst to have a sizable sample of a person's writing. Otherwise, this important feature of line spacing could not be noted.

Here are various examples:

CLOSE SPACING

Here, the lines are practically compressed together, representing a person whose thoughts are equally cluttered. This shows someone over-anxious to express himself, fearful that he cannot get enough into the space allowed, just as he might try to talk fast.

When the letters of one line actually encroach into the next, it shows that the writer has practically forgotten what he just wrote, or he wouldn't be jumbling into it.

Close

AVERAGE SPACING

This shows a clarity of thought, a person who meets issues as they come along and is never hasty about pressing his ideas on others. In some instances, it may indicate too casual an outlook, too easy an acceptance of things, but on the whole it is a sign of good balance, unless other features of the handwriting contradict this.

Average spacing depends somewhat on the size of the writing, but should run about as shown here.

Average

WIDE SPACING

Much emphasis has been given to such spacing as a symbol of great minds, and it is true that many famous personalities have preferred this style. Usually, however, such notables are writing on important subjects and therefore are more careful and methodical in their writing.

Wide spacing allows... room between the lines as in this specimen!

Wide

Also, as in the case of speeches or essays, the space between the lines is intended as an allowance for changes and other notations. Unquestionably, wide spacing is inspired by a feeling of importance. But in most cases it simply shows a person of a careful nature, who attaches much weight to everything he says and is often not only brief, but cautious in his statements. Wide spacing, it should be noted, enables few words to take the place of many—a good index to the writer's character.

EVEN SPACING

This should be carefully checked when analyzing the spacing between lines. Even spacing—whether cramped, average, or wide—shows a person with fair judgment. When spacings vary, they show a mind swayed by uncertainty.

Letter Spacing

This covers various features of a person's handwriting, all giving indications of character. First and most obvious is—

WORD SPACING

Which falls into one of two categories, either writing in which the words are uniformly spaced, or uneven, irregular spacing between the words of a sentence.

This handwriting shows even spaces between the words signifying a calculating nature.

Even word spacing

Here is a case of wider as well as variable impulsive spacing.

Uneven word spacing

These, more than line spacing, are a sure index to a person's flow of thought, whether his ideas are clear and calculated or subject to impulse and hasty decision. *Even spaces* show calculation; *uneven spaces,* impulse.

Connected Writing

This comes under the head of spacing, or the lack of it—as it is a form of writing in which all the letters of each word are connected.

It shows a person of a positive nature, firm in decision and very exacting, one who will not make allowance for repeated mistakes. It shows a good manager, all the more so if words—as well as letters—are connected. It is also the mark of the outright skeptic.

This shows a positive nature as evidenced by the connected letters.

Connected letters

BROKEN WRITING

Where certain letters are disconnected—not too frequently—we find a person who plays hunches and is a keen judge of human character. You can almost catch the rhythm in this writing, the occasional lifting of the hand, like a pianist moving to another key. A fine flow of thought but with quick, inspirational touches. Most talented persons use this style.

Do you follow hunches? Broken writing indicates it

Broken writing

DISCONNECTED WRITING

Here, practically no letters are connected. This represents the dreamer who lives in a world of complete fancy, depending upon intuition rather than reason, seldom descending to the dull realm of reality. This writing shows a poetic trend and a love of nature. It must not be confused, however, with printed lettering, which some people use in order to make reading easier.

This is utterly disconnected writing with few letters joined

Disconnected writing

CRAMPED VERSUS SPREAD

No greater contrast in spacing can be shown than in the following examples, one representing *cramped writing* and the other *spread writing*.

Both are totally self-expressive: the cramped style shows a desire to save space, particularly when words are jammed together at the end of a line. This, of course, shows an inherent urge to avoid waste, especially if the lines are close together.

Cramped writing is a space saver and some writers jam it very closely.

That, in turn, indicates caution in money matters, a keen bargainer, a person of a somewhat suspicious nature, who is always holding on to what he has. It is a trait that shows itself strikingly as well as quite unconsciously through this sort of writing.

In *spread writing*, we see sheer extravagance, a nature often given to abandon, one that places social life and good times at the top of the list.

Here you find writing that is not only spread but stretched!

This is the mark of the spender, the carefree spirit. As a result, it usually shows a friendly type of person, but one who is seldom at all systematic. These writers have a wonderful ability at forgetting what they do not want to remember.

As one experienced graphologist put it: "If you think there's nothing harder than getting a cramped writer to lend you money, just ask a spread writer to give you back what he borrowed!"

Cramped versus spread is just about the equivalent of cash versus credit.

Letter Formations

We come now to the finer points of graphology, which confirm the features already described. Some graphologists will tell you that the "quick glance" methods are "general but not specific," and that the "fine points" count most. That, however, is not the case.

All handwriting authorities favor the more general systems—size, spacing, angles, and the like—so it is obvious that they are the methods on which the science is founded. Now that we have come to the "fine points" we should not attempt to make them too fine.

Almost all these points have to do with letter formations or peculiarities. To discuss all of these in detail would be superfluous, as many of them never appear in the average person's handwriting at all. So this discussion of letter formations will cover those that are apt to appear in practically every specimen of handwriting that the reader may be called upon to analyze.

ROUNDED LETTERS

These are distinguished by certain letters which can be written in "rounded" style. This is a leisurely form of writing that shows a desire for duty and harmony, a love of comfort. When clearly rounded it personifies all that is wonderful and perfect—provided no effort is needed to get it.

Rounded writing follows the pattern shown here.

Rounded writing adds up to a lazy symbol, an urge for luxury, an avoidance of any disturbing activity that might lead to a trifling bit of hard work.

Study this type of writing and you will learn to an amazing degree just how much idle time some people have, or how far they will go toward writing long, beautiful letters to their friends and acquaintances, with the feeling that they are having a busy day.

The degree of rounded writing is important. In its modified form it indicates nothing more than a peaceful, law-abiding disposition, willing to accept the tasks of life, yet at the same time craving better things.

ANGULAR WRITING

In sharp—and we mean sharp!—contrast to the rounded style is the angular writing. Here is a quick disposition, filled with energy and the desire to accomplish things. Such people can't waste time on beautiful curves represented by m's, n's, and r's. They rush right through their writing and let the reader worry.

This is the angular type of writing, often very purposeful.

People with sharply angular writing are inclined to be aggressive. Whatever their chosen field, they expect to be leaders and are annoyed if others do not follow. Their weakness lies in expecting results too quickly.

Frequently they are opposed to the artistic, but only on the ground that it is impractical. Angular writers judge success by its commercial value. Ask them—and they will tell you just that—provided that they are extreme types.

Angular writing of a modified sort represents a wiser personality, lacking the aggressive quality, or at least not showing it too openly. These are people who profit by experience.

BLOCK WRITING

This is a style that is neither rounded nor angular. It shows a meticulous, painstaking individual, but decidedly on the practical side. It is the slow, careful manner of the steady worker who goes by blueprint rather than inspiration, but is always sure of results.

Block writing follows this pattern

You will find people with this style of writing very busy in their home workshops. They are also very capable as accountants or as treasurers of organizations. Block writing appears in various styles, but always the writer apparently is anxious to make his letters plain—another token of a persevering nature.

Letter Variations

Close study of the letters in a specimen of handwriting will show that they conform to one of the following patterns:

EXACT LETTERS, all the same size, show a person who is extremely conscientious, following every instruction to the last degree, never neglecting even the slightest duty.

Carefulness is indicated when letters maintain an exact size.

IRREGULAR LETTERS, changing from large to small, are a sure sign of a fickle mind, a person who will take whatever course seems most convenient. At the same time, such people are often clever. Being somewhat irresponsible, they are ready to try new things at which they often prove capable.

It is surprising how irregular some letters may become in size

SMALL TO LARGE LETTERS, when they appear, show a restrained quality, eager to express itself. Such people are eager to work their way up, and feel that success can only be gained through honest effort.

This style of writing actually grows on you, word by word.

LARGE TO SMALL LETTERS represent tactfulness, a good listener, someone who makes friends easily, then profits through such connections but
always in a fair way. Some of our keenest minds reveal their traits
through this style of writing.

In some handwriting each word seems to fade away.

Open and Shut Letters

Here is another case of two extremes in individual letters, the "open"
and "shut" seen mostly in such letters as "a" and "o."

good examples of open letters. no longer open but closed.

The interpretation of these two extremes is almost obvious: The *open
style* shows a frank and outspoken nature, with an open mind toward
everything, often to the extreme of thoughtlessness.

In opposition, the *closed style* indicates a closed mind, a person who is
secretive and opinionated, although very capable of keeping such facts
to himself, so that often, his secretive ways are not suspected.

a style both open and shut

An *open* and *shut style* incorporates both these features and shows a cordial, considerate nature, usually tempered with discretion. It can also show a somewhat uncertain disposition, trusting in some ways, suspicious in others.

In all such analysis, the degree of the "open" or "shut" letters has a definite importance. If very slight, the personality trends are apt to be less marked. In such cases, "open" and "shut" letters are apt to nullify each other, if found in the same handwriting.

Special Letter Variations

Practically all the letters of the alphabet show variations that lend themselves to personalized interpretation. The question is how far these should be carried, as such analysis can be more time-taking than productive. The best-known of letter variations are the dotted "i" and the crossed "t" which are subject to many interpretations; but other letters have noteworthy differences.

Since these are secondary features, the interpretations are brief, but pointed. In some cases, a single letter will show two features, each with its own significance; for example, a "t" with a long cross-stroke that is also set low. Occasionally, a letter variation may provide a key to some very distinctive trait; but often, these variations simply modify the broader findings covered by the more important phases of handwriting analysis.

Here are some of the more significant types:

Carefully formed letters—A capable, inventive mind.
Strongly looped "b"—A kindly, understanding manner.
Slightly looped "b"—Somewhat individualistic.
No loop with "b"—Decisive, determined personality.
Strongly looped "d"—Shy and easily influenced.
Low upright line—Self-effacing, but crafty.
High upright "d"—Strongly idealistic nature.
Formed like musical note—Great aspirations.
Backsweep with "d"—Intellectual attainments.
With added twist to right—Independence and imagination.
Overly curved to right—Egotistical tendency.
Widespread letter "d"—Silent, secretive manner.
Well-rounded "e"—Natural and unaffected.
Narrowed like an "i"—A somewhat uncertain nature.

Ornamental or Greek "E"—A vain, showy tendency.
A very ornate "f"—A self-sufficient individual.
Loop very slight—Urge for accuracy and precision.
Long below the line—A virile, active nature.
Short below the line—Lacking in stamina.
A "g" shaped like an "8"—Good vocabulary and literary ability.
A "g" with straight down line—Scientific trend.
A "g" long and rounded below line—Fanciful ideas.
A "g" (or other letters) with small loop—Petty tyranny.
High-looped "h"—Insight and imagination.
Low-looped "h"—Matter-of-fact nature.
No dot to letter "i"—A neglectful nature.
Light dot over "i"—Willingness to go along with others.
Heavy dot over "i"—Blunt, aggressive nature.
Rounded dot over "i"—A token of affectation.
Dot directly over "i"—Careful, methodical ways.
Dot to right of "i" or "j"—A very quick mind.
Dot to left of "i" or "j"—A retrospective nature.
Dot high above—Imaginative or mystical nature.
Dot placed low—A practical, painstaking trend.
Stroked dot over "i"—Impatience and petulance.
Curved dot over "i"—A keen, clever thinker.
An "i"-pointed like an inverted "v"—An eager disposition.
A low-looped "j" below the line—Similar to low "g."
A high, rounded "k" or "l"—Emphasis with exaggeration.
A high, but narrow "l"—Emphatic, but exacting.
A balanced, normal "l"—A balanced, normal nature.
Small "l" mistaken for "e"—Haste or indifference.
A well-rounded "m" or "n"—Precise ways or manners.
Angular "m" or "n"—Friendly and highly sociable.
Letter "o" like an "a"—A general lack of system.
A high-looped "p"—Imaginative, as with high "h."
A simple "p" only slightly looped—A practical nature.
An open "p" like an "h"—Love of tradition and old ideas.
Long-looped "q" below the line—Similar to low-looped "g."
A specially formed "q"—Tendency toward detail.
A well-formed "r"—Rather careful and precise.
A rounded "r" like an inverted "u"—Lacking inspiration.
A sharply angular "r"—A quick but keen intellect.
An "r" like a printed letter—Good power of expression.

An overlarge "s"—Tendency toward excesses.
Poorly or hastily formed "s"—Talkative and dynamic.
An "s" shaped like printed letter—An acquisitive streak.
Large printed "s" below and above line—A dominating trend.
A simple, well-formed "t"—Good decision and balance.
Simple "t" but small—A mediocre tendency.
A looped "t"—Sensitive and easily offended.
A pointed upright portion of "t"—Blunt and challenging.
A low-placed crossbar on "t"—Easily influenced or guided.
Even placement of "t" bar—Calm, unassuming nature.
High-placed "t" bar—Self-willed and opinionated.
Bar of "t" above upright—Demanding or overbearing.
A thinly formed "t" bar—A kindly, careful nature.
A heavy "t" bar—Rough, impulsive, and often quarrelsome.
Bar to left of "t"—A hesitant, doubting nature.
Bar to right of "t"—Good initiative, but overeager.
Bar starting thick, ending thin—Too much enthusiasm.
Bar starting thin, ending thick—Increasing determination.
No crossbar on "t"—Indifferent, inconsiderate trends.
A "t" formed in one action—Somewhat petulant or hasty.
A rising bar on "t"—A quibbling over trifles.
A descending "t" bar—An obstinate streak.
An upward curve of "t" bar—Kindly, amiable manner.
A downward curve of "t" bar—Desire for authority.
Variable curve of "t" bar—Fun-loving and humorous.
A "u" shaped like "n"—Easygoing, taking things as they come.
A well-rounded "u"—Careful and often finicky.
A pointed "u" like "n"—Overeager to please.
A "v" shaped like a "u"—A somewhat fastidious trend.
A "v" ending high at right—A conscientious nature.
An angular "w"—Sociable and generally cordial.
A "w" well-rounded—Painstaking but thoughtful.
A "w" with low center—Desire for efficiency.
A curved "x" with short straight bar—A hasty manner.
A sharp "x" with long bar—Challenging and forceful.
A "y" with straight down stroke—A firm or rugged nature.
A "y" or "z" long and rounded below line—Similar to "g."
A "z" like a printed letter—Care in matters of detail.

Many other variants could be included, so many in fact that some authorities are inclined to reject practically all of them on the ground that their differences are too trivial. This may be true in respect to a more general analysis; but letter forms betray little quirks and represent natural habits that the writer does subconsciously. Regarded as keys to unguarded traits, they may prove of real value in analyzing certain individuals, particularly as a check on more important findings.

Last Letters of Words

The final letter of a word often carries a habitual flourish that serves as a key to individual characteristics. This may be particularly marked in the last word of a sentence. Accepted indications of the last letter include:

Letter shortened—Prudent but self-centered.
Letter lengthened—Generally wasteful.
Rising straight—Easily swayed, but given to temper.
Rising with high curve—A mystical nature.
Angular rise—Friendly and inquiring.
Doubling back over word—Mental uncertainty.
Doubling back under word—An egotistical nature.
Downward droop—Seeking wealth or favors.
Downward slant—Firm, practical ideas.
Finishing in high curlicue—Love of nature.
Finishing in level curlicue—Self-satisfaction.
Finishing in low curlicue—An unpredictable type.
Large last letter—Pride and self-importance.
Many dots and dashes—Trend toward the romantic.
Heavy period or other punctuations—Poor taste.
Light period or other punctuations—Good taste.
No period at end of sentence—A trustful nature.

Capital Letters

The study of capital letters is highly revealing in itself, with many interesting facets. It is modified by the fact that many persons use some accepted style of penmanship with their capital letters, so they often show the results of training rather than personality, where types of capitals are concerned.

Thus a person trained to use old-fashioned capitals might continue with them, even though he had a trend toward something more ornate. However, after making due allowance for that, you will often find that some deep trait will creep into the simplest or most stylized of capital letters.

Keeping this in mind, capital letters can be considered in the following categories:

SIMPLE OR OLD-STYLE CAPITALS: These represent a well-developed mind, willing to accept the tried and true; a practical, reliable disposition.

PRINTED CAPITALS: A sign of artistry, often representing skill. If rather rapidly formed, they show a mechanical or scientific trend.

GRACEFUL CAPITALS: A more modern trend, getting away from the more simple style, showing interest in new ideas and a desire for personal advancement.

ORNATE CAPITALS: Too much elaboration, showing pride in small things and a feeling of self-importance. Sometimes an indication of an inferiority complex.

SMALL-SIZED CAPITALS: Not much larger than the small letters that follow, show a modest, often self-effacing nature that should crawl from its shell. The smaller the capitals in proportion, the more pronounced those traits.

LARGE-SIZED CAPITALS: More than twice the height of the small letters, are a symbol of vanity, coupled with a boastful, sometimes overbearing nature. The bigger the capitals in proportion, the more evident those points.

A capital by itself shows an independent, yet helpful and whole-hearted nature. This, however, is subject to certain modifications; namely:

If the capital is carried or extended over and above some of the following letters, it signifies self-sufficiency, with a lack of the usual sympathy toward others.

If the capital includes a sweeping stroke beneath the following letters, it indicates false pride.

Capitals of different types show a highly adaptable disposition, usually carefree and likable, especially when the same letter differs. This indicates a mingling of traits.

Certain capital letters carry a special significance of their own. Here are some examples:

An "A" beginning with a hook shows a grasping disposition which is accentuated if the letter also ends in a hook.

A "D" ending with a hook at the upper left is a sign of a critical but not unfriendly nature.

A wide "H" shows a strong, decisive nature; as it narrows, it denotes a retiring individual, doubtful of his ability.

The letter "M" shows independence if its first stroke is higher than the others; too high, self-grandeur.

An "M" with all strokes the same height shows an urge for culture rather than ambition.

An "M" with strokes descending is like steps going down to the level of pessimism.

An "M" with ascending steps to a high final stroke signifies ambition, but seldom of a very high order.

An "M" with only two downstrokes shows an obstinate disposition that often results in failure.

An "M" beginning with a hook is grasping, as with "A," and also boastful if the "M" ends with a hook.

The capital "N" shows similar characteristics to "M," particularly an "N" of the hooked variety.

A widespread "M" or "N" denotes a kindly but extravagant disposition; when very narrow, a person too cautious to risk anything. This applies to all styles of capitals.

Signatures

The study of signatures as a key to individual traits is almost a study in itself, and is worthy of close attention. Often, a signature is more revealing than a paragraph of regular handwriting. This may seem surprising, considering its brevity, but the point is that a person puts more concentrated thought and effort into a signature than in ordinary writing.

Thus the signature becomes the individual's trademark, so to speak. Many signatures have been traced through the years, showing how the signer has matured, implanting his personality more firmly in the final example, thus making a detailed analysis possible from comparatively trifling clues.

The usual rules of handwriting analysis can be applied to signatures where appropriate, but with certain modifications. Two of these are rather obvious. First, a signature is a formal piece of writing, and therefore may be somewhat stylized; second, a flourish may be added to give it individuality, or completion, much as an exclamation point might be put at the end of a sentence for emphasis!

Such features should not be disregarded; on the contrary, they provide some of the best possible clues to character, the sort not often found in ordinary writing. It must simply be borne in mind that slight affectations are both allowable and expected in signatures, and therefore should be interpreted in their own right.

The quickest and most effective way to cover this is by a study of some well-known signatures, stressing their salient points and giving due notice to their embellishments. Good examples are found among the signers of the Declaration of Independence, starting with the name at the top of the list:

(Signature of John Hancock)

By far the largest of all the signatures, taking twice the space of any other, this shows an active nature with the eagerness to sway others. Its self-reliance looms to self-importance, with grand ideas but strict integrity, these being signified by overly large writing.

Virility is stressed by the huge loop of the "J" below the line. The forward angle indicates a generous nature, looking toward future happiness and prosperity, but the ornate style shows self-sufficiency, with its natural pride accentuated by the large last letter.

The final flourish embodies several features: The straight line indicates pride of personality; the added backstroke shows an energetic fighter, but the curved lines supply a certain degree of tact.

These observations fit the personality of John Hancock, one of the most aggressive spirits of the Revolution, capable as President of the Continental Congress, yet described as a man of "vanity" and "jealous disposition" despite his ardent patriotism.

In the graceful capital letters, we see an interest in new ideas and their advancement, plus a self-importance because of their size, but tempered by self-sufficiency, as indicated by the long loops below the line. There is pride in the extension of the capitals beneath the letters that follow, but being part of a compact signature, it is not an affectation, as in ordinary writing.

Instead, it stresses the forthright patriotism that caused Charles Carroll to add "of Carrollton" to his signature. One of the wealthiest men in the Colonies, he was risking a huge fortune on the success of the Revolutionary cause and he added the name of his estate, Carrollton, so there would be no mistake as to which Charles Carroll had been bold enough to sign the Declaration.

The low curlicue adds the unpredictable element suited to his exact mood, for there was no telling at that time just what would become of either Charles Carroll or Carrollton. All turned out well, however, for Carroll outlived the other fifty-five signers of the Declaration and still showed his urge for the advancement of new ideas when he laid the cornerstone for the B & O Railroad at the age of ninety.

This signature is characterized by the forward slant of generosity and purpose. The "j" of "Benj" ends in a high curlicue, showing love of nature and simple things, while the high "k" and "l" reveal an emphatic personality, being just sufficiently rounded to account for Franklin's keen wit.

The roundish tendency throughout shows a devotion to duty, a desire for harmony, and an appreciation of comfort, all of which characterized Franklin. But most remarkable of all is the fact that this comparatively simple signature should be embellished with the intricate flourish that appears beneath it.

This "knotted flourish," as it is sometimes styled, had long been recognized as the mark of the firm but tactful negotiator, the symbol of the true diplomat. Franklin was noted for such qualities, more so than any other signer of the Declaration, and none of the others begin to match his flourish.

Here, the "open" capital B shows a frank, outspoken nature. Compared to an assumed modesty in Franklin's abbreviated "Benj" with its offsetting curlicue, the "Benj" of Benjamin Harrison is totally unassuming and therefore more genuine.*

In contrast, there is self-importance in the ornate capital H. The isolated capitals show strong independence, the "r's" of the printed type give power of expression, and the spacing between the letters indicates good judgment of human nature. Harrison had such qualities, for he was speaker of the Virginia legislature for five years and was three times elected governor of the state.

The final flourish gives further contrast to the first and last names, thereby denoting pride to the extent of great egotism where family is concerned, judging from the way it carries beneath the name, then finishes with an extended sweep, as though leaving it for future generations to tell.

If any man had a right to such opinions that man was Benjamin Harrison, for both his son and his great-grandson were elected to the Presidency of the United States.

As a striking comparison in handwriting analysis, here we have exactly the same name, even to the abbreviation of "Benj" for "Benjamin," in the signature of Benjamin Harrison, twenty-third President of the United States and the great-grandson of the signer of the Declaration of Independence.

Here, again, there is frankness in the open B, but the narrow H shows a retiring disposition. The abbreviated "Benj" with its open "j" could show the acceptance of tradition.

The real contrast begins with the connected capitals, showing cooperative effort rather than independent action. All the letters, including the names, are connected, emphasizing a positive, decisive nature. The ending is emphatic, signifying a fulfillment with its very slight downward slant. The angular writing symbolizes leadership and the "printed" r's carry the same power of expression shown by the earlier Benjamin Harrison.†

* The abbreviated "Benj" though commonly used, was not universal at the time and might even be regarded as an affectation, particularly in Franklin's case. Another signer, Benjamin Rush, a noted physician, used his full first name.

† The similarity in "r's" was not a family trait, for William Henry Harrison, son of the early Benjamin and grandfather of the later, used a conventionally rounded "r" in his signature.

Considering the signatures of other famous persons, we have:

Here there is a mingling, running from simple E, through printed A, to somewhat ornate P. These in themselves show both a versatile and indecisive temperament. The simple capital denotes a well-developed mind, definitely artistic, from the printed capital, and inclined to elaboration, from the ornate capital, which also indicates a wavering between self-importance and an inferiority complex.

The dipping "g" shows a fanciful mood; the disconnected letters, a flow of thought with inspirational moods, with enough gaps to denote a poetic trend. The upright writing shows an analytical mind, with indifference to surroundings, a creature of whim or of the moment, considering the corroborative signs.

Most remarkable is the flourish, complex, enigmatic, as though propounding a knotty problem, tangling the viewer, and then leaving him nowhere, with a final hook resembling a question mark. Typical of Poe, the father of the modern detective story. But this is in complete contrast to Franklin's intricate but traceable flourish that ended in a neatly connected link that denoted a satisfactory completion of whatever was at hand.

This is the signature of Benjamin Disraeli, after he became Earl of Beaconsfield. The high, distinctive letter B shows pride with a strongly individualistic nature. There is exactitude in the small letters, and their connected form shows energy and purpose, with a dash of ostentation or extravagance in the extension of the final letter.

Ambition is shown in the forward slant, indicating that Disraeli was still looking toward the future. Most graphic, however, is the line beneath. It combines the guarded nature of a strong statesman with the flowing curves of the literary skill for which Disraeli was also famous. It gives the impression of a firmness which is not inflexible.

8
Numerology

Although numerology has gained most of its present popularity within comparatively recent years, it is actually one of the oldest of the psychic sciences. In a sense, numbers form a language in themselves. Primitive tribes understand their meaning and communicate in terms of numbers. Among ancient alphabets, numerical values were ascribed or assigned to certain letters, giving them a special significance.

As one authority succinctly puts it:

"Every number has a certain power which is not expressed by the figure or symbol employed to denote quantity only. This power rests in an occult connection existing between the relations of things and the principles in nature of which they are the expressions."

Rather than delve into the intricacies of cabalistic cosmology and its esoteric doctrines, modern numerologists prefer a simplified numerical and alphabetical code, based upon the theories established by Pythagoras, the famous Greek mathematician and mystic, who rose to fame about the year 550 B.C.

Attributed to Pythagoras is the statement, "The world is built upon the power of numbers," and in keeping with that theory he and his followers reduced the universal numerals to the figures 1 to 9 inclusive, as the primary numbers from which all others may be formed.

These, as listed some twenty centuries later, by the famous Cornelius Agrippa in his *Occult Philosophy*, which appeared in A.D. 1533, possess the following significations:

1 is the number of purpose, evidenced by aggression, action, and ambition, all beginning with "A," the first letter of the alphabet. Straight as an arrow, its aim is to acquire fame or to rule by might.

2 is a number of antithesis, with such extremes as day and night. It stands for balance as well as contrast, and maintains its equilibrium through an admixture of positive and negative qualities.

3 shows versatility, as symbolized by the triangle, which represents past, present, and future. It combines talent with gaiety, making it the most adaptable of numbers.

4 stands for steadiness and endurance. Its solidity is represented by the square, the points of the compass, the seasons of the year, and the ancient elements of fire, water, air, and earth. It is the most primitive of numbers.

5 symbolizes adventure, attaining its ultimate through travel and experience. Its lack of stability may produce uncertainty, but it is the keystone of the group and therefore is the luckiest though most unpredictable of numbers.

6 is the symbol of dependability. It is in harmony with nature, representing the six colors of the rainbow. It is the perfect number, being divisible both by 2, an even number, and 3, an odd number, thus combining basic elements of each.

7 symbolizes mystery, with study and knowledge as its ways of exploring the unknown and the unseen. It represents the seven governing planets, the seven days of the week, and the seven notes of the scale. It combines the unity of 1 with the perfection of 6 to form a symmetry of its own, making it the truly psychic number.

8 is the number of material success. It stands for solidity carried to completion, as represented by a double square. When halved, its parts are equal (4 and 4). When halved again, its parts are still equal (2, 2, 2, 2), showing a fourfold balance.

9 is the symbol of universal achievement, the greatest of all primary numbers. It combines features of the entire group, making it their controlling factor, if developed to the full. As 3 times the number 3, the number 9 turns versatility into inspiration.

Various systems have been devised to reduce large numbers to one of these primaries. The simplest, as well as the most popular of modern numerological methods is to add the figures of the number; then, if they total 10 or more, to add those figures. This process is continued until a primary number (1 to 9) is obtained.

As a simple example, the number 125 would be treated as $1 + 2 + 5 = 8$. Thus 8 would represent the vibratory symbol for 125.

Take the "number of the beast" in the Book of Revelation; namely, 666. It adds to $6 + 6 + 6 = 18$. In their turn, the figures $1 + 8 = 9$. This is a very appropriate vibration, considering the universal influence represented by the number 9.

A more complex example is the number 684371. This adds to $6 +$

$8 + 4 + 3 + 7 + 1 = 29.$ $2 + 9 = 11.$ $1 + 1 = 2.$ So 2 becomes the vibratory symbol.

It should be mentioned here that many modern students of numerology regard the numbers 11 and 22 as having special significance of their own. Thus a number like the one just given would be checked first for qualities expressed by 11; then it would be finally considered as number 2.

In contrast, a number like 312563, which adds to $3 + 1 + 2 + 5 + 6 + 3 = 20.$ Here, $2 + 0 = 2,$ which becomes the vibratory symbol. But the influence of number 11 is not encountered during this reduction.

Similarly, a number reducing to 22 and then to 4 $(2 + 2)$ would be studied first as 22 and then as 4; whereas a total of 13 would also reduce to 4 $(1 + 3)$ as would 31 $(3 + 1)$, but neither of these would have any vibratory significance other than that represented by the final number 4.

Dates and Vital Numbers

Dates can be reduced to vibratory numbers by adding the day of the month, the number of the month (as January, 1; February, 2; and so on through December, 12) and finally, the figures composing the year.

As an example, July 4, 1776, the day on which the Declaration of Independence was signed:

Here we have the fourth day (4) of the seventh month (7) in the year 1776. The figures are 4 - 7 - 1776. Added, $4 + 7 + 1 + 7 + 7 + 6 = 32$. Further addition, $3 + 2 = 5$.

No numerical vibration could be more expressive of the hazard and uncertainty that went with the signing of that momentous document. The risk assumed by all the persons involved, as well as the launching of a new ship of state upon uncharted waters from which there could be no return, reflected to full degree the number 5, symbol of adventure.

Many other important dates of history lend themselves to such numerological interpretation. Whether they are propitious or ominous depends to a strong degree upon the attendant circumstances, as well as the underlying urge. As proof of this, we have the direct antithesis to the example just given; namely:

November 11, 1918, the day on which the Armistice was signed, ending the actual or immediate fighting in World War I.

The eleventh day $(1 + 1)$ of the eleventh month $(1 + 1)$ in the year 1918 (1, 9, 1, 8) add to: $1 + 1 + 1 + 1 + 1 + 9 + 1 + 8 = 23$. Further addition, $2 + 3 = 5$.

Again, hazard and uncertainty were the factors. But instead of treating the armistice as a step toward final and greater victory, it was accepted as the basis for a makeshift peace. As such, it fell prey to all the insecurity found in the vibration of number 5.

Fascinating though this study of memorable dates may be, the chief concern of numerology is in terms of the individual being; how each person may be affected by the vibratory influences attributed to numbers and how he or she can use them most to advantage. Certain dates harmonize with the individual's own vibratory numbers.

Of these, the simplest is:

THE BIRTH NUMBER

This is obtained like any important date, by adding the figures of the month (as given below) to those of the day and year, thus reducing a person's birthday to its vibratory number.

January	— 1	May	— 5	September	— 9
February	— 2	June	— 6	October	(10)— 1 (1 + 0)
March	— 3	July	— 7	November	(11)— 2 (1 + 1)
April	— 4	August	— 8	December	(12)— 3 (1 + 2)

Thus, a person born on March 12, 1957, would add the figures of 3 - 12 - 1957; namely, $3 + 1 + 2 + 1 + 9 + 5 + 7 = 28$. $2 + 8 = 10$. $1 + 0 = 1$. This produces 1 as the person's birth number.

The birth number is unalterable and therefore holds a fixed position in a person's life. It represents the vibratory influence existing at the time of birth. However, the extent to which it may shape an individual's character or govern his future depends upon other numerological factors that will be discussed.

In theory, two persons having the same birth number should be similar in many respects and in some cases almost identical, but it seldom works out that precisely. Rather, the birth number simply reveals a person's inherent traits in relation to controlling conditions, which serve as guiding factors rather than ruling forces.

In a primitive society, where wants are few and purposes lacking, the birth number might predominate; but in civilized company, its importance is generally lessened and may become little more than an underlying trend in relationship to the higher development expressed in the more complex phases of numerology.

Still, for that very reason, the birth number is of prime importance, as the person who goes against its natural inclinations will be handicapped in further fields of expression, such as those that are found in:

THE NAME NUMBER

In numerology, every name has a vibratory number, obtained by translating the letters of the name into figures, then adding their totals and reducing them to primary numbers, as already described. The name number, as an expression of a person's developed personality and a key to ambition or achievement, should either blend with the birth number or be geared to it.

In short, natural inclinations or influences are important in the development of both an outward and dynamic personality, so that a name, as it gains fame or recognition, will express the full force and true character that it represents in the public mind.

There are many fascinating facts to this phase of numerology, with many promising prospects for individual attainment, provided the rules are recognized and followed. The first step, of course, is to find the number represented by the name.

This is done with:

THE FIGURE ALPHABET

1	2	3	4	5	6	7	8	9
A	B	C	D	E	F	G	H	I
J	K	L	M	N	O	P	Q	R
S	T	U	V	W	X	Y	Z	

Actually, this is merely a listing of the letters in numerical order: A, 1; B, 2; C, 3, and so on up to Z, 26, which becomes 8 when its figures are added. (2 + 6 = 8)

By reference to the chart, any name can be transcribed into figures, letter by letter. When added, the totals can be reduced to the primary number representing the name vibration.

As an example: The name *George Washington*

$$G \quad E \quad O \quad R \quad G \quad E$$
$$7 + 5 + 6 + 9 + 7 + 5 \quad = \quad 39$$

$$W \quad A \quad S \quad H \quad I \quad N \quad G \quad T \quad O \quad N$$
$$5 + 1 + 1 + 8 + 9 + 5 + 7 + 2 + 6 + 5 \quad = \quad 49$$

Total	88
Reduced 8 + 8 =	16
Reduced 1 + 6 =	7
Name Number	7

In the case of a famous personage like George Washington, the name itself creates a strong impression. Enough facts are known about him to analyze his life and career in terms of 7 as a name vibration. This will be covered in the discussion of the meaning of the numbers, which follows.

But with an unknown name, only the vibration registers. It impresses itself upon people who hear the person's name; but if the person himself fails to come up to expectations, or his traits prove at variance with that vibratory message, the result is a disappointment or a total blank. That person, numerologically speaking, would do better with a name more suited either to his nature or to the impression which he is trying to convey to the world at large.

To the old question, "What's in a name?" the long-experienced numerologist will reply, "Much, much more than you suppose." He might even phrase his answer with the well-known quote: "There are more things in heaven and earth, Horatio, than are dreamt of in your philosophy." For here, the accent would be on the name Horatio, which adds up as follows:

$$H \quad O \quad R \quad A \quad T \quad I \quad O$$
$$8 + 6 + 9 + 1 + 2 + 9 + 6 \quad = \quad 41$$
$$\text{Reduced: } 4 + 1 \quad = \quad 5$$

And 5, as already mentioned, is the number of uncertainty, adventure, even the incredible, just the thing to overwhelm anyone with a number 5 vibration, who would naturally be skeptical until flattened with evidence to the contrary.

This raises the question: Are first, or given names, significant in themselves, from the numerological standpoint? The answer is: Normally, no. They are of importance chiefly as a component of the entire name. A name number of 7, composed of 3 + 4, has shadings, so to speak, that differ from a name number of 7 that is composed of 1 and 6. These may be studied to a nicety; but they both add up to number 7.

But in the case of a name like Horatio, or any other character, real or imaginary, who is known by a single name or title, that one name can stand as the mark of the individual.

The same applies to stage names, pen names, and the like. Often, these become the true vibrational expression of a personality that would otherwise be lost. Alterations, changes in a name; the use of an initial, or the act of dropping it, can have much to do with success or failure, so numerologists claim.

So, before delving deeply in such details, let us consider the meaning of the numbers 1 to 9, in regard to both the birth number and the name number, as given in the charts that follow.

Number One
And What It Signifies

As a birth number, 1 shows a driving, strong-willed nature that must be centered on a positive goal. People of this type dislike complexities and should avoid them; otherwise, their efforts will be scattered and their path strewn with pitfalls. This number is a good one,

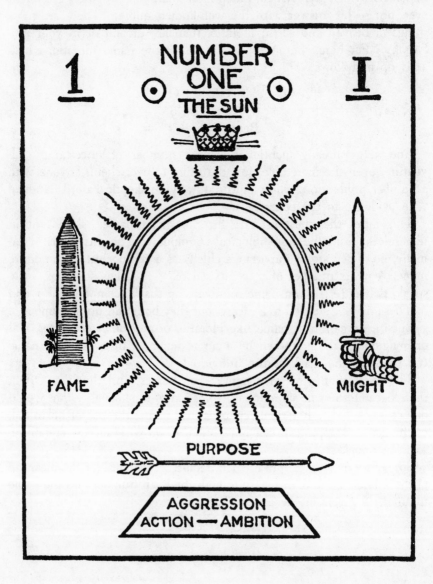

but it must be pointed in the right direction, or it may soar high but may fall low, meeting with ultimate disaster.

Once having set a right course, a person with birth number 1 should follow it, even if lesser aims and possible ambitions must be sacrificed. They should never change course or try to jump too far ahead, as persons with this vibration can rise to new and greater attainments only in a direct, progressive fashion.

Since number 1 is the symbol of the ego, such persons can become both selfish and self-willed. So they should be careful not to let their own interests conflict with those of others, or they will lose friends and make enemies instead. Forceful and untiring, number 1 as a birth number promises much, if well controlled and directed into channels that offer high development.

As a name number, 1 denotes a person filled with vigor and desire for action, but more suited to meeting immediate situations than planning far ahead. Such persons should give full time to any work or activity, avoiding anything of a speculative nature. Even lending their names to long-range projects is a mistake, as persons of the number 1 type are generally the ones to be called upon to deliver; and the first to be blamed when they can't, even though someone else may be at fault.

Persons with name number 1 should take the best opportunity that offers and then stick to it, in the confidence that they will open the path to bigger things through that very policy. Courage and self-reliance go with name number 1, but it signifies a nature that is more imitative than creative. These people often make money, but are apt to spend it just as freely. They should avoid making hasty decisions under the urge or excitement of the moment.

Number Two
And What It Signifies

As a birth number, 2 reveals a kindly, tactful nature, yet one given to gloom as well as happy moods. This is due to a desire for balance, inherent in this vibration. Persons with 2 as a birth number often recognize both sides of a question to such degree that they shift back and forth, never reaching a true or satisfactory decision.

This drives them to extremes, in the false hope of equalizing matters. Consequently, they exaggerate things and argue against themselves. The very sense of judgment that enables them to give good advice to

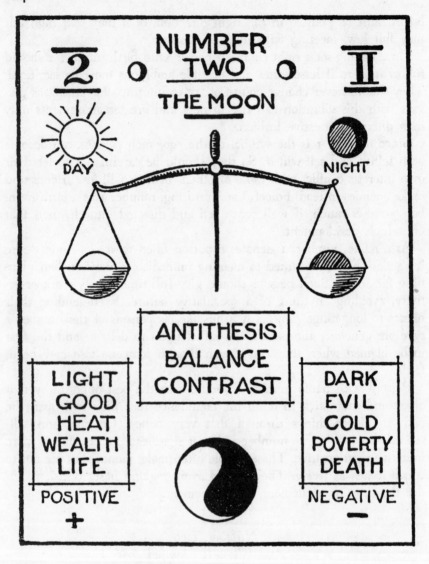

friends prevents them from making up their own minds regarding their own affairs. Sometimes they may do better to be wrong than right, if only for the satisfaction of coming to a quick decision.

Persons with birth number 2 should accept conditions as they are and try to adjust themselves to such conditions, rather than attempt to shape those conditions to their own desire. They should avoid extremes and any indecision. Their great fault is overgenerosity. They should give the same thought to themselves that they give to others.

As a name number, 2 reflects a quiet power of judgment. It marks a person as a good planner, or adviser, but without the power to execute. Anyone with this name vibration should seek associates who can carry out plans in a proper, helpful way. The judgment represented by name number 2 should be used in choosing such associates. Never should the choice be governed by sentiment. Indulgence toward others is the fault of number 2.

This name number shows a changeable disposition that can become emotional and restless to the point of complete uncertainty or outright fanaticism. The best advice for persons with name number 2 is to avoid all worry over small matters or minor actions. They should make the most of their agreeable, friendly qualifications and never indulge in argument.

With the right friends and associates, they will then go far. Otherwise, their spirit of fair play will shift to the opposite extreme of spite, bringing misery to themselves as well as others.

Number Three
And What It Signifies

As a birth number, 3 is one of the quickest to disclose its traits. It shows a keen, intuitive mind, with the ability to learn things rapidly, often at an early age. Many persons with this birth vibration are highly talented, but fail to use their ability to advantage. Being adaptable and capable in many ways, they are apt to give up their best prospects for something easier or more immediately profitable.

Persons with this birth number are often so free from worry that they fail to take life seriously. They like pleasant surroundings, interesting people, and good fun. Hence, their tendency is to think only of the present and let the future take care of itself. Their problem is to make the most of things that they have started, rather than let other people reap the profit of their original ideas.

This birth number shows an aptitude for doing the right thing at the right time, so the proper plan is to make the most of every opportunity, avoiding the neglect that will later mean regret.

As a name number, 3 shows ability in many lines, plus a confidence that adds to competence. Given a right start, anyone with this name vibration should go far. But this name number also shows impatience with small or trivial things. A new job or quick advancement may lure

such a person away from the less attractive path that leads to greater opportunity, where long-range planning is concerned.

Arts, sciences, sports, anything involving quick thinking or intuition, all are natural outlets for persons who fulfill the qualifications attributed to name number 3. If they accept advice or exercise good judgment in choosing a calling or planning a career, they may soon find themselves on the path to fame as well as fortune.

Number Four
And What It Signifies

As a birth number, 4 stands for a steady, plodding nature, which always favors caution rather than risk. Though persons with this vibration may be able to grasp new ideas quickly, they usually prefer to study them out. To have a thing right is of prime importance to anyone with the solid way of thinking represented by number 4.

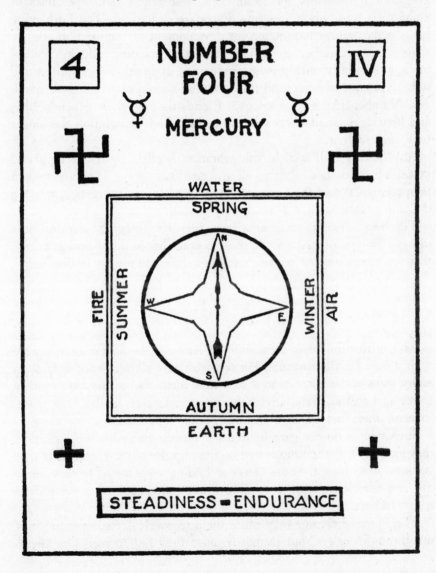

Honesty and reliability are normal attributes with this birth number, but they hinge upon the satisfaction or security that the individual may gain from patience and perseverance. If frustrated, the number 4 nature can denote the schemer rather than the plodder. Reduced to small opportunities, a person with this vibration may begin to think in small terms, too, so that number 4 can become the symbol of poverty and defeat.

Oddly, however, this birth number is coming more into its own with the modern demands for technicians, researchers, and specialists of many sorts from whom exacting duties are demanded. The birth number 4 makes a firm foundation for development of acquired abilities.

As a name number, 4 signifies success in scientific and mechanical fields, particularly with growing industries. It stands for steadiness and stability, hence persons with this vibration should cultivate those qualities. Number 4 persons often gain friends through their dependability; and honest, constant effort will bring them high recognition the longer they stay with it.

Any lack of brilliance in this vibration is offset by its strength and power of endurance. Persons of the true number 4 type are seldom temperamental and they are extremely good in an emergency, treating difficult situations in a normal, easy manner.

The best advice to number 4 is to keep on plugging, learning new things all the while. Above all, these people should never underestimate their own importance, for their strong qualities are always in demand.

Number Five
And What It Signifies

As a birth number, 5 represents an enthusiastic, adventurous nature with a flare for the unusual. Persons with this vibration are capable in many ways and are quick to accept new ideas. Often they are fond of travel and feel at home anywhere, even in foreign lands. As a result, some of them are quick at learning other languages.

Such people do not care for routine duties; and with this vibration, they are apt to do the unexpected on the impulse of the moment. If they get into difficulties, they are clever at finding ways out. They are versatile and vivacious, with a genuine interest in people that wins them many friends.

Their love of change may cause them to overlook real opportunities, not through neglect, but simply because they fail to recognize imme-

NUMBER FIVE

—

JUPITER

♃   ♃

ADVENTURE
TRAVEL – EXPERIENCE

diate possibilities. Always, they are looking ahead to something else, rather than what lies at hand.

As a name number, 5 shows independence of thought as well as action. It reveals a preference of learning from actual experience, rather than from the advice of other people. This may mean setbacks and even misfortune; but persons with this vibration are recuperative and usually make up their losses.

By curbing their restless trend and getting down to steady work, such persons can increase their chances of success. But their names literally vibrate the spirit of adventure; without it, they feel lost. If they can apply that dash to their daily work, so that their jobs and surroundings are dramatic, with promise of the unexpected, they may gain real results.

However, it is hard to pin them down, for the name number 5 denotes the speculator as well as the adventurer. Often, it has been a lucky star for those who are governed by its glint. But it is always unpredictable, so persons with this vibration should not tax their luck too far—or too often!

Number Six
And What It Signifies

As a birth number, 6 stands unsurpassed. People with this vibration are usually honest, sincere, and reliable. They are also progressive, yet anxious to establish themselves and to gain respect and good will. Consequently they tend to be tolerant in nature, always eager to promote harmony among their friends and to improve conditions around them.

Persons of this type are cheerful, optimistic, and fond of the finer things in life, which they are usually willing to share. They are often called upon to fill positions of trust; and in such capacity, they generally come up to expectations and more. If they do not find fame, it is often because they become satisfied with what they have, so they do not push on to higher pinnacles.

Their danger is complacency and self-satisfaction. Being so impartial, they may set themselves up as judges, and may even be swayed by false ideals. Such superiority lessens their natural sympathy and makes them seem hypocritical.

As a name number, 6 promises success in all undertakings, provided that they are conducted in a way that creates confidence. People with this name vibration have a way of attracting followers as well as customers. They can become important to their community, as they are usually popular both socially and politically. But to achieve such aims, they must live up to their reputation.

Persons with this name number never have to be too radical in their methods. But whatever they promise, they should be able and ready to fulfill. They will find that their friends and the public take their word

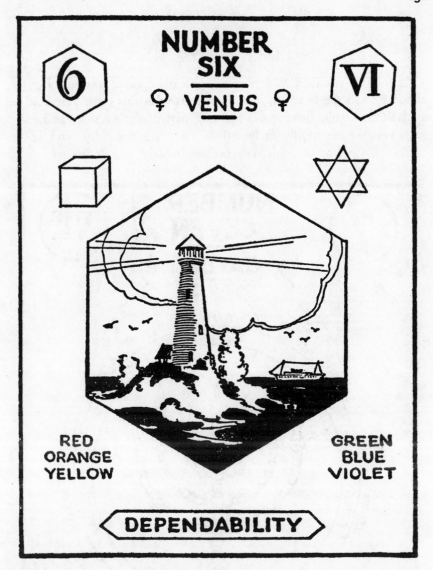

NUMBER SIX
♀ VENUS ♀

6   VI

RED
ORANGE
YELLOW

GREEN
BLUE
VIOLET

‹ DEPENDABILITY ›

as their bond, due perhaps to the subtle impression that this name vibration conveys. They will find that integrity is more productive than ambition and that honest effort will bring its own reward.

Through kindly action, these persons will attain their goals without radical methods or desire for immediate gain. They should remember that such results are cumulative; then they can go on to greater things.

Number Seven
And What It Signifies

As a birth number, 7 denotes a scholarly, poetic nature, often inclined toward the fanciful, though persons with this birth vibration are analytical as well. Intuition is a strong part of their nature and many such persons are highly imaginative. They are naturally fond of the mysterious and as a result may become moody and depressed.

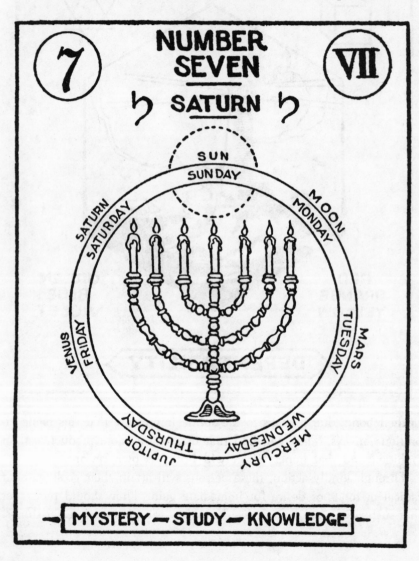

Solitude often inspires these people, but obscurity disheartens them, for they are apt to blame the world, rather than themselves, for their failure to gain prominence. This draws them into deeper despondency, to the point where they may refuse to mingle in the ordinary affairs of life. Though capable of solving intricate problems, they seldom really understand themselves.

Composers, musicians, students, philosophers, and outright mystics are nurtured by this birth number; and often they seek solace in such pursuits. But to be really happy, a number 7 person must become a part of this world, rather than seeking to be completely out of it.

As a name number, 7 has grand possibilities. A person with that name vibration can bend his natural talents to art, science, and philosophy, often attaining greatness in a chosen field. They may rise to dramatic heights, but should remember that their success will depend upon quiet planning and may often require deep meditation.

Gloomy thoughts, impractical dreaming, are a weakness of this name vibration. Therefore, such persons should devote effort to purposes that are possible of attainment, for there they can often go beyond all normal expectation, turning their intuition and imagination to great advantage.

Persons with this name number can become leaders and teachers of high order, for they possess deep understanding of others and thereby inspire loyalty. They will need the help of such persons to gain commercial success or financial independence, for these are not found in the vibration of number 7.

Number Eight
And What It Signifies

As a birth number, 8 means business. It is the token of the steady builder, who can go far in this age of vast commercial and industrial development. It symbolizes persons who put plans into execution, complete them, and then go on to something still bigger.

This vibration shows a person with a strong, forceful nature, who will demand and get the most from others. Opposition does not stop them; instead, it urges them on to greater effort. Persons with this birth number have embarked upon great military and political careers, because executive ability is needed in those fields as much as in the business world.

In social life, persons with this vibration are apt to judge friends by

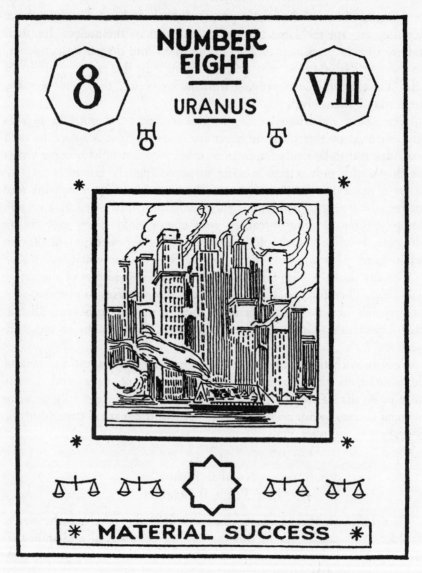

NUMBER
EIGHT
—
URANUS

8

VIII

MATERIAL SUCCESS

wealth and success, setting those as their standards. The more costly a thing may be, the more they admire it. In their quest for wealth and power they may be ruthless with rivals and subordinates; but at the same time, they often carry other persons along with them. So it is extremely wise to get on the good side of a number eighter—if you can find it!

As a name number, 8 spells Success with dollar marks ($UCCE$$).

It thrives on progress and activity. People subconsciously expect big results from a person whose name is tuned to this powerful vibration.

Persons with this name number should constantly build for bigger things, but always with good materials. When they have achieved an aim, they should continue on to another, for with them, easing up may mean slipping back. Often, they can pick up old or neglected enterprises and turn them to advantage and profit, but they should first make sure that the opportunity is there.

The weakness with this name number lies in petty jealousies, wasted efforts, indulgence in small things, when large opportunities are available. Think big, act big, and you will be big, if you have name number 8!

Number Nine
And What It Signifies

As a birth number, 9 combines influence with intellect. It should show a powerful personality, capable of high development. Like 8, number 9 promises success, but through artistic ability or creative channels, rather than the mundane fields of commerce and industry.

Persons who possess the wonderful, sometimes magnetic qualities of this vibration should centralize them and apply them in a practical way. If they manage that, their success may be unbounded. Their problem often is to recognize their own talents and to choose the course to follow.

Art, music, skill, inventive ability, all are found with number 9. Its only limits are the capability and desire of the individual person. Those two factors should be tuned and blended. Then, by summing his talents, a person with this birth number can set his goal, rather than shooting beyond his limit.

As a name number, 9 calls for a person to apply himself to high and honorable achievements, bringing out the best of his natural traits or talents. Such people must avoid drudgery and drab surroundings, as these things stifle the ambition that their name vibration represents.

Persons with this name number often can influence other people and guide them, so they should do this wisely and well. They must constantly be fair-minded and live up to the ideals that they express. They should never resort to petty tactics or behave out of character. Once they do, their whole strength is lost, and with it the confidence and respect that they created.

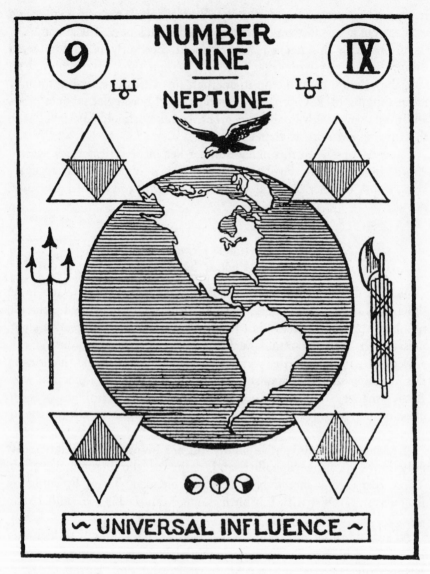

NUMBER NINE
NEPTUNE

~ UNIVERSAL INFLUENCE ~

Since this name number symbolizes power, a person having it should never demand more than his share. Pride, arrogance, and self-interest can prove serious pitfalls. The understanding of other people, recognizing their merits and desires is important to anyone with this name number, for it will then truly express the universal influence it represents.

Numbers Eleven and Twenty-two

Ardent students of numerology often delve into the meanings of numbers higher than the primaries 1 to 9. Some give special attention to the numbers 10 to 22, as represented by the letters of the Hebrew alphabet, a method also applied to the reading of the tarot cards, as described in another section.

Still higher numbers have been given special interpretations according to the Pythagorean system; but, as one authority aptly states the case, it is the unit value which is finally significant, even though the gross value is of some consideration.

The general theory among more practical numerologists is that any difference between two numbers such as 15 and 24 can be regarded as mere shadings, that are overshadowed by the stronger power of 6, the primary number to which both reduce. The same would apply to higher totals, as 33, 42, 51, and so on, under the Pythagorean system. All resolve into the number 6, which is the ultimate vibration, all-inclusive of the rest.

Exceptions are made with numbers 11 and 22 for a very definite reason. Number 11 reduces to number 2, which is both a symbol of balance and of contrast, making it very changeable, one way or the other. Hence the vibratory influence of 11, rather than merely being absorbed by the fluctuating number 2, is apt to become either a controlling or a deciding factor.

Similarly, number 22, in reducing to number 4, superimposes a strong though eccentric activity upon a solid base, thus changing the accepted standards of routine commonly found in the number 4 vibration. Or, to put it another way, number 22 contains elements which are not generally assimilated by number 4 and therefore may still function.

The special meanings of numbers 11 and 22 follow:

SIGNIFICANCE OF NUMBER 11

As a birth number, 11 shows initiative generally lacking in the number 2 vibration to which it reduces. It is forceful enough to end the indecision of number 2; but its influence is not too apparent in the case of the birth number.

As a name number, 11 adds determination, power, and vitality to the judgment represented by name number 2. Frequently, the quiet-mannered, self-contained number 2 personality will rise to inspired heights, achieving the seemingly impossible under the vibratory influence of 11.

This may often be traced to long, steady planning of the number 2 type, culminating in a much-desired achievement. Accordingly, it may be spasmodic, as the person thus activated may revert to number 2 form and rest content with the laurels gained. New, quiet preparation is needed to rouse the fiery spirit of 11 once again; and by then, over-caution or self-sufficiency of number 2 may curb new activity of 11.

SIGNIFICANCE OF NUMBER 22

As a birth number, 22 lends a touch of mysticism to the steady nature of number 4. Persons of this type may develop an inner life which causes them to ignore outward things. Whether this is to their benefit or disadvantage depends chiefly upon the individual concerned. Often, this is not too apparent with the birth number.

As a name number, 22 may waver between eccentricity and genius. If persons of this vibration develop the mechanical, somewhat inventive skill that is sometimes found in number 4, they are apt to turn it to fields that are unexplained or unexplored. This is the influence of number 22, but it seldom outgrows the methodical, plodding, and sometimes exacting demands of number 4.

Conflict of desires and goals must be avoided or curbed by persons swayed or tuned to this vibration. They must temper desire for fame or importance with solid effort and practical results. Otherwise they may overvalue their ability or their ideas and meet with difficulties and failure.

How to Analyze the Vital Factors in the Vibratory Numbers

Of the various methods used in analyzing individual traits through numerology, the following procedure is one of the simplest and best:

The birth number is first considered as representing the person's natural characteristics. It is formed from the figures of the birth date and is the *number of personality*.

The name number is taken next, to indicate developed traits. In early life, the full name is generally considered; but this is supplanted by the name as regularly used. This is the *number of development*.

If the name number continues in that form, its importance increases in terms of the person's career. If it is radically changed, or a pen name or stage name is taken in its stead, the new name is the one on which the later reckoning is based. In either case, whether the old name or a new one becomes all-important, it is known as the *number of attainment.*

Note that in many instances the person's original name becomes both his early number of development and his final number of attainment, without any change whatever. In other cases, the adding or dropping of a mere initial may cause an appreciable difference between the two.

From either name, but preferably the one finally chosen, added data can be gained from:

The vowel vibration, which is obtained by adding the numerical value of the vowels in a person's name and reducing them to a primary number. This is the *number of underlying influence.*

The frequency number, which applies only when a number recurs very often in a name and predominates strongly over the others. This is the *number of added influence.*

Examples of Numerological Analysis

Famous names have been taken for numerological analysis in the examples that follow. This makes it possible to check the numerological findings against known facts. Several instances of name changes are included, with sidelights on their correct interpretation.

One fact relating to birth and name numbers has been stressed by many numerologists and is worthy of note throughout. It is this: When the birth number is higher than the name number, a person is apt to follow his basic trends and therefore may meet with difficulties in developing the features of his name, or its expressed vibration.

In contrast, if the name number is higher than the birth number, the ambitions or purposes expressed by the name number have a strong tendency to predominate, so that natural traits and tendencies of the individual are directed toward circumstances of his own choice. His tendency is to establish conditions, rather than be governed by them.

Any person having the same birth number and name number is likely to develop an even, harmonious disposition, capable of taking all things in easy stride, but this is not especially desirable. Such balance is seldom found in the birth and name numbers of famous personages;

hence the net result of such harmonious numbers may be comparative obscurity.

Examples of analysis follow:

GEORGE WASHINGTON. Born February 22, 1732.

Birth number: 1 (2 + 2 + 2 + 1 + 7 + 3 + 2 = 19. 1 + 9 = 10. 1 + 0 = 1.).

```
7 5 6 9 7 5   5 1 1 8 9 5 7 2 6 5   Total: 88 = 16 = 7.
G E O R G E   W A S H I N G T O N
5 6     5       1       9       6     Vowels: 32 = 5.
```

Name number: 7 (both development and attainment).
Vowel vibration: 5. Frequency number: 5.

The birth number 1 clearly shows the personality of George Washington. As a boy, he was a surveyor; he became a military hero; then took up the life of a planter, only to answer the call to head the Continental Army. After that, he became the first President of the United States.

The name number 7, representing both development and attainment, also expresses Washington's career. Intuition of the highest sort is coupled with the idealism of this vibration. Washington bore a charmed life and his skill in the face of adversity was unequaled. He was everything that this Stoical, often mystical vibration implies.

The vowel vibration 5 shows the underlying influence of adventure in Washington's life. The frequency number 5 is noticeably apparent, appearing five times in the sixteen letters of Washington's name, so its added influence strengthens the adventurous vibration, offsetting its uncertainty.

HENRY FORD. Born July 30, 1863.

Birth number: 1 (7 + 3 + 1 + 8 + 6 + 3 = 28. 2 + 8 = 10. 1 + 0 = 1.).

```
8 5 5 9 7   6 6 9 4   Total: 59 = 14 = 5.
H E N R Y   F O R D
5     7       6         Vowels: 18 = 9.
```

Name number: 5. Vowel vibration: 9.

The birth number 1 shows the single, definite purpose in the career of Henry Ford. He gained mechanical knowledge and the ability to apply it in a practical way. Near the age of forty he saw the public need for a low-priced automobile and proceeded to fill it in a direct, productive fashion. He kept to that one purpose, always a step ahead in the expanding industry which won him fortune.

The name number 5 shows willingness to speculate along new and radical lines. Ford accepted uncertainty as the keynote in the changing world and its demands. Through his unity of purpose, he handled issues as he met them, turning the unexpected into reality. His commercial career became an adventure story in itself.

The vowel vibration 9 shows the underlying influence that promised Ford's vast success. High achievement, living up to expressed ideals, with confidence in the final result, are factors that 9 represents.

MARK TWAIN. Born November 30, 1835.
Birth number: 4 (1 + 1 + 3 + 1 + 8 + 3 + 5 = 22. 2 + 2 = 4.).
　　Higher vibration: 22.
Original Name: Samuel Langhorne Clemens.

```
1  1 4 3 5 3   3 1 5 7 8 6 9 5 5   3 3 5 4 5 5 1
S  A M U E L   L A N G H O R N E   C L E M E N S
1    3 5       1       6     5         5   5
```

　　　　　　　　　　　　　　　　　　Total: 92 = 11 = 2.
　　　　　　　　　　　　　　　　　　Vowels: 31 = 4.

Name number: 2.　Higher vibration: 11.
Vowel vibration: 4.　Frequency numbers: 5; also 3 and 1.

The birth number 4 shows the plodding nature that characterized Mark Twain from boyhood up. Despite his varied interests, his fame as a humorist, he was a hard worker who found life a grim struggle. Always, when faced with difficulties, it was through hard work that he won out.

The higher vibration of 22 played a hand in this, however. It shows the eccentricity of genius, the touch of mysticism in their budding forms. With the birth number, these are usually slight and sometimes unnoticeable, but in this case they are more marked, because:

The name number 2 not only injected indecision into the drudgery of the birth number 4; it also brought out a higher vibration of 11, which coupled initiative to imagination, yet could not overcome the peculiar practicality of that birth number 4 with its overtone of 22.

The vowel vibration 4 only stressed the plodding traits of the youthful Mark Twain, keeping him within the bounds of boyhood surroundings, which he peopled with fantastic dreams that ignored all outward things except the river steamboats that plodded the Mississippi in the true methodical style of number 4.

The frequency number 5 added a desire for adventure; and the noticeable frequency of 3 showed versatility, while there was enough frequency of 1 to supply immediate purpose.

In short, from the standpoint of numerology, it was inevitable that a youth with such complex vibrations fraught with both overtones and undertones, would take the short way out of his drab surroundings and seek adventure and importance in the most practical form. Mark Twain did that. He became a river pilot.

How Mark Twain happened to persist in that endeavor, as well as later efforts as a prospector and then a journalist, might seem puzzling in the light of his original name. But by the time he took to the river, he had shortened it to Samuel L. Clemens. That adds up to:

```
1  1  4  3  5  3    3    3  3  5  4  5  5   1   Total: 46 = 10 = 1.
S  A  M  U  E  L    L    C  L  E  M  E  N  S
1     3  5             5     5         Vowels: 19 = 10 = 1.
```

Name number: 1 (development).
Vowel vibration: 1. Frequency numbers: 3 and 5.

Here is a combination of drive and purpose that is hard to match. The name number 1, backed with the vowel vibration 1, could certainly goad the natural plodder (4) and eccentric dreamer (22) into action that would not be natural to such a birth number. Note, too, that the frequency of 3, with its versatility, now tops the adventurous 5, though the latter is still an apparent factor.

Without the middle initial (L) the name SAMUEL CLEMENS adds up to 43, which gives the name number of 7. This would be even stronger in its urge, since the river and all the distant scenes it offered would touch on the mysterious and the desire for knowledge. But the vowel vibration would still have been number 1, providing the incentive, with 3 and 5 balanced as frequency numbers, showing skill and longing for adventure.

Whether Mark Twain used the middle initial of Samuel L. Clemens at that time is a mystery in itself; but it works out either way. It is certain, however, that he became more simply known as SAM CLEMENS during his pilot and prospector days.

This produces another set of vibrations:

1 1 4   3 3 5 4 5 5 1   Total: 32 = 5.
S A M   C L E M E N S
1   5   5   Vowels: 11 = 2.

Name number: 5 (development).
Vowel vibration: 2. Higher vibration: 11.
Frequency numbers: 1 and 3.

All the uncertainty of this period of Mark Twain's life is reflected by the name number 5. It also represented a time of indecision, as represented by the vowel vibration 2. He had plenty of initiative, shown by the higher vibration 11, with unrecognized genius. The frequency number of 1 was enough to spur him to new fields, where he showed the talent indicated by frequency 3. But these were not enough to help. The great stroke came when he changed his name to:

4 1 9 2   2 5 1 9 5   Total: 38 = 11 = 2.
M A R K   T W A I N
1   1 9   Vowel vibration: 11 = 2.

Name number: 2 (attainment). Higher vibration: 11.
Vowel vibration: 2. Higher vibration: 11.

Originally, the birth number 4, with its higher number 22, had responded to the name number of 2, with higher 11, but the vowel vibration of 4 had been a drag. The changes, too, had disadvantages (as already covered), but the final choice proved different.

The name MARK TWAIN provided a dual vibration of the number 2, each with a higher 11. It proved the perfect balance. Whichever way the balance went, determination and inspiration went with it. The birth number 4, with its higher 22, turned all this into solid, painstaking effort that found its outlet in new and productive fields. From beginnings that seemed shaped to prosaic routine or scattered misadventure, Mark Twain scaled undreamed heights as an author, lecturer, and humorist. He had the ability to concentrate a double 11 into 22; and it added up to fame just as simply as the fact that 2 + 2 = 4.

This analysis of the vibratory influences in the career of Mark Twain has been treated in detail because it illustrates so many numerological points, particularly the importance of a name and what may result when it is changed. In contrast, however, there is the case of a later humorist, almost the modern prototype of Mark Twain, whose numerological chart is simply analyzed:

WILL ROGERS. Born November 4, 1879.

Birth number: 4 ($1 + 1 + 4 + 1 + 8 + 7 + 9 = 31.$ $3 + 1 = 4.$).

5 9 3 3   9 6 7 5 9 1   Total: $57 = 12 = 3$.
W I L L   R O G E R S
· 9   6   5   Vowels: $20 = 2$.

Name number: 3.   Vowel vibration: 2.

Here, again, is the steady, plodding birth number 4, showing painstaking effort and an interest in simple things. He became a cowboy in his native Oklahoma and through arduous practice became an expert with the rope. All this fitted with the personality number 4.

The name number 3 expresses the versatility and talent which brought Will Rogers from the obscurity of the ranch to the vaudeville stage. There, his natural flare displayed itself and soon he was adding witty comments to his act, which brought him to top rank as a comedian and later as a humorist.

The vowel vibration 2 showed ability to swing from one activity to another, so that Will Rogers was equally known as an actor and a writer, finding his balance point in the lecture field. His steady 4 (birth) and talented 3 (name) were ideally suited to the balance (2) of the vowel vibration, with its underlying influence.

Note that whereas Mark Twain, both in early boyhood and in his final career, was strongly governed by the numbers 4 and 2, in his case those were represented by the higher vibrations of 11 and 22, with all their unpredictable complexities. With Will Rogers, the numbers 4 and 2 were of the simple type, free from the vagaries of 11 and 22, as a study of his career clearly shows.

Now study the numerology of a famous and remarkable writer:

RUDYARD KIPLING. Born December 30, 1865.

Birth number: 8 ($1 + 2 + 3 + 1 + 8 + 6 + 5 = 26.$ $2 + 6 = 8.$).

9 3 4 7 1 9 4   2 9 7 3 9 5 7   Total: $79 = 16 = 7$.
R U D Y A R D   K I P L I N G
3   7 1   9   9   Vowels: $29 = 11 = 2$.

Name number: 7 (development and attainment).
Vowel vibration: 2.   Higher vibration: 11.
Frequency number: 9.

The birth number 8 shows a strong, forceful nature pointed to fame and commercial success. This was true in Kipling's case, for his early writings catapulted him to fame and made his name known with them. From there, he went on to one literary triumph after another.

The name number 7 was the most appropriate possible. It expresses the vibrancy of Kipling's writings, capturing the imagination as his stories and poetry did. The name of Rudyard Kipling is fitted to his work, showing how indelibly a vibration can impress itself upon the mind.

The vowel vibration 2 reveals the balance in Kipling's work, as he was one of the few great writers who could change from verse to prose with equal facility. The flare of genius is shown by the higher vibration 11, but there was an uncertainty—the sign of 2—that became evidenced in his later writing, where the spirit of 11 was lacking, or only spasmodic.

The underlying influence of 2 and 11, as represented by the vowel vibration, was encouraged and somewhat strengthened by the frequency number 9, which furnishes the added influence representing achievement and recognition, both of which Kipling gained. The frequency of 9 is not strong, however; and with the vowel vibration 2, it showed the tendency to dwell on past accomplishments rather than the urge for new glory.

Here is a brief but illuminating analysis of another famous name:

P. T. BARNUM. Born July 5, 1810.
Birth number: $4 \ (7 + 5 + 1 + 8 + 1 = 22. \quad 2 + 2 = 4.)$.

$$
\begin{array}{ccccccc}
7 & 2 & 2 & 1 & 9 & 5 & 3 & 4 \\
\text{P.} & \text{T.} & \text{B} & \text{A} & \text{R} & \text{N} & \text{U} & \text{M} \\
 & & 1 & & & 3 & & \\
\end{array}
$$
Total: $33 = 6$.
Vowels: 4.

Name number: 6.   Vowel vibration: 4.

The birth number 4 shows a steady, plodding, solid nature that kept building to completion in a style that truly characterized Barnum's early career. Note that this is the simple 4.

The name number 6 expresses the honesty and business integrity that became Barnum's forte, the human understanding which insured his success and was reflected in charitable activities. All these made the name Barnum a household word.

The vowel vibration shows the same simple 4 as the name number, which accounted for Barnum's ability to build anew whenever he encountered reverses and thus to maintain the standing of his name.

Note that the name BARNUM adds up to 24 = 6 so that it is exactly the same without the initials P. T.; the same applies to the vowel vibration 4. It was as "Barnum" that P. T. Barnum was generally known.

Barnum's full name was PHINEAS T. BARNUM, and he used it in signing contracts, as well as in his more important enterprises. Its letters total 62, making the name number 8, symbolic of worldly fame and commercial success, while the vowels total 19 = 10, making the vowel vibration 1, exceedingly appropriate as the underlying influence in a business career that was both direct and egotistical.

But the name BARNUM, with its established 6 and plodding 4 as the underlying influence, is the vibration by which P. T. Barnum has been most clearly recognized. "Barnum was right" is a quotation that still sums human gullibility.

As an interesting contrast, here is another name that has also survived as representative of its field of endeavor:

RICHARD A. CANFIELD. Born June 17, 1855.
Birth number: 6 (6 + 1 + 7 + 1 + 8 + 5 + 5 = 33. 3 + 3 = 6.).

```
9 9 3 8  1 9 4   1   3 1 5 6 9 5 3 4   Total: 80 = 8.
R I C H A R D   A.  C A N F I E L D
9        1       1   1       9 5        Vowels: 26 = 8.
```

Name number: 8.   Name number (without middle initial): 7.
Vowel vibration: 8.   Vowel vibration (without middle initial): 7.

The birth number 6 shows a reliable, progressive nature seeking establishment, good will, and respect. As the greatest gambling operator of his day, Canfield patterned his career on that policy, attracting the most exclusive clientele and putting less scrupulous gamblers out of business.

The name number 8 is indicative of worldly success, plus a desire for private esteem, which Canfield gained from those persons who were not opposed to gambling. Here, his stress of the middle initial "A" is peculiarly appropriate. It may have been pure affectation on his part, to lend more "class" to his name; but in any case, from the standpoint of numerology, it was sound indeed.

That name number 8, doubly emphasized by the underlying influence of the vowel vibration 8, raised his status from that of the gambler to the man of big business. The elegance of his establishments in New York and Saratoga, his careful, meticulous mode of operation, were marks of the merchandiser rather than the gambling proprietor.

But to those who opposed him and most of the public who read about him, he was Richard Canfield, whose name and vowel vibrations were both 7, the symbol of the successful gambler, for only 7 could express the intuition and imagination so necessary in that field.

However, this intriguing numerological study goes still further. To his close friends and great admirers, who included some persons of high importance, he was known as Dick Canfield. To posterity, he has become simply Canfield, a name synonymous with "gambler" just as Barnum stands for "showman." In Barnum's case, dropping the initials P. T. made no difference in the name number and the vowel vibration. The same applies to Canfield, with or without the nickname Dick.

In CANFIELD, the letters total 36, which reduces to 9, while the vowels total 15, which reduces to 6. Numerologically, this signifies that the name number 9 represented high achievement in a chosen field, regardless of moral issues involved. This is a highly significant phase of 9, which may lead either to fame or infamy.

The vowel vibration 6 shows a reversion to the type expressed by the birth number 6, and Canfield's later career fulfills this conservative desire for establishment and recognition as a community figure. His gambling career over, he became an art connoisseur and a manufacturer, while his famous casino at Saratoga was turned into a historic landmark.

An exceptional example of a person known by one name only is found in the case of:

HOUDINI. Born April 6, 1874.
Birth number: 3 (4 + 6 + 1 + 8 + 7 + 4 = 30 = 3.).

$$8 \quad 6 \quad 3 \quad 4 \quad 9 \quad 5 \quad 9 \quad \text{Total: } 44 = 8.$$
$$\text{H O U D I N I}$$
$$6 \quad 3 \qquad 9 \qquad 9 \quad \text{Vowels: } 27 = 9.$$

Name number: 6. Vowel vibration: 9.

The birth number 3 shows Houdini's remarkable versatility as a locksmith, acrobat, daredevil, and mystifier. His name number 8 expresses his tremendous success in a strictly commercial way, when he became a vaudeville headliner. But his vowel vibration with its underlying influence of 9 urged him on to higher and more lasting fame in his fight against frauds and his efforts to accomplish the supersensational.

Though the name Houdini was an adopted one, he used it through his entire career and was known by it exclusively, making it highly significant from the vibrational standpoint and an excellent study in numerology.

Numbers in Daily Life

Many people are firmly convinced that they have good days and bad days. Accordingly, they are interested in determining any advantages or disadvantages that may depend upon a particular day itself, as well as choosing a course of action suited to the existing conditions.

In numerology, each day is patterned after its vibratory number, as witness the influence of such a number upon persons having that particular birth date. How the individual may attune himself to each succeeding day, or any specific day, is therefore of interest to all students of numerology.

Through a simple formula, it is possible to form a composite number which may be reduced to a vital vibration showing the extent to which the individual harmonizes with the day. The process is as follows:

Take the person's birth number   1
(As March 5, 1946. Total 28 = 10 = 1.)
Take the person's name number   6
(Adding figures of name as regularly
  used. Example 33 = 6.)
Take the number of the day itself   3
(As December 26, 1972. Total 30 = 3.)
                          Add the Total   10
Reduce (10 = 1 + 0 = 1) to key number   1

Thus having combined the two most important numbers of the individual with that of the desired day, consider the harmonized result (in this case 1) in terms of the following table:

Table of Harmonious Numbers

1 A day for definite, direct action, with a single purpose. The time for attack upon any problem which must be settled as immediately and effectively as possible. A good time to seek advance or to start something new, provided it is of a practical nature. Contracts, legal matters, and business propositions can be handled effectively during this vibratory period, but only if a simple plan or prompt decision is feasible. Nothing complex or evasive should be considered on a day that shows this vibratory combination. It stands for opportunity.

2 A day for planning, for weighing problems, and often for making a decision, though it should not ordinarily be put into immediate action. Here, in harmonizing, the numbers produce negative aspects, and any one who tries to meet difficulties head on will be swayed by indecision. This is a day of contrast, that may start badly and end well; or vice versa. It teems with contrasts, so that good results are often offset by disappointments. It is better to sit back and let others carry the ball or wear themselves out on such a day. It may be their day, but it certainly is not yours, except to the extent that you can work out things calmly and to your own satisfaction.

3 A day that offers varied action, when many things can be accomplished. Business can be combined with recreation under these vibratory conditions. Various projects can be started, work allocated, and cooperation gained. It is not the time for concentrating on a single purpose; to do so may mean neglecting others. Troublesome tasks come easily on such a day; often, problems can be ended by quick, friendly decisions. It is a good day for meeting people, for travel, and most of all, for fun.

4 A day for handling routine matters and finishing up small jobs in a methodical way. No time for a trip to the racetrack; it would be better to stay home and concentrate on "do-it-yourself" projects. Similarly, visits to the golf course or a bowling alley may give you ups and downs where their respective scores are concerned. Fun and four just don't mix. Anyone trying to enjoy himself under this vibratory condition will often begin to worry about the practical things he should be doing instead. A hard, persistent worker likes this type of day. Others find it dull, so when there are unpleasant things to do, this is the time. But nothing very important should be attempted and all speculation should be avoided.

5 A day to expect the unexpected. It teems with vigor, excitement, and adventure. But don't get overeager with wild ideas, as they can backfire under these conditions. In taking risks, make sure they have some merit, for all other things being equal, they are apt to swing to a person's advantage at this time. New projects or travel may beckon, but make sure such things have some purpose—not just the desire to sever old connections or to be free and footloose. Avoidance of unnecessary chances is often doubly wise, because this is a day when things may come to you,

such as long-hoped-for success, or any results that are overdue. If you must take a chance, this is the day, but be sure the goal is worth it!

6　A day for good will and understanding. Ease, comfort, and harmony combine in this vibration. This is not a day for quick or direct action. It is not suited for new enterprise, excitement, or the acceptance of a challenge. It is a day for establishment, a time for business conferences, social meetings, consideration of friends and families, and the furthering of diplomatic missions, provided that none of these involve conflict. That is the important thing to avoid, as uncertainty can be ruinous; and any risk, deadly. This is a day of culmination, but only of those things that have been long and properly planned.

7　A day for meditation upon the deeper things of life. Good for study, research, inventive effort, and application toward higher or artistic subjects. Worry, moodiness, or morbid thoughts should be avoided at such a time, but these cannot be banished through merely superficial action. This is a day to think things out, to plan affairs which have already been decided upon but need further consideration; a good day to seek advice or to consult with persons whose opinions are truly worthwhile. Strange things can happen on a day like this, for the combined numbers add up to mystery. So "hunches" can be played, if they pertain to more important things. Often this is a "lucky" day.

8　A day for big things. Under this vibration, broad, sweeping action may bring results. Complex matters can be handled and solved as readily as simple ones; in fact, it may be wasting time to deal with small or immediate problems unless they are stumbling blocks to something bigger. In that case, the small can be swept along with the large. This vibration is attuned to finance; it is suited to solid investment, company mergers, the launching of advertising campaigns. Anything pertaining to constructive effort is at its best; and the larger the undertaking, the better.

9　A day that promises grand achievement. Don't depend on it, however, as often the vibratory combination is greater than any opportunity at hand. But it is always a good time to present attractive propositions, to announce important plans, or to make strong contacts. It is a day that promises personal triumph or the attainment of ambition, more often in artistic or competitive fields than in commercial undertakings, though the latter may be benefited thereby. Aim for the biggest things in sight when the vibratory combination totals 9!

Examples of Daily Vibrations

When John Hancock boldly affixed his signature to the Declaration of Independence, he was taking a great risk and he knew it. He was joining a cause that was desperate in its own right, the American Revolution. But he could not have picked a better day to attune himself to the tempo of the times.

John Hancock was born on January 23, 1737. Its figures total $24 = 6$, giving the birth number 6, the natural type to encourage confidence in his companions. The figures in his full name total $48 = 12 = 3$, so his name number stressed his versatility and capability. The Declaration of Independence was officially announced on July 4, 1776, which adds up to $32 = 5$, producing the date vibration 5.

Those vital numbers add to $6 + 3 + 5 = 14 = 5$. This shows daring, uncertainty, but with it the will to win, no matter how prolonged the struggle. That was the vibratory influence, 5, that inspired John Hancock on that day.

If Napoleon had studied numerology, he would have made the greatest decision in his career; one that could have changed history. He would have avoided the Battle of Waterloo, scene of his final defeat. Here is what the figures show:

Napoleon was born on August 15, 1769, which totals $37 = 10 = 1$. The letters in his name add up to $38 = 11 = 2$. The Battle of Waterloo was fought on June 18, 1815, which totals $30 = 3$. Add birth number, name number, battle date, $1 + 2 + 3 = 6$. That is the number of good will and harmony, when all conflict should be avoided.

Wellington, the opposing general, was born on April 29, 1769. This adds up to $38 = 11 = 2$. The letters in his name total $50 = 5$. Add Wellington's birth number, name number, and the battle date, $2 + 5 + 3 = 10 = 1$. That is the number of decisive action, that promises the attainment of an immediate purpose.

No wonder Napoleon lost the Battle of Waterloo to Wellington. But numerology held the answer before it became history!

9

Moleosophy
(The study of moles)

Moleosophy is based on the hypothesis that moles can be interpreted, in a small way, as indicators of a person's character and also prognosticate generalities for the future. The location of the mole, the shape and color are considered.

Round moles reveal the good in people; oblong, a modest share of acquired wealth; angular represents both good and bad characteristics.

Light-colored moles are considered the luckiest; black moles, many difficulties before favorable results are achieved.

The signification of the moles by location are as follows:

Ankle—On a man, a fearful nature. On a woman, a sense of humor, courageous, willing to share love and worldly possessions with others.

Arms—Courteous, industrious, happy conjugal relations. A man may have to fight many battles if the mole is near the elbow. He may also become a widower at an early age. A woman has the same characteristics but her problems are in her occupation.

Armpits—Under the left arm, the early years are a struggle but ample remuneration, even riches will make the later years very happy. Under the right arm, constant vigilance for welfare and security must be kept uppermost.

Back—Be sure you have all the facts before you enter into negotiation of any enterprise.

Belly—Tendency to self-indulgence. Avoid overeating and excessive drinking. Keep a rigid check on your economy. Choose a marital partner who has an even, calm temperament and the gift of understanding.

Bosom—A quarrelsome nature given to temper. This mole indicates a lazy, sometimes unsteady disposition. Lack of ambition may result in a colorless career. On a man, this area is the chest.

Breast—On the right breast, indolence and intemperance may destroy happiness for self and family. Need to exert will power and self-discipline so that you can enjoy the love and comfort of the children you might have. On the left breast, an active, energetic person, able to concentrate upon the acquisition of wealth and property.

Buttocks—Not very ambitious. Inclined to accept any mode of living, even poverty.

Cheek—On either cheek, a serious, studious, almost solemn person. A middle-of-the-road point of view on most theories pertaining to living, religion, and politics. Wealth is not necessary for your happiness.

Chin—Many people have a mole on the chin. Right or left, it designates people with enviable characteristics. These are people with loving, generous dispositions. They are conscientious workers, and love to travel and acquaint themselves with the habits and customs of other peoples in distant countries. They are capable, responsible citizens, willing to accept responsibilities for family and country.

Ear—Rare, but whoever possesses it may find riches far beyond expectations.

Elbow—Tremendous desire to travel. Always uncertain. Usually talent connected with one or more of the arts. Capable of earning a fortune in money but rarely having the urge to work for it.

Eye—Poverty overshadows unusual talent. If the mole is located on the outside corner of the eye it means an honest, forthright person, one who is reliable but needs love and admiration to offset the struggle for existence.

Eyebrow—Over the right eyebrow, a mole signifies perseverance. A very active life and successful in everything—business, home, and family. Over the left eyebrow or temple, the reverse is threatened. Disappointments will be due to selfishness and indolence. Only with a maximum of effort can poverty be avoided.

Finger—On any finger, dishonesty, inclined to exaggerate due to inability to face the hardships that must be confronted.

Foot—Inclined to brooding akin to melancholia. Prefers a sedentary life but really needs a balanced amount of activity to remain healthy.

Forehead—In the middle of the forehead, a mole predicts honors, wealth, love, and a happy, distinguished family. Right and left forehead mole interpretations are identical with "eyebrow" classification.

Groin—Despite prosperity, a mole on the right groin augurs ill health. On the left, frailty without much prosperity.

Hand—An abundance of almost everything, health, wealth, and happiness. Usually very talented.

Heel—Very active mentally and physically. Ability to accumulate a fortune if so inclined, but makes enemies who continuously plague and cause petty annoyances.

Hip—A mole on any part of the hips except the buttocks, contentment, fortitude, and ingenuity are the salient attributes that balance an otherwise overamorous nature.

Instep—Quarrelsome, often sullen. Generally a keen interest in athletics.

Knee—On the right knee, a friendly, amiable disposition. A great lover, desirous of family and home life. On the left knee, extravagant and inconsistent, but an excellent business acumen.

Legs—Many difficulties during early years but capable of surmounting them by sheer forcefulness. Resources must not be dissipated. Avert any tendency toward indolence.

Lips—A benevolent nature, always striving for better conditions.

Navel—On a man, very lucky. On a woman, desire to have many children.

Neck—Unexpected good fortune, if mole is on front of the neck. On either side, unreasonable. On the back, need to practice frugality.

Nipple—On a man, fickle and desirous of many amours. On a woman, always striving for social status.

Nose—A sincere friend. Will achieve success, make an excellent marriage. A person dedicated to amassing great wealth even though the struggle often seems impossible.

Shoulder—Generally, restless, needs to travel in order to be satisfied with home surroundings. A mole on the right shoulder brings prudence, discretion; a faithful marriage partner; very industrious. On the left shoulder, satisfied with any position in life, both occupational and social.

Wrist—Frugal, ingenious, dependable. On a woman, one marriage. On a man, possibly two marriages.

When there are twin moles such as a mole on one wrist in a certain spot and an identical one on the other wrist, this is called a Gemini duality. The person possesses a dual nature. This pertains to all dual moles no matter what the location, such as legs, arms, cheeks, and so on. Two moles, side by side, are said to indicate two loves.

10

Palmistry

The subject of palmistry, or the study of the human hand, is composed of two parts: chirosophy, or the mystical significance of the lines, markings, and developed areas; and chirognomy, or an analysis of the shape and formation of the hand, thumb, and fingers.

While the two are closely interwoven, the emphasis was originally on chirosophy, which was closely identified with astrology, as witness the names of the planets as applied to the areas called mounts. The lines, too, were generally interpreted in divinatory terms, as with other psychic sciences.

At the same time, formations were noted and used by experts in the art of chirosophy, and their readings became so accurate that scientific surveys were undertaken, resulting in a definitive classification of shapes and their indication. Thus chirognomy came into vogue.

In more recent years, studies of a purely physiological nature have indicated that lines and other features may be affected by retarded development, ill health, and other physical causes, thus further verifying the traditions of chirosophy by the findings of chirognomy.

Most interesting of these developments is the fact that character traits can be noted by a preliminary observation of a person's hands, even at a distance, and often at a glance. Unquestionably, the early chirosophists must have recognized those points, and the later chirognomists made special note of them. So in all hand analysis, these factors should be considered:

Large hands indicate an ability for detail. Small hands show the reverse, because of an impatient trend.

Mannerisms are easily observed and very revealing. The graceful, lightly moving hand denotes a person who is popular at social gatherings and at the office. It is a sign of affection and interest in others.

Clenched hands are the sign of a dynamic, restless, pushing personality, but one that is usually self-reliant.

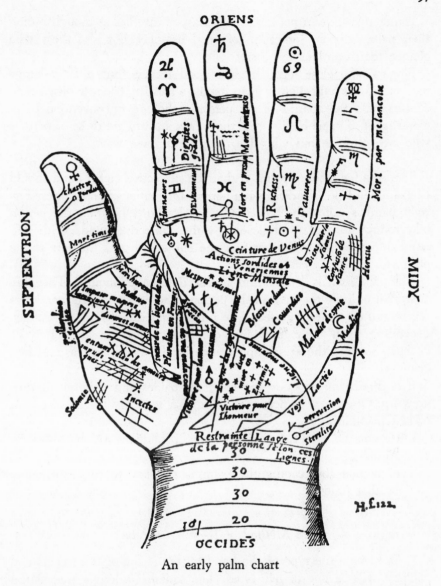

An early palm chart

Extended fingers show extremists who like attention, especially when the little finger is extended while holding a cup or glass. This is also a moody sign.

Nervous, gesturing hands are those of quick thinkers, but with an inclination to be overanxious.

Relaxed hands are the token of a practical person, who is apt to be interested in almost everything.

Hands that hide in pockets, or are clasped together as though hiding their palms, are an indication of good listeners, but also those who change their opinions too easily.

Fingers held close together show good leaders, but often a stingy nature. Fingers held slightly apart denote a trustful, friendly disposition. Fingers held far apart indicate persons who are unconventional but extravagant. Fingers held so that they curve inward are those of persons who are secretive, but who like things their own way.

The rule for reading palms is that the subjective (left) hand should be examined first. It indicates the natural inclinations and abilities. The right hand is called the objective hand. It shows how far the person may follow the pattern indicated by the subjective hand. With left-handed people the right hand is the subjective and the left is the objective.

The palm itself is divided into nine sections called mounts. These are areas that indicate the traits of the person. The lines and other markings tell how those traits are used. The fingers and thumbs add or detract, depending upon their individual qualities. Lines can and often do change. So does the entire appearance of the hand, just as the face changes.

It is interesting to study the hands of babies and children as they grow up. Often new indications will appear to verify the development of certain abilities.

Lines can be eradicated temporarily or permanently by shock or severe illness.

The method for reading the palm is the key to the explanatory sections that follow.

The Method of Reading a Palm

1. Determine the type of the hand by the shape of the fingers and palm. It will be one of five types. The square (orderly), the conical (inspirational), the spatulate (energetic), the pointed (idealistic), or mixed (adaptable).

2. Test flexibility and texture. Determine the angle of the thumb. Look for smooth or knotty finger joints. Type the fingernails. Note peculiarities.

3. Check the fingers for length. Long, for detail. Short, for impulsiveness. Compare phalanges for irregularities in size and shape.

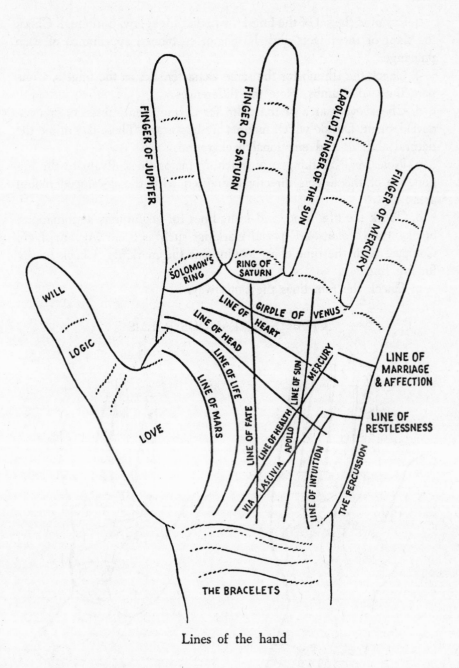

Lines of the hand

4. Examine the set of the fingers, whether high, low, or normal. Check the slant of the fingers and the flat or cushioned appearance of each phalange.

5. Check the thumb for the same characteristics as the fingers. Compare the two thumbs. Note the differences.

6. Check every area of the palm for development, absence, or over-development. Decide which mounts are important. These determine the natural abilities and emotional background.

7. Note small markings not touching major lines. Evaluate the importance of the fingers directly connected with the developed mount areas.

8. Check the life, head, and heart lines for beginnings, terminations, breaks, frays, color, and special markings such as a cross or an island. Compare with the time chart to pinpoint the markings. Check for influence lines.

9. Check the fate lines the same way.

CHARTS OF FAMOUS PALMS

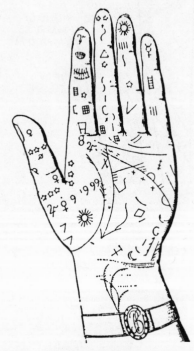

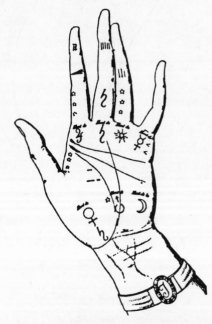

Napoleon's hand   Josephine's hand

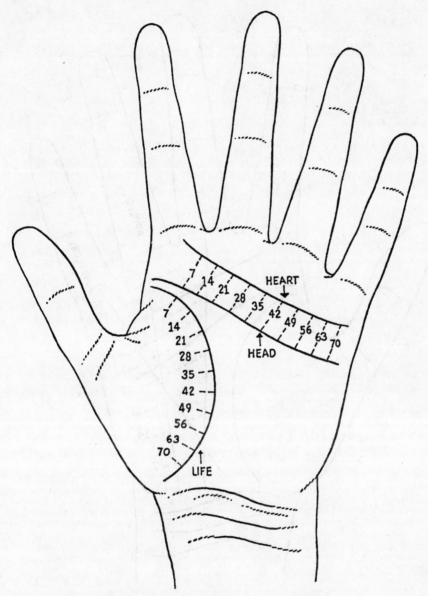

Time: On lines of life, head, and heart

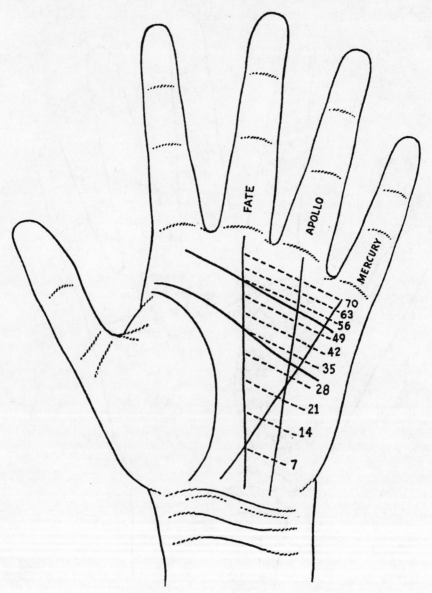

Time: On fate lines

10. Look for secondary lines and analyze them carefully, especially for their relation to basic lines.

11. Check all the findings and weigh them cautiously, bearing in mind the difference between the subjective and the objective hand. If a person is right-handed, the left hand is called the subjective hand representing the natural talents and characteristics. The right hand is called the objective hand, showing how those talents and qualities have been developed or neglected.

Time

Time is computed approximately by dividing the basic lines into segments totaling ninety to one hundred years, always starting from the beginning of each line. The life line starts the count from the point of beginning, which is between the thumb and forefinger. The head and heart lines follow the same way. The fate lines, Saturn, Apollo, and Mercury, start their time reading from the bottom of the plam to the top.

Types of Hands

Hands are typed by their shape. They fall into various classifications as follows.

THE ELEMENTARY HAND
(rare)

The elementary hand is easy to identify because of a short thumb, wide palm, short, thick fingers, and a clumsy appearance. The hand is stiff and awkward. It represents very little intelligence but is strong on brutal instincts. Fortunately it is rarely seen except among the most primitive of tribal people.

THE SQUARE HAND
(the orderly hand)

The square hand is the practical, the working hand. It is really rectangular over-all, but the palm is square and the fingers have a squared-off appearance at the fingertips. People with these hands want everything organized with specific plans. Very forceful and determined to fulfill the requisites for living and the pursuit of happiness.

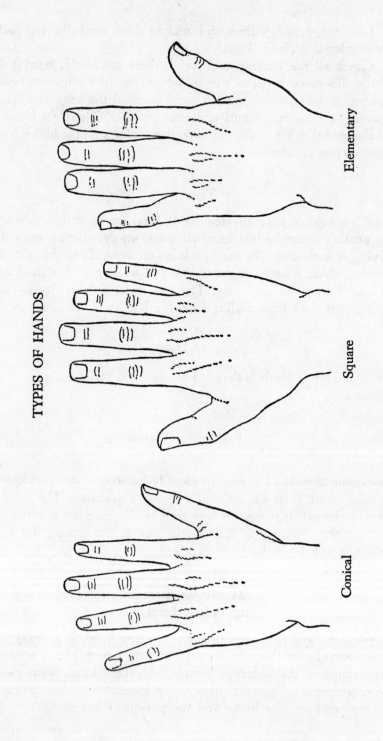

TYPES OF HANDS

Elementary

Square

Conical

THE CONICAL HAND
(the inspirational hand)

The conical hand tapers gently from base to fingertips. Each finger tapers to an elliptical tip. This is the inspirational type. They are exuberant and their enthusiasm for the artistic is very evident. They love companionship and are very social minded. They must be encouraged to activate their ideas.

THE SPATULATE HAND
(the energetic hand)

The spatulate hand represents a very active person. The entire appearance of the hand is suggestive of the spatula. There are two types. One palm is wider at the wrist than at the base of the fingers. The second type is the reverse, wider at the top than at the wrist. The fingertips are spatulate. The hand spreads out fan-shaped. It denotes great activity. It can be found in all kinds of work, from artisan to artist. The energetic laborer may excel in sports, the architect may have revolutionary ideas, but always there is the urge to be active, to do something more, to be original.

THE POINTED HAND
(the idealistic hand)

The pointed hand is also called the psychic hand. In its purest form the fingers are pointed. The hand is long, narrow, and thin. This is the intuitive mind, the idealist. Extremists of religious cults and philosophies may be found with these hands. They can become martyrs to their own ideas.

THE MIXED HAND
(the adaptable hand)

Most hands are mixed. The square hand may have two or three different types of fingers. The spatulate may have only two or so that vary. It is necessary to analyze the fingers carefully, then combine the findings. The thumb is the indicator. If it is square, just as an example, a practical aspect will modify or regulate any idealism that might be on a pointed first finger or a spatulate third finger which would partake in a speculative nature. This is the way to diagnose a thumb and finger relationship with a specific problem hand.

THE PHILOSOPHICAL HAND

This an old classification of hands that are really square or conical but always have knots on both joints of all the fingers and the thumb joint. The hand has a long, lean appearance. It represents the thinker, one who wants to weigh every question carefully. Many teachers have this type of hand. The fingertips can vary, square or conic. Either way, these are the men and women who seek knowledge.

FLEXIBILITY OF HANDS

Very flexible hands have fingers that bend backward, almost curling, some almost at right angles to the palm. These are extremists who like to live an unrestrained, almost unconventional life. Usually very talented.

Medium flexibility. These fingers bend back slightly, at least noticeably. These belong to people who are reasonable and willing to meet you halfway in a business agreement.

Stiff hands will not bend. Neither will their owners. They are unyielding and hard to convince, but once they give their word they abide by it.

TEXTURE OF HANDS
(also called consistency)

Flabby hands are loose-skinned and swollen in feeling them. Temperament is variable, sometimes genial, sometimes irritable.

Soft hands feel limp and listless to the touch. Although they detest manual labor they must not be underrated. Many successful and famous people have just such hands.

Firm hands belong to determined people who accept the good with the bad but work with conviction in every effort.

Hard hands are stiff to the touch. Their owners are resolute and hard to convince. Unusually obdurate, but with good lines and well-shaped thumbs they listen to reason.

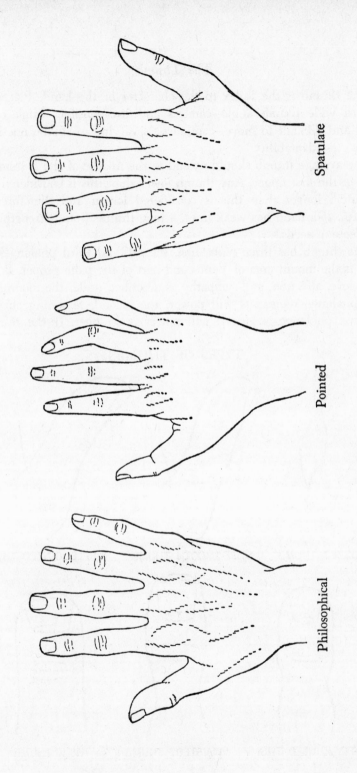

Spatulate

Pointed

Philosophical

The Thumb

The thumb is the index to the character of the hand. Placed low, with a wide thumb angle—careless and irresponsible. High on the hand and difficult to move—cautiousness varying to stubbornness. Medium set—adaptability.

The average thumb should extend to the middle of the bottom phalange of the first finger. Any thumb lower than this is considered short. A thumb longer than this is considered longer and therefore more forceful. If a hand has weak lines, a long thumb would strengthen the intellectual needs.

The thumb has three parts, first, second, and third phalanges. The third is the mount area of Venus and part of the palm proper. It represents love, affection, and sympathy as described under the mounts. The first phalange represents will power, the second, reasoning ability. If the first phalange is longer, will power is stronger. If the thumb is

TYPES OF THUMBS

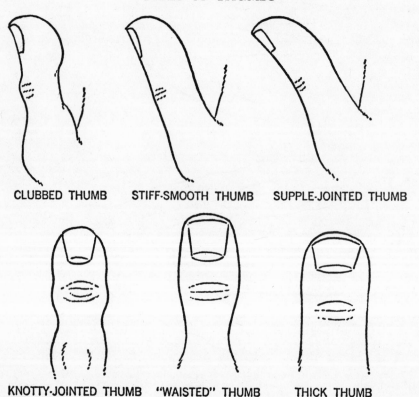

CLUBBED THUMB   STIFF-SMOOTH THUMB   SUPPLE-JOINTED THUMB

KNOTTY-JOINTED THUMB   "WAISTED" THUMB   THICK THUMB

square, there is practical application; if conical, the artistic viewpoint; if pointed, idealistic. A second phalange which is too short denotes a tactless person and a lack of reasoning.

The thumb is normally broader than it is thick. If it is as thick as it is broad—an unbalanced, violent nature; slender thumbs—patience; a "waisted" second phalange—great understanding and sympathy for both people and creatures; a knotty joint on the thumb—the analytical mind; a smooth joint—impulsiveness.

Flexibility of the thumb denotes the intensity of logic and will power indicated in the palm. A stiff thumb adds determination, stubbornness; extremely supple—talented, extremist; moderate pliability—reasonable, good understanding.

Fingers

To measure for length of fingers, measure the second finger from tip to knuckle. Measure the back of the palm from that knuckle to the wristbone. Measure the palm side from the bottom of the second finger to the wrist. The two latter should be equal. Compare this measurement with that of the finger. If the finger is longer you have long fingers. If shorter, you have short fingers. If they are the same in measurement, the balance is average.

Each finger has its own interpretation, following the meaning of the mounts directly below them. They also carry the same names, Jupiter, the first finger; Saturn, the second; Apollo, the third; Mercury, the fourth.

The fingers modify or direct the qualities of each mount. Long fingers increase the value. Short fingers decrease the value. Very long fingers exaggerate.

If the fingers lean toward Jupiter, the first—ambition—is most important. Toward Mercury—money is the aim. Toward Saturn—a scholarly or serious attitude toward life.

Knotted upper joints—reasoning ability. Knotted lower joints—practicality.

Long fingers—interested in every detail. Short fingers—impetuous, want to grasp the over-all quickly, leave details to others. Very short fingers—selfish, lazy, unconventional, can be brutal. Crooked fingers detract from the good qualities, chiefly by irresponsibility. Low-set fingers add indifference. Thin fingers denote delicacy. Thick fingers—self-indulgence.

TYPES OF FINGER JOINTS

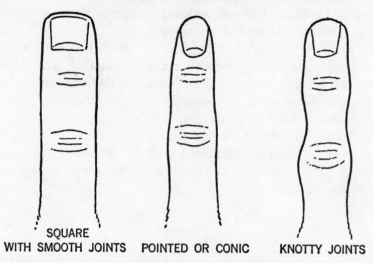

SQUARE
WITH SMOOTH JOINTS   POINTED OR CONIC   KNOTTY JOINTS

Very long first finger—desire to rule. Very long second finger—zealous struggle for religious aspiration. Very long third finger—urge to gamble. Very long fourth finger—money-conscious.

Fingers that are held close together—secretive. Fingers held apart—non-secretive, too outspoken. Bending back—clever, careless spender.

General meaning of the phalanges: first—mental; second—practical; third—materialistic. The latter includes sensuous desires such as over-eating, love of luxury, and ostentation to a varied degree. Padded first phalange—very sensitive.

A pointed fingertip adds idealism. A square tip, practicality. A spatulate tip, action.

The set of the fingers is important. The normal set for a square hand is almost in a straight line across the palm. All others make a gentle curve so the first finger sets a little lower than the second and third, while the little finger drops down slightly. Any finger that is noticeably low detracts greatly from the value of the mount area.

Nails

Nails, both finger and thumb, are classified as follows: Long—artistic, idealistic. Short—critical. Very short—irritable. Very broad—meddlesome.

Thick—indolence. Fluted—overexertion. A ridge crosswise—a physical weakness or period of illness. Hard—good physical endurance. Wedge-shaped—too sensitive.

Pale pink nails—even temperament. White—impartial. Red—impulsive. Purple—faulty circulatory system. White specks—lack of calcium, often nervous.

TYPES OF NAILS

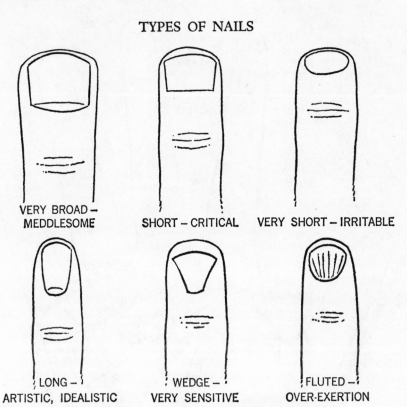

VERY BROAD —
MEDDLESOME

SHORT – CRITICAL

VERY SHORT – IRRITABLE

LONG –
ARTISTIC, IDEALISTIC

WEDGE –
VERY SENSITIVE

FLUTED –
OVER-EXERTION

The Mounts of the Palm
(the areas of the palm)

The palm is divided into nine areas. They are the key to our natural abilities and emotional traits. Each area is called a mount, which sounds as though there is a point or hump in each section. This is not the case. It has been a traditional term to designate the different qualifications of each area. Naming them, in order around the palm, they are as follows: the mount (area) of Jupiter, under the first finger; Saturn, under the second finger; Apollo, under the third; Mercury, under the fourth; Upper Mars, under Mercury, on the percussion side of the palm; Luna, occupying the rest of the percussion side of the palm; Venus, between the root of the thumb to the encircling line called the line of life and extending from the wrist to about three-fourths of the distance upward within the line of life; the rest of this area is called Lower Mars; the center of all these areas is called the Plain of Mars.

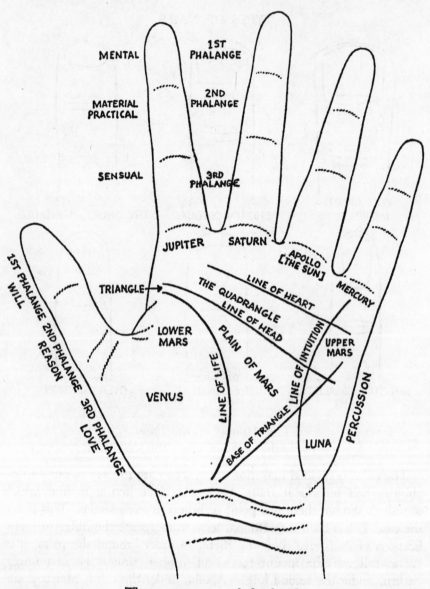

The mount areas of the hand

The higher or the more space that is developed, the more important are the traits attributed to that area. They are a fleshy elevation filling the entire area, or they can be off center. Each location has a variation of the meaning of the area and its relation to the entire analysis of the palm. The Plain of Mars is the plain or hollow center of the palm.

If the mount area is so high or spread out that it appears to unbalance the rest of the palm, the qualities represented by that mount must be kept under control. Lacking height, look for the center or apex of the whorl formation. Overlapping mounts partake of both areas.

The Interpretation of the Mount Areas

MOUNT OF JUPITER

The mount area of Jupiter normally represents ambition and social prestige. If the development is closer to the side of the palm, family pride is the chief ambition; closer to the head line, leadership, a desire for authority. Here, arrogance would have to be subdued. Placed nearer Saturn, scholarly attributes. If the area is very high or large, conceit. Generally, idealism is the keynote for Jupiter. Fanaticism, exaggeration, and lack of dignity cannot be tolerated by a balanced Jupiterian (sometimes called Jovian). One vertical line—success. Two lines—more than one ambition. A cross—a happy marriage. A star—fame. Too many lines—too many interests. The grille—very unfavorable, the reverse of all the good qualities of Jupiter. Absence of the mount—superstitious, vain, boastful, lack of respect.

MOUNT OF SATURN

This mount area is seldom highly developed. Usually it partakes of either or both Jupiter and Apollo. Saturn in itself is the epitome of sobriety. Love of solitude, cautiousness, and mental reserve are characteristics. Developed close to the heart line—the qualities magnify. Toward Jupiter—very serious viewpoint about life. Toward Apollo—genuine interest in the arts; sentiment becomes important. Very active Saturnians, those with spatulate fingers, have ability for sturdy occupations such as mining or agriculture. Absence of the mount—indifference, periods of morbidness, often antisocial, a realist with little care for anyone. A single small vertical line—luck in spite of self. Two small lines—unusual success, a philosophical mind. Crosslines—too much interference; Saturnians must have solitude. Delicate, fine lines—mental

problems. A cross—suicidal tendencies, prone to accidents. A star—
health problems. A square—danger from fire. A grille—unscrupulous,
entanglements with the law.

MOUNT OF APOLLO

This mount area represents the talent for and appreciation of the
arts. It stands for brilliance in achievement in any field of endeavor.
Developed toward Saturn—a serious aspect is uppermost. Toward Mercury—a practical, business mind is added to the talents; shrewdness in
all deals. One vertical line—fame or fortune, perhaps both. Two lines
—may have two good talents. Several lines, usually crossed by one or
more lines but not a grille—too many talents, causing a diversion of
interest. All Apollonians are versatile and enchanting. Overdeveloped
mounts—fantastic natures inclined to overrate their ability. Absence—
non-intellectual, despise culture in every aspect, reckless, but sometimes
one of this class has a tremendous acumen for high finance with great
possibilities for success. A star promises great fortune. Cross—if no line
of Apollo, poor judgment in speculation. A cross with the line of
Apollo—success after long and arduous work. A circle—fame. A grille
—exaggerated valuation of personal talent. Horizontal lines—many obstacles to overcome.

MOUNT OF MERCURY

The mount area of Mercury represents hope. Normally it adds gaiety
and cheerfulness to the clear-thinking, practical, managerial faculties
that make this area so important. Fortunately, many classes of people
can have this development. Top-bracket business executives, men and
women in every profession and business niche, the underrated but mag-
nificently capable housewife, all must possess some degree of the qualities of the mount of Mercury, otherwise they could not be successful.

Developed toward Apollo—love and appreciation for everything artistic; love of beautiful surroundings. Toward the percussion—a touch of
humor. Toward the base of the finger—business before pleasure. Toward Upper Mars—an indomitable spirit, willing to fight for a cause.
Very dependable under stress. Absence of the mount—lacking all business ability; an utterly purposeless life.

Overdeveloped—swindlers and criminals may have this driving force, though in good hands it furnishes the stimulus for inventive minds. Also indicative of a high-pressure salesman.

The horizontal lines on this area are the marriage lines, which are discussed elsewhere in this book. A single vertical line—promise of wealth, interest in scientific achievements. Two or three lines—varied interests that have a business possibility or that materially aid in the building of a career. Four vertical lines are called the medical stigmata. There may be a cross line with them. This is a very old term; nevertheless, many a nurse and doctor has these lines. More than four lines—very loquacious, also careless about money. A cross—a born diplomat, one who says the right thing at the right time; in a scheming hand—deceit. A grille—severe punishment or death due to malpractice or violation of the law. Square—great business foresight.

MOUNT OF LUNA

The mount area of Luna represents imagination, intuition, creative ability, and motivation. It is a large area so it must be examined carefully to determine the exact location of the apex or precise spot of development. Luna has varied physical forms. It can bulge in spots or all over. It can be thin and almost flat. There may be few lines or many. It may have the color of a lot of blood or a little. All of these things have a meaning. When developed toward Upper Mars—the practical dreamer able to apply imaginative ideas to everyday needs. If the entire percussion bulges—need for physical activity combined with some creative project. Near the wrist—sensuality, sometimes just imaginative. Toward Venus—romantic, emotional. Toward the Plain of Mars—aggressiveness to further one's ability. All of these types are intensified if the mount shows a reddish color. A bluish color—sadness, even melancholia enters the imagination such as the gloomy poet or composer. Pale color—may possess any one of the qualifications for the specific type, but indifference would be evident unless pressure were exerted. Absence of any development—the poseur, the imitator, usually satisfied with their place in life, no matter what it happens to be.

Lines on the area of Luna are very important because they are directional. Every talent will be corroborated on this area. Inventors, artists, writers, actors, musicians, builders, designers, in fact, every imaginative, creative talent is represented with a Lunarian mark or development. In excess, this talent becomes fanciful or foolish. If the imagination is too strong without a well-balanced intelligence, lunacy may result, or at least a very confused and erratic mind. The horizontal lines show many interests. Lines that extend to the areas of Jupiter, Saturn, Apollo, or Mercury automatically assume the names of those respective mounts and are explained under the major lines. The short lines starting on the percussion are lines of change often called travel lines, and are so interpreted as journeys. In a creative hand these lines can be considered as many interests. Slanting lines pertain to the same creative ideas.

Many fine lines—nervous tension.

Oblique lines—more important interests concerned with travel.

A cross—dreamy nature, superstitious, such as many theatrical people.

A large cross—wild imagination. A grille—inconstancy, fickleness, neurotic nature. Islands—fear and possible danger from water. Star—conflicting translations, i.e., meritorious achievement by risking life or fortune; serious accident or death on a perilous expedition. Triangle—unusual talents, brilliant success. Square—escape from dangers of water and sky.

MOUNT OF VENUS

The mount area of Venus represents love, sympathy, passion, and vitality. A well-centered, moderately cushioned area partakes of all qualities. The top section is the area of the mount of Lower Mars. A low, flat area—cool, calculating, dispassionate unless Lower Luna is very accentuated. In that case perverted ideas may rule the subject. If Venus is developed toward Lower Mars—antagonistic nature. Near the wrist—affectionate, sensual. Near Luna—self-indulgent. Near the thumb base—very emotional. Excessively cushioned—dynamic in love and friendship. If the area is hard, very muscular—resentful, will not tolerate interference.

Curved lines parallel to the line of life (not the line of Mars, which is described elsewhere in this book)—friends or relatives influential to happiness. Diagonal or horizontal lines that touch the life line—interferences. A grille—passionate nature. Many very small fine lines in crisscross effect—the constant worrier. A large cross—happy love and marriage.

MOUNT OF LOWER MARS

This area is really part of the Venus area since it lies within the line of life, filling the upper section of the enclosure. It is termed "lower" because it lies below the head line, as opposed to Upper Mars, which lies above the normal head line, on the percussion side of the palm. It represents the will to fight for a cause, for family, for country, or for personal reputation or aim. This can be mental activity or it can be physical, such as men in the armed forces. In a woman's hand it is aggressiveness for self and family. Overdeveloped—an abusive temperament. Hollow—fearful, reticent.

A star—death of a loved one. A grille—too sensitive. A square—quick thinker, very poised.

MOUNT OF UPPER MARS

This area, located between Mercury and Luna on the percussion side of the palm, represents endurance, bravery, fortitude, and resistance. This is a passive form as opposed to the activity of Lower Mars, but it takes both for balance. Higher or stronger toward Mercury— nothing can defeat this person in business or profession, very persistent. Toward the center of the palm, the Plain of Mars—guard against overaggressiveness. Toward Luna—takes advantage of imaginative inspirational qualities, such as an attorney who can sway a jury by his choice of words. Toward the percussion—physical reserve. Overdeveloped—cruelty. Absent—morbid, always on the defensive.

A single vertical line—bravery in face of death. Many parallel lines —brutality. A cross—quarrelsome. Short horizontal lines—obstacles or enemies. Long horizontal lines—lawsuits or participation in the legal profession. Triangle—honors in warfare. Circle—wounds.

Lines of Opposition

The lines on Upper Mars are also called the lines of opposition. They are the short horizontal lines that run straight across the area parallel to the line of heart. If any line is longer and reaches another area it takes on the characteristics of the other area. If, for instance, one line curves up to the area of Apollo, it is then considered as a line of Apollo and its interpretation falls under that nomenclature in this book.

If a long line from Upper Mars touches a major line, the Mars line then becomes an influence line and registers as a hindrance or deterrent force against the major line. If it touches the line of Mercury it threatens a health problem that would interfere with business. Cutting the Apollo line—financial problems connected with a profession.

THE PLAIN OF MARS

This is the area in the center of the palm. The two directive influences controlling it are Upper and Lower Mars. A high plain—good control of emotions, especially under argumentative or combat circumstances. A flat plain—great restraint as a result of a negative attitude toward everything. A hollow plain—fearful, nervous, need for cooperation from friends or family.

Signs and Small Markings

Signs and small markings add great interest to the interpretation of the palm. Usually they are an imperfect form such as an incomplete square or a two-sided triangle which looks like a dart. Their meanings vary depending upon location. The triangle is considered the best sign of luck. The cross, unlucky, except for the Mystic Cross, which consists of two lines forming a cross in the area between the lines of head and heart. This denotes the natural instinct associated with powers of the supernatural. Squares are good. Grilles are bad. The following gives detailed traditional information.

Triangles on the mounts. Jupiter—the diplomat, excellent leader. Saturn—scholarly attributes. Apollo—artistic success. Mercury—the executive mind. Luna—rare imaginative talent. Venus—fortunate in love and marriage. Mars—honors. On the wrist—wealth through marriage or inheritance.

Triangles on the lines. Life—eloquent speaker or glibness. Head—unusual perceptive powers. Heart—brilliant marriage alliance. Fate (this includes lines of Saturn, Apollo, or Mercury)—great achievement.

Crosses on the mounts. Jupiter—happy married life in spite of struggles. Saturn—fatalistic attitude toward life. Apollo—frustrations that mar success. Mercury—deceptive. Luna—exaggeration of abilities. Venus—disappointment in love. Mars—physical danger.

Crosses on the lines. Life—illness or danger at that period. Head—accident. Fate—financial reverses due to some business complication.

Crosses in the Plain of Mars—uneven temperament, quarrelsome. On thumb or fingers—petty quarrels.

Stars on the mounts. Jupiter—great honors. Saturn—in a strong hand, the sober-minded scholar such as the historian, the high-churchman; in a weak hand, tragic melancholia. Apollo—celebrity. Mercury—success. Luna—remarkable imaginative talents. Venus—great love. Mars—bravery.

Stars on the lines. Life—shock. Head—accident. Whenever the star is on a line, there is a warning of danger pertaining to the meaning of that line.

Stars on thumb or fingers—a lucky streak or will power in some particular project.

Squares. Squares and rectangles are marks of protection or preservation. On Venus or the life line—protection from unhappiness or some physical danger such as an accident or illness. On the fate lines—an averted business or financial problem. Anywhere it appears, it supplies protective measures when most needed.

Grilles. Grilles can be large or small, a simple crisscross or a dense mesh of mixed-up lines. It must be a definite patch. Wherever it appears it magnifies the bad traits of the area or the line it touches. On Jupiter it destroys ambition. On Saturn—morbid moodiness. Apollo—utter abandonment of talents. Mercury—deceitful, dishonest. Luna—lack of concentration, dissipation. Venus—maladjustment.

Islands indicate physical weakness on the life line and the hepatica. Head line—periods of mental strain. Heart line—illness or disappointments with loved ones. Fate lines—reverses. On the mounts, an island detracts from the evaluation of the area.

Dots and Bars are obstacles that detract or temporarily stop progress.

Circles are a hindrance except on the area of Apollo. There a circle signifies brilliant success.

A *small vertical line* adds ability to a given talent. Two or more vertical lines divide the energy. The person diverts ambition into too many channels. Two exceptions are: *lines of reputation,* on Apollo, adding to good fortune, and *the medical stigmata,* four parallel vertical lines on Mercury mount showing interest in medicine.

Horizontal lines diminish the valuation of the area. This is a nervous, scattering effort.

Diagonal lines on the mounts have the same interpretation as horizontals. They magnify the weakness of the area.

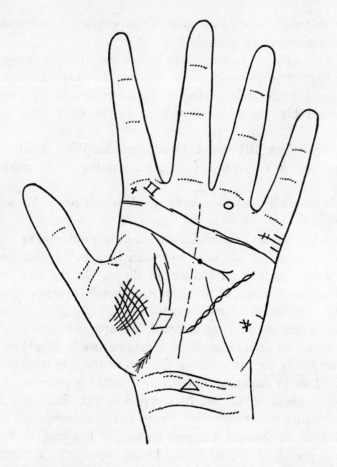

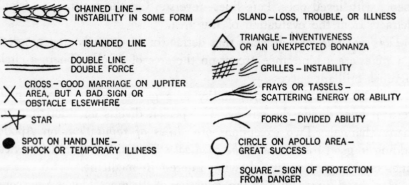

CHAINED LINE – INSTABILITY IN SOME FORM	ISLAND – LOSS, TROUBLE, OR ILLNESS
ISLANDED LINE	TRIANGLE – INVENTIVENESS OR AN UNEXPECTED BONANZA
DOUBLE LINE DOUBLE FORCE	GRILLES – INSTABILITY
CROSS – GOOD MARRIAGE ON JUPITER AREA, BUT A BAD SIGN OR OBSTACLE ELSEWHERE	FRAYS OR TASSELS – SCATTERING ENERGY OR ABILITY
STAR	FORKS – DIVIDED ABILITY
SPOT ON HAND LINE – SHOCK OR TEMPORARY ILLNESS	CIRCLE ON APOLLO AREA – GREAT SUCCESS
	SQUARE – SIGN OF PROTECTION FROM DANGER

Signs and special formations

Similar lines on thumb and fingers exert the same influence, in a lesser degree, relative to the nearest mount area.

Mount Combinations

Jupiter-Saturn   Scholarly ambition.
Jupiter-Apollo   Talent with ambition.
Jupiter-Mercury   Practical purpose.
Jupiter-Luna   Creative imagination.
Jupiter-Venus   Pride in achievement.
Jupiter-Lower Mars   Aggressive, dynamic leadership.
Jupiter-Upper Mars   Heroic ambition, endurance, forceful leadership.

Saturn-Apollo   Restrained vitality, wisdom.
Saturn-Mercury   Capability through knowledge.
Saturn-Luna   Mystical nature.
Saturn-Venus   Reliability and understanding.
Saturn-Lower Mars   Deep interest in nature.
Saturn-Upper Mars   Stolid acceptance of all conditions.

Apollo-Mercury   Flair for business.
Apollo-Luna   Imaginative talent.
Apollo-Venus   Artistic talent.
Apollo-Lower Mars   Urge for self-improvement.
Apollo-Upper Mars   Ability to meet emergencies.

Mercury-Luna   Inventive ideas.
Mercury-Venus   Ability to make friends.
Mercury-Lower Mars   Active participation in business.
Mercury-Upper Mars   Success after long effort; business stamina.

Luna-Venus   Desire to meet new people.
Luna-Lower Mars   Impulsive, overindulgence.

Venus-Lower Mars   Adherence to a cause.
Venus-Upper Mars   Tolerance; confidence in friends and family.

When there are more than two developed mounts, check the information from the particular mount area and add it to the interpretation of the combined mounts.

The Appearance of Lines

A line should be continuously, clearly traced, without variance of form or color. It should be medium in depth and width. Color, pinkish or medium pink. Red lines show impetuosity, unrestrained emotions. Very dark lines, vindictiveness, jealousy. Light-colored lines, indecision, inertia. Deep lines, intensity, determined. Wide lines, overactive. Very fine lines, lack of physical strength. Few lines, able to work without worry. Many lines, many interests, often harassed by worries and conflicts. A frayed line has many little lines emanating from it. This weakens the value of the main line. A chained line, periods of illness. A broken line, a change. A forked line has a fork at the beginning or the end. It draws help from the mount areas wherever the forked ends touch. Branches are lines stemming from the main lines and long enough to reach a mount area or touch or cross another line. These branches are described in the chapter on basic lines. A split line shows a weakening influence. This is not to be confused with an island formation.

Signs and Markings on the Lines

One or more dots on a line, detrimental defect or illness. A bar is a little short line that crosses a major line. This is a warning of a serious interference.

A small cross on a line, an unfortunate sign that interferes with health, happiness, or occupation.

A star consists of several little crosslines. It marks something extremely unusual, depending upon the placement. Usually some degree of shock or unexpected change is connected with it.

A circle, temporary illness. Very rare.

A triangle, ingenuity, quick perception during stress. An excellent mark alone or formed with other major lines.

A square or rectangle can be closed, open, or irregular in formation. On a line it is always a good sign of protection. Often found where a major line is broken.

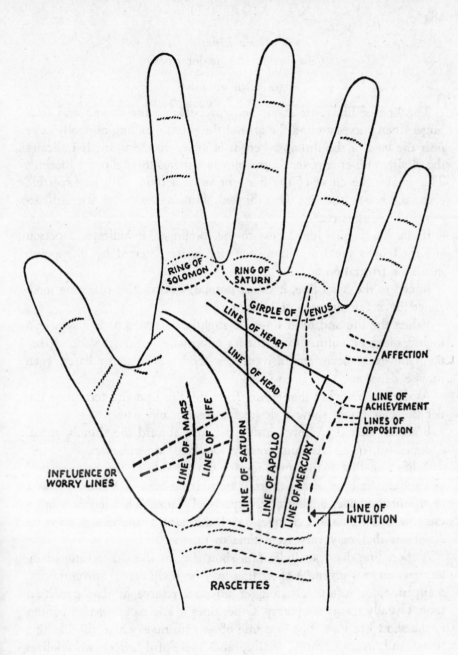

RING OF
SOLOMON

RING OF
SATURN

GIRDLE OF VENUS

LINE OF HEART

LINE OF HEAD

AFFECTION

LINE OF
ACHIEVEMENT

LINES OF
OPPOSITION

LINE OF MARS

LINE OF LIFE

LINE OF SATURN

LINE OF APOLLO

LINE OF MERCURY

INFLUENCE OR
WORRY LINES

LINE OF
INTUITION

RASCETTES

BASIC LINES (MAJOR) ————————
LESSER LINES (MINOR) ------------

Basic Lines
(Also called the major lines)

THE LINE OF LIFE

The line of life starts about halfway between the thumb and forefinger, then curves around the area of the thumb, ending normally at or near the base of the thumb where it is joined to the wrist. It indicates the vitality and energy that a person can expend throughout a lifetime. The greater the curve of the line, the more activity is to be expected, especially when the line is unbroken. Unusual physical strength accompanies this curve.

If the line begins high, close to the forefinger, it indicates a person governed by a great ambition, one not easily deterred by disappointments or frustrations.

Joined to the head line, it shows normal, constructive planning moderated by a fair amount of caution.

When the life and head lines are slightly separated, it is a sign of a highly energetic nature, excellent for any niche in life. A wide separation, however, means impulsiveness, a tendency to make hasty, even unwise decisions.

Ascending branches that spring from the life line and terminate under the first finger show a desire for wealth and power.

Branches that drop down inside the line, toward the thumb, reveal a desire for, or an absolute craving for, love and affection.

A life line that swings over toward the far side of the palm instead of circling the base of the thumb, around the area of Venus, partakes of the imaginative, adventurous aspects of Luna. This requires interests that mean constant change, travel, different surroundings, even occupations that may vary from time to time.

A short line does not indicate a short life, as the old traditional interpretation was given. A short line may be a change of surroundings, occupation, or just a lessening of physical reserve at that particular time. Usually this is temporary. Other lines in the palm act as a booster to the short life line. The fate line often continues where the life line stops, and many a busy, active, and successful career materializes through some inevitable change, marked one way or another on the fate line.

Life and head lines joined for some distance at the beginning should be studied carefully—by parents—because there may be timidity or shyness during these early years of childhood. Children having this line formation need extra encouragement.

Chained formations or broken effects warn of physical weakness. At the beginning of the line, any of the early childhood ailments are to be expected.

Double lines, either complete or partial, are tremendous strengtheners, adding great vitality to an already strong physique.

Triple lines can be good or bad, depending upon the mentality of the person. Great talent and passion, or the reverse, lust and deceit.

Irregularities of the Life Line

Wavy—delicate health, unable to make decisions.

Thin in parts, wide in other—unpredictable temperament; unreliable.

Very red—violent temper, or uncontrollable.

Broad and very pale—envious disposition and very likely a need to take better care of health.

Completely chained or linked—poor health.

Dark blue or blackish lines—resentful, rebellious under pressure.

Break or split—illness for a short period; if in both hands, a change of residence may be necessary or advantageous.

Terminations of the Life Line

Forked end—physical weakness; warning to provide for security in old age.

Tasseled—great financial losses and threat of mental shock.

Cross formation—threat of ill health late in life, but with care may be averted.

Unusual Lines Emanating from the Line of Life

A definite branch line at or near the beginning of the life line extending to the mount of Jupiter, under first finger—unusual marked success; can be a brilliant marriage or career, but avoid egotism.

A connecting line to Saturn, under second finger—desire for solitude; often deeply religious. If this line starts inside the life line, on the mount of Venus, domestic or personal grievances can deprive one or more persons of all the happiness in life.

A line to Apollo, under the third finger—usually wealth or fame through the aid of friends or family. This must be a straight line. Wavy or broken lines mean struggles that may hinder the ultimate goal.

A connecting line to Mercury area, heavy as the life line, with no breaks—prosperity in business or profession, usually through the help of loved ones. If this line cuts through a strong fate or Apollo line, the business outcome would be dubious because of interference with one or more projects, or too many people interested in the same thing.

Small lines that cut through the life line are usually annoying interferences that hinder business or inflict unhappiness. Sometimes called bad luck lines.

A line to Upper Mars—unusual bravery, physical strength, often in service to one's country.

Line to Luna—many interpretations. Strong life and head lines with it may mean love of travel, restlessness. With drooping head line, imaginative and creative ability such as writers, artists, musicians, etc. In a weak hand—lascivious tendencies. With a weak life line denoting illness, this line to Luna increases the hazard. If a cross formation is on this line to Luna, there is a desire to escape from problems, so habitual alcoholism or dope addiction is the result.

THE LINE OF HEAD

The normal starting point of the line of head is identical with the start of the line of life. They should be joined together, just touching. This start is about midway between the thumb and forefinger. The head line then proceeds across the palm toward the outside of the hand. It should slope gently downward so that it does not exactly terminate on the area of Upper Mars, nor on Luna below it. The line should not extend to the edge of the palm. This is a good head line. It represents mental power, intellectuality, good memory.

Joined to the life line, it shows a cautious nature; the longer the join, the more caution.

Separated, a very spirited quality, a desire to forge ahead.

Widely separated, restlessness. Willing to take chances without sufficient thought to consequences.

The normal, average head line that is straight across the hand reaching under the area of Apollo or as far as Mercury shows mental balance and a good intellect. Naturally, it must be remembered that these interpretations are for normal hands with a strong thumb and good fingers. Any abnormal marking would contradict a good reading. A clear, firm line gives common sense. A thin, light line, indecision. A red line, aggressiveness, strong determination. A short line, need for outside assistance to achieve success. Very short, insufficient ambition or lacking the energy to fulfill any ambition. Double head line, unexpected inheritance; two or more interests. Branches that are small and descending, distractions that divert and lessen the ability to work or concentrate.

Ascending branches are good. To Jupiter, wealth; to Apollo, intense interest in the arts; to Mercury, business acumen or a desire to benefit or aid fellow men.

Small lines or crossed formation that join the head line to the life line at the beginning of the lines, forced to earn a living contrary to early plans or desires. Delicate childhood, shyness.

Irregularities of the Head Line

Chained effect, mental problems, due to ill health, variable temperament. Wavy, uneven line, deceitful, unreliable, unable to cope with problems of life itself. Need for good companionship and guidance. Turned back at the end of the line, exaggerated egotism. Islands and slightly twisted, financial disappointments. Breaks in the line under Saturn, Apollo, or Mercury, unhappiness in personal or business relations. The more breaks, the more serious. If there is a parallel line underneath the break, complete harmony will resume. A square surrounding these breaks modifies the problem.

Beginning under the first finger, not at the edge where the life line starts, conceit, overestimation of abilities or importance.

Several branches under the first finger, ambition enters every phase of life, self, family, and business; desire for wealth.

Beginning under Saturn finger (below that area) and under the heart line, there is no pride, very little ambition, and often a state of morbidity.

Terminations of the Head Line

Under Saturn, very little intelligence, premature death if a poor health line is indicated. Otherwise, insanity.

Under Apollo, desire to obtain wealth in the easiest possible way. Often lighthearted, cheerful personality gifted for the theater or one of the arts.

Under Mercury, excellent manager in any field of endeavor.

On Upper Mars, fast thinking, presence of mind, ability or urge to fight for a cause.

Sloping to Luna, imaginative or creative, abiding by whatever occupational demands there may be. This could run the gamut from the housewife who wants her home to be a model of good taste, to the musical composer or the author who demand the ultimate of themselves.

An abnormally long, straight head line that extends to the side of the palm, actually on the edge of the hand, denotes selfishness, secretiveness, usually very demanding of others. It can be the result of fear. May possess an exceptionally brilliant intellect.

Curling up onto the mount area of Apollo or Mercury intensifies the qualities of those mounts.

A forked ending adds a marked degree of the imaginative of the Luna area and the common sense of the Upper Mars area, so there is tenacity of purpose, power, and ability to plan ahead. The larger the fork the stronger the aims.

A triple fork ending augurs a brilliant alliance, since the topmost prong adds the talent of the practical business mind.

Ending on heart line, sacrifice everything for loved ones.

Head and heart lines as one in path of head line, cool and calculating.

Unusual Lines Emanating from the Head Line

A strong, deep line from the head line to the mount area of Jupiter, ambitions that lead to success.

A heavy line, not just a fragmentary branch to Saturn, registers intense religious fervor.

To Apollo, wealth or success in chosen field of employment.

To Mercury, prosperous business relations.

Line leaving head line and dropping down on Luna area, strong imagination. This is a very important line in any hand, and its final interpretation lies in the type of hand and the sum total of all the lines, areas, thumb, fingers, and special markings. However, imagination plays a strong part in the final reading.

THE LINE OF HEART

The line of heart normally starts in the area of the mount of Jupiter, under the first finger, then runs across the palm at the base of the mounts to the edge of the hand. It is the first horizontal line in the palm. It represents the emotional and physical qualities dependent upon the heart. A clear line indicates a love of family, steadfastness, and human sympathy.

Starting high, almost to the base of the finger, jealousy.

Beginning low and running in a straight line, apparent affection for family with little demonstration of emotions.

Between first and second finger, love is sensual; a very tolerant nature; a generous attitude toward all people.

Between second and third fingers, a negative attitude toward love; the object of the affections must be a very understanding person.

The heart line that drops down at the start and joins the head line, the head then "rules the heart."

If the heart, head, and life lines are joined at the start, unreasonableness in affections and family life may cause unhappiness and disappointments. An extremist unwilling to use good judgment.

Extending around the percussion of the hand, very spirited, inclined to be too audacious.

Long and thin, revengeful when frustrated.

Wide and pale, inclined to dissipate because of indecision.

The higher the line lies, the warmer and more affectionate the nature. The lower it lies, the colder and more calculative.

If the line is missing, then extreme selfishness may exist. It may be part of the head line if only one line is visible. In this case, read it as a head line tempered by the affections.

A double heart line increases the capacity for love and affection. Unusual physical strength and endurance.

A fork formation at the beginning, a nicely balanced home life.

Small branches, lightheartedness, gaiety.

Downward branches that do not touch another important line, disappointments with those you love or admire.

Irregularities of the Line of Heart

Wavy line, uncertainty in love.

Small bars that cut through from beginning to end, disappointments with a loved one.

Chained, unable to make a choice of affections.

Faintly chained, emotionally unstable.

Islanded, infidelity. If the life line is also islanded then look for a physical defect.

White spots, happy in love.

Breaks in the line, inconstancy; under Saturn, a broken engagement; under Apollo, lucky parting of the ways for a mismated couple.

A circle, misunderstanding and final separation.

Crosses, interferences due to money matters such as debts.

Lines Emanating from the Heart Line

A line descending from the heart line to the head line, an engagement called off before date of marriage.

A line to the life line, disappointment and sorrow due to loss of member of the family.

A line to the Mercury area, collapse of business because of family or loved one. Extravagant tastes.

Line dropping to Luna, uncontrollable emotions, quarrelsome.

Line from heart line ascending to Saturn, unrequited love.

Line to Apollo, career may interfere with normal home life.

Terminations of the Heart Line

When the line of heart curls upward at the end on the mount of Mercury there is a keen interest connected with the affairs of the heart. Monetary matters must be taken into consideration.

Forked ending, danger of separation ending in divorce.

Tasseled ending, too many love affairs.

Secondary Lines
(Also called the minor lines)

THE LINE OF SATURN
(Also called the fate line)

The line of Saturn starts at the base of the palm near the wrist, normally between the life line and the edge of the area of Luna. It proceeds in a straight line to the mount of Saturn, the area under the second finger. A line like this has traditionally been considered a mark of good luck, though when studied it really signifies a steadfast desire to follow a definite pattern of living. It can be found in the hands of the rich and the poor alike, from the housewife or the cloistered nun to the seagoing official of the navy or famous personalities—in fact, in any station of life.

Absence of the line of Saturn does not mean failure. It means that the career, the way of living, can be chosen by the individual, with or without help. Often a new line will grow into the palm as the years pass by; however, the line of the Sun can be read as a substitute fate line.

A short life line may be transferred on a long line of Saturn, usually following some small line of demarcation on the latter.

Starting Points of the Line of Saturn

From the life line—success through one's own resources and efforts. Might have some help from relatives or friends. The date, approximately, can be gauged from the joining point on the life line. Marriages are sometimes calculated at this same point. For women this can also mean a very good career.

Starting inside the life line on the Mount of Venus—assistance from the family from the very start. This can be education and/or financial help to launch a business or career. There will, at least, be parental guidance, or an inheritance.

Cutting a beginning from the rascette, or the wrist lines—many difficulties to surmount before the ultimate is achieved.

From the mount of Luna—opportunity comes through channels outside the family circle. The imaginative qualities of Luna lend a restless urge that drives the mind to seek an unusual career. Many professional people have this type of line. If the line starts low on the mount, intuitive qualities are added. If the mount itself is large, or high, creative talent is present. If the line starts higher on this mount area, travel could be included.

On Mars area—an adamant, forceful trait is added, but there is usually a branch line with this to determine the direction this trait may lead. It may be in connection with physical activity such as sports, either professional or amateur, or with the military services. Will power and personal drive would bring the desired aim no matter what the career might be.

From the middle of the palm, the head line or the heart line—the duration of the career is shorter and later in life.

Terminations of the Line of Saturn

On the area of Saturn—responsibilities may begin early. For a woman, if marriage is her lot, she may be sheltered and protected throughout her years. A man's career may be charted through his own efforts and be successful to the end. If mishaps are marked elsewhere in the hand, then there exists a strong determination to understand people and situations and to maintain the best possible standard of human relations.

Near the head line—the pattern of living changes. Surroundings, career change. New things lie ahead. Avoid obstinacy.

Near the heart line or on it—everything can change and effect the emotional life to such an extent that a new interest is needed to fill the void. Avoid jealousy.

Forked, with one prong on Jupiter—add ambition; one prong on Apollo—add a brilliant, quick-thinking facet; lastly, add the cautious aspect of Saturn itself—the sum-up is success.

A Jupiter instead of a Saturn termination is not uncommon. The ambitions, whether for business, politics, a home, security, or profession should be attained.

Lines Emanating from the Line of Saturn

To life line—family connection or assistance to family.

To head line—another interest or business. Can be a hobby.

To heart line—emotional problems; disappointment and sorrow due to a loved one; need to seek new environment for work and pleasure.

To Jupiter—a brilliant marriage, great happiness, or an impending career with someone else.

To Apollo—artistic success, usually with financial gain. Socially aspirant.

To Mercury—business ability; eloquence or wit. Good, friendly contacts.

To Luna—avoid despondency over interference of any kind.

Irregularities

Small cutting lines—impediments.

Island—financial losses.

Breaks of any kind, anywhere on the line—a change of surroundings, home, occupation, one or all. A parallel line beside the break is good because it means the loss is temporary. A square may avert the change or disaster.

Wavy or chained—variable, quarrelsome nature.

Very red—avoid situations that arouse wrath.

Very deep and red—overwork, taking on too much responsibility that can end in a nervous ailment.

Frayed in any part—caution to take care of health.

THE LINE OF APOLLO

The line of Apollo has numerous alternative names, namely, the fortune line, line of luck, line of the Sun, solar line, second fate line, line of brilliance, line of success. All are indicative of the ultimate significance of the line itself.

The line of Apollo augments the line of Saturn, when present, and supplants it when absent. If you have both you are fortunate. This line adds brilliance and strength to an exceptional talent.

Absence of this line does not mean failure, nor a dull, uninteresting life. It means that the struggle for success may be harder, and so-called luck will be the results that accrue from laborious work and untiring effort.

The normal starting point for the line of Apollo is near the first line of the rascette on the wrist, and proceeds in a straight line to the area under the third finger, known as the mount of Apollo. It denotes generally a quick thinker and a promise of great popularity, even fame. Wealth usually follows. The clearer the line, the greater the amount of financial gain.

Starting from and joined to the life line—talent must be developed, sponsored or financed by family, friends, or some sort of organization. When this line pertains to a business career, the person's own money might be placed as an endowment of sorts in the field of arts, or for literary achievement.

Starting from the area of Luna—imaginative qualities govern the choice of career. Desire for travel may be present, but creative ability is the motivating force. Composers, writers, dancers, painters, architects, and innumerable other categories of creative people are likely to have this line.

Beginning within the triangle, or the center of the palm—success follows a rough struggle to surmount business and/or family obstacles.

From the head line—the subject usually attains financial security through self-planned ideas, due entirely to personal ingenuity. This is usually well organized so that an orderly progression follows without too much hard work.

If it starts in the area of Upper Mars, on the side of the palm—everything will be attained through slavish persistence and will power.

If the line seems to start from the heart line—success may not come until late in life. If this line is separated from the heart line, it then adds honors and wealth to a career indicated elsewhere in the palm.

Terminations of the Line of Apollo

Ending on the area of Apollo but close to the Mercruy area which is beneath the little finger—materialistic attitude regarding every aspect pertaining to career. Contracts, costs, and profits must be thoroughly considered before any performance or occupational venture. Lucky the artist or practitioner who has this business acumen.

Slanting closer to the Saturn area under the second finger—seriousness governs any decision. Whatever the chances of luck and the promise of great success, this slanting line means that a lot of thought is given to any project to protect one's reputation.

A forked ending—more than one talent, and probably capable of using both.

A triple forked ending—very unusual, but a remarkable ability to attain both fame and wealth. The carefulness of Saturn and the shrewd business instinct of Mercury give permanence to the great talent of Apollo.

Terminating at the heart line—often due to marriage or a sufficiency of an amassed fortune.

Modifying lines connected to other lines partake of the meaning of those lines. For instance, a line leaving the Apollo line and touching or crossing the line of life will indicate some interference from relatives. It would affect the finances also.

A line joining Apollo and fate (Saturn) lines—partnership.

A small line leaving the Apollo line and touching the heart line—a happy love affair that might resolve in marriage.

This same little line cutting through the heart line—a love affair that was broken or ends unhappily.

A cross close to the termination, toward Saturn—religious fervor or intense seriousness about career and personal life.

A star at the termination—excellent chances of success through teamwork or assistance.

A broken line—various periods of success. May be different types of interests, or changes due to marriages, change of surroundings, ill health, or causes beyond one's control.

THE LINE OF MERCURY

The line of Mercury is also known as the line of health, the line of liver, or the hepatica line.

The normal starting point is from the wrist, just above the rascette, then in a straight line to the area of Mercury, under the little finger. Its best form is a solid line. It represents an abundance of health and success in one's chosen occupation.

Starting from the line of life—digestive ailments.

Beginning in the area of Luna—restlessness, desire to travel, do anything other than the immediate occupation.

Absence of this line has always been considered a good omen with no fear of digestive troubles. Gypsy lore has carried this tale as far back as the beginning of fortune telling. Mercurians are well known for their good appetites and their vivacity. Those fortunate enough to have no portion of this line are able to control their craving for food and drink. They are quick thinkers, always aware of a good opportunity.

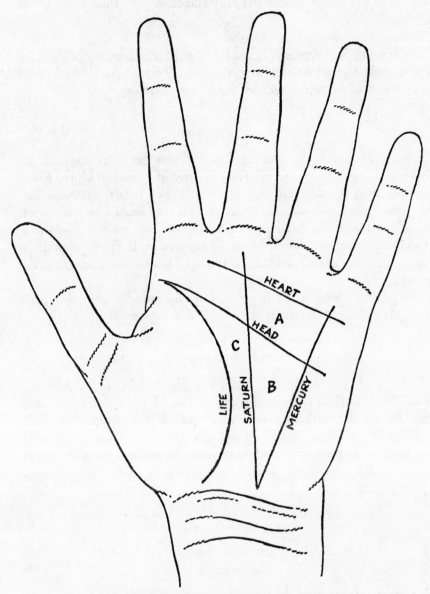

A–The quadrangle between heart and head lines
B–The triangle—formed by lines of Saturn, head, and Mercury
C–Another triangle—formed by lines of life, head, and Mercury

They have the ability to use wit and humor to gain their point in an argument.

Broken, short lines—poor health.

A wavy line—uncertainty, changeability, poor judgment, biliousness.

A triangle formed by this line, the line of Saturn, and the line of head—talent of so-called "second sight," premonitions.

THE QUADRANGLE

The quadrangle is the area that lies between the heart line and the head line. Lengthwise it extends from the area of Jupiter to Upper Mars. It represents good judgment and fair play. When narrow—jealousy and pettiness. If the narrowness is caused by a lowered heart line—penurious, fearful. If due to the head line rising toward the heart line—narrow-mindedness. Narrow in both hands—exaggeration. If the quadrangle is very wide—selfish, independent, perverse. Many cross lines—irritable, nervous.

The Mystic Cross, when it exists, is to be found within the quadrangle. It denotes interest in the occult and mysterious.

THE TRIANGLE

The triangle lies in the area formed by the life, head, and Mercury lines. This is rarely a completed triangle. The Mercury line must sometimes be supplanted by an imaginary line. If well marked—a well-balanced temperament, usually good physique and a strong mind. A very large area—bravery. Small—cowardice. A cross—a mark of action, such as soldiers may have. Many lines making a grille formation—too argumentative.

The Lesser Lines

THE RASCETTES
(the bracelets)

These are the lines on the wrist, not on the palm itself. Traditionally time was computed on them at the rate of twenty-five years per line. By today's gauge of longevity, the count must be thirty years per line, the average number of lines being three. A safer method of computation is the estimate that is indicated by the life, heart, and fate lines. The first line, clearly marked, not frayed, indicates good health.

Chained or frayed means hard work to achieve success or a lucrative position in life.

A badly chained and arched first line that touches the palm—chance of difficulty with the reproductive organism. This too is an old traditional saying, but a poor Mercury and life line would indicate a weakness if there were one.

THE GIRDLE OF VENUS

This line is a crescent- or arc-shaped line that starts between the first and second finger, then curves down toward the heart line, only to rise and terminate between the third and fourth fingers. It is a sister line, in a way, to augment the qualities of the heart line. It can strengthen deficiencies that are physical handicaps, but it can be too overpowering if the heart line is strong. It is the mark of sensuality in a powerful hand. In a very well-balanced hand it can mean an aesthetic disposition.

Broken or fragmentary—disappointments in love, reticent.

Double lines—nervousness, excitability.

Triple formation—tendency to hysteria.

THE RING OF SOLOMON

This is a line that encircles the area or part of the area of the mount of Jupiter under the first finger. It can be seen most frequently in partial formation in overlapping lines. This is a small line and not to be confused with the crease at the join of the finger to the palm. It starts near the beginning of the line of head, then curves upward, ending between the first and second fingers.

A solid curved line—great aptitude for the psychic, the occult, the mystical.

A straight line, usually a little indistinct—interest in performing magic or a curiosity in the occult.

Short, overlapping lines—understanding and appreciation of psychiatric problems in others.

THE RING OF SATURN

This is a semicircle under the second finger on the area of the mount of Saturn. It starts between the first and second fingers and makes a curve downward, ending between the second and third fingers.

A solid line—lack of purpose, depressed, unable to cope with life, irresponsible.

A broken line—tendency to suicide.

THE VIA LASCIVIA
(also called the cephalic line)

The Via Lascivia, known also as the cephalic line or the Milky Way, is a sister line to the line of Mercury. It lies parallel to the Mercury line toward the percussion side of the palm. When the Mercury line is weak, the Via Lascivia serves as a strengthener and is supposed to give the owner physical stamina to overcome any defects that may be registered on the weaker Mercury line.

When this line is absolutely parallel to the Mercury line and present in both palms it shows abnormal sensuality and a lust for money.

Starting from the line of life—immorality.

A wavy Via Lascivia—inconstancy.

A chained formation—worst form of lewdness.

A branch line starting from the Via Lascivia, crossing the line of Mercury, and just touching a short line of Apollo or extending into the area of Apollo—unexpected wealth, luxurious living.

Two equally strong lines—interest in two different enterprises; in a woman's hand, a home and a business interest.

A star on the Via Lascivia—wealth easily squandered in reckless living or associations.

THE LINE OF INTUITION

The line of intuition is a curved, crescent-like line, extending from the lowest part of the Luna area to the area of Mercury. Both the beginning and the termination are located near the percussion of the palm. The bend of the curve is inward toward the palm proper. This line pertains to psychic powers.

A solid line formation—natural ability to interpret the occult sciences; in both hands, a life devoted to the occult. Vivid intuition with possible mediumistic ability.

Reversed line of intuition—impressions or premonitions are usually wrong.

Line of intuition with a cross under Saturn finger—religious fervor added to occultism; psychometric powers.

Broken in small lines—nervous and unpredictable.

Terminating on Upper Mars—power of hypnotism, or a personality that influences others.

An island at the beginning of the line—somnambulism.

A star—psychic dreamer, an extremist. If the line of head drops down onto the area of Luna and actually crosses the line of intuition—temporary insanity. In a weak hand with a small thumb—little hope of sanity.

THE LINE OF MARS

This line runs parallel to and just inside the line of life. It is a sister line and serves as a strengthener to a weak or broken life line. To a strong life line it adds unusual physical stamina. It often appears as a short or fragmentary line which acts as a forceful reserve when most needed.

A short line—aids physically when nervous pressure or strain seems unbearable. Unusually brave.

A very long line—extraordinarily active life, possibly ending far from birthplace. This line is often found in strong hands like the military or police.

A branch ending in the Luna area—brutal, intemperate.

A star on this branch—lack of self-control.

Forked ending—violent, vicious disposition.

If the line appears only in the left hand—imaginative or psychic trends.

THE LINES OF AFFECTION
(lines of union)

The lines of affection, sometimes called the lines of union, are also known as the lines of marriage. They are located on the side of the hand under the little finger on the area called the mount of Mercury, running parallel to the heart line. There may be one, two, three, or more. They represent love affairs, marriages, and marital complications. Usually there is one line that is more clearly marked and longer than the others, denoting a marriage or the most important attachment.

A straight clear long line—a good marriage with happiness and contentment. If it continues to the line of Apollo—an exceptionally brilliant alliance for husband and wife promising fame and wealth. If it cuts through—misfortune and unhappiness.

If the line slopes downward—the mate will be the first to die.

If the line turns upward—no marriage, or a frustration that causes disappointment.

A broken line—divorce or separation, especially if a line runs from the line of union to the line of life.

Overlapping broken line—periods of reconciliation.

Forked at the beginning, on the side of the percussion—self-willed separation.

Forked at the end of the line—separation by the will of the mate.

Two parallel lines very close together—affectionately called the mother-in-law line. It may be a relative from either side of the family.

All of these interpretations must be identified on the life and/or fate lines by a cross line, cross, or break, depending upon the good or bad traits of the lines of affection.

Children are supposed to be promised by small cross lines on the important line or lines that indicate a marriage. Straight lines for boys. Slanting lines for girls. These lines can be on hands of people who have no children, but the desire may have been so strong that despite circumstances, the lines remain in the hands.

The line which is closest to the heart line—the earliest possible marriage or love affair.

If the most important, longest line lies closer to the little finger—marriage late in life.

Absence of lines—marriage does not change the lives of either husband or wife. Living conditions, social status, and economic basis remain the same.

An island on a line—unfaithful.

Many islands—irresponsible, not desirable for marriage.

Star on a line—hopeless infidelity.

LINES OF INFLUENCE
(also called rays of influence)

These are lines that start on the mount area of Venus and cut through the life line. It refers to someone in the family or a close friend who has great influence at the time indicated on the life line. If it reaches the line of Saturn, a liaison or marriage. To the line of Apollo, an influence on the career. To the line of affection on mount of Mercury, unhappiness in marriage. To mount of Jupiter, assistance for fulfillment of ambition. If the mount of Venus is low, irritation can be overwhelming.

The escape line is a single strong line starting from the mount area of Venus extending to the area of Luna. It is what it says, a way of escape from self or problems, leading to drug addiction, actually running away from responsibilities, or obsessed by sexual perversion. Frays, signs or breaks only magnify the awful situation.

Family lines are small curved lines that run parallel to the life line within the Venus area. They are not part of the line of Mars, which is a sister line and strengthener to the life line. The small lines represent family and friends who help morally or financially; their advice is helpful.

The thumb chain is a chained line or formation found around the place where the thumb joins the mount area of Venus. It means an argumentative inclination, a desire to exert will power.

LINES OF OPPOSITION

These are horizontal lines on the mount area of Upper Mars. They start from the percussion side of the hand. They represent opposition toward other people. This can be a financial problem or a personal complication that takes the form of enmity.

Short lines—unimportant quarrels or friction.

A long line reaching the life line or mount area of Venus—family problems that could be very serious.

Reaching or cutting through the line of Saturn or Apollo—a legal threat or danger of lawsuit. In the hands of people with long thumbs and strong head lines, the opposition lines pertain to lawyers, judges, and the many other appointees connected with law whereby they handle such problems. These lines can also be found in the hands of the wives of men in the legal profession.

Cutting the heart line—the affections will become involved.

One exception—if the line turns and terminates on the area of Apollo it becomes the fortune line—a successful career in spite of opposition due to personal effort alone.

TRAVEL LINES

These are the horizontal lines on the Luna area. Short percussion lines—travel by sea and air. On the area itself—travel by land. This is an old traditional reading for hands that have few lines. Generally, there are oblique lines meaning restlessness, hence the urge to travel. When such lines reach the area of Jupiter, Saturn, Apollo, or Mercury, they become one of the fate lines and are treated as such.

11

Phrenology

Once the most popular of all psychic sciences, phrenology was an off-shoot of modern physiognomy as propounded by Johann Kaspar Lavater (1741–1801). Among Lavater's admirers was Franz Joseph Gall, who was born in Baden in 1758, studied medicine in Strassburg, and became a practicing physician in Vienna, where, in 1796, he advanced his theories of phrenology, which he based on extensive research.

Just as physiognomy had its roots in ancient teachings, so could phrenology point to earlier findings. One dealt with general physical appearance as an index to individual traits; the other considered the formation of the skull as indicative of mental processes.

Both studies followed a similar pattern: With physiognomy, facial formations were checked against traits that they seemingly represented, which led to surveys of less obvious formations, which were accepted on the strength of positive—or negative—results.

With phrenology, Gall applied this same process of rationalization to the formation of the skull, dividing it into three major regions which offered rather obvious interpretations. Those areas were subdivided into many more, all identified by individual enlargements, or lack of such. Gall listed twenty-six of these, and compared the characteristics of persons having the same notable "bumps" or developments.

These were later classified as irregular areas, and their number was increased by Johann Kaspar Spurzheim (1776–1832), another Viennese physician and an ardent follower of Gall. In Scotland, Spurzheim's lectures impressed a lawyer named George Combe (1788–1858), who took up the subject of phrenology and later helped to establish it in America.

There, the number of divisions, which had jumped first to thirty-two and then grown to thirty-six, was increased to forty-two by the Fowler brothers, Orson and Lorenzo, who started giving phrenological readings in New York in 1835, and soon issued charts and sent lecturers throughout the country. Eventually they set up a phrenological museum containing thousands of models of human skulls, ranging from those of savages to famous historical personages, all of whose traits could be traced by a skilled phrenologist.

The three main divisions consist of:

1. The region of instincts or propensities, found at the lower portion of the back of the head.

2. The sentiments or moral faculties, which occupy most of the upper portion of the head.

3. The abilities or intellectual faculties, at the front of the head, including the forehead.

Such groupings gave phrenology a solid framework. It was generally conceded that the well-developed forehead of civilized man was the stamp of intellectuality, as compared to the sloping forehead of his early ancestors. Conversely, overdevelopment at the base of the skull was the mark of primitive man, indicative of unrestrained instinct. A high, large head showed a greater capacity for sentiments than a low, brain-cramping skull.

As each region was subdivided, appropriate titles were bestowed upon the smaller areas thus localized and defined. This nomenclature changed with the years, but the findings themselves remained substantially the same. With the aid of the chart shown here, anyone can locate the areas of the human head and give a phrenological reading, based on the development or deficiency of specific divisions, according to the listed traits.

At the outset, these readings are generally limited to the most noticeable bumps, which serve as keys to the individual's outstanding traits. But through comparison of different heads, minor differences become more noticeable and can be interpreted accordingly. In the heyday of phrenology, experts toured the country reading thousands of heads, and became remarkably precise in detail when giving an individual analysis.

In studying the accompanying chart and the list of traits given with it, you will note a similarity between some of the adjacent areas, one often blending into another, as with "veneration" and "spirituality." This is helpful in giving a reading, as the phrenologist will not be far off in his finding if he moves a trifle into an adjacent area. With others, however, there is a sharper line of demarcation, as between "friendship" and "combativeness." This can account for certain conflicts of nature, when the development of one area carries over into the next.

In addition to the grand divisions of propensities, sentiments, and abilities, special groupings have been formed for easier identification of the individual faculties, or organs, as they are sometimes termed. These special groupings are utilized in the list that follows:

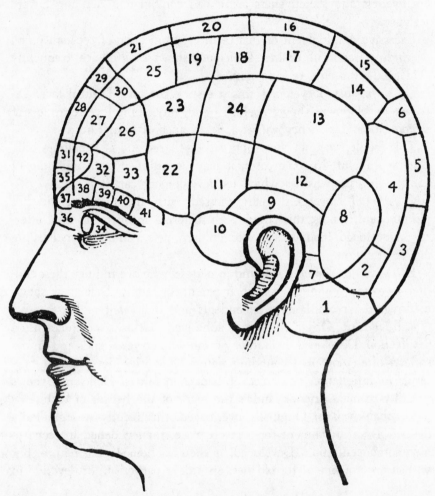

Phrenological chart with numbers corresponding to descriptions of faculties

Description of Mental Faculties

GROUP I: THE SOCIAL PROCLIVITIES

These are located in the lower back of the head, entirely within the region of propensities. When large, they often give a fullness to the entire area. There are six in all:

1. *Amativeness:* When developed, this indicates an ardent interest in the opposite sex, an excellent token when supported by helpful faculties, such as friendship, which is synonymous with affection. Conversely, amativeness and secretiveness are a bad combination, tending toward jealousy.

Excessive development of this faculty is indicative of sensuality and overindulgence in all desires. Deficiency shows indifference, frequently evidenced by a shy, retiring nature.

2. *Conjugality:* Developed, this stresses a constant, faithful love. Excessive development shows a selfish trend, unyielding love regardless of reciprocation. Deficiency shows a fickle, inconstant nature.

This faculty was not shown on earlier charts, and is sometimes difficult to pinpoint. In some cases, it may be nullified by a mingling of surrounding propensities which its development can indicate.

3. *Parental Love:* Originally blessed with the elaborate title of philoprogenitiveness, this covers both maternal instinct and filial affection. Developed, it shows a love of children, pets, and all others needing aid or attention.

Excessive development is found in persons who overindulge their children or expect too much from their parents or family. Deficiency shows a disregard for children or dependents and their welfare.

4. *Friendship:* Originally termed adhesiveness, this is sometimes listed as affection. Developed, it shows a person who craves friends and enjoys society—often one of a confiding nature. Excessive development may result in infatuation or choice of bad companions. Deficiency shows inability to make friends, and is the mark of the hermit or recluse.

5. *Inhabitiveness:* Originally overlooked, this faculty was gradually defined as an attachment for a given place, then widened in scope to include concentration. Developed, it shows a home-loving nature, but with it an attachment for old ties, an ardent patriotism, or devotion to a cause.

Excessive development brings homesickness and inability to adjust to new ways or surroundings. Deficiency is the mark of the "rolling stone," with a desire for change and travel.

6. *Continuity:* Once included with inhabitiveness, this faculty is a fuller form of concentration. Developed, it shows unity of thought, with the ability to keep to a subject. Excessive development indicates too much urge for detail or repetition; deficiency, too many interests and inability to complete work once started.

GROUP 2: THE SELFISH PROPENSITIES

These faculties are found at the sides of the head, above or around the ears. Excessive width or narrowness of the head in these regions may be the determining factor of their development, rather than any smaller, localized bulges.

7. *Vitativeness:* When developed, a token of vitality, with the ability to resist ailments. Excessive development shows worry over illness and fear of the future. Deficiency shows lack of stamina or a sickly individual.

8. *Combativeness:* Reasonably developed, this shows a courageous, energetic nature, with strong powers of resistance. Further development, however, marks the antagonist rather than a good competitor. Excessive development is accompanied by a quarrelsome, quick-tempered disposition, given to argument. Deficiency is the sign of a cowardly, fearful person incapable of self-defense.

9. *Destructiveness:* When developed, a hard, severe nature, yet efficient as well as ruthless, therefore indicative of executive capacity. Excessive development shows a vindictive trend, both cruel and malicious. Deficiency means inability to give orders and a general voidance of decision.

10. *Alimentiveness:* The faculty ruling the appetite, according to later phrenologists. Developed, the sign of the good eater, fond of food and drink. Excessive development marks the glutton and compulsive drinker. Deficiency, a light and finicky eater, frequently an abstainer.

11. *Acquisitiveness:* When developed, this shows a thrifty nature, capable of gaining great wealth, with great desire for same. Excessive development is the sign of a miserly, even thieving nature. Deficiency is found in the spendthrift and others who do not recognize the value of money.

12. *Secretiveness:* Duly developed, this shows a tactful, well-restrained nature, capable of discretion, but sometimes inclined to shrewd practices. Excessive development is often accompanied by deceit and double-dealing to the extent of outright prevarication. Deficiency of this faculty connotes an overtalkative, indiscreet nature, incapable of keeping a confidence.

13. *Cautiousness:* When developed, this shows a careful, watchful disposition, unwilling to take risks and therefore apt to be apprehensive in many ways. Excessive development causes a person to postpone plans indefinitely, rousing prejudice or even fear in a hesitant mind. Defi-

ciency denotes a reckless, careless nature that plunges into anything, including trouble.

Expert phrenologists are careful not to confuse the faculties of combativeness and cautiousness, though the positive phase of one resembles the negative of the other and vice versa. Combativeness involves physical action or some threat of violence, whereas cautiousness involves mental problems.

Still, cautiousness belongs with the selfish propensities, because it is a primitive instinct, as witness the fear shown by animals toward something unknown. So we are dealing with an innate trait in considering the faculty of cautiousness. There are instances, however, where cautiousness can be modified or governed to some degree, placing it in the next category:

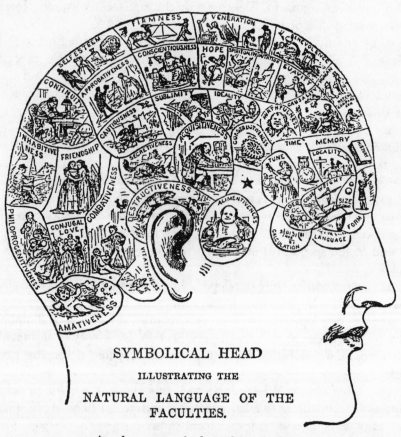

SYMBOLICAL HEAD

ILLUSTRATING THE

NATURAL LANGUAGE OF THE
FACULTIES.

Another type of phrenological chart

GROUP 3: THE ASPIRING FACULTIES

Starting from cautiousness, these faculties rise upward and backward from above the ears, approaching and reaching the crown of the head. They are sometimes termed the "lower sentiments" or the "self-controlling" group, as it is quite possible to elevate them from the involuntary to the voluntary stage.

14. *Approbativeness:* When developed, this shows appreciation of public acclaim and often the will to win it, along with fame and social position. Excessive development leads to self-praise, and denotes the publicity seeker who is often oversensitive to criticism. Deficiency shows an unconventional, Bohemian nature with disregard for popular opinion.

15. *Self-Esteem:* At the crown of the head. When developed, shows a commanding nature, with desire for authority and importance. Excessive development betokens arrogance, conceit, and a domineering manner. Deficiency shows an incompetent person, incapable of appreciating his own worth.

16. *Firmness:* Developed, shows purpose, endurance, and general stability of nature, coupled with an assertive manner. Excessive development is the mark of a stubborn, self-willed, and sometimes illogical personality. Deficiency shows an unstable disposition, yielding to any whim or fancy.

This faculty is farther forward than self-esteem, but earlier phrenologists carried it down the sides of the head as well, including the closely related faculty of conscientiousness, which at that time was undefined.

GROUP 4: THE MORAL SENTIMENTS

These are found in the coronal region and are regarded as dominating faculties in high, fully rounded heads.

17. *Conscientiousness:* Developed, an ability to recognize right from wrong, with a high sense of integrity, coupled by adherence to convictions. Excessive development results in criticism of others, which can lead to self-condemnation. Deficiency shows a lack of principle and a self-justification of one's own faults.

When first noticed, partly through its deficiency, conscientiousness was placed where firmness now stands and vice versa. Often, the two may be treated as one, but the more modern treatment is to set conscientiousness more toward the sides, with firmness centralized.

18. *Hope:* Once regarded simply as the concomitant of other faculties, hope was eventually assigned to this area, forward of conscientiousness. Developed, it marks an optimistic nature, confident of eventual happiness. Excessive development is the sign of the constant dreamer, whose extravagant expectations never are fulfilled. Deficiency denotes the pessimist, given to deep gloom.

19. *Spirituality:* An extension of the previous region, now defined as a separate faculty. Developed, a devout, intuitive nature, often with psychic overtones. Excessive development, a superstitious nature, sometimes fanatical. Deficiency is the mark of the complete skeptic.

20. *Veneration:* Akin to the last-named region. Developed, conformity to custom and tradition. Reverential, and highly admiring of greatness, with respect for old age. Excessive development, obsessed with lofty ideas, too inclined to hero-worship. Deficiency denotes a disrespectful, cynical type that belittles anything worthwhile.

21. *Benevolence:* When developed, a fine, humane, sympathetic disposition. Excessive development, oversympathetic, easily imposed upon. Deficiency denotes a calloused, selfish, unkind attitude, indifferent to the suffering of others.

GROUP 5: SEMI-INTELLECTUAL FACULTIES

Sometimes termed the perfective faculties, these are variously grouped, but are located in the region of the temples and are evidenced *in toto* with heads that are well developed in that area.

22. *Constructiveness:* Frequently classified as a mere propensity, this is the mark of mechanical ability, which may be largely an instinctive trait. When developed, however, it may show inventive genius and skills in design and engineering. Excessive development shows a trend toward the impractical, a love of gadgetry for its own sake. Deficiency is sometimes accompanied by a total lack of mechanical ability.

23. *Ideality:* Developed, this indicates the artistic sense, a love of beauty and perfection. It also symbolizes the truly poetic. Excessive development shows an overaesthetic nature, with a dislike for practical things. Deficiency is the mark of vulgarity and poor taste.

24. *Sublimity:* Developed, a love of nature's grandeur and the great creations of human art. Excessive development shows an extravagant nature given to exaggeration. Deficiency, an indifference to anything of a highly inspiring sort.

25. *Imitation:* Developed, this shows a flare for drama, acquired skills, and social graces. Excessive development denotes outright imitation, with no individuality. Deficiency marks a lack of capability, an inept nature.

26. *Mirthfulness:* Also listed as wit, this faculty, when developed, shows a cheerful, vivacious individual with a humorous disposition. Excessive development, the practical joker, given to ridicule. Deficiency shows a serious nature, unable to enjoy fun.

GROUP 6: THE REASONING FACULTIES

These are found in the upper forehead and presumably account for any great bulge noted there. They include:

27. *Casuality:* When developed, this is the sign of the thinker, with great ability at rationalization, a superior intellect. Excessive development, a mind given to theoretical rather than practical knowledge. Deficiency, poor powers of reason and judgment.

28. *Comparison:* Developed, this shows great analytical ability, with quickness at citing examples to prove a point. Good at quoting proverbs and appropriate sayings. Excessive development indicates a habitual fault-finder. Deficiency means lack of ability in forming sound conclusions.

29. *Human Nature:* Developed, this shows ability to judge people almost on sight. Excessive development, overcritical in judgment. Deficiency, a lack of discrimination in choice of friends and associates.

30. *Agreeableness:* When developed, the mark of the smooth, persuasive speaker with a winning personality. Excessive development indicates glib, empty talk. Deficiency shows an unpleasant, challenging manner.

GROUP 7: THE LITERARY FACULTIES

These run across the center of the forehead, beginning with the very center, then spreading on both sides. They include:

31. *Eventuality:* Developed, a remarkable memory for facts and experiences, often of a historical nature. Excessive development, a tendency to describe events in lengthy, redundant fashion. Deficiency, no memory for past events.

32. *Time:* Developed, this shows an uncanny sense of time and timing, with a good memory for dates. Excessive development, a stickler for punctuality and exactitude. Deficiency shows little or no regard for time in any way.

33. *Tune*: Developed, a remarkable memory for tunes and good appreciation of music. Excessive development, the urge to sing and play continually. Deficiency marks the person devoid of musical sense.

34. *Language*: This faculty is shown in the eye itself, evidenced by a bulge of the eye or the area just beneath it. Developed, it denotes skill in speech and writing, often with the knack of acquiring foreign languages. Excessive development, an overtalkative nature. Deficiency, lack of word memory, and poor expression.

GROUP 8: THE PERCEPTIVE FACULTIES

Identifying these requires considerable skill and careful comparison of different persons. Overhang of brows is not the only gauge; if brows are well forward from the ears, perceptive faculties are regarded as large.

35. *Individuality*: Above the eyes, on the line between. When developed, shows keen observation with ability to individualize or particularize on data thus gained, so other faculties can form ideas. Excessive development, a prying, inquisitive nature. Deficiency, a poor observer, who must focus attention.

36. *Form*: Between the eyes, at each side; when developed, the eyes seem wide apart. Good memory of faces, diagrams, and objects. Excessive development shows annoyance at any lack of harmonious form. Deficiency, poor memory of shapes; no ability at drawing or describing objects.

37. *Size*: Higher and outward. When developed, it shows recognition of proportions, in objects and measurement. Excessive development, constant urge for unnecessary comparisons. Deficiency, no recognition of proportions or distance.

38. *Weight*: The next area in order. Developed, shows good balance and ability to judge weights. Excessive development often shows a love of high altitudes. Deficiency denotes awkwardness and lack of balance or poise.

39. *Color*: Developed, a natural memory for colors and shades, with joy in blending them. Excessive development, sensitivity toward clashing colors. Deficiency shows little interest in colors; perhaps color-blindness.

40. *Order*: Developed, shows good planning, systematic procedure, a neat, well-regulated nature. Excessive development shows a fussy trend, waste of time in trivial planning and rearrangements, annoyance at persons who are less exacting. Deficiency, lack of method or regularity, generally untidy, even chaotic.

41. *Calculation:* Farthest out from the middle line, carrying beyond the eyes. Developed, the sign of a mathematical mind, quick at figures and mental summaries. Excessive development may show an interest in figures to the exclusion of all else. Deficiency indicates poor memory for figures, inability or distaste for even simple additions, and trouble in balancing accounts.

42. *Locality:* Placed higher than individuality and on each side of it. When developed, this shows the urge for travel, quick adjustment to new surroundings, and the ability to remember places. Excessive development shows an urge for exploration, often for its own sake. Deficiency indicates poor memory for places and little interest in new scenes.

SUMMARY OF PHRENOLOGY

From the detailed descriptions given and a study of the accompanying chart, it becomes all the more obvious that the expert phrenologist must depend on much more than mere bumps, protuberances, or even noticeable bulges to conclude his findings. An uneven skull naturally gave plenty to work from, as it showed many developments—frequently of the excessive type—with corresponding deficiencies in other faculties.

But most people were of more balanced types, anxious to learn their natural traits and how to further them while avoiding any pitfalls that phrenology might reveal. In dealing with such types, phrenologists used an over-all measurement, taking the center of the ear as the axis of the brain and using comparative distances to determine the development of the various faculties. At that, there is a chance of error, as the ear itself may be wrongly placed, but allowance can be made for such a factor.

Unfortunately for phrenology, it reached its peak of fame due to its widespread acceptance as a physical rather than as a psychic science. Comparatively modern, and initiated by physicians of the day, phrenology filled a void in the study of brain structure and functions, thus advancing the cause of medical science. Later discoveries, however, refuted the more extravagant claims of phrenology. Rather than backtrack to fundamentals and branch out along new lines, the neophrenologists preferred to sink or swim.

When their ship sank, they were too far at sea to swim ashore. This was probably for the best, as the widespread acceptance of phrenology had by then attracted too many quacks and faddists to its banner. As attempts were made to measure phrenological faculties more accurately, business organizations were inclined to hire and fire employees on the basis of phrenological readings. But as scientific support dwindled, all that was rapidly dropped.

The fact that Gall and others were mistaken as to the functions of the brain does not nullify the correlation between the shape of the skull and certain human traits. It must be remembered that it was from such findings that phrenology was founded. So the subject still forms an interesting field for study and research, particularly on an experimental basis.

This could lead to the rejection of later claims, eliminating some of the faculties more difficult or doubtful of analysis, for the closer the survey follows the original observations of such pioneers as Gall and Spurzheim, the more solid its groundwork becomes.

12

Physiognomy
Character Analysis from the Face,
Head, and Other Features

The art of studying heads and faces as a guide to individual personality is of very ancient origin and rather obviously so, since facial expressions can register every mood from kindliness to ferocity; and facial formations are frequently responsible for such expressions. As for head shapes, modern anthropologists have typed the skulls of mankind from prehistoric ages up to the present, finding them indicative of various stages in human development.

From the occult standpoint, physical appearance has long been linked with the various signs of the zodiac as studied in astrology; and persons have been classed as planetary types on a similar basis. But, like palmistry, which also was once closely allied to astrology, the subject of physiognomy has branched off in its own right; it is from physiognomy that modern methods of character analysis have developed.

The pioneer in this field was a Swiss mystic, Johann Kaspar Lavater, whose keen power of observation convinced him that the deepest of human traits could be determined from individual faces. He worked out a system of physiognomy which was published at the beginning of the American Revolution. Others took up the work during the century that followed; and modern character analysis, which developed during the early 1900's, was the result.

There is one strong keynote in the study of physiognomy, giving it a special value today. In Lavater's time, famous portrait painters were skilled at bringing out the characteristics of the subjects of their paintings. This is apparent when you view the masterpieces of that bygone era. Now, skilled photographers are doing the same thing a thousand times over, often capturing momentary moods far more revealing than any that would be possible with the painter's brush.

Through the medium of movies and television, it is possible to study many facial types and other details of persons who appear upon the screen, even to the matter of minor mannerisms. Thus, once the basic points of character analysis have been learned, they can be applied immediately, not only through observation of friends and acquaintances, but through a study of photographs in newspapers, magazines, and other media.

The first important factor to consider is:

The Shape of the Face

When viewed full-front, the entire face, from top of forehead down to chin, conforms to one of three basic types or their composites. The basic types are:

The round face: Almost completely circular, this is the easygoing type that likes comfort, luxury, and good times. Sometimes the round face is elongated, but if the curve is continuous, it means the same. However, a person of this type seldom becomes lazy or indolent except when he can afford it.

They are usually good bargainers and capable in business, because their aim is wealth and ease. They are convivial and make many friends, which is also helpful to their worldly progress. They accept losses as something to be anticipated and usually find ways to make up for them. These people make it a habit to come out ahead.

Though people of this type may be indulgent both to themselves and their friends, they have a strong sense of values, which is often accompanied by sound judgment, a combination that spells success. They have keen insight into the abilities of other persons, which makes them good middlemen in many transactions. Their sense of justice enables them to recognize another person's needs and desires without overlooking their own. Balancing of one purpose against another is one of their fortes. They are good advisers and know how to settle issues to the satisfaction of all.

Men of this type show a quiet confidence and rise to high positions in business and social life, but usually with very little fanfare. They are apt to sit back and let others take the credit while they reap their own share of the profit and establish themselves still more strongly.

SHAPES OF FACES

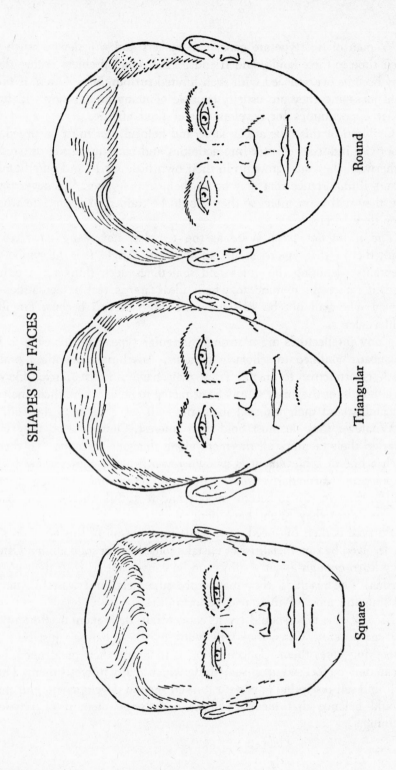

Round

Triangular

Square

Women of this type are good homemakers and will devote much of their time to their family and friends. Their chief problem is that they may become oversatisfied with such limited surroundings. Often, if they hold jobs—and they are usually capable of many kinds—they will find wider opportunities for development of their abilities.

Children of this type are amiable and helpful, but must be urged or otherwise induced to enter into activities and take up outside interests. Otherwise, they may grow up in their own little world and quietly take on a self-importance that may bring them trouble later. Whatever they get, they will want more, so they should be trained to appreciate whatever they receive.

The triangular face: Wide at the temples, narrowing down to a pointed chin, this type resembles an inverted triangle. It is the symbol of mentality, denoting the quick and sometimes deep thinker. In either case, it represents a mind to which ideas are as real as actualities—a person who will not be satisfied until those dreams become tangible achievements.

Many intellectuals are a strong triangular type, but this type is by no means confined to scholarly pursuits. Anything demanding brainwork is attractive to them. They may have inventive, scientific or legal minds; or they may simply be attracted to fields where their analytical ability and their unusual memories will serve them to the full.

Whatever they do must hold their interest. Once it does, they will develop their faculties all the more along that one direction. To them, such a line of achievement is its own reward; hence they are apt to be impractical, particularly from a business standpoint. Having strong minds, they are apt to become moody and regretful when looking back at the things they might have done.

Purpose is their big need, so in gauging a person of this type, do not be deceived by superficialities or mistake some flair for solid ability. Often they learn enough about a subject to be conversant with it; then go no further. The result is, they may prove superficial and wasteful, never making the most of their real opportunities.

Men of this type should try to concentrate their mental effort upon one real interest. Often they will swing to other channels just because something bores them. Concentration is therefore their great need, but it can only be focused upon something which really interests them. They will find self-discipline important to their mental development, and they should balance that mental activity with some amount of physical training.

Women of this type are soulful, thoughtful, and often highly sensitive. As a result, they may become introspective and listen only to those who seem to appreciate their abilities. They should seek jobs or forms of practical experience that will help them to develop their natural talents and mental abilities.

Children of this type are highly imaginative and can easily become self-sufficient; often too much so. They are avid readers and therefore quick to learn things and remember them. But unless they are guided in the right direction they may neglect their studies for hobbies or turn to whatever interest captures their fancy. Much of their later life depends upon well-directed early training. The more they are taught to direct their efforts toward something practical and useful, the better.

The square face: Width at the temple and width at the jawline are almost identical in the full-fledged square type; but some variance is allowable, provided the face is generally squarish. The heavier the jaw, the more rugged the individual is apt to be; but any face of a definitely square shape represents a person of an active mind and nature.

You will find scholars here along with businessmen, for the square type strikes an intermediate between the round and triangular. But their learning is more of a practical nature, not going to intellectual extremes, while in commercial pursuits they depend more on their own efforts than upon the management of someone else's talents.

That does not mean that people of this type always work alone. On the contrary, they have great directive ability and are often natural leaders. But always, their own activity is an important factor. They prefer to show people how to do things and set the pace for whatever is done. As a result they frequently rise to high positions through their sheer dynamic power.

Will power, firmness of opinion, and a constant urge for action form a powerful combination in the makeup of the square-faced type. Often they rely on physical strength or sheer drive to accomplish their aims. Mechanical skill is strongly present in the square type. They are prompt at taking up new things and carrying them through to a successful conclusion. The keener their minds, the more they feel that results are what mainly count.

Men of this type should plan ahead to make the most of their natural qualifications. They need mental stimulus toward the expansion of their efforts; otherwise they will favor brawn over brain. In our modern space age, where courage and physical prowess are so often needed as the concomitant of high intelligence, men of the square type are needed as pioneers as well as leaders. As technicians they are among the best, and the more ways they find to apply their ability the greater their chance of success.

Women of this type are also keyed to the modern tempo. With so many active fields to choose from, they are free from the restraints and limitations that cramped their style in bygone years. They should concentrate on whatever they undertake rather than relying too much on their versatility, with the ultimate aim of working up to a directive or executive capacity in their chosen field. At the same time, they should not neglect interests that are to their liking, as their success frequently hinges upon the proper blend of capability and personality.

Children of this type should have great prospects, considering the present emphasis on physical fitness, as well as technical and scientific training, for their bent is toward those directions. More than ever, they should be taught the practical side of whatever they undertake, so as to put it to later use. If they like a sport, they should learn its fine points. If they show aptitude in a mechanical or scientific field they should be urged to continue it.

COMPOSITE FACES

Though comparatively few faces conform exactly to the round, triangular, and square shapes, many approximate them sufficiently to be classed in a specific category. An oval face may be regarded as round; a face is triangular if it narrows to the chin, though it is not actually pointed; while a strongly oblong face belongs in the square type.

By picturing each visage in a frame of one of the shapes just described, over-all judgment may be made, with further analysis depending on a study of other features. But there are composite faces that show two shapes, or leave doubt as to their exact type. These should be modified accordingly.

The round-triangular: Wide at the temples, sloping inwardly, then rounding widely at jowls and chin. This shows mentality of the triangular type, tempered by the commercial sense of the round. Judgment is not always a strong factor, however. This blend indicates optimism, because of the many ideas coupled with self-confidence. The result may be complacency or indulgence, with a lack of action.

Where the upper face is rounded, with the chin coming to a strong triangular point, the calculating nature of the round type is more apt to be the dominating factor. Here, ingenuity is often keener than intellect, and quick thinking may supplant deeper thought. A good combination in the handling of business details.

The triangular-square: Wide at the temples, narrowing downward, but terminating in a strongly squarish jaw. This shows the person who has ideas and puts them into action. An excellent blend, much like the square type, but less impetuous. Versatility is apparent here, showing a person who may have many interests, with the ability to choose the best.

A squarish face with strongly pointed chin shows a trend toward impulsive action, with quick thinking as a follow-up. Such persons profit by experience and gauge their future actions accordingly. Many inventive and scientific minds are found in the triangular-square category.

The square-round: Such a blend starts straight down from the temples, with a definite widening and rounding toward the jaws and chin. If simply straight, with a noticeable curve, it must be regarded as either a square or a square-triangular type, for the rounding must be truly apparent to count.

This shows an active nature, with good business ability. It has a jolly, happy-go-lucky trend, but also a definite self-interest. The rounder, wider, and therefore the more bulbous the lower portion of the face, the more self-centered this type can become.

A typically round face ending in a square jaw comes in the same general category, but this type shows a more indulgent, easygoing nature, sparked by occasional periods of action and a definite trend toward firm though somewhat opinionated decisions.

Full Head Shapes

These are best gauged by studying the back of the head, to gain a different perspective than the facial outlines. Often, it is possible to obtain an inkling of a person's individuality from a brief and distant back view; hence, although this is no more than an index to very general traits, it is valuable nonetheless.

For convenience, head shapes can be classified in three simple groups:

Type A: This is a semicircular type, following an even, well-proportioned curve. It shows an impulsive, sometimes aggressive nature, with a willingness to take chances. This may be attributed in some degree to confidence in one's own knowledge or ability, which in turn means a lack of worry over consequences. This is a head shape common to men who handle big business matters.

Type B: This is a squarish or flattish type, block-shaped and there-

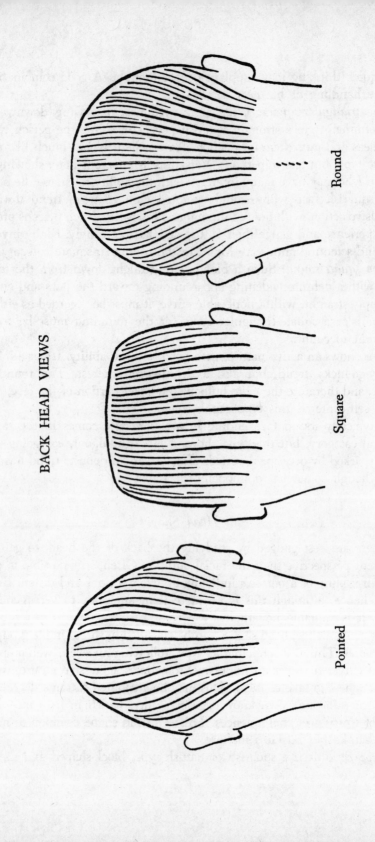

BACK HEAD VIEWS

Round

Square

Pointed

fore rugged. It symbolizes caution, which is sometimes classed as obstinacy. It also represents deliberation, which may be mistaken for indecision. But these actually add up to dependability. Once anyone of this type makes up his mind to a purpose, he almost always acts firmly and efficiently.

Type C: This is a pointed type, sometimes classed as egg-shaped. It shows intuition, with ability to chart a course according to circumstances and conditions, rather than following any fixed policy. Here we find a diplomatic nature, though persons of this type will also rise forcefully to an occasion when they feel that they are right. They are apt to accept artificial standards and govern their actions accordingly; hence they frequently stress their self-importance.

Wide and Narrow Heads

Width—or narrowness—of the head can be effectively gauged from the back and the resultant findings applied to the types just listed.

An average, well-balanced head—which can be judged by its proportions—usually shows a general conformity to the types as given. This width is measured on a cross line just above the ears, which corresponds approximately to the temples, when noted in a front view.

Wideness shows an energetic mind and is something of the mark of the extrovert, who is anxious to enter into many affairs.

With Type A, round, this accentuates the natural aggressiveness of the individual, particularly when the wide head is proportionately low. It shows a querulous disposition; a habitual annoyance over small things.

With Type B, square, width combined with squareness produces a challenging disposition. Antagonism toward any suggestions may result.

With Type C, pointed, wideness usually broadens the individual's outlook, enabling him to drop the superficial attitude common to the pointed head.

With all three types, wideness shows a calculating, ambitious nature; that of the social as well as the business climber. Sentiment is often lacking, except as a means to an end.

Narrowness shows definite restraint. It is found with the introvert, who shrinks from the public eye or is satisfied to move in small circles.

With Type A, this shows persons who are apt to worry about what other people think and thereby curb their normally impulsive natures.

It is apt, however, to keep them under too great a restraint, thereby preventing them from really great attainment.

With Type B, narrowness shows willingness to be swayed by sentiment. Caution becomes reticence, with an acceptance of outside ideas and suggestions. Hence persons of this type are easily imposed upon.

With Type C, narrowness simply accentuates the already narrow viewpoint of the individual. Here, self-importance in the smallest of circles becomes a personal triumph; any slight accomplishment is magnified as high achievement. Fads and notions are accepted as great philosophies.

With all three types, wideness shows a somewhat adaptable disposition, which is usually quite harmless, if that can be called an attribute. Once out of their respective ruts, they should improve their situations.

Facial Features

These represent an important branch of physiognomy, especially when studied from the profile. In the early days, faces were often likened to those of birds and animals, with any resemblances being classed as corresponding attributes. Thus a leonine expression would mean greatness and majesty; a foxlike face would denote cunning; and so on.

This has been supplanted by a form of profile study which can be covered with three over-all types: the convex, the plane, and the concave. These are sometimes seen in their complete form; but more often, there is some mingling of the component parts, so a person may have a plane forehead, a convex nose, a concave chin.

The simplest way to study profiles is to take each in turn, giving its full significance, then defining each part in brief. From this, it is possible to compose a complete list of profile traits for each individual.

THE CONVEX PROFILE

So-called because it forms an outward semicircle, or convex curve, consisting of frontward sloping forehead, pointed nose, strong upper lip, and receding chin.

Such a profile signifies a quick mind, interested in quick results and therefore one that concentrates on practical things. This leads to enthusiasm that often borders on impatience. Glib salesmen are found in this category along with fast-talking comedians. Sharp of wit, eager for action, these people naturally do not go for sustained effort,

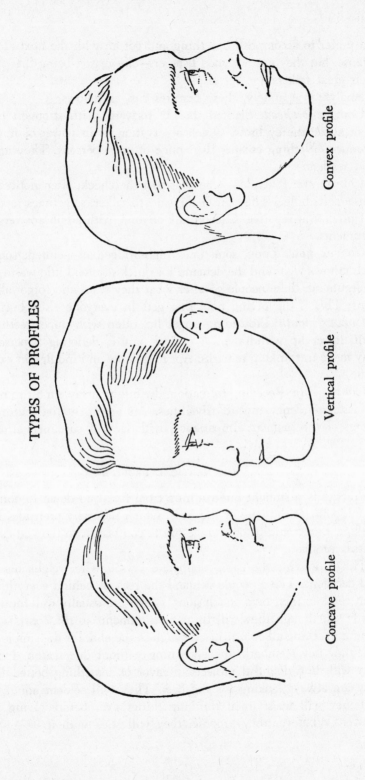

TYPES OF PROFILES

Convex profile

Vertical profile

Concave profile

but prefer to accomplish one thing and get on with the next. They are intense; but they are not good listeners—one reason being that they are such great talkers.

Analyzed separately, these features run as follows:

Convex forehead: Slanted sharply forward, with strongest development above the eyebrow. Quick observation, with power of immediate retention. Nothing escapes the notice of such persons. They are often avid readers.

Convex eye: Extended somewhat past the cheek; often noticeable because of its bulge. The sign of the smooth talker, sometimes repetitious, but prompt at repartee. Can outtalk anyone, with ad-lib answers for all arguments.

Convex nose: Long, sometimes high-bridged or pointed; sometimes both. Shows vigor and the demand for quick results. Little waste of time in argument; these people go after what they want and forget all objections. This is the prying nose that gets in everyone else's business.

Convex mouth: Protruding upper lip, often with upper teeth prominent; lower lip withdrawn. A critical nature, denoting a person who may make unthinking remarks. Apt to quibble and indulge in exaggeration.

Convex chin: Receding formation, dwindling away almost to nothing. Shows a tendency toward trivialities. An argumentative nature, over things of the moment. Impatience, with lack of sustained effort.

THE VERTICAL PROFILE

Practically a straight line running from forehead down to chin, with its midpoint at the base of the nose, which naturally protrudes beyond the line, but should be of average size to conform with the vertical effect of this profile.

This represents the calm, deliberate person who weighs his speech and decisions. These people demand the reasons behind everything and then come to their own conclusions, which are usually well-formed and firmly set, though they will listen to arguments to the contrary. They believe in seeing all enterprises through to the end, for the simple reason that they never embark upon anything without due reason. However, they will drop doubtful projects in favor of something better, because they are always looking for the best. They will seldom admit failure and they will insist upon thinking things over before giving a final answer. Whatever they propose, they will stick with it.

Vertical forehead: Practically a straight line from hairline down to eyebrows. Shows careful observation and cool deliberation. Ability at concentration, always with the aim of thorough understanding before coming to a final decision. Sometimes slow in thinking, but exacting in detail.

Vertical eye: Noted in relation to a normal cheekbone, the pupil of the eye should be on the same vertical line. It shows a good talker, often an excellent salesman, but only on subjects with which he is fully familiar. During other discussions they become good listeners. Their ability to weigh matters makes them convincing speakers when they assert themselves.

Vertical nose: One that is almost in exact proportion to the other features of the profile; not too conspicuous, yet noticeable. It shows a steady nature, with a willingness to accept routine. They would rather work on a problem than waste time in useless conferences. Given a task, they will go through with it, if given reasonable time.

Vertical mouth: Of average size, set directly beneath the nose, with neither lip noticeably protruding. Restrained in speech, but willing to become assertive if occasion demands. Being analytical, they may criticize people, but usually in a moderate or whimsical way.

Vertical chin: On a straight line with the base of the nose; but the chin itself may be slightly rounded, rather than strictly blunt, which it often is. However, it should neither recede nor protrude.

Such a chin shows a firm, stolid nature, but one that will rise to high indignation should the person's patience be overtaxed. Calmness in such individuals applies to trivialities only; often it is apparently deep-set, but is actually a surface expression.

THE CONCAVE PROFILE

This follows a slight but noticeable inward curve from the bulge of the forehead to the point of the chin, both of which must be prominent to show the fully concave profile. Similarly, the base of the nose must form the innermost segment of the constant curve. The nose itself should not be too prominent in the true concave pattern.

Here is the person who is careful both in manner and speech, always weighing matters before coming to a decision and then always expressing a reserved opinion. Sometimes, such a nature seems deeper than it really is; and such people, though outwardly satisfied with conditions or contented with circumstances, may be brooding inwardly. In short, their

seeming concern with important matters may be nothing more than annoyance over trivialities. They absorb what they see or hear and remember most of it, so if they can override inward dissatisfaction and morbid
trends, they can accumulate ideas and put them to a practical use. They
can prove themselves loyal and long-lasting friends, helpful in times of
trouble and capable in emergency.

Concave forehead: Actually, this is a bulging forehead, which could
be termed "convex" in its own right, but must be classed as "concave" in
relationship to the over-all profile. It is the mark of the listener, who
reasons out everything before making a decision. A thinker, but not
necessarily a deep one, as such persons may form false conclusions.

Concave eye: Deep-set, with the pupil definitely behind the vertical
line of the cheekbone. Denotes a slow, careful talker; one who chooses
a subject with which he is familiar, or else remains silent. Also convincing in speech, the longer he continues.

Concave nose: Since the base is set well back, the nose usually appears short or snubbed. The more it recedes, the more it shows its accepted traits. These include an easy, friendly disposition, but one that is
secretive, often in small ways. Also the mark of the plodder, who is
satisfied with slight but consistent accomplishments.

Concave mouth: Small lips, that seem tight and reticent; though a
larger or protruding lower lip may be in evidence. With either type,
there should be a noticeable outward curve down toward the chin. This
denotes a pleasant disposition, that of the person who gives consideration to the feelings of others, usually speaking nicely or not at all.

Concave chin: Strongly projected at the lower portion, whether
pointed or curved. Conspicuous and easily recognized. This shows deliberation in action more than thought. Purposeful, but in a self-
sufficient way, ready to await results. Such people seldom, if ever, can
be swayed from a determined course.

Frontal Features

Study of frontal features forms a valuable adjunct to physiognomy,
as lesser observations corroborate the more important findings and sometimes supply distinct points of their own. These run as follows:

Forehead: When high, this denotes a strongly mental type; if wide, a
tendency toward theory and philosophy, hence the expression "high-
brow." High but narrow, an analytical scientific mind. When low,
it shows a practical, direct nature, given more to action than to theory;

hence the expression "lowbrow." Most foreheads are between these extremes, so they can be gauged proportionately.

Eyebrows: If heavy or bushy, an intense, strong nature, but inclined to domineer and become blunt in manner. If light or pencil-thin, they show a fastidious but sometimes fussy nature.

When wide apart the eyebrows show adaptability, but indicate that the person is easily influenced. Close together, of the "beetle" type, they show nervous energy, often coupled with emotional outbursts.

Straight eyebrows mark an alert, active nature, while curved eyebrows show a more inquiring type. Downward slopes show petulance or resignation; upward, considerable ambition. A double curve connotes artfulness; while arched eyebrows indicate an imaginative nature.

Eyes, when roundish, show a trustful, often naïve person. Oval in shape, good humor, yet with a canny outlook and readiness to believe rumors. Slanted eyes symbolize a secretive, self-sufficient disposition.

Wide-open eyes show a friendly, confiding person. If partly hidden by the upper lids, a scheming nature tinged with envy. If partly hidden by lower lids, an unyielding, sometimes harsh disposition. Narrowed lids go with a keen, retentive observer, often suspicious and inclined to misgivings.

Width between the eyes indicates a broad-minded person, but one inclined to believe that he is always right. Narrowness between denotes a small nature, often given to trifles, but with a strict sense of responsibility.

Vertical lines between the eyes are interpreted to mean: one line, a person with a single aim, who dislikes interruptions; two lines, a changeable nature, shifting from practice to theory, always trying to balance up; three lines, the mark of the practical idealist, accepting work and responsibility for their own sake; four lines (or more), a person given to many interests.

The Nose: If large, an aggressive nature, with a liking for worldly things. Small, a quiet, unassuming disposition. A thin nose shows a nervous type, easily annoyed; a wide nose, a boisterous, exuberant, and often careless nature. A long nose betokens a careful, worried disposition; a short nose, a cheery person who may ignore consequences.

The Mouth: If large, a liberal, sometimes extravagant nature; small, a selfish, even penurious sign. Large lips, a love of pleasure and excitement. Narrow lips, lack of emotion or enthusiasm. Straight lips represent self-control; curved lips, a changeable, unpredictable temperament. Upward-curving features, observable chiefly by the lips, are naturally a happy sign, while downward curves show moodiness or discontent.

The Chin: If long, shows a resistant nature that will not give in. If short, a changeable person who will switch to other things if thwarted. A pointed chin is the sign of a quick, keen nature; a blunt chin, a person slow in decision. A cleft chin shows a self-centered individual, who is outwardly gracious and highly sociable, but is strongly intent on personal gain. A double chin indicates an amiable but indulgent nature.

Side Head Views

Viewed from the side, the head may show unusual height, or lowness, in contrast to its length or shortness from the nose to the back of the head. Ears also enter into such observations, but since their placement is governed largely by the shape of the head, they will be considered only in terms of their own shape and size.

A large head is one that is both high and long in proportion to the average for a person of a given stature. It shows vision and ambition, usually of a high nature. Frontal development shows a desire for personal achievement; development at the back of the head tends more toward tradition or devotion to a cause.

A small head, both low and short proportionately, denotes the person who lives chiefly for today and wants quick results rather than long-range returns.

From these contrasts, it is easy to define the components: A high head shows aspiration and formalities; a low head, a person who deals only in tangibles. A long head reveals foresight, with retentive ability needed in long-range planning. A short head makes the most out of every opportunity and prefers new things which can be discarded once they have served their purpose.

Ears: If large, they indicate a person who hears much and uses it to advantage, for this is an intellectual sign, though the wisdom acquired may be worldly rather than altruistic. Small ears, in contrast, show the person who lives by instinct rather than intellect. If tall, the ear denotes a person who may be keen but impractical; while a wide ear is just the opposite, showing natural capability, even though limited. If pointed, it shows an artful person, sometimes with a conniving mind.

Large lobes, complete in themselves, show an independent nature. Strength of purpose is evident, but if overlarge, such lobes may denote a crude nature. Small lobes, less fully formed, show a more dependent

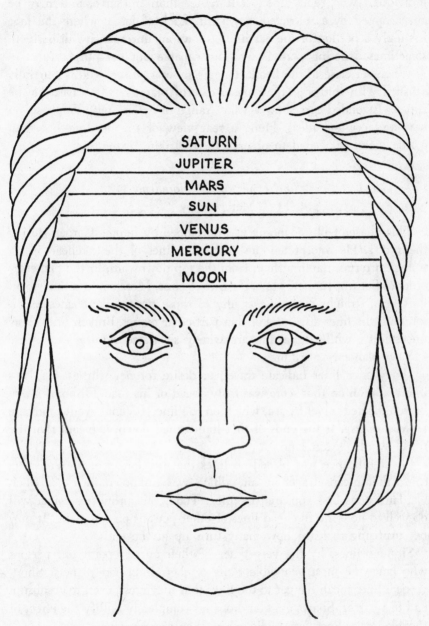

The lines of the forehead

individual, who relies upon skill rather than initiative, and may be handicapped by a restricted viewpoint. Lack of lobes, where the lobe is simply a portion of the ear itself, shows an unresponsive disposition, sometimes denoting persons who are capable but not purposeful.

When set close to the head, the ears show a person who is generally satisfied with things as they are, a careful planner, who saves for the future. Extended ears show a wider range of action, with emphasis on new and original ideas. Here, a rear view of the head, rather than a side view, is needed to observe these striking extremes.

The Lines of the Forehead
Metoposcopy

This phase of physiognomy was developed by Jerome Cardan during the 1500's. He interpreted the horizontal lines of the forehead in astrological terms, naming them from the top downward, in the planetary order of Saturn, Jupiter, Mars, the Sun, Venus, Mercury, and the Moon.

A firm, straight cross line at any of those positions indicates a person with the finer attributes of that particular planet. Broken lines show uncertainty, while those that are widely separated signify a complete lack of planetary attributes.

Wavy cross lines indicate travel, or desire for new things. Cardan's interpretation on that score was truly ahead of his time. Ordinary wavy lines indicated travel by sea, which on the line of Venus would indicate a pleasure trip. If the ends of that line turned down, it meant that the travel would be on land.

No significance was placed on lines that turned up at the ends, because that means travel by air, which was unknown in 1558, when Cardan's opus first appeared in print. Today, an airline passenger will do well to note the forehead lines of other persons on the plane. It may be surprising to learn how many turn up at the ends.

Sinuous lines, by the very grace of their curves, point out persons who have the most adaptable traits of their indicated planets. Short, vertical lines mean danger to the lines that they cross, even to an abrupt end to a career. Sharp, angular crossings completely nullify the effect of the planetary lines, especially when they are repeated.

So a frown, a narrowing of the brows, can reveal much, according to metoposcopy, a psychic science which may be coming into its period of full development and appreciation.

13

Radiesthesia

and Other Phenomena

One remarkable form of divination that has continued through the centuries is that of the "divining rod," which is still used for finding underground streams of water. Some authorities have tried to link the modern art of "dowsing," as it is sometimes termed, with the ancient science of Rhabdomancy, or divination by use of wands, but while the two have points in common, they apparently differ somewhat in purpose.

In fact, when the divining rod emerged from obscurity during the early 1500's, it was used for locating mines. A forked stick was cut from a tree, preferably the hazel, which was small and frequently grew in terrain where minerals might be found. The rod was gripped by the forked ends, one in each fist, with the fingers above and pointed toward the body, so that the stem of the rod extended forward and upward.

The diviner then walked about, often muttering incantations, until the stem of the wand began to dip. That was the place where the miners were supposed to dig, and the fact that they often found veins of precious metal brought fame to the divining rod and fortune to the diviners. Naturally, the odds favored those diviners who knew the sort of ground where ore was most likely to be found; but that still did not explain the action of the rod, which often thrust itself downward so forcibly that the forks were known to break in the diviner's hands.

The fact that the mines were presumably haunted by goblins and other demons may have helped spread the legendary powers of the rod, and by the late 1600's, it was used for finding treasure, springs of water, and even the bodies of missing persons. The forked wand, it seemed, could uncover whatever its handler "willed" it to find, provided there was some such substance in the vicinity; otherwise it wouldn't respond.

Divining for metals (from an old print)

But by the late 1700's, "water witching" had become the chief purpose of the rod and it has remained so ever since.

As early as 1790, spurious dowsers were at work, and books were published telling them how to fake the motion of the rod while locating water sources through patches of green grass, or by following gullies where water was apt to flow. Confederates, acquainted with the area, were also used as aids. All this proved harmful to the honest dowsers, who were also handicapped by the inept members of their craft who operated on a somewhat "hit-or-miss" basis.

Kenneth Roberts, the noted author, who did much to encourage expert dowsing up until the 1950's, encountered much of this prejudice and fought valiantly and rightfully against it. For the fact stands that the scientifically minded critics, who "explain away" the results of the divining rod, are never able themselves to duplicate or even approach the achievements of a really "gifted" dowser. If the whole thing were purely imaginary or simply mechanical, it should be easy for anyone to do. But it isn't that easy.

Unquestionably the mental and the physical combine with the diving rod, but the sum total may carry over into the domain of parapsychology. The interesting fact is that anyone can try it for himself and see to what degree he may be "gifted," though a word of warning is needed here; namely, that no one should go on a few chance results or brief experiments. A dowsing test held with a group of friends is a good preliminary experience, nothing more.

Almost any wood will do for a dowsing rod. Hazel was chosen because of its availability and its flexibility. The latter is important, as the rod should be pliable enough to spread the ends of the fork, thus giving the rod a certain tension. This is essential to success, as the rod is "on a balance," so to speak, ready to respond forcefully, once the diviner "picks up" a subconscious impression of water or whatever else he is counting upon the rod to find.

Instead of a forked stick, you can use a wire coat hanger, by bending in the center, so that the hanger forms a Y. Bend the ends of the Y slightly outward, grip them in the usual fashion, and use the hook of the hanger as the pointer. Another excellent rod can be formed from two strips of whalebone, or plastic. Simply tape them together about a third of their length, using that end for the pointer; then bend the loose ends outward as the points of the Y.

Many persons can find water with such a rod, by going back and forth over ground where springs or hidden streams are known to be. People familiar with the terrain can check and tell them if they have found the right spot, when the rod shows a powerful dip. Some can find water pipes or wells in the same fashion. But there seems to be a variance among diviners. Some can only pick up springs or streams.

Trying the rod on hidden objects, such as an imaginary "treasure" or some spot in a yard that has a special significance, can often be a rewarding practice. But where the divining rod often becomes most spectacular is in map work. Here, it is moved slowly above a map or chart—particularly one on a very large scale—to see where it dips. Water has been found in this way, and other things presumably can be located. For such work, however, many persons prefer:

The Exploratory Pendulum

This device can be traced back to a form of divination called coscinomancy, that utilized a crude sieve or strainer, which two persons held suspended between their fingertips. In lieu of a handle, the strainer was gripped by a pair of pincers, this clamp being the portion balanced between the fingers.

Due to the uneven pressure, the suspended strainer had a tendency to turn, but the holders did their best to maintain its equilibrium, while names of other people were recited aloud. The name on which the strainer turned, indicated the person involved in some crime, or whatever else the sieve was being used to test. Almost always, it was something bad.

Other similar devices were utilized for such purposes, but the real refinement came in divination by a key, called cleidomancy. One person held the key suspended by a thread, and if the key began to revolve, any question was answered in the affirmative. Working along the same line, a finger ring could be used instead of a key; and modern experimenters found a small ball even better.

From this, the exploratory pendulum acquired more refined forms, such as that of a small crystal ball suspended from a gold chain, or a pear-shaped pendulum carved from ebony or ivory. Plastic pendulums have recently come into vogue, and these, like some of their predecessors, are hollow, so that they can be filled with a sample of the substance sought.

Thus, in going after water, you would fill the pendulum with water. If divining for gold, you would use gold. But many capable pendulum operators forego such auto-suggestive aids and rely on a solid pendulum. For some purposes, the pointed type has advantages over the spherical, so in that case, a child's top can be suspended from a string instead of using a rubber ball. But in either case, a tack can be inserted in the pendulum and the end of the string wound around it. The pendulum should balance nicely; that is all. Hence a simple finger ring suspended on a thin cord is still satisfactory.

When the upper end of the string is held between thumb and forefinger, with the pendulum dangling five or six inches below, a mysterious motion gradually takes place. This varies according to the length of the string; with a long string, up to say eighteen inches, it becomes greater, just as with the pendulum of a clock. But the exploratory pendu-

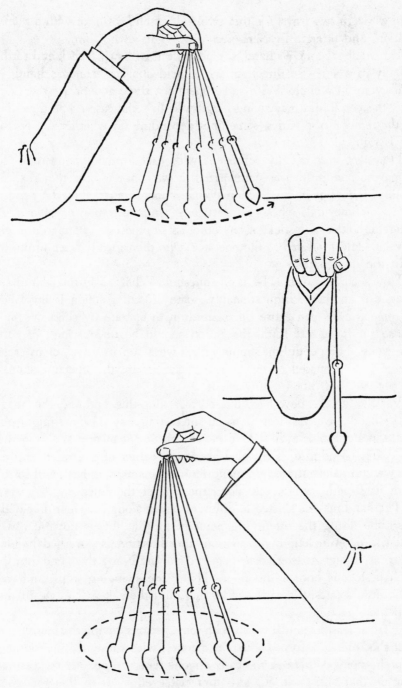

A pendulum in operation

lum works in two ways; it either swings back and forth, or with a rotary motion, and often this seems according to its own whim.

If held above a man's hand, the pendulum will swing back and forth, usually in a sidewise direction; when held above a woman's hand, it will gyrate in a circle. With some operators, these actions are reversed; also, the pendulum may swing lengthwise in some cases. The direction of the rotation also varies, sometimes depending on whether the operator is right- or left-handed.

However, it is usually consistent with each individual operator, so when the pendulum was popularized, it was once termed the "sex detector" because of its dual action. What is more remarkable, the pendulum sometimes tells whether an article belongs to a man or woman. A cigarette holder, a lipstick, or any other small object can be placed in an envelope and proffered to the operator, who then uses the pendulum to gain the impression.

How accurate this may be, is one question. What makes the pendulum operate is another. Unquestionably, some muscular action is involved, as some persons can cause the pendulum to operate by conscious motions. But in correct form, the action should be unconscious, or subconscious. The pendulum should either work "on its own," or in cases where it is supposed to move in a specific way, the operator should simply "will" it, not try to push it.

Various theories have been offered regarding this, and one, the "magnetic theory," can be "tested" in an interesting way. Use a straight object, say a ruler, or even a long pencil, placing it at any angle on the table. The pendulum is dangled above the center of the ruler, and as the operator concentrates, the pendulum begins moving back and forth, with its straight swing, but along the line of the ruler.

The hand may be shifted to different places along the ruler, but with the same result, the interesting point being that this is not the usual sidewise or even lengthwise motion; the direction is governed by the ruler, as though it exerted a magnetic power. Now, the pendulum is brought to one end of the ruler. There, the swinging stops, and the pendulum rotates. Go to the other end, and there it will rotate in the opposite direction.

That, at least, is how it works with some persons, giving the impression that the ruler is a form of mental magnet, with the ends representing opposite poles. Whatever the case, anyone who can operate the pendulum on that basis, without any appreciable effort, is in line for more serious experiment.

Such experiment consists in locating mines, springs, or any other desired spot on a map, as described with the divining rod, but much more easily, as the pendulum is far less awkward. The usual procedure is to move it about a map, pausing at intervals, trusting for it to gyrate. When it begins to do so, the spot at which it just pointed is supposedly the right one.

Often, the pendulum is put to tests that can be more easily verified. An operator may use the pendulum with a road map, to find the way to a place where he has never been. He is told the main highway to start; from there, he is on his own—and the pendulum's. He moves his hand slowly, pausing at every crossroad or turnoff, trusting on the pendulum to gyrate when needed.

Thus he literally explores the road, with the pendulum indicating whether he goes right or wrong. Again, individualism prevails, the pendulum "talking" to each operator on his own terms. Some operators claim they can use the pendulum as a compass: First, they let it swing and its line indicates due north and south. To tell which is which, the operator faces one way, then the other, letting the pendulum gyrate. Clockwise, it means one direction; counterclockwise, the opposite, as determined by previous test.

Many other remarkable results are attributed to "pendy," as the device is sometimes nicknamed. The pendulum can be caused to stop, either by "willing" it to do so, or by gripping the wrist with the other hand. Presumably, lost objects can be traced, missing persons found, the whereabouts of friends ascertained, all through the power of the pendulum. This is technically termed "radiesthesia," and even the most ardent champions of such a psychic force agree that the full faculty is possessed by very few, though it may be latent in most members of the human race.

For those who feel quite latent, the simpler the test, the better. The "magnetic" test with a ruler has already been described. Here is something even simpler; a way to make pendy increase its gyrations. The pendulum is dangled above a drinking glass and the operator "wills" it to rotate. Soon, the pendulum is swinging in a circle, while the operator keeps his eyes fixed on the glass, much as though sighting on a target.

Frequently, and quite surprisingly, the pendulum will increase its circle, swinging wide of the glass rim. Power of suggestion is the logical answer, but the effect still is remarkable, for the swing seems far beyond normal range.

A glass is also used in the time-telling test, one of the oldest in the history of modern radiesthesia. Here, the pendulum—preferably an ordinary finger ring—is dangled down into the glass. The operator calls upon pendy to tell the time in hours, and the device obligingly does so. It swings back and forth, increasing its speed until it begins to clink the sides of the glass—"one, two, three, four, five"—ending on the exact hour and slackening its swing immediately thereafter.

Sometimes it will add a trifling "plunk" for a half-hour, perhaps to the surprise of the operator himself. Indeed, when this time-telling test was in its heyday, a few generations ago, skeptics used to get up in the night and try out the pendulum for themselves, without looking at the clock. According to the majority of the reports, the dangling ring gave them the right time. That, of course, could be due to a "time sense" in the persons themselves, but it still speaks well for the pendulum.

Table Tipping

Further evidence of subconscious muscular activity accompanied the "table-tipping" craze of a century ago, when "spirit circles" gathered about a table and pressed their hands upon it, hoping for a message from beyond. Soon, the table would begin to move, then bounce about, rearing upon two legs and banging down upon the other pair.

Next, the "sitters"—as the members of the circle were called—would be spelling out the alphabet, "A-B-C-D-" and so on, hoping for the table to stop on a letter, which it always did. So they would start the whole thing over, hoping for another letter, which would also come. Next, the table would be spelling out words, sentences, and complete messages.

Often, this was attributed to "spirit" aid, which put table tipping in bad repute. Usually, some member of the group was responsible, for by clamping hard at the right moment, it was definitely possible to "spell out" messages. This put an unfair burden on other members of the group, whether or not the "clamper" was operating subconsciously or consciously.

But what of cases where the group itself was working toward the same end? That question raised many others in the minds of sincere "sitters," who felt that they were all tuning in on the same "influence." Fortunately, confidence in table tipping lessened, but it was replaced by:

Planchette and Ouija

These devices really spell out messages. Planchette is a name applied to a triangular plate mounted on tiny wheels with a pencil projecting down from the center. Several persons place their fingertips on the plate and wait for it to move above a sheet of paper.

It moves, all right, and if properly inspired, it writes out messages, but with too many mental impulses at work, those are apt to be a mere scrawl. So the planchette declined in favor, except in a few circles—probably those where a dominating impulse prevailed!—and the ouija took over.

The name "ouija," coined from the French *oui* and the German *ja*, means "yes, yes," when translated into English, but the ouija board can respond with either "yes" or "no." Both of those words are emblazoned on its surface, along with all the letters of the alphabet and the numerals 1 to 0 inclusive. A three-sided device is mounted on little felt-tipped legs, and consultants of the "ouija" put their hands on the sides and await results.

The ouija table responds by moving from letter to letter, spelling out words, adding up figures, and responding yes or no. Often it becomes a routine process, much as though someone had something in mind and wanted to say it. In fact, a person can use a ouija alone, which offsets some of the stigma applied to table tipping.

What gives the ouija status is its answers. They seem to come from beyond the knowledge of the operators. It's the pendulum, but on a higher scale, which raises the question: Why haven't the two been combined?

The answer is, they have been. Some authorities have placed that coalition back in Roman times, when a pendulum was dangled above letters, and wiggled over those that were needed to spell out auguries and portents. So today, boards are obtainable for pendulum work, instead of the ouija tripod.

Automatic Writing

This is truly a step beyond, in tapping the subconscious. The operator takes a pencil in hand and lets it inscribe messages or even drawings on a sheet of paper. Very remarkable information, pertaining to past, present, and future has been obtained through such a procedure. Often, the integrity of the operator is unquestioned, though skeptics have often cast doubt as to the value of the revelations.

The most remarkable feature of automatic writing is that it often lives up to the term "automatic." A gifted person may keep on writing lengthy dissertations, even the manuscripts of entire books, long after they should have tired physically. The hand of the operator seems to be actuated by an outside force, making the results all the more impressive.

Unquestionably, automatic writing is an important study in the newly developed field of parapsychology. The same applies to:

Crystal Gazing

The art of "scrying," which includes crystal gazing, dates back to antiquity. Blobs of ink, opaque mirrors, bowls of water, and even flames have been used to induce visions of a supposedly clairvoyant nature. Sometimes these visions are spontaneous; in one instance, a woman viewed the enactment of a distant crime in a glass of water that happened to be at her bedside. Other persons have seen visions by simply staring into a water bottle. But it is generally agreed that a crystal ball is the best implement for the development of such imagery.

Even there, considerable choice is involved. Veteran scryers prefer spheres of genuine crystal, particularly with a blue or purplish tinge, at least two and one half inches in diameter. Larger crystals may increase the size of the picture and are therefore more desirable. So-called crystal balls composed of clear glass are less expensive in the larger sizes and are therefore often used.

The general purpose in choosing the right crystal is to avoid tiring the eyes, which may induce a hypnotic condition. Some persons claim that all crystal gazing is a form of autohypnosis, but scryers generally dispute this. They watch for a clouding of the crystal, which causes changes in the images.

Some remarkable cases of precognition have been attributed to the crystal ball. One woman saw and described an elderly man whom nobody present recognized; yet a few hours later, she met and was introduced to a stranger who fitted the description perfectly. Others have had repeated visions, like a series of events, which have proven accurate in regard to coming scenes.

One authority, however, regards the crystal chiefly as a device for reviving the memory, bringing past scenes into focus, and linking them with the future in coincidental and wishful fashion. This coupling of imagery with imagination has never proven itself harmful, but it tends toward exaggeration, and cannot be taken too seriously. Most of the really evidential crystal visions are of a spontaneous sort, often being seen by persons who have not made scrying a constant habit.

The term crystallomancy is applied to divinations gained through the crystal ball. Persons who practice this usually see partial pictures or symbols emerging from the milkiness, rather than complete scenes. These take the shapes of objects, as anchors, animals, and the like. Any which are fairly definable are given some specified significance, as with the patterns noted in tea leaf reading. Hence the list given under that head can be applied to crystal gazing as well.

14

Superstitions, Omens,
and Lucky Signs

Man's earliest forays into the realm of the psychic probably had to do with portents—good and bad—which seemingly had a bearing on his future. How these arose was often a question; but it seems most likely that the occurrence of some unusual event, followed by another happening, logical or illogical, led to the belief that such a combination would take place again.

If it did, the portent was established, and after a few more repeats it was unlikely to die out. If it failed to deliver, the same type of reasoning caused people to suppose that some antidote had been provided, usually in the case of a counterspell. This, too, could be the result of chance occurrence. But the practitioners of occult science, as it existed in those early days, were prompt to take credit for it, one way or another.

A vast compendium could be assembled, covering charms, spells, auguries, incantations, amulets, talismans, and the like; but their why and wherefore would be too obscure and obsolete to be of interest to modern readers. Rather, our list has been confined to popular superstitions which have survived to the present day, and in many instances still hold sway over certain persons, whether or not they care to admit it.

Some of these are doubtless of ancient origin; others have a groundwork of common sense. When Julius Caesar was told to "Beware the Ides of March," the soothsayer who gave the warning may have been hazarding a long guess that Caesar would be in for danger on that date. Today, telling someone not to walk under a ladder has a similar significance; the person may have something coming to him, sooner or later, if he persists in that habit.

Other portents, like those to do with weather, sometimes include factors of true prognostication. Others, particularly in the realm of lucky

EXAMPLES OF ANCIENT TALISMANS

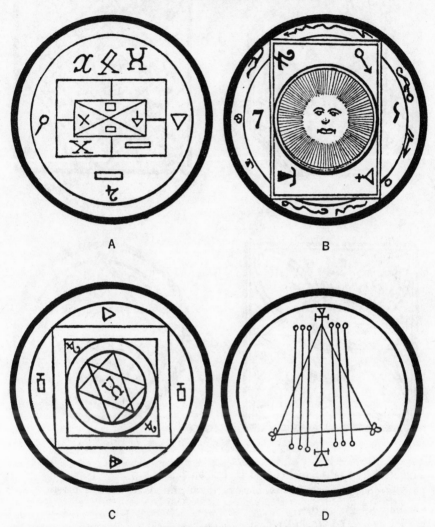

A

B

C

D

These talismans, carefully copied in ink on heavy paper or parchment, presumably bring specific types of luck to persons who carry them.

A. Designed as an aid in wagering and games
B. A token of good health to its owner
C. Helpful in business and financial affairs
D. An assurance of honor, riches, or both.

TALISMANS USED WITH INCANTATIONS

E

F

G

H

These ancient talismans, copied in ink on heavy paper or parchment, supposedly give power to all who carry them and recite certain mystic words on required occasions.

E. To make schemers disclose their secrets, carry this talisman and recite the words "Noctar" and "Raiban." This should outwit all enemies.

F. A man carrying this talisman should impress any lady whom he meets, provided he first repeats the magic formula, "Nades, Suradis, Maniner."

G. Good for luck in games and lotteries. When shuffling a pack of cards, pronounce the word "Pilatus" to gain an ace or winning hand. In other games, the word "Rokes" helps hit a winning number.

H. Scholars will appreciate this talisman. All who carry it will shine in classes, and success in examinations is often assured by declaring, "Ritas, Ambas, Zamarath" during study and prior to the test itself.

Various types of talismans

charms, may have no rhyme nor reason whatever, unless it could be that they give confidence to persons who could gain it in no other way. There are a few, perhaps, that were coined to coax children into better behavior, and even influence adults into improving their manners.

Today, they come under the general head of superstitions, that may hold little truth, but some have been given the more dignified titles of "omens" or "lucky signs." Those of general prevalence have been selected, rather than little-known localisms, quaint though some of the latter may be. Many uneducated persons still believe in such things, and more intelligent people enjoy laughing at them, so the more of them the merrier.

For those who do intend to take them seriously, it should be mentioned that most of the spells can presumably be broken by spitting, walking backward a specified number of steps, going around in a circle three times, hitting one palm with the closed fist of the other hand, or alternately with the thumb and fist.

Medicinal remedies also are encountered in conjunction with existing superstitions, but these survivals from a less enlightened past are foolish, dangerous, or contrary to modern medical practice, so they have been eliminated from the alphabetical listing that follows.

Apples figure in many superstitions, the most noted being the phrase, "An apple a day keeps the doctor away."

When apple trees bloom, it is considered lucky to plant seeds of other trees and plants.

If you peel an apple in one long piece and count off the twists by calling the letters of the alphabet, the last letter will represent the first initial of the name of a sweetheart or future spouse.

Another way is to peel an apple in one long piece, throw it over your left shoulder, and see what initial it most resembles as it lies on the floor.

To cut an apple in eight or nine pieces, throw the last piece over the left shoulder, then count off the letters of the alphabet until the piece has dropped to the floor, carries more or less the same prediction as the peeling procedure, except that it can refer to a friend or a visitor.

Slice an apple in two without cutting a seed and your wish for love will come true.

If an apple breaks apart while eating it, bad luck is close at hand.

Ashes in the days of the barbarians were used as a charm to produce large crops. A token amount of ashes blown over the seeded farm, with incantations, was sure to bring luck to the farmer.

Later, through the centuries, ashes were mixed with the seeds or the soil to increase the fertility.

An old saying which is not so lucky goes as follows: "Empty ashes after dark, double trouble will you stalk."

Baldness There is an old saying that you'll be bald if you cut your hair when the moon is waning.

Bats that fly around at twilight predict good weather.

If they come near you someone is trying to betray or bewitch you.

A bat that hits your window or enters your home warns of death or very bad luck to someone you know.

When a bat hits a building it is a sign of rain.

Bed If you are accustomed to getting out of one side of the bed in the morning, getting out on the other—or "wrong" side—is supposed to bring you bad luck during the day.

Placing a hat on the bed is supposed to be very bad luck, particularly in theatrical circles.

Always finish making a bed once you have started, otherwise you will have a bad day.

Bees that buzz before the first of spring bring more cold weather. When bees stay in their hive it is a prognostication of rain. It is lucky to receive a hive of bees as a gift, but unlucky to sell them. Bees must be told of the death of a person in the household, or you must turn the hive around. Otherwise bad luck may follow.

Birds vary where omens are concerned. Sometimes the species of the bird is the important factor. The bluebird is the harbinger of springtime and signifies both fair weather and good luck.

If a robin flies into the house it brings good luck to the owner.

When a cuckoo cries, take out your money and spit on it for good fortune.

If an owl hoots near a sick person, death may be near.

A white dove or pigeon that hovers near a house or person augurs happiness.

Shoot a dove and you'll have only bad luck.

To rob a bird's nest means sorrow.

A bird that hits a window is an omen of death. If it flutters its wings and tries to come in it is in danger, but it is considered very lucky for the occupant of that room.

Birthstones Birthstones have been worn as a lucky charm by both men and women through many centuries. There has been considerable variance in the birthstones due to availability, selectivity, or appropriateness for the people who wear them. Each stone has an imputed virtue of its own which it gives to the bearer. Hence those most appropriate were assigned to certain months. Real students of occult lore carry the stones to meet their needs.

These are purely traditional customs but they seem to grow much deeper with the passing of time. If you need strengthening of the qualities of your birth month, carry a stone that can lend these increased virtues to you. Some people like to carry birthstones of other months to absorb the extra attributes that they can bring to the wearer.

The following is a list of birthstones for each month.

January—garnet
February—amethyst

March—bloodstone or aquamarine
April—diamond
May—agate or emerald
June—pearl, alexandrite, or moonstone
July—ruby
August—sardonyx or peridot
September—blue sapphire
October—opal, tourmaline, or rose sapphire
November—topaz
December—turquoise or blue zircon

The Symbolic Meaning of the Precious and Semi-Precious Stones

Agate The agate is helpful to a happy, prosperous career. It is a protection against danger or plotters and brings sympathy to the wearer.

Alexandrite The alexandrite is a form of beryl called chrysoberyl. It changes color, sometimes blue, or amethyst or green, so in turn it symbolizes the combined qualities and virtues of the sapphire, the amethyst, and the emerald.

Amber Amber protects the wearer against secret poisons and has the power of attracting compassion and understanding.

Amethyst The amethyst brings contentment and sincerity for the wearer. In ancient days it was carried to prevent the desire for drinking. It is also worn to attract favor of people in high office or importance.

Aquamarine The aquamarine should be worn by those who are unhappy. It symbolizes hope.

Beryl promotes love, especially between man and woman. The person who wears it is given the power to attract the affections of the opposite sex.

Coral lends preservation from misfortune and illness. It wards off fear and temptation toward violence. It imbues reason and wisdom. White coral adds modesty; black coral, fortitude and perseverance.

Crystal induces serenity and poise. It shapens the mentality and balances the emotional qualities.

Diamond The diamond brings peace and serenity. It also signifies constancy, fidelity, and innocence. These qualities have been the reason for its use as a symbol of faithfulness for engaged and married couples. It is also used as a token or gift for reconciliation between estranged lovers.

Emerald The emerald enhances love. It adds to fortitude and strength, especially in old age. It increases the gift of understanding, and brings gaiety, eloquence, and popularity to those who wear it.

Garnet The garnet has many virtues. Foremost is constancy; then follow frankness, sincerity, friendliness, and charity.

Jade Jade is a symbol of forthrightness and immortality. In past centuries, in India, only men of integrity and highest moral character were permitted to wear jade. It is a sacred stone for the Chinese and Japanese. It is characterized by many curative powers and a preventative for disagreeable dreams.

Jet Jet has the attribute of warding off exorcisms and unpleasant apparitions or mental fears. It symbolizes sadness and grief, so it has long been used as jewelry during the period of mourning.

Lapis-lazuli represents tenderness, sympathy, and love. It was long used as the lucky birthstone for people born in December. Its particular virtue is that it gives the owner the power to transmit love to another person.

Moonstone The moonstone is the symbol of purity and chastity. It lends reverence and respect for conjugal love.

Onyx The onyx is a symbol of discordance, fear, and sadness. It promotes chastity but induces quarrels, fitful dreams, and ominous forebodings.

Opal The opal is considered unlucky for all except those people born in October. Originally it was attributed with the power to give wealth and beauty to its owner, even the ability to become invisible. It is known to grow dull if it is unlucky for the wearer. This quality makes it a symbol of infidelity or fickleness. The milky-looking opals are symbolic of sadness, melancholia, and a subsequent turn toward seclusion and prayer.

Pearl The pearl symbolizes tears of sorrow and of gladness. It is the symbol of patience, purity of mind and soul, faithfulness, and an abhorrence of violence and temper.

Ruby The ruby sometimes changes its hue to a slight degree, at which time it brings misfortune or unhappiness to the wearer. In its normal state it symbolizes loyalty, charity, and courage, but in its most virile mood it imbues boldness, anger, and cruelty.

Sapphire The sapphire transmits peace and humility. It symbolizes truth, loyalty, and justice.

Topaz The topaz in ancient days made the wearer invulnerable to injury or attack. It symbolizes sobriety, clemency, faithfulness, and idyllic love. It appeases anger, turns sadness into happiness, brings wealth and honors. The topaz also is used as a divining rod to locate water, buried treasures, and precious metals.

Tourmaline The tourmaline is the symbol of vitality and is said to give the wearer exhilaration and potency akin to the power of electricity.

Turquoise The turquoise is a charm that voids assassination, accidental death, or violence of any kind. It brings courage and love. It is the symbol of youth and innocent love.

Zircon The zircon is the stone of luck that grants the wearer all desires for health, prosperity, and honors. It is a silent protector against all danger on land, sea, and air. It promotes sound sleep and brings happiness and strength.

(Alphabetical Listing continued)

Breakfast You'll weep before evening if you sing before breakfast.

Bride Lucky is the bride who wears old shoes, a bit of blue, or her mother's wedding ring at her wedding.

If the bride wears earrings she will be happy; but pearls will bring her unhappiness.

Orange blossoms are regarded lucky for the bride.

It is unlucky to give away a wedding present.

Rice thrown at the bride brings luck for the future. Old shoes tied to the bridal car bring more luck.

It is unlucky to postpone a wedding.

Rain on the wedding day means unhappiness for the bride and groom; snow, happiness; thunder, a bad omen.

To place a piece of the bridal cake under a pillow brings dreams of a future spouse, for a young unmarried girl.

Bridge   Make a wish while going over a bridge and it will be granted if you do not speak until you are across.

Broom   If you sweep under someone's feet that person will not get married—at least not for a year!

Keep a broom outside the door to keep witches away.

Persons who sweep after dark will never be rich; also such a person will lose a friend.

Sweeping before sunrise brings bad luck.

If a child starts to sweep, guests will come that day.

You will have bad luck if you borrow a broom, lend one, or burn one.

Never step over a fallen broom. It means bad luck, and so does a broom which falls while you are walking by it.

Butterfly   The first butterfly means the beginning of spring. If it is white, it brings health and happiness; yellow, it predicts illness.

Button   Find a button, make a new acquaintance.

Candles have figured in many superstitions which have dwindled with the introduction of modern lighting. Once a drip of wax down the side presaged bad luck or even death to the person nearest to that side.

More generally a death is indicated if a candle is allowed to burn itself out. In contrast, killing a moth flitting about a candle denotes good luck.

A tall straight flame indicates the arrival of a stranger.

Today the old traditions of candles on a birthday cake still hold. There should be one for each year of a person's age, as this symbolizes good luck for the coming year. If a person makes a wish and blows out all the candles on the birthday cake in one breath, the wish will be fulfilled.

Cat   If a cat washes its face and paws over its ear three times, company will come. The direction in which the cat is looking is the one from which people will supposedly arrive. Black cats bring luck if they come to your house. Gray cats bring very good luck. White cats are doubtful; some claim they bring good luck, others sickness. If a cat follows you, expect to receive money.

If a black cat walks under a ladder, the person who climbs that ladder will have bad luck.

It's bad luck if a black cat crosses your path, but there are various ways to counteract this:

One is to go home and start out again. Another is to take twelve steps backward. Still another remedy is to turn around, walk backward past the spot where the cat crossed, and count to nine.

However, if you see a black cat starting to cross in front of you, one procedure is to turn away and, if the cat is gone when you look again you will avoid the spell, because you have no visible proof that it crossed. Cats of other colors are more helpful. To see a black and white cat cross your path indicates good luck; a gray cat, very good luck. A white cat crossing your path is variable. Sometimes it brings good luck, other times sickness.

Christmas omens are numerous and varied. A white Christmas indicates that deaths will be fewer during the coming year; lack of snow signifies the opposite.

A child born on Christmas is lucky, and supposedly is able to understand the speech of animals. An announcement of an engagement made on Christmas presages a happy married life.

Clover Picking a four-leaf clover means good luck except in the month of May. Putting the clover in your left shoe insures the indicated luck. It sometimes means that you will find or inherit money.

Picking a five-leaf clover will bring you bad luck, though throwing it away may counteract this. A better plan is to give it to someone else, as that will bring you good luck. If passed along from person to person, each will have good luck, until the last, who will be unlucky. A six-leaf clover is generally regarded as bad luck.

Coins Flipping a coin for heads or tails has long been regarded as a lucky way to decide a question. Finding a coin is naturally good luck; but if you continue to carry that coin you may find more, which is still better. It is also good luck to carry a coin that bears the date of your birth. Another good luck charm is a coin with a hole in it, or a bent coin. To wear a coin in each shoe on New Year's Day means that you will have money all year; while to receive pennies in change on Monday means that you will have money all week.

Crickets Crickets in the house are often regarded as a sign of good luck. To hear them chirp or sing presages still more luck and contentment. To kill a cricket therefore means bad luck, while if a cricket stops chirping and leaves, an illness is to be anticipated.

Dog A howling dog is a sign of death. If a strange dog comes to your home it is generally considered as a sign of good luck, though some people claim the opposite. A dog whining beneath a window is regarded as bad luck. A dog lying in a doorway facing inward means someone is coming into the family; facing outward, someone is leaving the family.

Dress You will get a new dress or a gift if you accidentally put your dress on inside out.

Ears, eyes, and *eyebrows* have the same meanings when they burn, itch, or ring. If the left ear burns, itches, or rings someone is saying something complimentary about you; the right, the contrary. This is also told vice versa, the left meaning bad, the right, good. Other sayings refer to good or bad news and good or bad luck.

Eggs are the subject of many old-time superstitions. Once opened, the shells should be completely broken to avoid bad luck. If egg shells are burned in a fire, the hens will stop laying.

Horse owners should always eat an even number of eggs for good luck, while bringing eggs into the house after dark is generally regarded as unlucky.

Finger Cross your first and second fingers behind your back if you have to tell a white lie to avoid hurting someone's feelings.

To remember something, tie a string around your finger.

Fingernails Burn your fingernail parings in a fireplace to bring good luck. It is lucky to cut your fingernails when the new moon begins, or to file your nails on Monday, Tuesday, or Wednesday. Bad luck to cut your nails on Friday.

Flowers An old superstition that still holds with some horticulturists says, Plant flowers during the new moon and they will bloom and bloom. It is unlucky to pick Mayflowers unless you were born in May. If a dandelion or buttercup reflects yellow when held under your chin, you like butter. Sunflowers and sea-onions bring luck if you grow them. Tuberoses are generally considered unlucky.

Pluck the petals of a daisy saying with each successive petal "He loves me, he loves me not" and you will learn if you are loved.

Flowers that bring luck for the month of your birth are as follows:

January—carnation, snowdrop	July—water lily
February—primrose	August—gladiolus
March—daffodil	September—aster
April—daisy	October—dahlia
May—lily of the valley	November—chrysanthemum
June—rose	December—holly

Certain flowers have recognized qualities and are often worn or chosen as gifts to express a sentiment. The most popular ones are in the following selection:

Carnation—fidelity, trust, and virtue
Daisy—humility
Forget-me-not—remembrance
Honeysuckle—constancy
Hyacinth—friendship
Lily—steadfastness
Marigold—wisdom
Mayflower—anxiety, hatred
Pansy—good will
Poppy, white—faithfulness
Rose, red—nobility
Rose, white—valor and bravery
Rose, yellow—infidelity
Rosemary—love and tears
Violet—patience and hope

Frog When a frog croaks in the day it means rain within three days. It is unlucky to kill a toad or a frog.

Glove Drop your glove and you will meet with a disappointment.

Hair Cut your hair on the start of the new moon to make it grow fast. A cowlick is a lucky omen. Many sailors consider it lucky to cut their hair during a storm. Rain makes your hair grow faster. Carry a little lock of your sweetheart's hair for luck. A stray hair on your shoulder means you will receive a letter. If you drop your comb while combing your hair it means a disappointment.

Hairpin If you find a hairpin, you will make a new friendship. If a hairpin slips out of your hair, someone is thinking of you. If you lose a hairpin you will make an enemy. If you find a hairpin, hang it on a hook for good luck.

Hands If the palm of your right hand itches you will receive money, a letter, news, or a call from a person long absent. It is also said that you will make a new acquaintance. When the left hand itches you will have to pay out money. To break the spell, rub the hand on wood.

It is bad luck to shake hands with the left hand. If three people start to shake hands simultaneously it is a sign of good luck and happy times for all three.

If two couples cross hands while shaking hands, there will be an unexpected marriage.

A cold hand indicates a warm heart. A moist hand, an amorous nature.

If two people simultaneously wash their hands in a single basin of water they will have a quarrel. Similarly, if two persons dry their hands on a towel simultaneously, they will have angry words with each other. To break the spell, spit in the water or make the sign of the cross.

Hat It is very unlucky to place your hat on a bed. It is bad luck to wear two hats on your head. A quarrel usually ensues.

Hay To see a load of hay, or pass it, means good luck for the day. A wish made at the same time will be granted. Some people say that it is bad luck to pass a load of hay unless you spit and make a wish.

Horse If you see two white horses together, they will bring you luck. One white horse may be unlucky for you unless you cross your fingers or stamp your foot once, then make a wish.

Horseshoe Horseshoe superstitions date back to the ancients. When a horse lost his shoe it was usually bad luck for the rider. This may account for the fact that the finding of a horseshoe may be regarded as lucky. Frequently such horseshoes were hung over doors of houses or barns, though any horseshoe so hung may be regarded as lucky. A horseshoe should be hung with its points upward in order to hold luck. Most horseshoes have seven nailholes, also contributing to the lucky notion.

Finger rings made of horseshoe nails are said to ward off bad luck. Rubbing two horseshoes together is said to bring good luck—a good thing to try when pitching horseshoes. Miniature horseshoe pins are also regarded as lucky.

House When visiting, be sure to leave a house by the same door through which you entered. Otherwise you will take the owner's luck away and most likely bring bad luck upon yourself too.

If a door opens by itself, expect an unwelcome guest.

If you forget your key and are forced to enter the house through a window, open the door from the inside, then crawl out the same window and enter by the door, otherwise you will be hounded by bad luck.

Insects Busy ants predict bad weather. A ladybug brings good luck. Help it out of the house carefully or you will have bad luck. If a firefly enters the house it is a sign of good luck, or unexpected guests.

It is unlucky to kill a cricket, daddy longlegs, katydid, ladybug, wasp, or spider. One omen says, to kill a spider brings rain.

If you see a spider weaving a web you will soon have new clothes. If a spider drops down on a thread that it is spinning you will have good luck, but if it drops down to the floor, bad news is on the way. If a spider gets on you or your clothes you will receive a letter or money or both. *See* Bees.

Itching If your head itches it means good luck soon. An itching right elbow means good news; left elbow, bad news. An itching right knee means good news; left knee, gossip. An itching right ankle means that you will receive money; left ankle, need to pay out money. If your feet itch you will walk in new surroundings or take a journey.

Journey If you start on a journey, then turn back for some reason, it means bad luck throughout the day. You can avert this bad luck by taking another road or turn around three times before entering the home. If you see a spider working on its web in the afternoon, you will make a journey. Wear black agate to avert danger while traveling. It is bad luck to start a trip on the thirteenth. It is bad luck to postpone a journey.

Key If a housewife's key rusts, someone is saving money for her.

Knife and *fork* A knife dropped on the floor indicates a male guest will arrive; a fork, a woman.

Never give a knife to your sweetheart. It will break the engagement. Some say that if a plain pin is given in exchange, the bad spell will be broken. It is unlucky to cross two knives, or a knife and a fork.

If a knife or pointed object is offered as a gift, the recipient must give a pin or a penny in return to avoid bad luck. A new knife must be tried out on paper or wood to avoid bad luck.

If you drop either a knife or a fork during a meal stop eating to avert bad luck.

Ladder To walk under a ladder is bad luck. Some believe that if you go back under it, that the bad luck will be nullified. Others, that if you are having bad luck, walking under a ladder will bring good luck. Climb a ladder with an odd number of rungs if you want to be successful. To lose your footing means a loss of money.

Leaf Catch a falling leaf in your hands and you will avoid a cold in the subsequent winter.

Lightning Sheet lightning warns of hot weather. An old saying that lightning never strikes twice, has been disproven. If it lightens and thunders before the trees leaf, spring will come late. If it thunders on the last day of February it will bring more frost at the end of May.

Lilacs Bad luck will hound you if you take white lilacs into the house. *See* Flowers.

Locks When a person is dying all the locks of the doors should be opened so the soul (spirit) can leave the house with ease.

Match Three on a match means bad luck. If you light a match and it burns to the end without stopping, your sweetheart loves you. If you dream about a match you will receive money.

Mirror Break a mirror and you will have seven years' bad luck. It is bad luck to look in a mirror by candlelight.

If a mirror falls down steps or from a great height in your home, a relative or a member of the family will die.

A bride will have bad luck if she looks in the mirror after she is dressed for her marriage.

It is bad luck to make your dog look in the mirror.

Money Two-dollar bills are generally regarded as unlucky. Carry money in two different pockets and you are likely to lose it! Turn your money over in your pocket when you see the new moon and it will increase with the moon. Never take all your money out of your pocketbook or savings box. Leave a little, even one coin, for luck.

Moon It is unlucky to look at the new moon over your left shoulder. Look at it over the right shoulder for luck. It is unlucky to look at the new moon through a windowpane. If you see it for the first time through the branches of a tree, make a wish. It will come true.

The crescent moon, when upside down, is a sign of rain—called the wet moon.

A circle or halo around the moon—rain, rain, rain.

Moving When you move, leave a little something in the old residence for luck.

New Year's Day It is bad luck to take anything out of the home on New Year's Day. If you wear new clothes, keep a little money in your pocket or pocketbook, for good luck in the ensuing year. Empty pockets bring no luck.

The person who drinks the last drink left in a bottle will have a lucky year. Some people also blow into the neck of an empty wine bottle for good luck.

Nail If you find a nail that is pointed toward you pick it up and you will have good luck that day.

Nose An itching nose has a variety of superstitious interpretations. The most common one is that someone is thinking of you. Another is that you will be kissed by a fool, or that you will receive a letter and have a quarrel.

If your nose bleeds it is a sign that you are in love.

Numbers See "Numerology" chapter, or individual listings.

Onions Throw onion skins on a fire. While they are burning make a wish and it will come true.

Onions should be hung in a sickroom.

To find the name of a future husband, a young girl should scratch or label the name of a boy on each of five to nine onions. Write a different name on each onion. Next, set them in a warm place. The first onion that sprouts will have the name of the future husband.

Opals are unlucky for everyone except people who have the opal for their birthstone.

Owl If an owl hoots during the day it means bad weather. To break the bad weather spell, burn salt, or take off one shoe and turn it upside down.

It is bad luck to see an owl in the daytime. If a very young girl hears the hooting or screeching of an owl in the daytime she should stay at home to avoid an accident.

Peacock feathers are considered an unlucky omen, especially bad luck for theatrical people. The fans bring misfortune to a home.

Peapods If you find a peapod with nine peas, make a wish, then throw the pod over your right shoulder for luck.

Pearls are considered unlucky except for people who have them for their birthstone.

Pencil If you find a pencil on a road or street, pick it up for luck.

Penny If you find a penny, keep it for luck. This is true of all coins that are found. Some sailors believe in throwing a penny across the bow of a ship before sailing to insure good luck.

Picture When a picture falls it is an omen of bad luck. If it is a photograph or a painting of a person, that person is supposed to die very soon.

Pigeon If a stray white pigeon comes to your home or grounds it is a warning of a death in the family.

Pin If you see a pin, pick it up to have a lucky day. If you do not pick it up it means bad luck. If the pin points toward you, make a wish for luck. If you give a pin to someone else you give away your luck. To break this spell lay the pin down, then let the other person pick it up. If pricked by a pin in your clothing, pull it out, make a wish, then put it back. Needles have the same superstitious meanings.

Playing cards To be lucky at cards many players wear a lucky pin. Those who are lucky at cards are unlucky in love and vice versa. It is unlucky to play on an uncovered table. A green cloth brings the best luck. To change your luck, change the order of your dealing or call for a new deck. Dropping cards causes you to lose your luck.

Among unlucky cards are the Nine of Diamonds, known as the "Curse of Scotland," and the Four of Clubs, called the "Devil's Bedposts." The Ace of Spades is sometimes regarded as the death card, if drawn while cutting cards.

In poker, two pair consisting of aces over eights is regarded as unlucky, as this was the famous "Dead Man's Hand" held by Wild Bill Hickok when he was shot down during a game.

Pocket You'll have luck if you keep a piece of oyster shell in your pocket or pocketbook. Keep a piece of raw fresh potato in your pocket to ward off rheumatics.

Poker Never keep both poker and tongs on the same side of the fireplace. Put one on each side to bring luck to your home.

Rabbit's foot   If you wear or carry a rabbit's foot it is supposed to bring you luck. An old theatrical superstition is that you should use a rabbit's foot to apply makeup. Today the rabbit's foot is in the makeup kit as a token of good luck, but is rarely used. Many young mothers keep a rabbit's foot near a young infant, especially in the carriage, presumably to ward off accidents.

Rain   If you walk in the rain you will be lucky. *See* Weather.

Rainbow   A bag of gold can be found at the end of the rainbow. A rainbow on Saturday means a week of rain. Make a wish three times when you see a rainbow and your wish will come true. Rainbow in the east, dry weather; in the west, wet weather.

Rats leave a sinking ship. It means good luck if you catch two rats in the same trap. Rats that leave a house predict a death of someone living there.

Ring   A birthstone ring brings good luck. *See* birthstone list. It is bad luck to remove your wedding ring. Make a wish if you put a ring on the finger of someone else.

Rooster   If a rooster crows during the day, you may expect a guest or unexpected visitor. If a rooster crows at night it is a bad omen. Roosters are known to be excellent "watchdogs" and, like geese, will warn all the barnyard as well as the owners that someone or some unwelcome animal is approaching.

Ruby   *See* Birthstones.

Salt   If you upset or spill salt on the table, throw a pinch of the spilled salt over your left shoulder and make a wish for good luck. Too much salt makes for sorrow.

Scissors   If you drop a pair of scissors, step on them gently before picking them up. This avoids a disappointment. Hang your scissors on a hook or nail and they will bring you good luck. If you receive scissors as a gift you must give the donor a penny in return to break any bad spell.

Seagull   Never kill a seagull. It will bring you bad luck. Sailors say there will be a death if they see three gulls flying over them.

Sewing   It's bad luck to sew anything onto a garment that you are wearing. You will weep if you sew something new on something old such as a dress or a suit. If your thread knots when you are sewing, you will quarrel before the night is ended. If a seamstress loses a thimble while working on a garment it means good luck for the wearer. If the material is sewed wrongside out, so that it must be ripped, this also means good luck for the wearer.

Shirt If you put your shirt on inside out, it means a bad day ahead.

Shoes It is a bad omen to put your shoes on a chair or a table. Throw an old shoe after newlyweds for luck, or fasten it to their car.

Shoestrings If your shoestrings are untied it is a sign that you are in love. If the left comes untied, someone is saying something unkind about you; if the right comes untied, something flattering. Make a wish when you tie another person's shoestring.

Skirt Kiss the turned-up hem of a skirt or petticoat and you'll have good luck. Some say it brings a new dress. If your underskirt hangs out, make a wish, then adjust it. Your wish will come true.

Sleep on unironed sheets for happy dreams and a lucky day. If you have a tooth pulled, sleep on it for luck. Luck comes to those who sleep facing the south. Always get in and out of bed on the same side to avoid bad luck. Always put your right foot out of bed first and you'll have a happy day.

Slipper It is bad luck to keep your slippers on a shelf over your head. Never cross your slippers lest the crossing bring bad luck to the household. *See* Shoes.

Smoke Smoke that rises straight up in the air means clear weather. If it accumulates close to the ground it predicts a change in the weather, usually rain in mild weather or snow during the cold months.

Snails If many snails abound, they'll bring the rain around.

Snakes If snakes crawl to high ground, rain will soon abound.

Sneeze Sneezing, like many other superstitious omens, has contradictory meanings. For instance, to sneeze three times in succession brings good luck, or it may bring a disappointment. Still another meaning is that it will cause someone to write you a letter. If you sneeze just once, make a wish and it will come to pass. Sneeze twice and you'll be kissed.

Spider If a spider makes a web in a doorway, you may expect a visitor. If you see one climbing up a thread you will have good news or good luck. It is also lucky to see a spider spinning a web in the morning. Killing a spider at night is unlucky.

Spoon Dropping a spoon at the table means a visitor soon. If it is a large spoon, a whole family may walk in on you. The direction in which the handle points tells where such visitors may come from. It is supposed to be unlucky to stir anything with the spoon held in the left hand.

Stairs It is unlucky to meet someone on a flight of stairs. Stumbling while going upstairs means a wedding; downstairs, loss of money or bad luck during the day.

Stars You can wish on the first star that you see in the evening by saying "Starlight, star bright, the first star I've seen tonight." Some people claim that to make the wish come true you must not speak to anyone until you see another star. If you see a shooting star make a quick wish and it may come true.

Thirteen Thirteen has long been considered an unlucky number. For thirteen people to meet together will shortly bring bad luck to one of them. This is all the worse if the thirteenth of that month happens to be a Friday. In an effort to break this jinx, people have formed Thirteen Clubs and their meetings have not been followed by dire results.

Toad Handling toads results in warts. If you kill a toad your house will catch fire. A toad hopping across the path of a bridal party means a happy marriage. The call of a tree toad is a sign of rain.

Toasts To spill a drink while making a toast means happiness and good health. If the glass breaks in the hand it is an omen of death.

Towel If two people dry their hands simultaneously on one and the same towel, they will have a disappointment or a quarrel. Dropping a towel or dishcloth means a visitor. You can thwart this by stepping over it backwards.

Umbrella It is unlucky to open an umbrella in a house. Carry an umbrella and it won't rain. If you drop your umbrella, let another person pick it up so that you will not have bad luck.

Weather superstitions are based upon keen observation or recognition of certain atmospheric conditions. Therefore they cannot wholly be regarded as superstitions but rather rate as indications. However, mystical omens have traditionally crept in among sounder prognostications. Some of the more bizarre are given here:

If a groundhog sees his shadow on February 2 there will be six more weeks of snow, rain, or cold weather.

A spade stuck in the ground will bring rain. An itching corn means rain. Bubbles in the puddles, three days of rainy troubles.

If you drop a piece of buttered bread there will be rain.

Burn ferns if you want rain to fall. It is a sure sign of rain if chickens or cattle go into their shelters during the daylight. When a cat climbs up and down screens or across upholstery it means rain. Swarming, biting, crazy flies mean much rain. If the leaves turn up, it means rain.

When horses or ponies or any other farm animals play or run around vigorously, there will be a change in the weather. If swallows fly low, if spiders leave their webs and run for cracks, if the soot flies down the chimney or there is a halo around the moon, you can expect a change of the weather.

The weather will be clear if there is enough blue in the sky to make a handkerchief or a pair of Dutchman's pants.

An east wind brings warmer weather.

If the frost holds on the trees till noon, there will be snow by night. If the wild fruits and nuts are abundant, there will be a cold, hard winter. Katydids that sing in August bring heavy frost in twice three weeks. If it snows on Christmas there will be another month of snow and cold.

Wedding Losing a wedding ring means losing a husband. If a cat sneezes in the bride's home prior to the wedding it is bad luck.

Wedding Anniversaries

Wedding anniversaries are supposed to carry good fortune if a person receives a gift or token made of the material for which the anniversary is named. These listings vary, but the important ones are as follows:

First, cotton or paper; second, paper or straw; third, leather or candy; fifth, wooden, woolen, or floral; tenth, tin; twelfth, silk or linen; fifteenth, crystal; twentieth, china; twenty-fifth, silver; thirtieth, pearl; thirty-fifth, coral; fortieth, ruby; forty-fifth, sapphire; fiftieth, golden; sixtieth or seventy-fifth, diamond.

Whistling Never whistle in a dressing room of a theater. It brings bad luck.

Windows Climbing through a window is bad luck unless you climb back out through the same window. It is also bad luck to break a window or if a window drops shut of its own accord.

Wishbone A wishbone is regarded lucky because it resembles a horseshoe. If two persons hold a dried wishbone between them and each makes a silent wish before snapping it, the one with the long end will have the wish come true provided the wish is unspoken. Some claim that the person with the short end will be the first to marry.

15

Tasseography or
Teacup Reading

Teacup reading is one of the simplest and most entertaining forms of divination. It allows great play of the imagination and so-called "hunches." The reader must interpret the shapes or forms that are made by tea leaves that remain after the tea has been drunk. The preparation of the cup and the meaning of the symbols are as follows.

The cup must be very wide at the top, the sides must slant, the bottom not be too small. A white cup is preferred, but any pastel, undecorated cup will do.

The best results are obtained from China tea or a very good grade of tea that has a minimum of tea dust. Tea should be brewed in a teapot without a strainer, obviously to pour sufficient leaves into the cup for a reading.

The person whose fortune is to be read must drink the tea, leaving a little in the bottom of the cup. Then, with the left hand, take hold of the handle and slowly move the cup around from left to right, three times. This should distribute the tea leaves around the sides of the cup, sometimes reaching the rim, and still have a few on the bottom.

Time is differentiated by the parts of the cup. The rim represents the present or things that may happen within a few days or weeks. The sides predict the future. The bottom augurs the very distant future.

The leaves, stems, and tea dust take on various forms around the inside of the cup, and these are called symbols. They denote fortunate or adverse happenings.

The *handle* of the cup represents the house or surroundings of the consultant; hence the closer a symbol in relation to the handle, or house, the sooner the event may take place.

Numbers represent time such as minutes, hours, days, or weeks, depending upon the relativity of the other symbols.

Letters of the alphabet mean people such as relatives, friends, or associates. The closer to the handle, the more importance.

Dots formed by little specks indicate a journey. Larger dots—money gained through extra effort.

Wavy lines—uncertainty. *Straight lines*—plans must follow a pattern or definite course.

Clear symbols are considered very lucky. *Poorly outlined*—indecision, obstacles that hinder progress or contentment.

Stars and *triangles*—fortunate. *Circles*—success. *Squares*—protective.

The Meaning of the Symbols

Airplane—Near the handle—improvements in the home; on the side—desire to travel far; on the bottom—disappointment in plans; a broken airplane—accident.

Anchor—Near the rim, abundant love; on the bottom, business success concerned with water or air; on the side, a commercial venture involving travel. If indistinct—unfortunate in love.

Angel—Good news.

Ants—Many difficulties before goal is achieved.

Anvil—Conscientious effort toward financial gains.

Apple—Achievement.

Arrow—Disagreement contained in a letter or message. With dots or dashes near, money involved.

Ax or hatchet—Impending danger.

Baby—Near the handle, another member added to the household; on the side—honors; bottom—trouble ahead.

Ball—Desire to move due to uncomfortable situation.

Basket—A pleasant surprise; with dots—legacy of money.

Bat—Fearful of some higher authority or enemy.

Bear—Misfortune.

Bed—Inertia, desire to rest or escape from problems.

Bell—News. Could be a wedding.

Bird—Good luck. Often promises a journey; wings spread—air travel; with leaves near—good companions.

Bird cage—Avoid conflicts.

Boat—Wanderlust.

Bottle—Threat or warning of illness.

Bouquet—Marital happiness.

Box (two-dimensional)—Uncertainty in business or social affairs.

Bracelet (or ring)—Loyal friends gather to congratulate you.

Branch—Omen of a birth or a new friendship is made.

Bridge—Obstacles that will be overcome.

Broom—New prospects ahead.

Building—Desire for change of habitation.

Bull—Avoid quarrels.

Butterfly—Much happiness. Unexpected pleasure.

Cab—Secret desires.

Cage—Proposal of marriage.

Car—Unexpected changes for the betterment of surroundings.

Castle—An inheritance.

Cat—A deceitful or treacherous friend.

Chain—News of marriage.

Chair—Need to relax; entertain a friend.

Church—A ceremony of some sort.

Circle—The perfectionist in one field that brings great success. Small lines or dots nearby or touching retard these efforts.

Clouds—Trouble; with dots or dashes, financial complications.

Clover—The happy sign of fortune and happiness.

Coffin—Sad news, often a death.

Comet—Too much excitement, tension, or unnecessary worry.

Compass—Travel.

Cross—Misfortune, sacrifice; on bottom of cup—very serious problems; within a square—trouble can be averted.

Crown—Highest honors and success often through luck itself.

Cup—A new friend.

Dagger—Symbol of danger or loss.

Daisy—Desire for love and affection.

Deer—Avoid arguments.

Dog—Symbol of a true friend; on bottom of cup—a friend needs your help; a dog's head—you are a true friend to someone near.

Donkey—Need for patience while waiting for assistance.

Door—Look for something unusual to happen.

Dragon—A new year or new venture ahead.

Drum—Expect a change. Look for some other interest.

Duck—Tenacity of purpose brings excellent results.

Eagle—This must look very very large. Desire for new home.

Elephant—Need for a trustworthy friend.

Eyeglasses—Prepare for a surprise. Be cautious in business.

Faces—Friendships.

Fan—A flirtation already begun. Warning of an indiscretion.

Flag—Be ready to defend yourself.

Flies—Annoyances.

Flowers—Honors, love; on side of cup—new love or marriage; on bottom—unhappy love affair.

Fountain—Great, enduring happiness.

Fox—A deceitful friend.

Frog—Be ready to make a drastic change.

Fruit—Ambitions gratified. A fortunate sign.

Gate—A problem will be satisfactorily solved.

Goat—Obstinacy causes a conflict of ideas.

Grapes—Very ambitious for a love match.

Gun—Avoid quarrels. Active service for those in the armed forces.

Hammer—Laborious effort rewarded by sufficiency.

Hand—Aid from an understanding friend.

Harp—Romance, happiness.

Hat—Honor; on side of cup—unusual diplomacy; on bottom—matrimonial bliss.

Hatchet (ax)—Impetuous nature causing many arguments.

Heart—You have a lover or there is someone close to you in whom you can confide.

Heavenly bodies—These are pictured as the Moon, the Sun, stars, Milky Way, and so on, but requires imagination to see them. All represent a state of happiness and good luck.

Hen—Take care of your nest egg.

Horseshoe—The good luck symbol; with prospects in the other symbols, could be applied as a "go-ahead" sign.

Hourglass—Need to mark time before making a decision; on bottom of cup—warning of danger.

Initials—Refer to people you know or are about to know.

Jug—Avoid extravagances or excesses. Also a token of conviviality about to take place.

Kettle—Strive for domestic tranquillity.

Key—Symbol of enlightenment. Look for new interests.

Kite—Do not take chances.

Knife—Avoid misunderstandings, take care of your health; pointed toward the handle—warning of separation from family or business connections; on bottom—lawsuits.

Ladder—Advancement through personal ideals and ambitions.

Lamp—At the rim, a celebration for a special event; on the side, loss of something personal; on the bottom, postponement of a social engagement. Two lamps—two marriages; near the handle, an inheritance or unexpected bonus.

Leaves—These must be formed by several tea leaves—a sign of renewed hope; on bottom of cup—ambition attained in later years.

Letters—If untouched by dots or marks, good news, sometimes about money; a heart with it—emotional problems concerning love or marriage.

Lines—Straight lines, usually journeys; wavy lines—indecision, frustration.

Man—An unknown person may be expected; if an initial is close, the person may be identified by the consultant.

Mask—Be careful. Do not divulge personal secrets. If a flower or bell is near, you may be invited to a grand party.

Moon—Full moon, romantic period; first quarter, look for new projects; last quarter, do not be impetuous, do not make hasty decisions.

Mountains—Rugged work that must be completed.

Mushroom—Possible complications in business or home; a disturbance either mental or physical that must be adjusted.

Numbers—An indication of time such as days or weeks, always relative to other symbols in the cup.

Owl—Trouble emanating from illness or death of friend or relative.

Palm tree—A happy and contented married life.

Pipe—Don't look for trouble; keep an open mind.

Ring—The marriage symbol; look for a number and an initial near the ring. On bottom of cup—postponement of an engagement or marriage.

Saw—Warning of an impending obstacle or interference.

Scissors—Near rim of cup, quarrels ending in separation; near handle, domestic unhappiness; on bottom, estrangement or reversals in occupational problems.

Ship—Generally means journeys; near rim, very unexpected, need to leave in a hurry; near handle, in reference to business or the home.

Snake—Represents an enemy or small misfortune.

Spade—Be industrious; usually rewarded with plenty of money.

Spider—Secretiveness; warning of an unpleasant artifice or ruse.

Square—A protective agent in case of danger or accident.

Star—The symbol of destiny, the promise of fulfillment of one's fondest hopes and aspirations.

Sword—Complications in both personal and business life.

Tent—Desire to travel far away; need for rest or retreat from present surroundings.

Tree—Promise of good health and comfort; several trees—a practical wish will materialize.

Triangle—Near the rim, time to begin new enterprises; near the handle, successful ventures can be followed; an upside-down triangle—bad luck, need to diligently reason and weigh every step before starting any new project.

Umbrella—Open, seek your friends in time of trouble; closed, temporarily unable to get what you want.

Vase—Service to friends brings you great peace of mind.

Wheel—Symbol of advancement through personal effort; near rim, unexpected money, rebate, or increase of salary and dividends.

Windmill—Schemes of gigantic magnitude could turn your industrious plans into money for yourself and others.

Woman—Desire for wealth and a happy family.

It requires a little study to become familiar with the shapes that make the symbols formed by the tea leaves, but after a few attempts your imagination takes over. From then on, weave a story, starting at the handle. If you go left, identical with the consultant's left, the immediate area of the cup deals with the past. As you proceed the future builds. A leaf on the rim, which is the present time, indicates something that is happening at the moment at a different location. A long stem that is very noticeable at first glance represents a man who is interested in something that pertains to the consultant. A short stem is for a woman who is planning something for the consultant.

Any obviously striking symbol lying on the bottom of the cup should be noted immediately because this shows the importance it bears to the consultant at some very distant date. Check all the easily discernible symbols first, look for initials, numbers, dots, lines. Note the clarity of each symbol, remembering that if they are cloudy or indistinct their importance is greatly lessened. If very cloudy their meaning becomes the reverse.

Coffee grounds can be used instead of tea leaves, but the results are never as good, the obvious reason being the lack of leaves which increase the number of symbols.

16

Telepathy

There are two predominant factors in all forms of psychic science. One is "clairvoyance," the ability to view the distant or unseen; the other is "precognition," an awareness of the future. How consistently and how accurately these faculties can be demonstrated, has long been a matter of contention; but many skeptics who doubted the methods used in certain psychic sciences have been impressed by the results.

By that token, the correct reading of a horoscope, the interpretation of the lines of the palm, or the recognition of moods through facial expressions, could be due to clairvoyance or precognition on the part of a "gifted" demonstrator. The skeptics, having gone that far, tried to find a physical rather than a psychical explanation for such phenomena.

They decided that in a majority of cases, a clairvoyant gained thought impressions that were already in another person's mind, while a prophet frequently voiced someone's unspoken hope or wish. Supporting this were many instances where a person had received a mental "flash" from a distant friend. This was classed by Mark Twain and others as "mental telegraphy," and students of the subject finally bundled it in with other similar phenomena under the head of "telepathy."

Simply defined, telepathy is the "transmission of thought independently of the recognized channels of sense." As such, it was studied and tested for many years, but no one was able to isolate it as a distinctive function. On the one hand, it seemed to be a "booster" to the faculty of clairvoyance; on the other, some supposedly telepathic results could be charged to "hyperesthesia," a straining or intensification of the normal senses, which through their concentration produced apparently supernormal results.

Thus the psychical and physical schools drew farther apart, until the subject of parapsychology was developed at Duke University during the 1930's. There, telepathy was treated simply as one phase of Extrasensory perception, popularly known as ESP, which has long been under widespread survey and study. But it still stems from the telepathic tests of the previous century, which were highly convincing because they could be worked or demonstrated to some degree by almost anyone.

Indeed, many of the most skillful operators in this field began as either skeptics or doubters, who were simply trying it out, like a game. When they found how well it worked and that their aptitude developed as they repeated the tests, they kept on until their ability became phenomenal. What was more, they were able to teach others the art of "mentalism," a word coined to include such tests.

One simple way to appreciate all this is to try it yourself. Some people are naturally good "demonstrators" who can pick up impressions intuitively. Others are excellent "subjects" who can subconsciously guide or assist in carrying a test to its climax. A combination of the two may bring about results that are almost uncanny. Like radiesthesia, telepathy is a highly demonstrable form of psychic science, suited to one and all.

Contact Telepathy

About a century ago, experimenters introduced "mind reading" experiments which required physical contact between the demonstrator and a person serving as his subject. In simple form, such tests involved the finding of an object hidden in a place unknown to the demonstrator, but known to the subject, who in a sense mentally guided the demonstrator to his goal.

Skeptics soon argued that these demonstrations were not "mind reading" at all, but actually "muscle reading," because the subject involuntarily exerted pressure on the demonstrator, thus pushing him along his way, or in some cases, restrained him. But as time went on the tests were greatly elaborated, and today skilled demonstrators of "contact telepathy" present experiments so complex that merely to term them "muscle reading" would be ridiculous.

In fact, a good contact mind reader never likes to have an eager subject, who provides shoves or other muscular actions, whether conscious or unconscious. Such "cues" are apt to prove more harmful than helpful. Sometimes they can actually be misleading, and in any case, if they are noticeable to onlookers, they spoil the demonstration.

The ideal subject should be something of a human transmitter, who merely *thinks* of what the performer is supposed to do. The demonstrator then concentrates deeply, often keeping his eyes half closed, and tries to pick up the thought. When handled perfectly, there is no conscious effort on either person's part and the result is sometimes uncanny.

At the same time, "contact telepathy" is basically quite easy; the simpler tests may be worked by many persons. The matter of contact is important, however. One system is for the demonstrator to grip the subject's wrist, right upon left, or vice versa, so that they can move around the room side by side. Often, this may be helped if the demonstrator raises the subject's hand, pressing its back against the demonstrator's forehead.

Still another way is for the demonstrator and the subject to lock arms, rather loosely, either left to right or vice versa. Some demonstrators prefer to slide their arm under the subject's, then bring their hand over to grip the subject's wrist from above. But all this may be varied according to individual choice, the best way being the one that proves itself by test.

Some simple experiments follow, along with comments on what may happen during their performance.

TEST NUMBER ONE: PICK THE OBJECT

This is the simplest of tests. It should be performed in a fairly large room, where there are plenty of objects to pick from, all of a type belonging there, such as a lamp, a telephone, an ashtray, pack of cigarettes, a few books and magazines, some matches, a box of candy, and so on. A regular living room or a sunporch makes a good setting.

The demonstrator leaves the room and the persons present decide upon the object that he is to pick. One of the group then acts as subject. The demonstrator is recalled, he grips the subject's arm in whatever manner he prefers, and they start about the room together, until the demonstrator begins to "sense" certain objects until he finally decides on one and announces it to be the right one.

The demonstrator is allowed to pick up objects and reject them, but once he announces his choice it is final. Almost invariably, a capable demonstrator will pick the chosen object.

Beginners are apt to fail if they neglect the early stage of the test. An experienced demonstrator takes his time in going about the room, actually sensing some portions as "hot" or "cold." If doubtful of any areas, he returns there, to see if the subject will mentally pull him away.

Thus he finally settles on one small area and applies the "hot" and "cold" procedure to the objects there.

TEST NUMBER TWO: COMPLETED ACTION

This is an extension of "picking the object." It does not stop at that point; instead, the demonstrator must do something with the object, as agreed upon by the group beforehand. For example, he might be "willed" to pick up a box of candy, open it, and offer some to specific persons present.

Here, again, he will sense a restraint if he starts to do the wrong action; and will get the "go-ahead" if he is right. Oddly, he gets a sense of *completion* or *incompletion* during this procedure. How that can be written off as "muscle reading" is hard to say. There is no "push" or "pull," but just a tension or relaxation, that will often cause the demonstrator to look up triumphantly, knowing his job is done.

Even when beginners fail, these tests can prove impressive. In one case, a person was "willed" to pick up a pack of cigarettes—which was not his own brand—and take out a cigarette and light it with a pack of matches from another table.

After the person acting as transmitter had led him around the room a few times, the inexperienced demonstrator gave up, saying he was too nervous to proceed. He slumped into a chair for a few moments, then walked over and picked up the *very pack* of cigarettes that everyone had in mind. He took out a cigarette, lighted it with a match from the pack on the other table, looked about the group, and asked, earnestly:

"Tell me, just what was it I was supposed to do?"

TEST NUMBER THREE: FINDING HIDDEN OBJECTS

This is a favorite with skilled demonstrators. It is like picking an object, except that the object is hidden. Hence when the demonstrator becomes "warm" he must keep looking further, as under a rug, or in a person's pocket, or wherever else he feels impelled to search. Again, he must draw this information mentally from the transmitter.

Sometimes this test is quite simple, the purpose being to find a specific object, such as a pin, which is not difficult, once the transmitter has guided the demonstrator to the hiding place. However, it can be presented as a highly spectacular test, say with the pin being hidden in a desk drawer in an office somewhere in a twenty-story building, a mile away from where the test begins.

Even that does not have to be specified. It can all be done with "step-by-step" impressions, following certain streets, turning corners according to the transmitter's guiding impulses, entering the right building, pushing the elevator button for the proper floor, stopping at the door of the office where the pin is hidden, and so on.

TEST NUMBER FOUR: SOLVING THE MURDER

This is an intriguing combination test, that requires a fair-sized group. One person plays the part of murderer, while another is the victim. An odd object, say a pocket comb, is chosen as the murder weapon, and a spot is chosen for the body. Usually this is simply a chair, where the "victim" can take his place like any other person present, though he might be taken into another room, or actually hidden in a closet.

The "murderer" and "victim" put on their act for the group, while the demonstrator is absent. The man acting as transmitter is, of course, present, and watches the "crime." The killer stabs or shoots his victim with the weapon, the victim clapping his hand to the spot where he is wounded. The murderer hides the weapon, and then hides the body, the victim obligingly cooperating in that process.

The demonstrator is then brought in, and gripping the transmitter's arm, he re-enacts the entire crime, due to the usual guidance. This is generally done in reverse, the demonstrator first finding the "body," then the "wound," then the "weapon," and finally the "murderer."

This test was a favorite with Washington Irving Bishop, the famous mind reader of the 1880's, who could even trace the "weapon" from one hiding place to another, if the "murderer" tried to throw him off the trail. Yet it can be worked today by anyone fairly proficient in contact telepathy.

TEST NUMBER FIVE: THE BLINDFOLD DRIVE

This was another of Bishop's great demonstrations. He would drive through the streets blindfolded, with a horse and carriage, to some destination known only to a subject—or transmitter—who was riding with him. In recent years, people have done the same with automobiles, but they have had to use "trick" blindfolds through which they could actually see.

However, you can try this test for yourself in a perfectly legitimate and safe manner. Suppose that you are taking a person somewhere in your car, and that he knows the way, but you don't. Instead of having him tell you where to turn, how many blocks to go, and so on, have him rest his hand on your shoulder or arm and keep thinking ahead, step by step. Often, you can pick up the impressions so perfectly that you can pull up in front of the exact house he has in mind.

This can be worked the other way about. With someone else driving the car and thinking of the route, you can sit beside him, resting your hand on his arm, and call the turns before he comes to them, sensing what is in his mind, without receiving an appreciable signal.

TEST NUMBER SIX: THE CHOSEN BOOK

This is an advanced version of "picking the object." In this case, the object is known in advance. It is a book, but the question is, which book? The test is worked in a room with a large or fair-sized bookcase. One volume is taken out and replaced during the demonstrator's absence.

Working with a subject or transmitter who knows the book, the demonstrator runs his hand along the shelves and picks the right one, then continues back and forth along that row until he finds the chosen book. Again, the "hot" and "cold" process is involved, but it is more exacting than in other tests.

Some demonstrators let the group pick an actual page from the book, and the demonstrator opens to that page and reads it. To keep this within bounds, it can be limited to the first page of a chapter. In that case, the demonstrator, after finding the book, can open to the contents page and run his finger down the list of chapters, pausing on each, until he gets an impulse.

Or he can thumb through to the start of each chapter, trying to sense "hot" or "cold" as with picking an object; then going back to certain chapters, according to the impulse gained from the person acting as transmitter.

Some expert demonstrators go to the extreme of having the group select any word on any page in the entire book. In that case, the demonstrator must work through the book page by page to get the right one; then line by line; and finally word by word.

This is a lengthy process, but when performed successfully, it seemingly goes far beyond the limitations of the "muscle reading" theory.

Non-Contact Tests

In most of the tests so far given, the presence of a group, concentrating on the same aim as the transmitter, is considered helpful to success. That raises the question: "Why not work from group to demonstrator through concentration only, without a transmitter or intermediary?"

That would stress the mental rather than the physical, thereby strengthening the telepathic theory. The next question is, "Are such tests possible?" and the answer is, "Yes." Here are some examples:

TEST NUMBER SEVEN: THE WILLING GAME

One of the earliest of telepathic tests, this is a version of "picking the object," but without the transmitter. A group thinks of an object in the room, the demonstrator comes in alone, and tries to "sense" it from the massed impression. One way is to move about, touching objects or handling them; but some demonstrators prefer to take a fixed position and "think" their way around.

If this test becomes difficult because of the large size of the room, or the variety of objects, it is better to switch to a test of a more concentrated type, such as:

TEST NUMBER EIGHT: AROUND THE CIRCLE

A group of objects is placed on a table, so that they form a fair-sized circle. These can be similar; in fact, some can be alike; at a dinner table, for example, you could use objects found there, say two coffee cups, two drinking glasses, a salt shaker, a saucer, a catsup bottle, a cream pitcher, and a sugar bowl.

Other items might be laid out on a card table, such as a pencil, a pack of cigarettes, a dollar bill, a notebook, and the like. In either case, the persons present decide upon one object while you, as the demonstrator, are absent from the room, or have turned away.

No one looks directly at the chosen object, but all keep it in mind. Upon your return, you extend your hand and move it slowly around the circle, in either direction, while people "will" you to stop at the chosen object. Sometimes you may get a quick impression, but it is better to keep circling awhile in case it changes.

Often, the best process is elimination. You may find a "pull" toward one portion of the circle, indicating that the "wanted" item is in that area. So pause and remove the objects elsewhere, stating that none of them is the chosen one. If you are right, spread the circle somewhat, and continue, eliminating other objects as they become "cold."

When you have narrowed it down to two, keep moving back and forth until you have the right one.

TEST NUMBER NINE: ONE RED CARD

Playing cards are the items used in this test. Seven is a good number, and you do not have to bother about suits or values. Just make sure that six of them are *black cards* (clubs or spades) and that the seventh is *red* (a heart or a diamond).

Have someone shuffle these cards and deal them in a row, face down. The people present look at the cards one by one, so they know where the red card lies in the line, although you do not. You then approach the table and run your hand slowly back and forth along the line, being sure to go *clear beyond* each end, before making the reverse trip.

Tell the group that while they watch you, they are to *think* the order, "Stop!" whenever you come to the one red card. As you proceed, you will find that your hand is drawn downward, as though by a magnet, as you pass over a certain card. Again, don't be too quick about that being the red card. A crossed thought or your own eagerness for results may bring a wrong pull.

But when it becomes stronger and definitely denotes one card, there are times when you can turn that card up with positive surety that it will be the red one. Keeping the cards well spaced is helpful; if they are too close, it may be difficult to tell which of two cards is the right one.

The hand should be at least three or four inches above the cards, in order to note the pull. Some persons have trouble noticing the downward motion of their own hand; in such cases, they should have someone watch for it, and announce when it indicates the card. Like the demonstrator, the watcher should be a person who does not know where the red card was placed.

TEST NUMBER TEN: SCORING THE CARDS

This is simply an extension of the "red card" test, but with a scoring system. If you hit the red card on your first try, it counts 7 points. If you turn up a black, move the face down cards a little closer together, and try again, with the six. If you hit the red, you score 6; if you miss, try again with five cards.

Keep on, scoring 5, 4, 3, 2 for respective hits. If you are caught with the red card at the finish, it counts 1 point. Mark down your score, have the cards shuffled, and repeat the test, continuing through a series of ten, in which 70 would be a perfect score. Some persons have come close to that total, but the breaking point is 35. Anything above that is evidential in a positive way, where telepathy is concerned; below 35, it is negative.

Visualization Tests

While all types of telepathic tests involve some degree of visualization, where picking objects or duplicating actions may be concerned, there are others that can be said to depend on visualization alone. That is, there is no physical contact with an intermediary; no presence of a group, whose combined tension might become a guiding force.

These, again, include early tests, which have proven their worth and efficacy through the years, as:

TEST NUMBER ELEVEN: REMOTE CONTROL

A form of the "willing game" that evolved in a very interesting way. Some demonstrators, instead of moving around the room or thinking their way about, found it preferable to study the objects briefly, then close their eyes and try to visualize one from the mass impression of the group. Since the demonstrator did not cue the group, either by handling an object or staring steadily at it, there was no way of "picking up" a "tension" thus created.

Granting, therefore, that the result might be purely telepathic, there seemed no reason for the group to be present; or if they did have to be close, they could at least be out of sight and hearing of the demonstrator. So the test may be worked thus:

The committee picks an object during the demonstrator's absence; then they move to another room. The demonstrator enters the first room, picks what he thinks is the right object, and takes it to the group.

TEST NUMBER TWELVE: THE UNSEEN OBJECT

This is a reversal of the previous test. The committee never leaves the original room; instead, they concentrate on an object elsewhere in the house or apartment, "willing" the demonstrator to find it and bring it. The group does not have to see the object in question at the outset; and if so agreed, they can choose something of a general nature, as a pencil, a key, or a spoon. Some very surprising results have been gained with this test.

TEST NUMBER THIRTEEN: TRANSFERENCE OF SENSATIONS

Here, a "sender" or a group actually undergoes a physical sensation, hoping to transfer it mentally to a "receiver" or members of a group in another room. In this test, you can literally go "hot" or "cold," as one favorite stunt is for the sender to pick up a hot cup or a cold glass, hold it a while, and find out if the receiver sensed "hot" or "cold."

Because of the limit of two choices, such a test should be repeated, say five to ten times, to get away from the element of chance. The same applies to "light" or "heavy" objects, or those which are "sharp" or "blunt."

Sensations of pain may be transferred; for example, a sender could pinch his right ear, or scratch his left ankle; the receiver would then seek to experience that sensation.

Transfer of taste has also figured in these tests. A person takes a pinch of salt, a spoonful of vinegar, or a bit of sugar, and endeavors to "project" the sensation. With certain senders and receivers, the "taste test" has been known to work surprisingly well.

TEST NUMBER FOURTEEN: VISUALIZED DIAGRAMS

This test has been highly successful under exacting conditions. Its very simplicity makes it all the more effective. It is the sort of experiment that two persons or a group can undertake almost any time, anywhere.

One person, the "sender," draws a simple diagram or sketch. A "receiver" stationed elsewhere—even at a great distance—attempts to reproduce it, while both are concentrating on the diagram.

Results fall into these categories: (a) exact reproduction, or nearly so; (b) reproductions containing most of the essential elements; (c) those with incomplete elements; (d) those with little similarity and obvious mistakes. The first two groups [(a) and (b)] are highly evidential. In addition, the third group (c) may be evidential with this proviso:

The receiver, in reproducing the diagram, should pause when he becomes uncertain and make a note to that effect. This shows that he is positive up to that point, but doubtful beyond it. Yet if he feels he should go on, he should have the right to do so, without jeopardizing what he has already accomplished. So the final result should be judged accordingly.

This is amply illustrated in:

TEST NUMBER FIFTEEN: PICTURE PROJECTION

Here, the sender goes beyond the diagrammatic stage. He visualizes a three-dimensional object, or concentrates upon a full-fledged picture, such as "Washington Crossing the Delaware" or something simpler, like the most recent ad for a popular brand of cigarettes.

During a period of mutual concentration, the receiver tries to sketch in the components of the picture, in much the same way as the diagram test (Number Fifteen). There are two differences, however: He is dealing with a three-dimensional object, and must visualize it as such; also, the picture, particularly a photograph, may be too difficult to draw. In that case, he can simply write in the details as he visualizes them.

One plan is to specify whether an "object" or a "picture" is being projected, thus enabling the receiver to concentrate on the right track. In recording any successful tests, such limitations should be mentioned.

Card Reading Tests

In early telepathic tests, playing cards were used, with the receiver calling their names as the sender looked at them. Some very phenomenal scores were recorded with highly "sensitive" receivers. One reputedly hit 202 correct cards out of a total of 382 trials, though by the law of averages (1 out of 52) only 7 or 8 correct calls should have been made.

Such tests generally proved unsatisfactory for two reasons: Even a "good" score, say 6 out of 52, could be somewhat discouraging; and the similarity between certain cards, say the six, seven, and eight of diamonds, made it difficult to visualize a card exactly.

So many of these tests were confined to calling suits—clubs, diamonds, hearts, and spades—which gave 1 out of 4 chances. One very remarkable receiver was credited 14 consecutive correct calls of suits; and the chances against this were mathematically computed as 4,782,-969 to 1. Suits offered problems, however, particularly with face cards, which could easily be confused.

So eventually, cards with symbols were designed, the most famous of these being the ESP cards introduced at Duke University in the early 1930's, and with which literally millions of tests have been made. There are five different symbols: Circle, plus, star, square, and wavy lines. A pack consists of twenty-five cards, five of each symbol.

With these, a sender can concentrate solely on a symbol as he looks at it, while another person, acting as a receiver, notes down his impression. A score of 5 out of 25 is average; hence higher scores, if they occur consistently, may be classed as evidential.

These cards also have been used in clairvoyance tests, in which five cards—one bearing each symbol—are placed face up and the "subject" tries to match them with face-down cards from the shuffled pack. These tests have even been carried to the point where the five "key" cards are sealed in envelopes, which are mixed before the matching is tried. This means that the subject undertaking the test must in some way sense which card is in each envelope in order to sense the face-down cards that match them!

To be fully effective, these tests should be made under laboratory conditions, so they can be checked against the mathematical factors involved. In some tests, the entire pack of twenty-five cards is run completely through, recording the cards as they turn up. In others, the test is stopped after a specified number of cards—say five—and the result is recorded and the entire pack thoroughly shuffled before trying another series.

This applies both to clairvoyant tests and telepathic tests. Certain factors favor the telepathic tests, particularly when tried informally, ouside of the laboratory. Some people who doubt their clairvoyant ability still feel that they are good telepathic receivers; hence it gives confidence to work with a sender. Two-person tests are often more interesting and therefore encourage needed concentration, whether clairvoyance or telepathy is responsible. Finally, there is the well-supported theory that even if clairvoyance is the basic faculty involved, telepathy may be a "booster" that will increase the positive results, bringing higher and therefore more significant scores.

When two persons try the cards on their own, the surest procedure is to shuffle the pack and pick a random card after each try. In that way, there will always be five chances out of twenty-five, or exactly one out of five, as the pack does not diminish. At most, no more than five cards should be used in these informal trials, for the following reason:

Suppose the pack is well mixed and the first five cards happen to be square, circle, waves, plus, star. The "sender" looks at these and the "receiver" happens to call off: waves, circle, plus, star, square. The sender and receiver each mark their cards down, but the receiver is not told if his calls are correctly "tuned" to the sender's. In this case, the receiver has so far hit the average of one out of five (by calling "circle" when it was dealt) and the pack is in its original status.

There are twenty cards to go, four of each variety. The receiver, moreover, has actually named the five cards already dealt, though not in their correct order, so he can only be credited with one hit, the circle.

Now, in contrast, assume that the pack came out freakishly despite the shuffle, and the sender, to his surprise, found that the first five ran plus, plus, plus, plus, plus. The receiver, calling in the same order as before—waves, circle, plus, star, square—would get his one out of five average. But the status of the pack has changed. There are only four varieties of symbols in the next twenty cards, with five of each variety. But there isn't a plus in the entire lot!

Mathematically, this may work out over an extended series of tests; but we are not dealing only with mathematics. It is conceded that the faculties of clairvoyance and telepathy are elusive, going "hot" or "cold" at intervals. In the instance just given, the receiver obviously wasn't "hot" or he would have hit more than one plus symbol out of five. But suppose he should go "hot" soon afterward. It would be like a new test, and the absence of plus cards would distort the mathematical probabilities.

Ending at five tries lessens this objection; shuffling the whole pack between each try eliminates it completely. Also, it saves the receiver from having to keep track of calls he has already made, which is disconcerting to some persons. Objections have been raised that the symbols on ESP cards are arbitrary and not suited to everyone. That may be true, but they are as easily recognized as the suits of playing cards. Also, parapsychologists using the regular ESP cards have suggested that people prepare cards with symbols of their own if they prefer.

Some "sensitives" claim that they need to become "emotional" to obtain clairvoyant or telepathic results. They say that they can't get emotional over symbols. But colors have been recommended as a suitable substitute, and it is easy to make up a set of five colors, with circles of red, orange, yellow, green, and blue, imprinted on blank cards. Colors in themselves stir emotions and have strong psychic interpretations, so they should be ideal.

The ESP cards can be used in visualization tests by having a sender create a "mental image" that can be interpreted as an ESP symbol. He might concentrate on a city square, or a baseball diamond, while studying a square symbol. Or a ship at sea would represent the waves symbol. By having the receiver think in terms of motion or action in order to get to the right symbol, the visualization becomes stronger, but it can't be repeated too often or the images will become strained. Here, telepathy is the logical test rather than clairvoyance, as the sender must first create the image for the receiver.

Years ago, tests with ESP cards were criticized on the ground that the backs of the cards might be readable, perhaps unwittingly, by some of the persons tested. A British experimenter brought out a pack with similar symbols, but with the unusual feature of a "sunburst" design on the back, which produced a razzle-dazzle effect that made it impossible to read.

But tests conducted in parapsychological laboratories were even at that time being held under conditions so stringent that specially printed backs were unnecessary with ESP cards. In most tests, the cards themselves were screened from view of the person trying to name them telepathically, and so many packs were used that none was in circulation long enough to betray any slight differences in the cards themselves.

17

Yoga and Its Powers

Much of our psychic science comes from the Far East, where mystic powers have been recognized since time immemorial. The Wise Men of the East were versed in astrology, and much of their lore was brought westward through the centuries. Meanwhile, in India, generations of scholars and adepts have continued to contemplate life in a timeless fashion, classing all manifestations of the mysterious as within the realm of their natural philosophies.

This is particularly true with yoga, which has been defined as a "union" between man and the higher planes. This means detachment from one's own personality, on the theory that our lives are clouded by a form of illusion termed *maya*. Once those higher planes are attained, the incredible becomes reality, as the individual controls forces that to the uninitiated are unseen and even unknown.

Such is the reputed power of yoga. Skeptics may argue that it merely consists of supplanting illusion with delusion, that the lower planes may have their fallacies, but that the so-called higher planes may themselves be purely imaginary. Still, yoga has maintained its pace, and there is no doubt that persons adept in its practice have achieved physical and mental results beyond generally accepted limitations.

There are various types of yoga, each regarded as a path toward spiritual attainment, such as karma yoga, which involves good works, bhakti yoga, which stresses worship, and jnana yoga, which seeks wisdom. All have points in common, but the two that are of chief interest to students of the occult are hatha yoga, which deals with physical development through breathing exercises and bodily postures, and raja yoga, the "kingly path," which deals directly with mental control and the development of latent psychic forces.

These two, hatha and raja, are interlocked because the practice of hatha yoga so subjugates the physical body that the mind can function more freely in the field of raja yoga. There is some conflict here, however: Many ascetics have so trained themselves in hatha yoga that they believe it functions in the higher realms; whereas the proponents of raja yoga regard hatha yoga as a mere stepping stone to real attainment.

According to Patanjali, who codified the philosophy and practice of yoga about the year 200 B.C., there are eight steps to such attainment, the first four being:

1. Control of self, or *yama*, which requires fair dealing toward others in everyday life. 2. Purity of thought, or *niyama*, as an accompaniment to outward action. 3. Control of the body, *asana*, through the adoption and practice of certain bodily postures. 4. Absorption of vital forces, or *pranayama*, through rhythmic breathing and breath retention.

Those four constitute a "fourfold path" that can be summed under the head of hatha yoga. This is the form of yoga that gained wide popularity in America as a means toward attaining physical health and strength, along with a serenity of mind. The great stress is placed upon the *asanas* or bodily postures.

These include headstands, body twists, back bends, and a variety of poses that supposedly resemble such living creatures as the cobra, eagle, locust, lion, peacock, turtle, and even a tree. But the basic form is *padmasana*, or the lotus posture, in which a person is seated cross-legged with hands extended beyond the knees, each thumb and forefinger forming a circle.

There are variations of the lotus posture, one favorite being *shirshapadmasana*, or the upside-down lotus, which combines the basic posture with a headstand. Some students of hatha yoga assume such positions for hours. But for practical purposes, the regular lotus posture is all that is required to reach the fourth stage of *pranayama* or rhythmic breathing.

Here, the psychic factor comes into play. In rhythmic breathing, which includes a form known as the "grand psychic breath," the idea is not merely to develop lung power and chest expansion. According to yoga, the air is charged with a subtle but vital force known as *prana*, which can be stored in the brain and nerve centers and transmitted to all parts of the body, much like an electric current.

The supposed power of this vital force can be put to the following test: One person lies flat on his back, preferably on a couch, keeping his body rigid. Four other persons take positions, two at each side, and extend their forefingers beneath the first man's body at intervals from neck to ankles.

All five breathe rhythmically in unison, taking in a long breath, re-

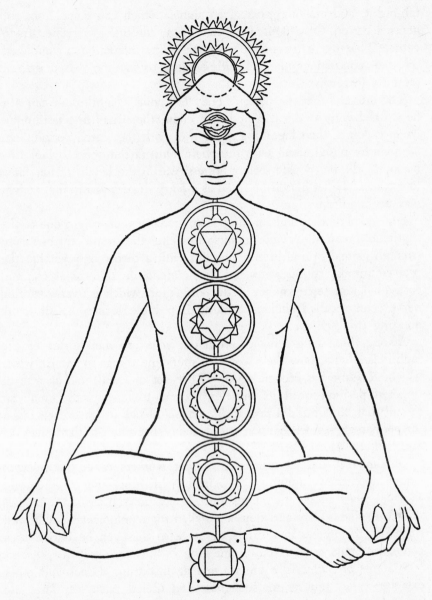

Padmasana or the "lotus posture" of yogic contemplation. The circles represent mystical wheels called "chakras" whereby the vital force is drawn from the base of the spine to the top of the head, achieving a higher consciousness with each of the seven levels.

taining it, and exhaling at a given signal, which can come from still another person. On a designated breath—say the fifth—everyone lifts together. This, too, can come on a signal, as the inhalation is completed. To their amazement, the four lifters bring the supine person upward on their fingertips.

The effect is that the person's body has gone weightless. It can also be worked with a person seated in a chair, the lifters first testing the balance points, then breathing in rhythm with the seated person, who is promptly raised along with the chair. During the period when Elsa Maxwell, the portly cafe society hostess, was at the height of her fabulous career, she let herself be lifted as a party stunt, proving that weight was no handicap.

Some experimenters claim there is an actual loss of weight due to the rhythmic breathing, while others attribute the result to increased strength gained by the lifters. This fits with a theory of yoga that the prana currents, running up and down alongside the spinal column, arouse a latent force known as the kundalini, which activates psychic nerve centers called chakras, making it possible to accomplish many amazing things.

Among those long schooled in hatha yoga are mendicants of the sadhu class, who show their scorn for mundane things in bizarre ways. To them, asana has become a way of life, for one will hold an arm in upraised position until its muscles become useless; another may sit so still that birds build a nest in his hair; and sadhus have even taken up permanent residence upon a tightrope, spending all their sleeping and waking hours there.

Of similar breed are itinerant wonder workers called fakirs, who demonstrate their immunity to pain by thrusting long needles and thin daggers through their arms and cheeks, as well as lying on beds of sharp spikes. They also stop or quicken their pulsebeats at will, and some put themselves in a cataleptic stage so they can be buried in a coffin for hours or even days, emerging as alive as ever.

Students of hatha yoga are warned against using asanas and other exercises called mudras for such base and useless purposes. They are advised to continue beyond the stage of pranayama into the higher steps of raja yoga. This constitutes the "eightfold path," and through it, the awakening of the kundalini is supposed to take place gradually, making it possible to accomplish genuine marvels of far greater worth than the hackneyed and sometimes dubious claptrap of the fakirs.

The first four steps, already given, are 1. *yama.* 2. *niyama.* 3. *asana.*

4. *pranayama.* Having practiced them enough to acquire bodily control and rhythmic breathing, the student of raja yoga goes into the next steps:

5. Introspection, or *pratyahara,* where thoughts, freed from physical shackles, turn inward. As *asana* aids physical control, *pratyahara* produces mental control. The mind is put through prescribed exercises until it is immune from outside impressions. That training is preliminary to:

6. Concentration, or *dharana,* in which the mind is pinpointed on a single idea. 7. Meditation, or *dhyana,* wherein an idea can be examined in minute detail under constant focus. 8. Ecstasy, or *samadhi,* a superconscious state that permits complete detachment from all worldly surroundings.

The three highest stages are known collectively as *samyama,* and by the time a yogi reaches that goal he has acquired such psychic powers as clairvoyance, telepathy, and ability to vision the past and future. If he continues on to attain the status of an adept, he can develop eight "superior" powers, namely:

1. *Anima,* or the ability to shrink to the size of an atom. 2. *Mahima,* to increase in size as greatly as desired. 3. *Garima,* to become extremely heavy. 4. *Laghima,* to become light, so the body will float in air. 5. *Prapti,* the ability to bring anything within reach. 6. *Prakamya,* or immediate realization of desire. 7. *Isitva,* or creation of matter through power of thought. 8. *Vasitva,* the dominion over all objects, animate and inanimate.

There is no doubt whatever that sincere practitioners of raja yoga not only believe in these amazing powers, but are often positive that they possess them. Stories are told of yogis dwelling in the Himalaya Mountains, warding off wild beasts by power of mind, such as *vasitva.* Others are said to float seated in midair during their contemplations, an example of *laghima.* Awed witnesses have even described parades of sky-walking adepts marching in from the snowy ranges.

When skeptics scoff, believers admit that such marvels are seldom seen because yogis are reluctant to perform them publicly. However, some have given private showings for privileged patrons, and over the years there have been reliable reports of instances where yogis have made tree leaves flutter without a breeze, and have restored dead birds to life, as evidences of *prakamya.*

One adept produced the scent of any perfumes that strangers requested mentally, without expressing their wishes aloud. This would appear to be *prakamya,* with telepathic overtones, unless it could be charged off as hypnotism on the yogi's part.

But there are also reports of a wonder worker who laid a mere feather on one side of a scales and caused it to counterbalance a man's weight on the other, a case of sheer *garima;* and the same adept could also make water boil in a vase by merely moving his hands toward it.

Often, such adepts have reputedly undergone prolonged living burials while in a state of *samadhi,* and there is a remarkable tale of one such yogi being seen in a big city like Calcutta while his body was entombed in the vault of a maharaja's palace a thousand miles away.

Such a case, if actual, would presuppose the power of astral projection on the yogi's part, coupled with *isitva,* whereby the thought would take form at the desired spot. Astral projection is a matter of routine with these adepts, though their excursions through the upper reaches are often purely mental. As proof of their ability to project an actual idea, or illusion, authorities cite the "astral call bell," a ringing sound that one adept causes another to hear at a far distance, so he can concentrate and open telepathic communication.

Practically speaking, that is the prototype of our modern telephone bell; but from the metaphysical standpoint, a yogi might just as well project his own mental image, as an illusion of sight rather than sound. Granting him that faculty, he could employ *isitva* during a demonstration before a group, causing physical objects—even living creatures and human beings—to appear and disappear at will. Whether these were actual creations or mere thought images would not matter. Either way, the onlookers would believe that they had witnessed the incredible.

This has been offered as an explanation of the famous "Indian rope trick," wherein a fakir tosses a rope in air and causes it to remain suspended while a boy climbs it and suddenly disappears from the top. Elaborated versions claim that the fakir, too, climbs the rope and disappears. In other accounts, he chases the boy up the rope with a big knife; then, from nowhere, pieces of the boy's body fall to earth, whereupon the fakir reappears at the top of the rope, comes down and covers the boy's body with a cloth, promptly assembling the fragments and magically restoring the boy to life.

That really would be taxing the "higher powers" of yoga, so an alternate proposition has been offered; namely, that "mass hypnotism" is responsible. Actually, this amounts to the same thing, since all yogic powers are probably hypnotic to begin with. But skeptics for years spiked that argument with the glib pronouncement that "Mass hypnotism is an impossibility."

True, perhaps, as hypnotism was known and practiced in Europe and America during the early 1900's, when that claim was current. But that did not prove that mass hypnotism was impossible among the yogis of India. Then, while the controversy still simmered, along came Hitler and proved that mass hypnotism was possible anywhere almost at any time.

Hypnotic annals of America include the celebrated radio broadcast of the "men from Mars," where thousands of listeners thought they were hearing an authentic news report and began calling up newspapers, as well as police, saying that they had seen Martian spaceships landing in their own backyards with little green men clambering out. The wave of hysteria that followed the so-called discovery of flying saucers was another case of mass hypnotism.

Yet this can be simplified still further, if we regard the rope trick and kindred marvels simply as a case where the individual members of a small group are hypnotized separately but simultaneously. This has been demonstrated by stage hypnotists, and it has long been a practice among fraudulent spirit mediums, when dealing with susceptible clients. Once the lights are out, the sitters will accept the crudest ventriloquial tricks as "spirit voices" or imagine that a waving curtain is an "ethereal breeze."

So it goes in India, or so it once went, back in the days when people claimed they had seen the rope trick. Again, skeptics will demand: "If the rope trick is the result of group hypnotism, granting such to be possible, why do the fakirs restrict themselves only to that one super-miracle?"

The answer is, they don't. Reports of equally fantastic marvels have come from witnesses quite as reliable as those who have described the rope trick. The only difference is that these other wonders have been seen much less frequently. Some have already been listed, such as levitation and sky-walking. There have been reports of fire-walking and water-walking adepts, too, and other fanciful demonstrations.

Usually these are hard to trace, and like the rope trick, the descriptions turn out to be second- or thirdhand. But whenever you do catch up with an actual witness to the feat—and several instances could be cited of this—his description is partly vague, partly stylized. Seldom, if ever, does it contain corroborative facts, or the essentials of sound investigation.

The witness may remember the place, but not the name of the fakir. He may recall the names of other witnesses, but if so, he has now lost track of them. Often, he is not sure as to the time of day, nor even the exact surroundings. He is apt to include details that he heard from some other source, such as the business of a photographer taking a picture of the boy at the top of the rope, only to develop it and have the print show the boy still on the ground with the rope coiled beside him.

In short, the witness who saw the rope trick talks just like the man who goes up on the stage during a hypnotic act and lets the "professor" mesmerize him. He knows he was at the theater, he remembers others who were there, but the crazy things that happened are just a jumble in his mind. He talks like he had come out of a trance, which he actually did. Apparently, the witness to the rope trick remembers what the fakir wants him to remember, just as the hypnotized subject recalls only what the hypnotist told him.

The rope trick follows a pattern, like all well-tried hypnotic stunts. Probably the fact that it has been reported so often in comparison to other marvels is because people are "conditioned" to it. They have heard of the rope trick, they want to see the rope trick, so the fakir shows them the rope trick. It can definitely be that simple.

Most certainly the hypnotic explanation is far more satisfactory than efforts to explain the rope trick by fake or mechanical means, such as the fakir tossing the rope up to a hidden balcony in a smoke-filled courtyard, or over a wire stretched between two tall trees, or by use of an articulated rope that stiffens like a bamboo pole, due to the operation of an interior device. Anyone accepting such absurdities as the secret of the rope trick in its full-fledged form may very well have been hypnotized into believing them.

One fact is certain: However far modern science may advance in the exploration and recognition of human abilities beyond the limits of the ordinary senses, the farther it will go toward establishing the higher claims of yoga, whose devotees have been following the "psychic path" long before anyone else ever heard of it. If our Western savants prove that parapsychology has much to offer and succeed in cracking down its riddles as they have done with atomic energy, the clearing clouds of doubt will reveal the Oriental mystics floating serenely in the midst of their own aura, as they always have!

Index

ABOUT THE AUTHORS

WALTER B. GIBSON is the author of many books in the field of magic and the occult, as well as literally hundreds of magazine articles about magic, true crime, mysteries, and the mystic sciences. His works include *Blackstone's Card Tricks*, *Blackstone's Secrets of Magic*, *Thurston's 400 Tricks You Can Do*, *What's New in Magic*, and *Hoyle's Simplified Guide to Popular Card Games*.

LITZKA R. GIBSON has written at least a half dozen books, as well as many articles, all on the subjects covered in this book. Her works include *How to Read Palms* and *Lessons in Palmistry*.